RES
3/3/89

P9-BJU-901

13 25

*Penfriends from Porlock*

*By the same Author*

The Sweets of Pimlico
Unguarded Hours
Kindly Light
The Laird of Abbotsford
The Healing Art
Who Was Oswald Fish?
Wise Virgin
The Life of John Milton
Scandal
Hilaire Belloc
How Can We Know?
Gentlemen in England
Love Unknown
Stray
Tolstoy

# Penfriends
# from
# Porlock

by

A. N. Wilson

W·W·Norton & Company
*New York     London*

Copyright © 1988 by A.N. Wilson
First American Edition, 1989

All rights reserved.

Printed in the United States of America.

Library of Congress Cataloging-in-Publication Data

Wilson, A. N., 1950-
Penfriends from Porlock/by A.N. Wilson.
p.      cm.
I. Title, II. Title: Penfriends from Porlock.
PR6073.I439P46   1988
824'.914—dc19                              88–15055

ISBN 0-393-02647-7

W. W. Norton & Company, Inc., 500 Fifth Avenue, New York, N. Y. 10110
W. W. Norton & Company Ltd., 37 Great Russell Street, London WC1B 3NU

1 2 3 4 5 6 7 8 9 0

# Contents

CONTENTS

# Preface

Life is full of situations where being good at one thing is thought to be a preparation for doing something else completely different. The life of the clever barrister, all of whose training teaches her or him to see only one side of a case, and to argue it in as devious and aggressive a manner as possible, leads, if it is successful, to the judge's bench, where the opposite qualities of balance and moderation are needed. Similarly, a woman whose real talent is interesting sixteen year olds in French literature is 'promoted' to being Headmistress, a job which is largely administration and public relations.

Something like this happens to authors. A person writes a book. Almost no one buys it, but it makes an impression, and the author is in demand. The demand is not for more books. Rather, it is to give a talk, to make a broadcast, to lecture at a seminar, or to pass judgement on another writer – all very different skills from those required in the author of a book.

Writing a book is a full-time occupation. You are thinking about it all the time. Sometimes you will wake up in the morning and realise that the book's problems have been with you even in sleep. Before conscious thought has dawned, even before you open your eyes in the morning, you realise exactly what is wrong with that chapter you were struggling to finish the day before. Or so it has been with me. Until a typescript is actually out of my hands, and with the printer, I am mulling over it ceaselessly. For this reason, the question of how long it takes to write a book is an unanswerable one, particularly in the case of novels, where years of meditating upon a particular theme will suddenly bear fruit. 'It didn't take long to write that,' someone will say, upon hearing that the actual *penning* of a story took only a matter of weeks. Well, no it didn't: only about twenty-seven years.

Writing of this kind needs to be obsessive or it does not work. It requires the ability to carry a whole book in one's head at once. Only when most of the technical problems of a book have been resolved can you really start to write. Up to this point, you can only do sketches for the work; you can't see it whole. The essence of the main work is its bigness, and if you start the writing too soon you will get it out of proportion, like a child drawing an enormous head on a piece of paper and not seeing that if he wants to draw a full-size body, he should have left room for the legs. Moreover, one knows that, however lucky one is, and however carefully one selects the right moment to start, no book will ever be perfect. The flaws – quite as obvious to the writer as to anyone else – are often ineradicable at an early stage of conception, so that however hard one labours to expunge them, one plods on with the rather gloomy sense that the finished artefact is not going to be all that one dreamed of when the first inspiration for the book dawned in one's mind. The big conception gets bothered by a host of tiny problems: over-all chronology, structure, or the tone of some particular scene which won't come right, or the need – unforeseen at the outset – to insert some explanatory matter at an earlier stage of the narrative. Such thoughts make writers bad company. The problems, uninteresting to anyone else, won't go away until they are resolved and you find yourself thinking about them when, to all outward appearances, you have stopped working and are 'relaxing'.

And it is perhaps at such a point in the life of a book that the telephone rings and someone asks you to give a lecture, to write an essay, to review a book. You know that they are like the person from Porlock, who interrupted Samuel Taylor Coleridge while he was writing *Kubla Khan*. But everything in their suggestion is tempting. First it is tempting, because what they are suggesting is something which, unlike writing a book, can be done with comparative speed. Often they are in a hurry and want your few thousand words within a fortnight or a month. For someone involved in the larger task of writing a book, there is something very tempting about the idea of a *little* writing chore, whose beginning and end can be rounded within a single fortnight. And then, very often – in the case of lectures and talks, – there is the possibility of travelling to agreeable places. The essay on page 3 began life as talks at the Gritti Palace in Venice. The longer of the two essays on satire was addressed to an audience of Turkish dons at Haceteppe University in the Anatolian plateau outside Ankara. The essays on C. S. Lewis and G. K. Chesterton were read to audiences nearer home, but I am no less grateful to the persons from Porlock who asked me to write them.

Stevie Smith wrote a haunting poem called 'Thoughts about the Person from Porlock':

> Coleridge received the Person from Porlock
> And ever after called him a curse,
> Then why did he hurry to let him in?
> He could have hid in the house.
>
> It was not right of Coleridge in fact it was wrong
> (But often we all do wrong)
> As the truth is I think he was already stuck
> With Kubla Khan . . .

I have certainly found this to be true in my own case. How easily one understands the temptation, not merely to open the door to the person, but to link arms with him, abandon home and stroll back towards Porlock for an extended holiday. How often I have stared through the darkness, when wrestling with some apparently insoluble little technical difficulty, and looked with envy at the lighted windows and the fairy lamps of Porlock, twinkling its welcome in the distant valley. On clear summer nights you can even hear the noise of revelry which comes from it. The place is full of writers, but the very word 'writer' means something different there. They won't bother you to write a *book*. All you have to do is to judge a literary prize, or eat a literary lunch or chat with a literary editor – never produce a literary work. When the speech at the conference is over, or the review handed in, you can settle down to all the serious business of getting drunk at book launches, making passes at publicity girls, signing letters to the newspapers about the plight of fellow writers in less liberal lands and jabbering about the latest fashions in fiction until it is time to collect the O.B.E.s and D.B.E.s which are regularly dished out to those who have chosen to live in this way.

> I long for the Person from Porlock
> To bring my thoughts to an end,
> I am becoming impatient to see him
> I think of him as a friend

Only an ardent Parnassian could object to such goings on. And though I hope that I shall never have to review another book, and I have no desire to take up permanent residence in Porlock, there usually comes a moment when I am only too happy to be interrupted.

Rachel Boulding kindly collected up all my old reviews for me, and I was appalled not just by their bulk but by how few of the books, about which I had expressed myself so certainly, had stayed in my memory. Usually I have been extravagant in my praise and the books about which I have been rude look as though they have deserved it. But how little impression of them remains!

The better the author, however, the more memorable the book. I remember quite vividly all the books mentioned in the following pages. I have made a selection of reviews which stand or almost stand as essays in their own right, but I have not tried to disguise the occasional nature of the writings here collected. Nor have I tried to update them. I write as if John Braine were still alive and David Lodge were still a professor. I have given its origins and date at the end of each piece, but I cannot conclude this prefatory matter without thanking the many persons from Porlock who asked me to write what follows, or who have been 'begetters' in one way or another of my occasional writing. They have all given me not merely welcome diversion but pleasure. And a large number of them have brought me meals or paid my hotel bills: Mark Amory, Clare Asquith, Nicholas Bagnall, Glen Black, the British Council in general (Christine Street in particular), Alexander Chancellor, Jeremy Dyson, Richard Holloway, Walter Hooper, Julie Kavanagh, Patrick Marnham, Charles Moore, Blake Morrison, Andrew Motion, Ferdinand Mount, The Ohio State University, Kathy O'Shaughnessy, Jane Rylands, Emma Soames, Jeremy Treglown, Geoffrey Wheatcroft.

Those are the persons from Porlock who asked me to write these miscellaneous pieces. I don't keep a scrapbook, so the journalism all had to be retrieved by Rachel Boulding. She also helped me to make the selection and gave me invaluable advice. She typed some of the book, and the rest was done by Pam Hewitt whose secretarial skills make such a difference to my life. To all, but especially to these last two, many thanks.

# Venice

# Browning's Parrots:
# Venice and the English Poets

How differently we would think of Byron and Shelley if they had survived into old age. How differently Byron would seem to us if our grandparents had known those who remembered him as a silver-haired fat old man, hobbling into dinners and even being, unimaginably, a bit of a bore. What a difference it would make to our feeling about The Odes if Keats had grown old, or wandered into London clubs and heard a gouty old figure in the corner complaining about the dangers and growth of radicalism, and said, with a desperate desire not to be 'caught' by him, 'Oh, that's Shelley'.

The old age of Robert Browning is, for me, a bit like that. His early poetry may not be penetrable. Was it Tennyson who said of *Sordello* – 'Who would, will hear Sordello's story sung' – that he only understood two lines in the whole work, the first and the last, and they were both lies? But the early Browning is burningly Romantic. He carried the torch of Shelley with fervour, and for one reason or another seized on the story of Sordello – in Asolo – to embody the strivings of the Romantic spirit. Then, after this impenetrable, if Romantic beginning, we see Browning living out the most beautiful love story in literary history, bringing to his middle-aged bride all the excitement and romance (in the vulgar sense of that word) which had been so ruthlessly denied her in her youth, bringing her love, and a child and bringing her, moreover, to Italy where, although she was to become a Florentine through and through, she was overwhelmed by Venice, 'the fantastic beauty of the buildings, the mysterious silence of the waters, St. Mark's piazza by gaslight, with its great populace swept up and down as if by a breath of music, the moon on the lagunes and the gondolas passing in and out of the shadows with their little twinkling lamps'.

It is all familiar to us; the romance of Elizabeth Barrett and Robert Browning. And yet how distressing the declining years of Browning are, the triviality of his social chitchat, the predictability with which he falls in love with one foolish woman after another, the sheer boringness of his later poetry. It is not purely wishful thinking on the part of his admirers, however, which sees in the poet's end a flaring up once more of the old flame. Like Galuppi, he had made his own crazy sort of music.

Then they left you for their pleasure; till in due time, one by one,
Some with lives that came to nothing, some with deeds as well undone,
Death stopped tacitly and took them where they never see the sun.

But when I sit down to reason, think to take my stand nor swerve,
While I triumph o'er a secret wrung from nature's close reserve,
In you come with your cold music till I creep thro' every nerve.

Yes, you, like a ghostly cricket, creaking where a house was burned:
'Dust and ashes, dead and done with, Venice spent what Venice earned.
'The soul, doubtless, is immortal – where a soul can be discerned.

'Yours for instance, you know physics, something of geology.
'Mathematics was your pastime; souls shall rise in their degree;
'Butterflies may dread extinction – you'll not die, it cannot be!

'As for Venice and her people, merely born to bloom and drop.
'Here on earth they bore their fruitage, mirth and folly were the crop:
'What of soul was left, I wonder, when the kissing had to stop?

'Dust and ashes!' So you creak it, and I want the heart to scold.
Dear dead women, with such hair too – what's become of all the gold
Used to hang and brush their bosoms? I feel chilly and grown old.

The Venice of Browning's *Galuppi* is literally a decadent place, almost rotting about one's ears. Its brightness is illusory, its pleasures transitory, its beauties vanished or faded. It is above all a city of death, full of chilling reminders of mortality, and this it remains in our mind if we think of it through the eyes of so many poets and novelists – a decadent place, a dying place, a perfect setting for the morbid marriage of love and death which is the hallmark of the Romantic approach to life.

How appropriate, then, that Browning (who, in spite of becoming such a dull old man, is one of the great Romantic poets) should by a natural instinct have rounded the ending of his story in this

4

corner of Italy. His last, very nearly posthumous poem is *Asolando* and in the autumn of 1889 he had revisited Sordello's old town, and then come into Venice to stay with his son Pen at Ca' Rezzonico. There, we are told, he would come, evening after evening, into what was called the Pope's room, overlooking the Grand Canal, carrying a little piece of cake or fruit to feed to Jacko the parrot. Here, to a certain extent, Browning held court, while in other houses, he gave exhausting readings for as long a two hours at a stretch. When he finally collapsed, he was too ill to read telegrams from England which assured him that reviews of *Asolando* were 'most favourable' which was more than you could say for most of the reviews he had received in the course of a long writing life. Nevertheless, when the contents of the telegram were read to him, he semed pleased, and gasped, 'I am dying, my dear Boy. My dear Boy'. And then he died.

The cemetery in Florence where Elizabeth Barrett is buried was closed, and so it was necessary to take Browning's body back to England for burial. In many ways it would have been more appropriate had the Venetians been granted their wish of burying him in the city where he died. An Italian Admiral's launch towed Browning's coffin on a magnificent funeral barge to San Michele, followed by an immense crowd of gondolas, all the chief officers of the city, members of his family and friends, and illuminated by a splendid sunset. It was then, somewhat less ceremoniously, dumped on a train and rushed across Europe for the obsequies in Westminster Abbey.

While that is happening, let us pause for a moment and map out our ground. I want to consider with you the Venice which crops up in poems and novels.

> Ay, because the sea's the street there; and 'tis arched by — why d'you call . . .
> Shylock's bridge with houses on it, where they kept the carnival:
> I was never out of England — it's as if I saw it all.

The first appeal of Venice to travellers is obvious, or seems to us obvious. Its appeal to poets has been, in historical terms, a little different over the years and in order to get, as it were, from 'Shylock's bridge with houses on it' to the funeral barge of the man who wrote those lines, we have to make a considerable leap in consciousness and imagination. So come back with me, if you will, on an imaginative journey of four hundred years, to one of the most magically beautifully Gothic cities in Europe, linked by narrow alleys, streets but above all by waterways, adorned with towers, bridges, castles, halls, palaces, abbeys and, over all, its brooding, strange, dark shadowy cathedral. In this thriving commercial capital of one of the most enterprising mercantile sea powers to emerge in modern times, there is an abundance of human activity, and its over-populated streets and squares are further swelled with the presence of foreigners, the richer of whom paid lavishly for the upkeep of the city's waterways, the repairing of bridges, the re-digging or draining of conduits or canals, the freshening and refurbishing of wells, the cleansing of pools. For their trade and profit largely depended on this city in whose waters so many beautiful pieces of architectural tracery were reflected. Nor, for the native citizens, were the waterways a mere amusement. It was the ordinary means of getting about, the ordinary, everyday traffic of the city passed by water; thousands of its inhabitants earned their living as boatmen. It was estimated in 1603 that there were as many as three thousand 'wherryes and other small boates, whereby . . . poore men bee set on worke and maintained'.

The waterway I am describing is the River Thames, and the city which I am describing, as you will have recognised, is Elizabethan London. John Stow, who completed his survey of the capital of England in the same year that Shakespeare's Venetian tragedy of *Othello the Moor* was first performed, describes a town almost all of whose major traffic was water-borne. Half a century and more later we find in the pages of Pepys's diaries the same state of things, with over two thousand watermen plying for hire as private taxis, quite apart from the other commercial vehicles with which the Thames was crammed. Pepys's London, more crowded even than Shakespeare's, was not built to accommodate the amount of traffic which was forced into its mean streets. If you wished to get anywhere fast, you had to go by water. 'By coach to the Temple and then for speed, by water thence to Whitehall' is a typical entry in Pepys's diary. It is a point worth remembering as we begin our survey of Venice – not a strictly historical or topographical survey, but our survey of it as a place which has haunted the imagination of playwrights and poets and novelists and aesthetes and dreamers. To us, perhaps lolling in a gondola as it bobs up and down on the lagoon or weaves its way into Venice and through its intricate warren of canals, there can be no more romantic mode of transport imaginable. If our first experience of Venice was not exactly like John Ruskin's, there is something in Ruskin's excitement which must have touched us all. Ruskin, for whom the love of Venice was more or less a religion, recalls his first grown-up glimpse of the place in tones which others would reserve for disclosures about the mystical life or memories of erotic awakening. He can hardly find words to express 'my own joys of 1835 and 1841, when there was not even the beginning of a railway bridge; when everything, muddy Brenta, vulgar villa, dusty causeway, sandy beach, was equally rich in rapture, on the morning that brought us in sight of Venice: and the black knot of gondolas in the canal of Mestre, more beautiful to me than a sunrise full of clouds all scarlet and gold.' The beginning of everything, he says, 'was in seeing the gondola beak come actually inside the door at Danieli's, when the tide was up, and the water two feet deep at the foot of the stairs; and then, all along the canal sides, actual marble walls rising out of the salt sea, with hosts of little brown crabs on them, and Titians inside'.

No such lyrical passage occurs in the Venetian plays of William Shakespeare. Beyond the vague sense that Venice is a port, from which Othello can take ship and Antonio can lose ships, there is not a very informed sense of Venetian topography in Shakespeare. It is true that Portia, at one stage of the *Merchant of Venice* (Act III, Sc. iv), speaks of 'the common ferry/Which trades to Venice'. But at the end of the same scene she appears to be intending to travel back to the city by coach. In *Othello* there is a similar lack of topographical interest or reference. There is no reason to suppose that Shakespeare had ever been to Venice. Had he done so, his two great Venetian plays might have contained descriptions of St. Mark's Square or the Grand Canal sufficiently lyrical to rival Ruskin's. Also, more tellingly, it is hard to believe, had he been to Venice, that Shakespeare would have been unable to resist jokes about it of the kind which W. S. Gilbert put into the mouth of the Duke of Plazatoro: 'As a Castilian hidalgo of ninety-five quarterings, I regret that I am unable to pay my state visit on a horse. As a Castilian hidalgo of that description I should have preferred to ride through the streets of Venice; but owing, I presume, to an unusually wet season, the streets are in such a condition that equestrian exercise is impracticable' (*Gondoliers* Act I).

But this is only something which *might* be so. Although we should not expect topographical accuracy in a dramatist who provided Bohemia, in *The Winter's Tale*, with a sea coast, Shakespeare very rarely goes in for detailed descriptions of specific places. He gives us no description of London, for instance. Had he visited Venice, he would have been coming, as I have already indicated, from a city much more *like* Venice than we could imagine. For Ruskin, as for us, a gondola is a romantic object. For Shakespeare it would probably have seemed as commonplace as, for a modern English observer, a number 19 bus. 'Sir Philip Sidney goes to Venice,' moans Ruskin, 'and seems unconscious that it is in the sea at all.' The sentence reminds me of an old friend, a veteran of the Spanish Civil War, to whom I lent a copy of Rose Macaulay's *Fabled Shore*. Though not devoid of an aesthetic sense, my friend cast the book down in disgust, saying, 'This is all about architecture and scenery. We had more important things to think about when we were in Spain.'

I question this pompous assertion – very few things are more important than scenery or architecture – but an Elizabethan traveller to Venice would have been excited by the place for reasons which seem strange to us now. The Elizabethans saw in Venice a prosperous, autonomous, island sea power, the mightiest in the Mediterranean. And of all models, it was evidently that one which they found most desirable to grow into themselves. The Venetian system of government was, in particular, the envy of these members of the new gentry, such as Essex, or the Herberts, or the Sidneys, who were to provide, many of them, the backbone of the republican movement in the next generation. A man of Shakespeare's age saw Venice not as a dreamy, idle, decaying sort of place, but as vibrant, prosperous and efficient: a place where money was made, where power was exercised by a rich oligarchy highly comparable to the rich oligarchy who dominated life in the Court and Parliament of Elizabeth I. For many in Shakespeare's London, Venice, where the Doge got the gondolas to run on time, was a realised embodiment of all their political and commercial aspirations. It is no surprise, therefore, to discover that Shakespeare does not find in Venice a city of dreams. In fact, on the contrary, in *The Merchant of Venice*, the dreamers, the lovers, the sentimentalists, the seekers-after-good retreat to Portia's pleasure palace of Belmont, a fairy-tale world, where the young man who chooses a leaden casket is given the golden reward of Portia's hand, and 'moonlight sleeps upon the bank' on which Lorenzo and Jessica lie down. The Rialto, by contrast, is the world of Shylock the Jew, the world of moneys and usances, and men there are held uncompromisingly to their

8

commercial agreements, a world where sentiment plays no part. The Rialto for Shakespeare is the same sort of place as Wall Street might be for us. Shylock makes it perfectly clear that Antonio, though annoyingly less grasping than himself, inhabits the same universe of getting and spending:

> I hate him for he is a Christian;
> But more for that in low simplicity
> He lends out money gratis, and brings down
> The rate of usance here with us in Venice.
> If I can catch him once upon the hip,
> I will feed fat the ancient grudge I bear him.
> He hates our sacred nation, and he rails,
> Even there where merchants most do congregate,
> On me, my bargains and my well won thrift.
> Which he calls interest.

This was language which would have been perfectly familiar to Shakespeare's audience, and they would have heard it, not on the lips of Venetian Jews, but on that of City merchants in London. Shylock's unforgiving, grasping nature is part of what makes him and the play so interesting. But we cannot enjoy *The Merchant of Venice* unless we can enter into the unrestrained innocence of Elizabethan capitalism. Venice in the title of the play reminds us at once that we are in the world of commercial reality, in an admirable, prosperous, efficient world of trade, commerce and finance.

Similarly, in *Othello*, we glimpse this Elizabethan idealisation of Venice both as a commercial and as a political entity. Brabantio, Desdemona's father, is seen as a 'super-subtle Venetian' by Iago, but he chooses to reveal himself as an even cleverer man, a man yet more Venetian: 'If sanctimony and a frail vow betwixt an erring barbarian and a super-subtle Venetian be not too hard for my wits and all the tribe of hell, thou shalt enjoy her,' he promises Roderigo. And just as the point of *The Merchant of Venice* is completely lost if we do not *admire* the commercial world which Shylock, albeit wickedly, represents, so in *Othello* we recognise that Venice is not only a great republic, presided over by 'most potent grave and revered signors', but also a place where wits and self-reliance and pushy self-enterprise and subtlety are all rewarded: in other words, an ideal place for those with the values and ideals of the go-getting Elizabethan merchant class, the first-generation gentry of the Cecil – Walsingham – Essex – Sidney calibre. Iago is a bad man. But we should recognise in him at once those qualities of cunning and enterprise which in a less malevolent character the Elizabethan audience would have admired. Volpone the Fox, you recall, is a Venetian in Ben Jonson's play; the Venetian mountebanks are in the gullible opinion of Sir Politick Would-be

> . . . the onely knowing men of *Europe*!
> Great generall scholars, excellent phisicians,
> Most admir'd states-men, profest favourites,
> And cabinet-counsellours to the greatest princes!
> The onely languaged men of all the world.

But his friend Peregrine is not so easily taken in and replies,

> And I have heard, they are the most lewd imposters:
> Made of all termes and shreds; no lesse belyers
> Of great-men's favours, then their own vile medicienes;
> Which they will vtter, vpon monstrous othes:
> Selling that drvg, for two-pence, ere they part,
> Which they have valued at twelve crownes before

In this exchange, as in the character and antics of Iago, there is the same mingling of horror at and admiration of Venetian deviousness and of the openly commercial nature of Venetian values. *Put money in thy purse* is the motto of Venice; as far as Elizabethan writers are concerned it is the motto not merely of Iago, but also of Antonio, Shylock and, yes, of Portia too, as it is of Volpone and Sir Politick Would-be. Money and power are so closely interrelated that it is hard to disentangle them. But we see in the Elizabethan Englishman's veneration for Venice something very like the twentieth-century Englishman's adulation of European power maniacs: George Bernard Shaw extolling the merits of Stalin and Hitler alike; Hilaire Belloc shouting himself hoarse in praise of Mussolini; droves of 1930s poets identifying with the struggle of the Spanish Republic. In the sixteenth, as in the twentieth century, it has been the more sinister political experiments in Europe which have excited the most enthusiastic support among the English. The ruthless commercialism and power-efficiency of the Doge and his councils, and of the multi-national skullduggery of the Rialto, naturally attracted the warmest enthusiasm from families whose fortunes had been founded on stolen monastic land, a mercantile coup d'état without European parallel at that date, and upon a secret police force and the use of torture. Sixteenth- and seventeenth-century Venice, which seems to us to be an alarming combination of the devious and the piratical, of the august and the ruthless, would have impressed the audiences of Ben Jonson and William Shakespeare.

Where Ruskin is wrong, of course, is in his suggestion that Elizabethan travellers to Venice returned wholly untouched by those 'actual marble walls rising out of the salt sea, with hosts of little brown crabs on them, and Titians inside'. The crabs might mean little to Sir Philip Sidney, but not so the Titians.

There can be few more indicative object lessons in how differently the Victorians and the Jacobeans looked at Venice than in the single parable provided by Turner's painting of Juliet's wedding night. Shakespeare, as I have said, saw Venice as a place which was almost an embodiment of worldly values, of deals, exchanges, ships, agreements. It was the most anti-Romantic of his Italian towns. And yet in order to emphasise the supreme romance of Shakespeare's most romantic play, the post-Byronic Turner transposes Juliet from Verona to Venice and has her leaning out of a window which overlooks the splendid torchlit Grand Canal. Between the time that the play was written and the painting painted, a revolution in taste has occurred.

The revolution, it can hardly be doubted, was effected quite largely by Turner himself, and yet more by his fervent apostle, John Ruskin. And I was in two minds whether to devote all my introductory remarks to the subject of Ruskin's *Stones of Venice*. There would be a case to be made out that it is the only fully successful work in modern English which takes Venice as its subject, and even more is there a case for regarding it, in the most important senses, as a work of the imagination. Nevertheless, what I really want to touch upon is the use to which Venice has been put in the works of poets and novelists. I am on the lookout not simply for works which are set in Venice, but for poems and novels which actually *use* Venice, grow out of it organically, as it were, rather than simply dropping it prettily as a backcloth to the otherwise irrelevant concerns of the writer.

\* \* \*

It would be as much a mistake to suppose that all Romantic poets felt about Venice as Browning had done, or as Ruskin supposed they had done, as it would to believe Ruskin's assertion that 'My

11

Venice, like Turner's, had been chiefly created for us by Byron.'
That is to say, while Ruskin's love of Venice may well have begun by
reading *Childe Harold*, it would be ludicrous to suppose that Byron
ever felt the faintest twinges of a Ruskinian thought while he was in
Venice. Ruskin quotes with amused disapproval the travel writings
of Elizabeth Lady Craven in 1789, who 'expected to see a gay, clean
looking town, with quays on each side of the canals, but was
extremely disappointed; the houses are in the water, and look dirty
and uncomfortable on the outside; the innumerable quantity of
gondolas too, that look like swimming coffins, added to the dismal
scene and struck me with horror rather than pleasure'.

Shelley, coming to Venice thirty years later, reacted in much the
same sort of way, as he confided in a letter to Thomas Love Peacock.
Not that the circumstances of Shelley's visit were altogether easy,
for he insisted on bringing with him, on his journey to visit Lord
Byron, his mistress and Byron's ex-mistress Claire Clairmont. She
was frightened by the dark – they sailed in at night – and we can
imagine that they felt somewhat seasick, since there was a driving
rain, and Venice, in so far as it was visible at all, bobbed up and
down as a prospect through the glass windows of their coffin.

The young idealists were profoundly shocked by the political
system obtaining at the time, and when he had had time to recover,
or gain his sealegs, Shelley explored the Doge's palace in whose
dungeons, he wrote home, 'the sufferers were roasted to death for
madness by the ardours of the Italian sun, and others languished in
the Pozzi, or wells, deep underneath, and communicating with those
on the roof by secret passages where the prisoners were confined
sometimes half up to their middles in stinking water.' He hated the
Austrian troops who swaggered about the place, but also, if the
truth was known, he was rather shocked to discover quite how Lord
Byron was behaving since his exile from London two years before.

Canto iv of *Childe Harold* had already appeared. It struck Shelley
as

> if insane, the most wicked and mischievous insanity that ever was given
> forth. It is a kind of obstinate and self-willed folly in which he hardens
> himself. I remonstrated with him in vain on the tone of mind from which
> such a view of things alone arises. For its real root is very different from
> its apparent one, and nothing can be less sublime than the real source of
> these expressions of contempt and desperation. The fact is, that first, the
> Italian women are perhaps the most contemptible of all who exist under

the moon; the most ignorant, the most disgusting, the most bigoted, the most filthy. Countesses smell so of garlick that an ordinary Englishman cannot approach them. Well, LB is familiar with the lowest sort of these women, the people his gondolieri pick up in the streets.

Nor, as Shelley was doubtless aware, was 'LB' entirely averse to the occasional dalliance with the *gondolieri* themselves. So one is bound to include, in any comments one makes about the Venetian motif in Byron and Shelley, that neither of them 'discovered' Venice in quite the sense that Ruskin maintained. There is the famous passage in *Childe Harold's Pilgrimage* where Byron

> Stood in Venice on the Bridge of Sighs;
> A palace and a prison on each hand:
> I saw from out the wave her structures rise,
> As from the stroke of the enchanter's wand.

But as one of his most affectionate and elegant biographers observed:

> Not once, during the years he was to spend in Venice, is there any descriptive mention in his letters of its most conspicuous glories. The great murmuring grotto of St. Mark's, where every surface gleams with a smooth subaqueous lustre and the rolling pavement imitates the wave-worn floor of a submarine cavern; Verrochio's presentation of Colleoni, with its *vista superba* and 'piercing and terrible' eyes: the vast devotional fantasies of Tintoretto and Veronese if not unregarded, they remain uncelebrated (*Byron, the Years of Fame* p. 79).

But this opinion of Mr. Peter Quennell's is highly Ruskinian, and might well have prompted a remark from the poet himself analogous to the moment when he and Tom Moore stood together watching a sunset so lovely that the Irish poet felt it necessary to say so, provoking from Byron the response, 'Damn me, Tom, don't be poetical.'

Byron came to Venice neither for the Tintorettos nor the architecture, but to get away from the scandals he had left behind him in England. It provided him with a perfect combination of privacy – compared with London, or even with Paris or Rome – and society; and moreover, as a student of Beckford and Casanova, Byron would hope to find here (he was not disappointed in the hope) the opportunity to gratify the image of himself as a hopeless *roué*, cynic, drunkard and lecher. How completely typical of the man it is, however, that, having arrived in time for the Carnival and enjoyed it so totally, he should have grown bored, as he admitted in the celebrated letter to Moore of February 28th 1817.

> The Carnival, that is, the latter part of it, and sitting up late o'nights had knocked me up a little. But it is over and it is now Lent, with all its abstinence and sacred music . . .

Notice, incidentally, how much the persona of the letters and of the narrative poems overlaps. 'With all its abstinence and sacred music' would scan perfectly as a line in *Childe Harold* or *Don Juan*. The letter goes on:

> The mumming closed with a masked ball at the Fenice, where I went, as also to most of the ridottos etc. etc.; and though I did not dissipate much upon the whole, yet I find 'the sword wearing out the scabbard' though I have just turned the corner of twenty-nine.

> So we'll go no more a-roving
> So late into the night,
> Though the heart still be as loving,
>   And the moon be still as bright.
>
> For the sword outwears its sheath,
>   And the soul outwears the breast,
> And the heart must pause to breathe,
>   And love itself have rest.
>
> Though the night was made for loving,
>   And the day returns too soon.
> Yet we'll go no more a-roving
>   By the light of the moon.

This exquisite, melancholy lyric is one of the best examples of what makes Byron's life and poetry so fascinating. For he approaches physical indulgence on the one hand wholeheartedly, almost with the enthusiasm of someone taking up a new sport or learning a language, and on the other with a wistful sense that he is a stranger and a sojourner on this earth. His determination to be thought wicked, his actual inability most of the time to be wicked, are alike products and symptoms of his natural honesty. It is his love of the truth which makes Byron such a funny writer as well as such a scabrous one.

The details of his life and loves are too familiar to be worth rehearsing. In both, there are reminders not only of the archetypal figure of Don Juan, but of the extraordinary character of Casanova. Both inhabited the peculiar, solipsistic no-man's-land where dissipation, pursued with the fervour of a religious votary, almost took on the character of spirituality; where the craving to become legends in their own lifetimes in no way seems contradictory to a profound need for solitude; where awaking and finding oneself famous was little more than the best way of falling asleep and making oneself anonymous. It was Casanova who wrote:

> Sans mystère, point de plaisirs,
> Sans silence point de mystère.
> Charme divine de mes loisirs,
> Solitude! que tu m'es chère!   (bis)

Byron, no less self-regarding, self-contemplative, self-ignorant, could easily have written the same.

We find him in Venice at an emotional crisis in his career, more stridently anti-English than at any period, perhaps in his life, more violently in pursuit of pleasure, more vulnerable in emotional affairs. This would have been so even without a visit from Shelley and Claire Clairmont, with all the painful memories which she resurrected. Yet once Claire had been dispatched to Este, it was an enjoyable reunion of the two friends. And the few weeks Byron and Shelley spent together in Venice in 1819 deepened their friendship. For Shelley, the hours they spent together talking or exploring the lagoon in a gondola, their evenings at the Palazzo Mocenigo, confirmed his sense that Byron was one of the great poetic geniuses, a view strengthened by the glimpses Byron allowed him of *Beppo* and *Don Juan* in progress. Moreover it led to Shelley writing *Julian and Maddalo*, his most accessible, though perhaps the least satisfactory of all his great poems.

Its unsuccess, from the artistic point of view, derives from the dramatic interest of the maniac, enwalled in the asylum, upon whom Count Maddalo has taken pity. What drove him mad

> I cannot say:
> A lady came with him from France, and when
> She left him and returned, he wandered then
> About yon lonely isles of desert sand
> Till he grew wild — he had no cash or land
> Remaining — the police had brought him here —
> Some fancy took him and he would not bear

>     Removal, so I fitted up for him
>     These rooms beside the sea to please his whim,
>     And sent him busts and books and urns for flowers . . .

It is this dramatic vein in Shelley (I mean in the Shakespearean sense dramatic) which Browning was able to exploit so brilliantly in all his own post-Shelleyan work. But in *Julian and Maddalo* the violence and the detail of the madhouse, and of the lunatic's ravings, are wonderfully irrelevant to the seriousness of Julian/Shelley's political and philosophical debates with Maddalo/Byron. The 'cause' itself, the idea of there being a cause, and of the melodrama with the woman which encases it, is all itself something of a cliché and wrapped up, in the end, in two lines:

>     I urged and questioned still, she told me how
>     All happened but the cold world shall not know.

Venice, in other words, retains its mystery. Shelley/Julian has been sufficiently impressed by the beauty of the place, as well as its threatening darknesses, its isolated darker quarters. There is the statutory glimpse of tourist Venice:

>                         The broad star
>     Of day meanwhile had sunk behind the hill,
>     And the black bell became invisible,
>     And the red tower looked gray and all between
>     The churches, ships and palaces were seen
>     Huddled in gloom; – into the purple sea
>     The orange hues of heaven sunk silently . . .

And these were matched with a wonderful incongruousness to the 'clap of tortured hands' which they hear later on in the madhouse having journeyed 'Through the fast falling rain and high-wrought sea' and felt 'the else unfelt oppressions of this earth'.

If Venice has produced a great poem in English, then *Julian and Maddalo* must be it. And yet most readers feel reasonably sure that it isn't it, that its greatnesses are all at war with one another.

I do not think these flaws are to be ascribed either to biographical causes – Shelley's ambivalence about Byron, for example, or about his own visit to Venice in 1819 – nor to the simple fact that the poem was written in some haste. Rather, I think the problem might have something to do with the very setting of the poem. The thing which seems to be such a splendid added advantage or backdrop,

16

this wonderful 'set' – the lagoon, the orange light, the purple water – break into the poem, which begins almost as a Platonic dialogue, and start taking over. It is an amusing coincidence that so many of the problems (both in his work and his personal life) which beset Shelley on this visit to Venice in the second decade of the nineteenth century should, as it were, be held by Providence in abeyance for some sixty years, until another visitor, also preoccupied, like Julian and Maddalo, with the sorrows caused in a demented mind by the pangs of despised love, should tell a story with the Venetian setting in which content and form are more perfectly and more miraculously married, should use almost the same formula, not of a lunatic, it is true, but of someone walled up in Venice with a 'story' attached to their unhappy past, and so handle or mishandle matters that he is at last assured that 'the cold world shall not know'; but that he should make of this failure – or rather the author, rather than the narrator of the story should make of it, a story not merely concerned with the frailty of human happiness and the nature of trust and confidence, but also an exercise and an exploration into narrative itself; so that we find in the hopelessly difficult quality of Venice – the fact, bluntly, that one is always getting lost if one tries, as a stranger, to explore, and the fact that – though waterlogged, it should be so largely, in high summer at any rate, arid and therefore infertile and unfruitful – we find I say in all this a certainly conscious paradigm on the artist's part of the narrative process itself. All this arose (and I am talking of course of *The Aspern Papers*) from Henry James hearing the story how Claire Clairmont survived into old age in Italy. Thus, to quote Betjeman at his least kind,

> . . . the new world meets the old world and the sentiments expressed
> Are melodiously mingled in my warm New England breast.

Venice, while being an appreciably delightful place for a poet, or for that matter anyone else, to be, is not actually a place which has inspired directly any very great English poetry. Shakespeare, as we have seen, probably never came here, but the uses which he made of Venice as a notion, as an idea, were altogether very different from the aspirations of the Victorians. The Romantics arrived in Venice when any such picture of it was not recapturable, for they saw a Venice in decay and decline, its architectural glories beginning to crumble, its political triumphs long since vanished. Browning, who saw the romance of Casanova's Venice from the safe distance of a hundred years and the happy security of a much more monogamous disposition, could play his Toccata of Galuppi's, and rather enjoy asking:

> Dear dead women, with such hair too – what's become of all the gold
> Used to hang and brush their bosoms?

His only answer was to say, 'I feel chilly and grown old.' The exploration of Venice in the eighteenth and yet more in the nineteenth centuries took, on the whole, narrative forms.

Browning's most remarkable narrative poem with a Venetian setting is the extraordinary *In a Gondola*. It is highly significant of the Victorian preoccupation with Venice as an idea, which did not necessarily bear any relation to Venice as a real place, that the poem was inspired by a painting, the 'Serenade' by Maclise. A modern poet, Philip Larkin, has made it a rule of life that he should never write a poem based on another work of art. Romantics had no such qualms, and *In a Gondola* is based not just on a painting, but on John Forster's commentary on the painting. In fact, the opening stanzas of the poem were written before Browning had even seen the painting.

The power of the thing derives from the luridly sensual stream of consciousness which passes through the male speaker's head, and by the violent and completely inevitable twist which is given at the end to the story.

The pair in the gondola seem at first sight to be a pretty stereotyped couple. He is serenading her:

> For the stars help me, and the sea bears part:
>   The very night is clinging
> Closer to Venice streets to leave one space
>   Above me, whence thy face
> May light my joyous heart to thee its dwelling place.

In other words, they are in the dark, and they can hardly see one another. But the second speech of the piece, spoken by the lady, reveals that they are not ordinary lovers. They are, to start with, adulterers who will be in trouble with the Three if they are found out. And she is chucking gold rings and jewels, trinkets evidently, given her by a detested husband, into the water.

The lady implores her lover to call her by her pet name now, while they are in the gondola together, for if the Three were to hear it, the use of the endearment

18

> would proclaim
> At once our secret to them all.

The gondola (and I think we are to imagine an *enclosed* gondola with windows, of the sort that Browning and his wife would have travelled in, the sort which made Shelley and Claire Clairmont so seasick in 1817) is a little world of love, where the lovers can be themselves, unthreatened by the jealousy of her husband and the threats of the sinister sounding Three. Meanwhile, with the combination of extreme compression and novelistic expansion which is one of Browning's hallmarks, we catch glimpses of the whole other world, the world of Venice, as the gondola glides by:

> Past we glide, and past, and past!
>    What's that poor Agnese doing
> Where they make the shutters fast?
>    Grey Zanobi's just a-wooing
> To his couch the purchased bride;
>    Past we glide!
>
> Past we glide, and past, and past!
>    Why's the Pucci Palace flaring
> Like a beacon in the blast?
>    Guests by hundreds not one caring
> If the dear host's neck were wried:
>    Past we glide!

In fact, this apparently random glimpse of the outside world of Venice reflects most vividly the inside world of the gondola. We can be sure that our heroine is as unhappy, sexually, with her husband, as poor Agnese, behind her shutters, or the child bride of grey Zanobi, whoever they may be. There is enough, from the things that the male voice tells us he sees, to discern what the world of love looks like from inside, from inside the gondola. They are in that state of peculiar and delicious erotic egoism in which it seems that they alone are happy, and they alone have the power to make each other happy. At the same time, the throwaway social observation, that someone is throwing a large party with none of his guests caring whether or not his neck were wrung, gives a first little breath of chill to our narrative of suspense.

After the lady sings the most famous lyric of the poem,

> The bee's kiss now!
> Kiss me as if you entered gay

> My heart at some noonday,
> A bud that dares not disallow the claim . . .

we return to narrative and learn that our hero is a Jew, carrying her

> farther than friends can pursue,
> To a feast of our tribe.

Browning derives as much excitement as he can from the contact between the pallor of the lady and the dark arms and legs of her adorer. He wishes that he had angelic wings with white feathers:

> Snow white they must spring, to blend
> With your flesh.

As he asks her to lie back, during this wing fantasy,

> Till both wings crescent wise enfold
> Your perfect self, from 'neath your feet
> To o'er your head, where lo, they meet
> As if a million sword-blades hurled
> Defiance from you to the world.

It is a little difficult to decide what, precisely, is going on: are we merely looking back, through Shelley, to an idealised, Platonic vision of the union between two souls, or is the pale naked form of the lady being literally enclosed in an archangel's arms?

All too soon, whatever is going on, the idyll is over, and he is once more wondering what will happen should the Three get him. And this time he imagines Paul's cloak cast over his head, Gian pinioning him while Himself (that is the lady's husband)

> has past
> His stylet through my back; I reel;
> And . . . is it though I feel.

In other words they are groping about, in some sense of the word, in the dark. He can't see her, as he speaks. Afterwards, and there is, at this stage of the poem, a distinct afterwards, she trails her hand in the water and says

> Dip your arm o'er the boat side, elbow deep,
> As I do; thus: were death so unlike sleep,
> Caught this way?

What is she suggesting? I dare say Browning himself would not have wanted the matter to be completely clear at this stage. A suicide pact?

20

Or is she agreeing with him that he will, all too likely, meet his end when her husband exacts her revenge? Or does she *know* that her lover is going back to his death?

They turn for home, and, only now, at this stage, do we get any inkling of how they met or what the nature of their love affair has been. The lover remembers the autumn day when he came along the canal and saw her trying to catch her pet parrot (called bafflingly, a lory) as it flew up into a peach tree over her balcony.

> I scarce could breathe to see you reach
> So far back o'er the balcony
> To catch him ere he climbed too high
> Above you in the Smyrna peach
> That quick the round smooth cord of gold
> This coiled hair on your head, unrolled,
> Fell down you like a gorgeous snake.
> The Roman girls were wont, of old,
> When Rome there was, for coolness' sake
> To let lie curling o'er their bosoms.
> Dear Lory, may his beak retain
> Ever its delicate rose stain
> As if the wounded lotus blossoms
> Had marked their thief to know again!

It is a most delicious moment, as is the long extended passage when he imagines her, in her naked beauty, rivalling the Titians and the Giorgiones which hang on the walls of her husband's house. Once more, as in the very conception of the poem in Browning's mind, we see her as a painted beauty. And then the dénouement, as terrible as anything Browning wrote; she agrees to meet her lover on the morrow, and to hang out the usual sign. If a harp string has been used to tie back the jasmine at her window, then all is clear, but if a black ribbon has been used, then it is a sign that the Three are on the lookout.

The arrangement made, they are about to step out of the gondola, out of the idyllic world, that is, of their *affaire*, and back into the artificial selves which 'real life' compels them to be.

> Resume your past self of a month ago!
> Be you the bashful gallant, I will be
> The lady with the colder breast than snow.

Then, we are told by a stage direction, he is 'surprised and stabbed' –

21

by the Three, or so he assumes. Rightly, surely. But did she know that she was leading her lover to his death? Is she, in fact, a Judas? In the immensity of the moment it does not matter whether she has betrayed him or not with a kiss. As in so much of Browning's morbid early love poetry, all that matters is the kiss itself. The hero dies with these splendid, if slightly ridiculous, words on his lips.

> Still kiss me! Care not for the cowards! Care
> Only to put aside thy beauteous hair
> My blood will hurt! The Three, I do not scorn
> To death, because they never lived: but I
> Have lived indeed, and so – (yet one more kiss) – can die!

Browning so delights in sexual experience that it is axiomatic with him that it is worth dying for: indeed, in a ghoulish way, it is perhaps even better if it is accompanied by death. Perhaps, when we remember that *to die* was Elizabethan slang for the experience of sexual ecstasy, the identification of the two experiences should not be dismissed. It probably relates to some widely held feeling about both. One's feeling on finishing *In a Gondola* is that poetry is too narrow a medium for the wide and strong matters of Browning's narrative. He is pouring too much into the pint pot, and meaning itself inevitably gets lost as it becomes refined and compressed. *In a Gondola* is a deformity. It isn't really a poem, in spite of its lyricism. It is a lyric shrieking and writhing to be turned into something else, a novel, perhaps. And it is time we turned to novels.

# Publishing Scoundrels:
# Novelists in Venice

*Sans mystère, point de plaisirs!* Our Venetian poet's assertion is
never truer than when we turn from the poets to the novelists.

> I loved her from my boyhood; she to me
> Was as a fairy city of the heart,
> Rising like water-columns from the sea,
> Of joy the sojourn, and of wealth the mart . . .

Byron's hymn of praise to the place makes it perfectly clear that
Venice is beautiful enough and exciting enough not to need an idea
being placed upon it, even though, as it happens

> Otway, Radcliffe, Schiller, Shakespeare's art
> Had stamp'd her image in me.

Byron, for a later generation, as we have seen, stamped the image of
Venice in a thousand hearts, making it a place, in the Victorian age,
which was equally alluring to innocent water-colourists hoping to
catch a perfect sunset over the lagoon and far from innocent way-
farers who hoped to find behind its rotting shutters and crumbling
façades a range of decadent pleasures of the sort which Byron or
Giovanni Jacopo Casanova themselves enjoyed.

But while a poem can be made of a town, and a painting can be
made of a sunset, a novel most unfortunately can't. The novelists
can no more resist the place than anyone else can, but it is not
always to their advantage, I think, that they are lured here. Place, in
a novel, is something which has to be absorbed into the whole
texture of the fiction, and Venice, as we have already seen in our
consideration of the poets, is not something which easily gets
absorbed. It tends in fact to do the absorbing. Proust, as we shall
see, felt defeated by the place precisely for this reason. There has

been a very great tendency, in lesser writers who have set their stories in Venice, to cascade into mere prettiness, to travel writing, even to travel brochure writing.

Another problem, not insuperable, but a problem nevertheless, is that a novel has to have people in it, and if the people are in Venice they have to have a reason for being here. This is not so of novels set in Rome (I mean *Italian* novels set in Rome) or St. Petersburg or New York or London. These are all places where people *live*. And although I know there are those who are lucky enough to live in Venice the great preponderance of novelists have neither known them, nor been of their number. Evelyn Waugh, Muriel Spark, L. P. Hartley, Ronald Firbank, Baron Corvo, Ivan Turgenev, Marcel Proust, Anthony Powell, Daphne du Maurier, Thomas Mann and Patricia Highsmith have all written Venetian novels about people who were not Venetian. The classic example of the sort of difficulty this poses is to be found in *Brideshead Revisited* where the Venetian passages are, to my mind, completely irrelevant to the main plot and are merely included because in a self-indulgent way Evelyn Waugh wanted to write about Venice.

Where the setting and the matter of the story are perfectly matched, by contrast, we do not always get a perfect story. Taking a *vaporetto* across the 'foul smelling, cholera ridden lagoon on a sultry afternoon', cannot Thomas Mann fill us with the full sense of mortality which the rotting place gives off, a sense fully allied to Browning's feeling of chill in the Toccata of *Galuppi*?

> There was a hateful sultriness in the narrow streets. The air was so heavy that all the manifold smells wafted out of houses, shops and cook-shops, smells of oil, perfumery, and so forth – hung low – like exhalations, not dissipating . . . His eyes rebelled, his chest was heavy, he felt feverish, the blood throbbed in his temples. He fled from the huddled, narrow streets of the commercial city, across many bridges, and came into the poor quarter of Venice. Beggars waylaid him, and canals sickened him with their evil exhalations . . .

Yes, there is no doubt that Venice is a natural place to die in. If we were to search through the works of the European novelists we would find a lot of death in Venice. There's a lot of it about. Is not this the place where Wagner's funeral barge came swooping down the Grand Canal, and where the perfect, morbid Romantic identification between love and death can be made?

Well, yes, of course, but the theme is not really exploited by Thomas Mann, or certainly not in *Death in Venice* itself, which if it is stultifying or crushing, is really stultifyingly *boring*. When we start asking ourselves why we should care about a character in fiction, then the novelist has failed. We never ask why we should care about the Brothers Karamazov; we go on suffering with them and following their every thought and passion. We don't ask why we should be wading through two thousand pages in order to find out about some unreal people called Natasha and Pierre and Prince André. But we do, I am afraid, keep putting down *Death in Venice*, and thinking that seventy-five pages is about as much as we can stand of the morbid Aschenbach and the wretched Tadzio.

> Yes, this was Venice, this is the fair frailty that fawned and betrayed, half fairy-tale, half snare; the city in whose stagnating air the art of painting once put forth so lusty a growth and where musicians were moved to accords so weirdly lulling and lascivious.

It is really very hard to take this self-indulgent string of platitudes seriously. And yet what else do you do with Venice, if you are not bold enough to put it into a story? You can realise, as Daphne du Maurier did in *Don't Look Now*, the thrilling potential to be got out of one's tendency to get lost in Venice. The dénouement of that tale *is* pretty terrifying, but it is at the opposite end of the scale from Thomas Mann. Daphne du Maurier's purpose is so modest. She is, as it were, being just cinematic, setting an extraordinary story in an exciting context. Mann is trying to make some sort of point but not telling a story which is, to me at least, very interesting. Is there no middle ground, in Henry James, for instance, or in Proust?

Of Henry James's visits to Venice, his biographer Leon Edel singles out two as being of singular importance. The first was a gloomy spell of 'seven unsuccessful weeks' in which he was depressed by the 'glutinous and malodorous damp' of the place, and by the appalling weather. 'Yesterday,' he wrote on this occasion (the month was March), 'there were sinister carts in the Piazza and men who looked like Irishmen shovelling away snow. One was almost sorry to have left.' Eight years later in 1894, however, visiting Venice in hot summer weather he was dismayed by the fact that it had become, 'if I may be allowed the expression, the mere *vomitorium* of Boston'. The Americanisation of Venice which occurred in the late eighties and early nineties was something which for James 'disitalianized this dear patient old Italy till one asks oneself what is at least left of its sweet essence to come to, or for. The accent of Massachusetts rings up and down the Grand Canal and the bark of Chicago disturbs the siesta.' This final phrase, 'the bark of Chicago disturbs the siesta', could almost be the opening line of a poem. I commend it to the insomniac among you as an exercise for the small hours to complete this haunting refrain.

For Professor Edel, however, these two particular visits to Venice, the gloomy one of spring 1887 and the hot, disgruntled one of 1894, are both full of meaning in relation to James's art. There are many other visits in between, of course, but it is upon these that Edel's attention rests in his monumental biography of the Master. And that is because he is one of those critics who likes wherever possible to link the impenetrable workings of a novelist's imagination to the external events of his life. What makes his biography of James so fascinating – a thing which in itself is almost a Jamesian exercise in fiction – is that James only most notionally *had* an external life. In the vulgar sense, he didn't 'do' anything, and we can only speculate, though since Leon Edel's researches how much more richly, fully, elaborately, about the movements of James's inner man. But it would seem likely as though the intimacy formed between the great novelist and a lesser practitioner, Constance Fennimore Woolson, was a source of great anxiety to James on that, his first visit to Venice in 1887.

With emblematic appropriateness, Fennimore was afflicted with deafness, and was unable to receive the signals, doubtless ambiguous enough by any standards, which the Master gave out. One is reminded of the old servant in the Reform Club in London in the early years of this century being asked if he remembered a Mr. Henry James. 'Mr. James? Mr. *James*. Would that be the gentleman who always gave his orders in a round*about* way?' Fennimore was, to put it brutally, very probably in love with James. He was aware that he had, as they would say, encouraged her attentions and advances, but had done so in the careless flirtatious spirit of a man who was so certain of his own celibacy that he could view relations between the sexes as 'safe'. These thoughts came to him particularly acutely, Professor Edel would believe, in that dank, miserable visit of 1887. Only a month before, in January 1887, he had been told the extraordinary fact that there had lived in Florence, to a ripe old age, Byron's mistress Claire Clairmont, the mother of Byron's daughter Allegra. She had had as a lodger a Bostonian, but one very different from Henry James himself. This Bostonian was one Captain Silsbee who had an interest in Byron and Shelley (particularly Shelley) and had been anxious to lay his hands upon any papers Claire Clairmont still had in her possession.

What struck James immediately was how extraordinary it was that the mistress of Byron should have been still alive when he had first got to know Florence. He must often have walked past her door.

'Certainly there is a little subject there,' James wrote, 'the picture of the two faded, queer, poor discredited old English women – living on into a strange generation, in the musty corner of a foreign town – with these illustrious letters their most precious possessions. Then the plot of the Shelley fanatic – his watchings and waitings – the way he covets the treasures . . .'

One sees here all the germs of *The Aspern Papers*, but the distinctive, the truly magnificent inspiration, was to transfer the story from Florence to Venice. For not only does James's story contain some of the finest descriptions of Venice, but it is also an entirely Venetian tale. The canals, bridges, *campi*, baffling little alleys and dark corners of the place are not merely a decorative backdrop. They are almost a character in the story. It is James's greatest drama, perhaps, of concealment – a constant theme running through all his novels. Europe is always at pains to conceal itself from itself – in *The Europeans*, the American visitors are aghast by the extent to which everything is draped and covered up – and also to conceal itself from the innocent affections or prying curiosity or both of the Americans.

Jeffrey Aspern, the unnamed narrator's hero, and the object of his ultimately unscrupulous literary quest, had been not a European like Byron and Shelley, but an American, and it had been his aim, you will remember, 'to feel, understand and express everything'.

One of the underlying ironies and assumptions of this densely meaningful story is the narrator's diminishing ability to feel, understand or express anything. Venice gets to him, but he (he, note, not James) is not clever enough, as Proust was, to resist it. This is what redeems what I disparagingly regard as the temptation to travel writing and purple prose which generally speaking assails the novelists as soon as they come bobbing over the lagoon. Take this paragraph, for example:

> I was seldom at home in the evening, for when I attempted to occupy
> myself in the apartments the lamplight brought in a swarm of noxious

insects, and it was too hot for closed windows. Accordingly I spent the late hours either on the water – the moonlights of Venice are famous – or in the splendid square which serves as a vast forecourt to the strange old church of Saint Mark. I sat in front of Florian's café eating ices, listening to music, talking with acquaintances: the traveller will remember how the immense cluster of tables and little chairs stretches like a promontory into the smooth lake of the Piazza. The whole place, of a summer's evening, under the stars and with all the lamps, all the voices and light footsteps on marble – the only sounds of the immense arcade that encloses it – is an open air saloon dedicated to cooling drinks and a still finer degustation, that of the splendid impressions received during the day. When I didn't care to keep mine to myself there was always a stray tourist, disencumbered of his Baedeker, to discuss them with, or some domesticated painter rejoicing in the return of the season of strong effects. The great basilica, with its low domes and bristling embroideries, the mystery of its mosaic and sculpture, looking ghostly in the tempered gloom, and the sea breeze passed between the twin columns of the Piazetta, the lintels of a door no longer guarded, as gently as if a rich curtain swayed there. I used sometimes on these occasions to think of the Misses Bordereau and of the pity of their being shut up in apartments which in the Venetian July even Venetian vastness couldn't relieve of some of their stuffiness. Their life seemed miles away from the life of the Piazza. And no doubt it was really too late to make the austere Juliana change her habits. But poor Miss Tina would have enjoyed one of Florian's ices, I was sure: sometimes I had even had thoughts of carrying one home to her. Fortunately my patience bore fruit and I was not obliged to do anything so ridiculous.

James is never so self-confident as in this story in his use of the first person narrative with the multiplicity of chance it affords for ambiguity and irony. For he, the Master, can gaze over the narrator's shoulders even as he speaks, and catch our eye and no, well, I would not say wink, for it is not possible to imagine Henry James winking. But we know that in his fashion the narrator has already made himself ridiculous in our eyes without his committing the ultimate absurdity of buying Miss Tina an ice cream. 'The accent of Massachusetts rings up and down the Grand Canal and the bark of Chicago disturbs the siesta.' The narrator is not properly speaking at home in Venice. Although Mrs. Prest, at the beginning of the story, promises him introductions, we find him still sitting with the tourists in St. Mark's Square by the fifth chapter. His reactions to it all are commonplace, banal, obvious; James thus covers his traces.

28

No one can accuse him of beautiful 'travel writing' here, for it is all seen through the eyes of his intrusive investigator. And yet of course, the man is right. The Venetian vastness has not been appreciated by the two ladies hemmed up in their crumbling *palazzo*. The evil is not all on the narrator's side. There remains in him, even to the unscrupulous end when he tries to rifle Miss Juliana's desk, a genuine sense of hero workship for Jeffrey Aspern, who wanted life to be 'free and not at all afraid'. He becomes a publishing scoundrel, but rather in the same way that it is impossible to grow any flowers in Miss Bordereau's garden. That sterile garden is another of these emblems which James manipulates so deftly throughout the book. We laugh at the Pooterish way in which the narrator is so jealous of his dignity. We are put into the position, from James's lofty ringside seat, to despise him for his Baedekerish view of Venice. And yet he is right. Miss Bordereau has lived a life of stultified desires, wasted ambitions, imprisoned hopes. With the innocent part of himself he would release her. With the unwitting, blundering part of himself, the part that offers a young (or not so young) lady flowers and ices, he is given the power to meet Miss Tina. But the prospect of a union with her is horrible to him, and so he loses everything; he loses the chance of seeing the papers, he loses his self-respect, he certainly loses our respect. He has become himself a withered garden in the midst of all the 'Venetian vastness'. Venice, as much as Miss Bordereau, and what James would call dear patient old Italy has won.

All these things, Leon Edel would say, were sharpened by James's own feelings of awkwardness and guilt about Constance Fennimore Woolson. Into the strong little anecdote about the survival of Claire Clairmont in Florence he has fed his own complicated responses to the European scene and to the emotional life felt in Venice in the month immediately following. So the twist is given to the story of the narrator leading Miss Tina on, and being unable to respond to her final, bold offering of herself, in exchange, as it were, for the papers.

Furthermore, Edel speculates that James, 'probably had an opportunity to see that Fennimore, with her innumerable trunks of possessions, was unable to throw anything away. And for all their promise to each other that they would destroy their correspondence, the thought may have occurred to him that somewhere among her accumulations were impulsively scribbled pages he had dashed off to her at various times, filled with his spontaneities of affection and irresponsibilities of feeling. *The Aspern Papers* may have been a screen for deeper thoughts, nourished by the novelist, that somewhere in the Brichieri, there might lurk some James papers.'

Well, maybe, is the most we can say to that. I think there is a bit of having your cake and eating it if you are going to force James into dreading union with Fennimore, and being worried that posterity could read his letters to her. But we shall never know the truth or not of this theory. That is because Henry James got there before us, and read the James papers, or these particular ones, and destroyed them.

For we now move forward seven years, to 1894, where we find the Master in a gondola far out in the lagoon, surrounded by what appear to be baby porpoises or balloons, or swollen parachutes, black, and growing momently more bulbous as, with the assistance of his friendly (but no more than friendly) gondolier, he attempts to sink the offending objects in the waters. At length, they have to return to land for some stones. The objects in question, swelling like great balloons to greater and greater proportions until, with the prod of a barge pole and the weighting of some old bricks they are sent to their watery grave, are, lugubriously enough, Miss Woolson's clothes. Henry James has come to visit her sister and brother-in-law, the Benedicts, and to assist them with clearing up Fennimore's 'effects'. For, as is notorious, she committed suicide. It is not exactly clear what led up to Fennimore killing herself, nor indeed, whether it was strictly speaking a suicide at all. She was in all probability delirious when she did it, suffering as she was from profound deafness aggravated by a very bad bout of influenza. It would certainly be ludicrously sensational to say that she threw herself out of a window of the Casa Semitecolo out of love for Henry James.

Together with her relations, Henry James went through her papers and things, and we do not know what he destroyed there. We know that this death, like the slow lingering death of his sister Alice some years before, was a bitter blow to him. He says as much. An example, however, of where Leon Edel goes one stage further than this and begins to write (admittedly plausible) fiction can be seen in his description of this particular bereavement.

'Fearfulness and trembling are come upon me; and sorrow hath overwhelmed me,' the Psalmist had sung. 'Oh, that I had wings like a dove!

for then I would fly away and be at rest.' In the coming months James may have read this psalm; for in it he probably found his deepest feelings of this terrible moment in his life; and in it he found the title of the novel that he would ultimately write about a death in Venice.

This is a very powerful piece of speculation, and a very powerful piece of writing in its own right, and in so far as it summons up a picture of James with a Psalter in his hand, it touches in us the inevitable curiosity we must feel about the religious sensibilities of the brother of William James. That particular line of enquiry is a dead end. If one tried to find out what, religiously speaking, Henry James 'believed' one would get nowhere. But Edel does not give us a single piece of evidence to suggest either that he read this psalm at the time of Fennimore's death more than at any other time (presumably he had known it by heart since childhood); nor that the fictitious death of poor little Milly Theale in *The Wings of the Dove* has a very close connexion with poor Miss Woolson's. Indeed, had there been such a connexion, would it not have been too painful for James to use? By analogy with his transference of the Florentine Claire Clairmont story to Venice in *The Aspern Papers*, would we not expect the tragic death of Fennimore to appear somewhere other than the town where it actually took place?

But perhaps I make all these provisos, these clearings of the throat, rather than plunge into the complexities of that, for me, the most difficult of all James's novels. I do not by that mean that it is difficult to follow, particularly, what is going on in *The Wings of the Dove*, as it is, for example, in *The Awkward Age*. I mean that for me there will always be a difficulty in believing that anyone, even a woman as devious as Kate Croy, would deliberately arrange for the man she loves to woo another woman, and to marry her (on the understanding that this other woman has only a frail hold on existence) simply in order to guarantee their future financial security. There would be so many other ways of doing it. Common theft would be less fraught with hazards. It is not, of course, that James plays down those hazards once his story is under way. And this, like so many of his books, began with an anecdote in real life in which someone was alleged to have done exactly what Kate Croy and Merton Densher attempt to do. But for all that, I feel a great yawning psychological implausibility at the heart of this magnificent work.

That does not prevent it, however, from being a wonderfully powerful book and, in simple sentimental terms, one of the most affecting James ever wrote. The death of Milly in Venice is heartbreaking. And more heartbreaking even than her death is the scene enacted in her hired *palazzo* overlooking the Grand Canal in which Lord Mark asks her why she does not go downstairs into the courtyard:

> 'Ah not to go down – never, never go down!' she strangely sighed to her friend.
> 'But why shouldn't you,' he asked, 'with that tremendous old staircase in your court? There ought of course always to be people at top and bottom, in Veronese costumes, to watch you do it.'
> She shook her head both lightly and mournfully enough at his not understanding. 'No, even in Veronese costumes. I mean that the positive beauty is that one needn't go down. I don't move in fact,' she added, 'now. I've not been out, you know. I stay up. That's how you happily found me.'
> Lord Mark wondered – he was, oh yes, adequately human. 'You don't go about?'
> She looked over the place, the storey above the apartments in which she had received him, the sala corresponding to the sala below and fronting the great canal with its gothic arches. The casements between the arches were open, the ledge on the balcony broad, the sweep of the canal, so overhung, so admirable, and the flutter towards them of the loose white curtain an invitation to she could scarce have said what. But there was no mystery after that moment; she had never felt so invited to anything as to make that, and that only, just where she was, her adventure. It would be – to this she kept coming back – the adventure of not stirring. 'I go just about here.'
> 'Do you mean,' said Lord Mark, 'that you're really not well?'

The contrast between the sickroom pathos of *What Katy Did* and the P. G. Wodehouse silly ass hero is brilliant. It is one of the finest moments in the book, and it is noticeable, as in *The Aspern Papers*, how James really uses Venice. It really makes sense that Milly should be here. This is not merely because she is viewed as an artefact, just as in England when she was unflatteringly compared with Bronzino. Milly is certainly a spoil or a commodity in which the other characters can trade. How Venetian! Not merely that, since she is going to elude her predators in the only way possible – by dying – what better place to die in than this place where the beautiful has always been up for sale, and where, in the midst of society, the very architecture itself conspires to immure and to isolate? She cannot come down. That is Milly's drama. The *mystère* and the *plaisirs* (if it is right to use the word *plaisirs* of this terribly sad book), the *mystère* and the *plaisirs* for which we were seeking were never more fully met than here.

Proust is much blunter about such things than Henry James and gives us his aesthetic predicament stamped, as it were, on a visiting card.

'When I went to Venice I found that my dream had become — incredibly but quite simply — my *address*!'

That is how Marcel Proust described his first sojourn in the Danieli, when he went there in the early summer of 1900, accompanied by his mother.

In Proust's fiction, Venice is a sort of spiritual or aesthetic Elysium after which the narrator is always pining. Indeed, there is complete appropriateness in the fact that Monsieur Swann's announcement of his own imminent death to the Duchesse de Guermantes should take the form of a confession that he will be unable to come with her to Italy. The narrator has been following Swann's Way from the beginning of the story. Whether it is into the torment of unrequited love or into the salons of Madame Verdurin and/or the Faubourg St. Honoré, Swann had been there before, his own existence providing a sort of strange commentary on Marcel's. So, in the famous scene (trans. Scott-Moncrieff, vii. p. 391) the Duchess asks him if she can expect his company in Italy the following year. She reminds him that he has been to Venice with Mme. de Montmorency. What possible excuse can there be for not going with herself? He is ill, he says. '"Yes, my little Charles, I don't think you look at all well. I'm not pleased with your colour, but I'm not asking you to come with me next week, I ask you to come in ten months . . . Give me in one word the reason why you can't come to Italy." The Duchess put it to Swann as she rose to say goodbye. "But, my dear friend, it's because I shall then have been dead for several months."'

There follows, as you will remember, the touching scene of the Duchess being sent from the room by the Duke to change her black shoes to red, but in reality to cover the blank unanswerability, the sheer embarrassment of Swann's admission. For us, however, who have lived by now with the narrator for six volumes, we see that Swann's inability to go to Venice is the perfect expression of the death of his mind, his imagination, his soul. For Swann before all other things, before he is a wounded lover, or a figure in society, or a Jew, is an aesthete: the man with the perfect eye; the man who has secretly been worshipping in the Palace of Art all his life, as the narrator aspires to do. In Proust's scheme of things, therefore, Venice is a sort of spiritual home from which Swann must be excluded. It is a place from which Marcel himself has already been excluded by illness. Places, and the individual artefacts within them, are all invested with peculiar private meanings in Proust's book. Combray, obviously, represented the depressingly violable world of his childhood, as well as being the mysterious place in which his first snobbish impressions of France were formed – the 'real' France, that is, of the snob's imagination, the France of peasants like Françoise, and the aristocrats like the Duchesse de Guermantes, the France untouched by the bourgeois realities of his own memories, his aunts, his parents and so on. Balbec, the Norman seaside resort where they go for holidays, is associated with sexual awakening and the Jeunes Filles en Fleurs. But Venice is the land of art; and when the youthful Marcel is told that he will be going there, he

> reflected that the spring sunshine was already tinging the waves of the Grand Canal with so dusky an azure, with emeralds so splendid that when they washed and were broken against the foot of one of Titian's paintings they could vie with it in the richness of their colouring. I could no longer contain my joy when my father, in the intervals of tapping the barometer and complaining of the cold, began to look out which were the best trains, and when I understood that by making one's way after luncheon, into the coal-grimed laboratory, the wizard's cell that undertook to contrive a complete transmutation of its surroundings, one would awaken the next morning, in the city of marble and gold, in which the 'building of the wall was jasper and the foundation of the wall an emerald'. . .

The Biblical quotation comes from Ruskin, whom Proust was avidly reading even as he himself made that transmutation in 1900, from the sooty laboratory of his Paris station to that of Venice. As it happens, however, his illness puts a visit to this Ruskinian fantasy world out of the question, and Marcel does not actually get to Venice until ten volumes later, after he has lost his beloved Albertine. Most conspicuously, Marcel is really rather disappointed in Venice. He provides a few pages of standard guidebook descriptions, of little-visited *campi*, picturesque canals and pretty churches. Like every tourist before and since, he forms the impression that he has found out a secret Venice which the idiots who have been there before have somehow missed. But in the end he is forced to confess that his egoism is reproached by the place. As they are preparing to go, Marcel tells his mother that he will not be leaving; and she, sensibly refusing to believe him, sets off for the station with the luggage, leaving him alone.

> Things had become alien to me. I was no longer calm enough to draw from my throbbing heart and introduce into them a measure of stability. The town that I saw before me had ceased to be Venice. Its personality, its name, seemed to me to be lying fictions which I no longer had the courage to impress upon its stones. I saw the palaces reduced to their constituent parts, lifeless heaps of marble with nothing to choose between them, and water as a combination of hydrogen and oxygen, external, blind, anterior and exterior to Venice, unconscious of Doges or Turner. And yet this remarkable place was as strange as a place at which we have just arrived, which does not yet know us – as a place which we have left and which has forgotten us already. I could not tell it anything more about myself. I could leave nothing of myself imprinted upon it. It left me diminished, I was nothing more than a heart that throbbed, and an attention strained to follow the development of 'sole mio'. In vain might I fix my mind despairingly upon the beautiful and characteristic arch of the Rialto, it seemed to me, with the mediocrity of the obvious, a bridge not merely inferior to, but different from the idea that I possessed of it as an actor with regard to whom, notwithstanding his fair wig and black garments, we know quite well that in his essential quality, he is not Hamlet . . .

By the time Proust wrote the Venetian sections of his novel his powers were failing and he was more than half dead. In fact, we don't know how he would have reworked these passages had he lived to see the whole novel collectively through the printer. But the drift seems pretty clear. The whole strength of Proust's fiction depends upon the success with which he can impose his own vision on the material world, a strength which is testified by the rather absurd burghers or villagers of Illiers in Normandy who have changed the name of Proust's childhood home to Combray, as he calls it in the book. (It would be rather like the aldermen of Coventry renaming the city Middlemarch – an unheard of compliment to the power of the novelist.) In Venice – true Venice, that is to say, rather than the imagined Venice which has appeared to Marcel for nearly eleven volumes as a Promised Land – in Venice, the narrator's egoism breaks down.

The reason for this, in biographical terms has been explained very convincingly by Proust's biographer George Painter, who reminds us that Proust first visited Venice in the year of Ruskin's death. The visit also coincided with Proust's growing disillusionment with Ruskin. Though it would have been contrary to his nature to put anything so succinctly, we might believe that Proust would have agreed with Virginia Woolf's judgement, coming to Venice: 'That old fraud Ruskin, he was too virtuous. That's a great pity. Everything had to be squared – even those finicking palaces must be morally Good – which they're not – oh no – merely slices of coloured stone.'

Proust who had been wholly disciple of Ruskin felt his loyalty to the master weakening when he was confronted with the actual thing, with the slices of coloured stone. He never quite admitted to himself that *The Stones of Venice* is a remarkable work of fiction, but he came halfway to doing so. Moreover, his feelings about the place which Ruskin describes must have been complicated by his second solitary visit in the autumn of 1900. We would not know that he had come back five months after he came here with his mother had not his biographer found out his signature (dated 19 October 1900) in the registry of the Armenian monastery at San Lazzaro. He hints, in his maudlin way, in *Contre Sainte-Beuve* that he wept with guilt, passing his mother's bedroom window in the Danieli, at the memory of some piffling quarrel that they were supposed to have had in the spring. But if George Painter's speculation is right, we may assume that there were murkier reasons for his tears. 'Perhaps,' Painter writes, 'for Proust, Venice was linked with the Cities of the Plain; and perhaps he sought and found there on the second visit the sinister enchantments known to Byron and John Addington Symonds, Henry James, Housman and Baron Corvo, of which Ruskin had nothing to say'.

We need not take seriously the absurd injustice of this imputation against Henry James. But of the other names in the list, all, as is notorious, visited Venice in search of the pleasures offered by compliant gondoliers who doubled as male prostitutes, a fact which cannot conceivably have escaped Proust's notice but of which he would have had small chance to take advantage while accompanied by his mother and various other friends from Paris. If the narrator's memories of Venice in À *la recherche du temps perdu* suggest an inability to reconcile the fact that his dream had become, incredibly, his address, we should not assume that the reasons for this are purely aesthetic. Venice eludes the novelist's imagination because it goes on being itself; it won't become Proust's Venice in the way that Ilier becomes Proust's Combray. But also it must be said that the slices of coloured stone which Ruskin's imagination could persuade Marcel to be 'morally good' are inevitably associated in Proust's memory with depressing homosexual sordidities. The whole raison d'être of À *la recherche du temps perdu* depends upon Proust's desire to pull wool over the public eyes. What seems to be the most self-regarding and self-contemplative novel in the history of literature is actually a highly elaborate piece of projection and self-protection. Proust's Jewishness, for instance, about which he felt so intensely awkward and ashamed, is all projected on to Monsieur Swann. Marcel the Gentile surveys Swann's quandary in the matter with the pity and kindness of an outsider. In exactly the same way, the Baron de Charlus's crypto- and eventually increasingly overt homosexual behaviour, his picking up of shopboys, his chasing of bus conductors, his frequenting of the male brothels, is viewed with horrified disapproval by the heterosexual Marcel. It is, of course, all a direct transcription of Proust's (far from exclusively) homosexual life. The slices of stone as they actually come jutting out of the brown waters of the lagoon and the canals cannot be as morally good as the great Ruskin wanted them to be. By the same token, what his biographer has called 'Salvation through Ruskin' was not to be found. Poor Proust had other things to occupy him. His narrator wanders alone 'through humble *campi* and little abandoned *rii*' in search of working-class girls of the kind who might have appealed to his bisexual lover Albertine when she came to Venice. Although it is facile to assume that all the girls in Proust are really boys in disguise, it does not require too much imagination to be able to see a process of transferance at work here. It was a short visit. Ruskin's Venice, as well as being a great generalised vision, is also an abundance of detail, lovingly and long contemplated. They are not the same details as those which, we may safely conjecture, attracted the eyes of Marcel Proust. Thus, when he came to 'remember' Venice for his novel, he remembered sensations of disillusionment and self-disgust, but he did not really remember the detail of Venice as Ruskin had drawn it for him. This was partly no doubt due to the fact that Proust's memory was curiously bad. That is why he had to construct a whole 'artificial' memory in his novel. (In order to write the famous passages recalling the apple blossom of his childhood, for instance, Proust had to have himself driven to the suburbs of Paris where some particular apple trees had taken his fancy, stare at them from the back of the car, and then be whooshed back at great speed to his cork lined bedroom before he forgot about them.) If he had actually viewed Venice through a haze of lust on his second visit in 1900 it would be a very good partial explanation for the fact that he is unable to give us anything more than the most commonplace guidebook impression of the place. There is only one good bit in his chapter on Venice. So often, in Proust, he is at his best not when he is contemplating the sufferings and sensations of Marcel but when he is turning his wonderfully comic and sympathetic eye on the social scene. Yet we must not dismiss Proust's picture of Venice without treasuring the scene in one of those palaces in the Grand Canal which had been turned into a hotel and where we meet again our old friend the Marquise de Villeparisis. Years ago, Marcel had visited her in Paris, in a scene memorable if only for the social detail that in those days, gentlemen when calling took their hats into the drawing room of a lady. Monsieur le Prince de Norpois, who is (we later gather) the lover of the old *marquise*, makes the ludicrous pretence of having left his hat, whereas he has spent the afternoon in the *marquise*'s bedroom.

And here she is, years later, an old woman in a grand hotel in Venice, munching her way through a meal. The waiter asks her if she would like to wait for M. de Villeparisis, and the narrator waits with amused anticipation to see who is claiming to be this woman's husband, the real M. de Villeparisis having long since quit the scene. He does not have to wait long before old M. de Norpois appears. The narrator is touched by their devotion to each other, but even more by their ability to go on deceiving the world. For the latest newspaper from Paris (a newspaper where M. de Norpois has friends and influence) reports that Norpois was at that moment in the French capital attending upon the Emperor, and justifying by his exemplary behaviour as Minister of War the absolute reliance which public opinion placed upon him. There is nothing particularly Venetian about the scene (it could have happened anywhere abroad) but it is a good example of the way Proust manipulates coincidences for comic effect.

For one last little glimpse of Venice in the novel it would be tempting to move forward and consider the work of some writer more modern. But I hope you will forgive me if, instead of coming forward in time, we go a little bit back; and if, instead of going west of the Paris bedroom where Proust, in the small hours, sustained by a repulsive diet of hot milk and fried potatoes, scribbled down his Venetian memories, we turn east to that thoroughly Europeanised Russian, Ivan Sergeyevich Turgenev.

I do so because *On the Eve* is such a delightful novel, and one which uses scenes so effectively – I almost said so shamelessly. Everything in the book happens in its perfect setting: students wrestle with intellectual problems in austere bachelor lodgings; young love flourishes in the springtime and in the countryside; and when it is time for the lovelorn hero to die, he is conveniently ready in his gondola. We know, from the moment that Bersyenev asks the young Bulgarian revolutionary Dmitri Nikanorovich Insarov to lodge with him in the country, that the young man will be introduced to the prosperous Stahov family, and that young Elena Nikolayevna will fall in love with him. And yet the very artlessness and simplicity of the plot does nothing to diminish the intensity with which we enter into Elena's feelings for Insarov. The prose is wholly economical, spare; and yet the most violently operatic of emotions are expressed, and a degree of physical passion is allowed the characters, which at this date – 1859 – would have been almost unthinkable in an English novel. I am thinking of the two occasions when Elena visits Insarov in his squalid lodgings in Moscow. On one occasion, before he is ill, she comes to his room and tells him that she loves him, and that he loves her; she is innocent and direct enough to be able to express these inexpressible truths which have been tormenting Insarov, and then she goes.

> For a moment Insarov stood in front of the closed door and also listened. He heard the door into the yard bang downstairs, then went to the sofa and sat down, covering his eyes with his hand. Nothing like this had ever happened to him before. 'What have I done to deserve such love?' he thought. 'Am I dreaming?' But the faint odour of Mignonette which Elena had brought into his mean dark room reminded him of her presence. With it, there still seemed to linger in the air the sound of that young voice and those light footsteps, and the warmth and freshness of that virginal body.

This physical directness – the reader's intense awareness of Elena as a physical being – is even more noticeable when, having attended upon him during a fatal illness, she visits Insarov again, and he begs her to go, for the passions she excites are too overwhelming. Once more, it is she who takes control of the situation.

> 'Elena, have pity on me, you must go, I feel I might die . . . I can't bear these feelings – all my being is longing for you . . . to think that death nearly parted us . . . and now you're here in my arms . . . Elena.'
> She trembled.
> 'Then take me,' she whispered, so that he hardly heard.

Ten words in English, fewer in Russian, to convey such a wonderful moment. The lovers are of course doomed to be separated by death. Cut off by the outbreak of the Turko-Russian War in the spring of 1854, Insarov is determined to get back to Bulgaria, if necessary by sea, which is what brings our lovers to Venice.

> And just as the spring stirs us and fills us with longing, so does the loveliness of Venice; she provokes and tantalises the innocent heart with a sense of some imminent joy, a joy which is both simple and mysterious . . .

There could be no fuller expression of Casanova's ideal 'Sans mystère, point de plaisirs!'

Do you remember when they finally get to their bedroom in the hotel, they look out

> on the broad lagoon which stretches from the Riva degli Schianovi to the Guidecca. Almost opposite their hotel rose the pointed tower of San Giorgio; to the right, high up in the air, shone the golden ball of the Dogana, and the most beautiful of churches, the Redentore of Palladio stood like a bride adorned; to the left, masts and sails and funnels of ships looked black in the night; half spread sails hung like a great wing, with the pennants hardly stirring. Insarov sat down by the window, but Elena did not let him admire the view for long; he had suddenly become feverish, and he was seized by an overpowering feeling of weakness. She put him to bed, and when he was asleep, quietly returned to the window. Oh, how peaceful, how tender the night seemed! The azure air stirred with the softness of a doze; surely all pain, all grief, must needs be silent and sleep beneath the holy, innocent light of that clear sky. 'Oh God,' she thought, 'why must we die, why must we suffer separation and illness and tears?'

In the unlikely event of there being anyone present who cannot

40

remember what happens to this delightful girl, I do not wish to upset you by any further reminiscence. But it is part of Turgenev's magnificent and touching achievement that one of his readers at least cannot see that picture postcard view of the lagoon without thinking of Elena in her distress, without feeling, as her lover did, that 'there seemed to linger in the air the sound of that young voice and those light footsteps and the warmth and freshness of that virginal body'.

Venice, February 1985

# Johnson, Boswell, Wilson

# Samuel Johnson's
## *A Dictionary of the English Language*

A lady, calling at number 17, Gough Square one afternoon during the period when the great lexicographer was compiling his *Dictionary*, was surprised when the front door was opened by Samuel Johnson himself, bleary-eyed, in a nightshirt. In one hand, he carried a brimming chamber pot, while with the other, as she stood in the hall, he retrieved a dirty little brown wig from the bottom of the banisters and placed it, with an awkward *politesse*, on his great head.

The incident is one of many which illustrate the Great Cham's almost preternatural indolence. Like all depressives, he found it impossible to regulate his sleep; in spite of his repeated resolutions to rise early, he was seldom out of bed before noon. A vast appetite compelled him to gorge a long and greasy dinner at about two in the afternoon, and his evenings were devoted to conviviality: at the period of the *Dictionary* (1746–54) this was largely enjoyed in the company of his friends in the Ivy Lane Club. These years, too, marked the last wretched phase of his marriage. After repeated illnesses and separations, his beloved Tetty died at the Gough Square House in 1752. Though he watched her being placed in the coffin, Johnson was, to his everlasting regret, unable to bring himself to make the journey to Bromley for her funeral.

This, too, was the period of his most energetic hackwork. From 1750 to 1752, he scribbled out twice-weekly essays (always at the last minute) for *The Rambler*, while in the early days of his widowerhood, he was writing *The Adventurer,* which fills four volumes.

When one considers the miserable outward circumstances of life in Gough Square, Johnson's own temperamental melancholy, bordering ever on lunacy, the pressures made upon him both by journalism and by the ceaseless (and never repulsed) demands on his infinite charity by the grotesque lame ducks with whom he was always surrounded, it seems miraculous that his *Dictionary* was finished at all. The boast and apologies in the concluding paragraph of his Preface to the great work are not hyperbolic. 'In this work, when it shall be found that much is omitted, let it not be forgotten that much likewise is performed; and though no book was ever spared out of tenderness to the author, and the world is little solicitous to know whence proceeded the faults of what it condemns; yet it may gratify curiosity to inform it, that the *English Dictionary* was written with little assistance of the learned, and without any patronage of the great; not in the soft obscurities of retirement, nor under the shelter of academick bowers, but amidst inconvenience and distraction, in sickness and in sorrow: and it may repress the triumph of malignant criticism to observe, that if our language is not here fully displayed, I have only failed in an attempt which no human powers have hitherto completed.'

All this is very largely true, even though Johnson's was not the first dictionary of the eighteenth century. He drew heavily, for the general shape and structure of his work, on Nathan Bailey's *Dictionarum Britannicum* of 1736. Where Johnson's *Dictionary* improves upon Bailey is in the wealth and range of its literary allusions, as in the sheer number of words he managed to include and define. An ever-changing team of hacks was employed at Gough Square to help him assemble the quotations. Johnson would go through the works of favourite English authors – Shakespeare, Pope, Dryden and Addison predominate – scribbling in the margin or underlining passages which might be of use. In many cases, he chose a passage which throws little light on the sense or etymology of a word, selecting lines which are merely beautiful in themselves. Thus, having told us that *mohair* is 'thread of stuff made of camel's or other hair', he quotes Pope's strikingly novelistic lines:

> She, while her lover pants upon her breast
> Can mark the figures on an Indian chest,
> And when she sees her friend in deep despair,
> Observes how much a chintz exceeds mohair.

The profusion of quotation makes the *Dictionary* one of the most rewarding anthologies in the language and shows us what we could be forgiven for disbelieving if we read only the *Lives of the Poets* –

Johnson's high feeling for poetry. Again and again, the lexicographer's eye lights upon poetry which is exotic, euphonious and delightful, where the critic's seems only eager to pounce on, or to create, absurdities. Nowhere is this more striking than in the quotations from Milton in the *Dictionary*; their extent reveals an obvious and loving acquaintance with Milton's work which the Tory biography of the regicide would not allow himself to show. One would not guess, from the number of times that the lexicographer quotes from Milton, that he was a poet whose diction was 'easy, vulgar and therefore disgusting'.

Once the passage had been marked, the book would be handed to the amanuensis to copy it onto a slip of paper, and Johnson would set to work with a definition. The caprice with which this part of the labour was completed has passed into legend. Because Lord Chesterfield had let him down badly at the beginning of the enterprise and not provided patronage, a patron is defined as 'a wretch who supports with insolence and is paid with flattery'. Likewise, everyone knows that *oats* are 'a grain which in England is generally given to horses, but in Scotland supports the people'. Sometimes he made simple mistakes, but was honest enough to own them, as when a lady in Plymouth asked him why he had defined *pastern* as the knee of a horse. 'Ignorance, Madam, pure ignorance.' Addicts of self-inflated Johnsonese likewise delight in the complex latinity with which he attempts to explain quite simple words such as *network*: 'any thing reticulated or decussated, at equal distances, with interstices between the intersections'; or *cough*: 'a convulsion of the lungs, vellicated by some sharp serosity. It is pronounced *coff*.'

Of etymology, Johnson was largely ignorant, and in words not of Latin or Greek origin, he was often wide of the mark. He was aware of knowing nothing of Germany philology (a subject so embryonic as not to have reached its infancy) and he went to Oxford in 1754 — when the bulk of the *Dictionary* was finished — to look for help in his *History of the English Language* with which the work is prefaced. He seems to have known nothing of the scholarship of such men as George Hickes or Thomas Hearne, and he does not appear to have spent more than a few weeks acquainting himself with philological problems which it was to take a lifetime of several German and English scholars in the nineteenth century to solve. The inadequacies of Johnson's history of the language need not, therefore, surprise us.

They did not prevent the dictionary becoming a monolith, a monument, and there was complete justice in the reverence with which, for some seventy years after its compilation, it was regarded. Since it is the biggest of Johnson's works it is not surprising that it should exemplify one of the great paradoxes of his character. Insofar as it is monolithic, bossy and latinate, it seems to embody all that we understand by the word 'Augustan'. The eighteenth century, we are told, was the age in which English spelling and orthography were ossified. And Johnson's *Dictionary* was partially responsible for this, seeming to fulfil many of the prescriptive offices which the *Academie Française* so comically carries out to this day over the Channel. It was this staid, pedagogical work, we remember, that Becky Sharp threw out of the carriage window as soon as she left behind her the constricting tyranny of the Semiramis of Hammersmith.

But Johnson, although he liked to represent himself as a stern moralist and a linguistic purist, was in fact a well of the volcanic chaotic idiosyncrasies with which we associate Romanticism. There was nothing orderly, or staid, or symmetrical about him. He possessed none of the neoclassical refinements. His ill-suppressed passions, his obsessive dread of death, his uncontrolled egotism and his high emotionalism are all qualities which we would associate more with Dickens or Beethoven than with Boileau or the Earl of Chesterfield. The *Dictionary* defines a lexicographer as a 'harmless drudge, that busies himself in tracing the original, and detailing the signification of words.' The book as a whole, however, is very obviously not that of any such being. Now that it has been superseded by the work of true drudges, we can appreciate its bubbling, imaginative wealth. For it is a tribute not merely to the range of Johnson's reading, but also to his profound sense of poetry. Though his own poetry is almost all disappointing, one sees from the quotations in the *Dictionary* that he was not merely steeped in the poems of his predecessors. He read them with a poet's eye.

*Spectator*, 30 July 1983

# James Boswell

Johnson once said to Boswell: 'Were you to die, it would be a limb lopped off.' And it is certainly hard to think of Boswell as anything but an appendage to the Great Cham. A biography with Boswell as its chief subject would seem to be on a par with the solitary adventures of Doctor Watson, with little reference to Sherlock Holmes; or the chronicles of Little Noddy without Big Ears.

It was only in 1950, one and a half centuries after Boswell's death, that his copious journals began to be published, and the reading public was gradually made aware of the extraordinary character of Johnson's biographer.

He was credulously religious, but terrified of exposing himself to rationalist arguments on the subject (with Hume for example) for fear of falling into scepticism. He was desperately anxious to get on in the world, but he invariably quarrelled with the people who might have helped him the most. Nor could he resist drunken and raucous behaviour which scarcely impressed potential patrons.

He was a devoted Scot (though Johnson called him the most unscottified of his countrymen) and he was really happy only when he was away from his native land. He was passionately proud of his ancestry but violently antipathetic to his father, Lord Auchinleck, (who opined that Johnson was merely 'an auld dominie').

And, as is notorious, Boswell was torn between a Christian love of his pretty young wife and an uncontrollable 'exuberance of amorous faculties', as he himself phrased it. His present biographer recalls that Boswell's premature death aged fifty-five was caused by uraemia, 'the result of acute and chronic urinary tract infection, secondary to post-gonorrheal urethral stricture'.

As readers of the *Journals* will know, Boswell was an erotomaniac who was almost incapable of walking home from work or a dinner party without taking in a prostitute on his way – unions which were often of the most perfunctory and depressing kind, achieved in darkened alleys or doorways. The primitive sheaths he wore were no protection.

But perhaps the most extraordinary thing about this mass of human contradictions was the extent to which Boswell was so purely a literary man. By that I do not mean merely that he was one like Silas Wegg, to whom you couldn't show the piece of English print that he wouldn't be equal to collaring and throwing. Rather, Boswell, although he *was* a *littérateur*, was himself the creature, almost the prisoner, of his own writing. His diary was much more than something sensational to read (as it were) on the train. It was almost his very reason for existing.

He makes the astonishing observation: 'I will go through almost anything with a degree of satisfaction if I am to put an account of it in writing'; and again, 'I should live no more than I can record'. In other words, so long as an incident makes a good page in his journal, he is prepared to accept any number of rebuffs of his ambitions, either in the military, or at the English Bar, or in the bedchamber.

Boswell's merciless Scottish power of total recall has guaranteed that we now know more about his inner life – his passing fears, his merest bodily sensations, his little fads, his moods of exultation and despair – than about any other man of his time. But do we want to know so much?

Well, we do and we don't. On the one hand, it has to be admitted that Boswell's Scottish life, which he himself found so hellishly boring, reads even more boringly when it is recounted by a pains-taking modern scholar from the university of Yale. Boswell's dis-appointments and mistakes at the Scottish Bar, or his concern with his estates at Auchinleck, can be of interest only to Scots antiquaries.

Similarly, as in the case of Simenon's *Mémoires Intimes*, you quickly reach the point where you think you will vomit if the man picks up another whore and then goes through the misery of yet another dose of clap. It is the sort of thing which, for the English reader, can be dealt with succinctly in a few paragraphs, rather than in two fat volumes of six hundred pages each.

Two fat volumes, however, were decreed to be worthy of the man by the directors of the Boswell industry at Yale. The first was published in 1966 and it was by the doyen of the trade, Frederick A. Pottle. It took Boswell up to the age of twenty-nine. Frank Brady has now completed the task,* with the admirable diligence which one expects from American academic biographers. It is the story of the last years of his marriage, the last years of his friendship with Johnson, his decline into melancholy, alcoholic collapse and disease. Above all, they are the years in which he wrote the *Life of Johnson*.

In writing that book, Boswell was inventing a new sort of biography which had never been written before. Hitherto, biographies had been succinct summaries of a great man's life, with a judicious commentary on his merits and virtues. Boswell anarchically supplies us with hundreds of densely detailed pages, and he was only able to do so because of his compulsive habit of journalising.

The *Life of Johnson* is the most companionable book in the world. In *The Hypochondriack* Boswell once condemned the habit of eating alone, and said it was the mark of a 'brutish disposition'. He is only happy when he has 'good social intercourse'. And it is this which he gives us in his biography of the lexicographer in page after page.

It is one of the greatest pieces of literary good fortune that Boswell, with a preternatural memory for speech, should have befriended the greatest of English conversationalists. As his journals show, he was equally happy to transcribe the humdrum talk of lawyers in coffeehouses. Instead, he immortalised Johnson, and because this book is largely the account of how he did so, it is rewardingly full of familiar and unfamiliar Johnsoniana.

Johnson's talk is an inexhaustible mine. 'I am quite restored by him,' Boswell wrote, 'by transfusion of mind.' And so are we.

*Sunday Telegraph*, 11 November 1984

---

* *James Boswell: The Later Years 1769–1795*, Frank Brady (1984).

# The Scotch Plato

'By far the greater part of the readers of the *Spectator* have always been of a class that is not affected by partisan spleen: its circulation being chiefly, as it must always aim to be, among the men of culture, who like to listen to all sides of controversies, provided the argument is conducted with fairness and moderation.'

Those words were not written by a modern editor of the *Spectator*, but by the first, Robert Stephen Rintoul, who came to London from Dundee and founded the paper in 1828. He wrote them after he had been editor for thirty years. Whatever his Victorian readers made of Rintoul's political reasonableness, they would not always have found 'fairness and moderation' in the 'literary' pages of the paper. Under Rintoul's editorship, and that of his redoubtable successor, Richard Holt Hutton, the *Spectator* published violently hostile reviews of Tennyson, Matthew Arnold, Charlotte Brontë, Carlyle, Dickens, Leigh Hunt and George Meredith.

Much of the splenetic tradition of early *Spectator* reviewing derives from the fact that its first editor was a Scot, who learned his trade on the fierce old days of 'English bards and Scotch reviewers'. The Scottish Academic Press has published a selection of Francis Jeffrey's criticism, culled from his articles in the *Edinburgh Review*. It serves as a reminder of how harsh criticism used to be. Jeffrey hated the egocentricity of the Romantic poets. He attributed 'ideas of schoolboy imbecility' to Wordsworth; and of the *Lyrical Ballads*, he wrote that 'their peculiarities of diction are alone enough, perhaps, to render them ridiculous'.

Rendering people ridiculous is an important part of the journalist's function and the great writers of the *Edinburgh Review* were pioneers in the field. Sydney Smith who, with Francis Jeffrey, helped to found the magazine in 1802, was once upbraided for having poured scorn on the sermons of Archdeacon Nares. He retorted, 'In these literary executions I do not care for justice or injustice a fig. My business is to make the archdeacon as ridiculous as possible.'

Jeffrey and Sydney Smith were staunch Whigs. The *Quarterly* was founded as a Tory counterblast to their outpourings. Much more conservative in politics than its rival, it borrowed from the *Edinburgh Review* the habits of critical asperity. Sir Walter Scott's future son-in-law, John Gibson Lockhart, became the editor when he was not much more than twenty and after he had published a few reviews, he was dubbed 'the Scorpion'. Lockhart mellowed in time. It is only fair to recall that he was barely out of his teens when he wrote his famous notice of John Keats: 'It is a better and a wiser thing to be a starved apothecary than a starved poet; so back to the shop, Mr. John, back to the plasters, pills and ointments.'

It was that sentence which Shelley believed had hastened the early demise of the author of *Endymion*. 'Poor Keats is dying of a review in the *Quarterly*,' wrote Miss Mitford maliciously. Nasty as Lockhart's review obviously was, it is hard to work up any sympathy for Keats, or for any other thin-skinned author who fails to understand that no literary judgement can, or ought to be, 'fair'; and that the purpose of literary, as of any other sort of journalism, is to entertain. People rushed to buy the *Quarterly* rather in the spirit of modern crowds who huddle at the dangerous corners of Brand's Hatch, agog for the next grisly casualty.

Lockhart was a mild reviewer in comparison with his colourful friend John Wilson, who wrote under the pseudonym of 'Christopher North' and deserves to be more widely known today. 'Though averse to being cut up myself,' he frankly averred, 'I like to abuse my friends.' Wilson rose to prominence with the appearance of *Blackwood's Magazine* in 1817. He was a big, athletic figure whose father had made a fortune out of gauze in Paisley. Wilson himself, after a brilliant career at Glasgow University, went to Magdalen College, Oxford, where it was alleged (probably falsely) that he had contracted a secret marriage with a gypsy woman. Confident of a leisured future, he settled on the shores of Lake Windermere, married the daughter of a rich Liverpool merchant and bought a few acres. He was driven to the desperate expedient of literary journalism when a wicked uncle somehow swindled him out of £50,000; and once he started writing for *Blackwood's*, he remained a prolific contributor until his death. He was also made Professor of Moral Philosophy at the University of Edinburgh.

Sir Walter Scott was right to see Wilson as 'an eccentric genius'. Nobody in the history of journalism has written more rumbustiously destructive reviews, but it is a mistake to believe that he did so out of malice. His pen ran away with him. The object of his ridicule became a figure of fantasy who was fair game for any amount of insult. Once the words appeared in print, Wilson was frequently stung with extremes of remorse. And reading these words today, one can see why.

Wordsworth's *Excursion* is described as 'the worst poem of any character in the English language'. He suppressed the obituary of Wordsworth in which he called the poet 'a fat ugly cur', but he published the article in which he said, with an admirably commercial judgement, that Wordsworth could not be forgiven for encouraging swarms of tourists to infest the Lakes. 'Who does not shudder to think that they may have given ostentatious alms to "the old Cumberland beggar", as the Kendal coach was passing by with twenty outsides? These are the reptiles that, if not trod upon, will occasion a fall in the price of land in the northern counties.'

He had particular fun attacking the 'young poets' of his day and remarked that many people from the provinces would be surprised 'on their introduction to "one of the most promising of our young poets" at beholding a bald or bush-headed man of middle age, in spectacles, and if not with an indisputable pot belly, yet "corpulent exceedingly" and, by rude guess, fourteen stone avoirdupois'.

Many of his generalisations are perfectly sensible, as when he wrote that 'one of the saddest misfortunes that can befall a young poet is to be the pet of a coterie'. This was what he believed had happened to the young Tennyson, and he dismissed Arthur Hallam's enthusiasm for 'The Lady of Shallot' as 'the purest mere matter of moonshine ever mouthed by an idiot-lunatic'. Hallam's mind might once have been human, he continued, warming to his theme, but now it was 'sensibly and audibly reduced below the level of the Pongos' (i.e. Apes). Tennyson retaliated with a rather damp squib:

> You did late review my lays,
>   Crusty Christopher;
> You did mingle blame and praise,
>   Rusty Christopher;
> When I learnt from whom it came,
> I forgave you all the blame,

> Musty Christopher,
> I could not forgive the praise,
> Fusty Christopher.

Tennyson had originally written 'Tipsy Kit', which was a better nickname than 'Crusty Christopher'. Wilson was a jovial boozy man. 'The animosities die, but the humanities live forever,' he said, looking back on a lifetime of slanging matches. And we can believe it, for his lasting memorial is the little volume called *Noctes Ambrosianae*, transcribed pub conversations between himself and James Hogg, the Ettrick Shepherd. The fact that they are written in dialect means that they are little known in England. But the light-hearted way in which they discuss everything under the sun appealed to Wilson's compatriots who named him, with pardonable hyperbole, 'the Scotch Plato'.

*Spectator*, 5 March 1983

# Victorian

# Lord Macaulay

Cardinal Newman believed that the best literary portrait of a man was to be found in his collected letters. The judgement sounds an odd note today, since the epistolary art has so lamentably declined. But for the Victorians, copious and frequent letter writers, there was a possibility of unselfconscious and full disclosure of the contents of the correspondent's mind.

Since 1876, when George Otto Trevelyan published *The Life and Letters of Lord Macaulay*, the delightfulness of the great Whig historian's character has been widely appreciated. Apart from anything else, his letters provide such a marvellous commentary on the public scene in which he played a part. Here are splendid dinners at Holland House, sparkling with the conversation of Sydney Smith; here is the pomp of Parliament — the letter describing the coronation of William IV is one of the most superb accounts extant of a public ceremony. Here are the excitements of the Reform Bill. And then, after Macaulay's very lucrative exile in Calcutta on the East India Company's Board of Control, we see the incipient Empire; our presence in India, which had begun as a purely commercial affair, taking on all the moral weight of an imperial ideal. And then, on his return, we read once more of the fashionable scene, literary and political, in early Victorian London.

Witty and hilarious as his letters so often are, they are much more than just a journal of 'high life'. For they are mostly written to members of his family, first to his parents, then to his sisters, nephews and nieces. Macaulay's love for his family was intensely strong, so that nearly all his commentary on the great affairs of his day is presented, not with the detachment of the historian so much as the informal and highly diverting *raconteur*, laughing, with much interruption, around a large family hearth. He wrote to his sister Hannah in 1883, 'I will say for myself that I am the only *parvenu* I ever heard of who, after being courted into splendid circles, and after having succeeded beyond expectation into political life, acquired in a few months a profound contempt for rank, fashion, power, popularity and money – for all pleasures in short but those which arise from the exercise of the intellect and of the affections.'

Nor, to judge from all external evidence, was he deceiving himself. It is the pleasures of the intellect and of the affections which his letters exuberantly celebrate. For he was, of course, not primarily a politician but a man of letters: a reviewer in the days when reviews were a form of literature; an essayist; the poet of *Lays of Ancient Rome*; and above all, the historian who 'need not despair of equalling Gibbon'.

To that, one might harshly retort that he need. He was the first man to be ennobled for what would now be called 'services to literature'; and it is not difficult to see why. He had a florid narrative brilliance (lumpy as a pseudo-Jacobean sideboard, overtinted as a canvas of Winterhalter) which lends a kind of technicoloured plausibility to his ridiculous historical distortions. Macaulay, more than any other historian, was responsible for the myth that the coup d'état of 1689, by which a few rich families hounded the rightful monarch out of his realm and replaced him with their own Dutch puppet, William III, was dignified with the name of 'Glorious Revolution'. And in order to make the picture a little more glorious, Macaulay paints William (whom we know to have been a cold, pederastic sadist) in the most glowing colours.

The implication behind much of Macaulay's historical thinking was highly agreeable to the generation hungry for Darwin's theory of evolutionary progressivism. Macaulay believed that since the country had been governed by rich cliques such as the Holland House set, and administered, in the Church and the law, by clever families such as his own, it had progressed out of the darkness into a glorious light. In 1844, he addressed an unknown correspondent, 'I will venture to say that if only the London of 1744 could be called up before us, and if we were to take a Sunday walk through it from St. James's Street to Moorfields, the spectacle of irreligion, of bestial stupidity, of obscenity, of barbarity, would utterly appal us, and make us thankful for the age in which we live.'

For my part, I would infinitely rather inhabit the London described in Boswell's *Journals* than be waif in the world of *Oliver Twist*. But thankfulness for the age in which he lives is one of Macaulay's most persistent and, ultimately, rather lovable qualities

60

of mind. He is supremely confident that the 1840s are superior in every way to the 1740s and that the 1850s will be better still. The fact that the industrialised slums of Victorian cities were worse than anything known in the days of Doctor Johnson could not occur to the mind of Lord Macaulay, which shone with progressive optimism. From where he sat in Albany, the nineteenth century felt very beautiful, and he probably did not know that there were children starving on the streets not far from his parents' old house in Great Ormond Street.

'Every generation imagines that it is of special importance in the great scheme of divine government which goes on slowly unrolling itself through thousands upon thousands of years.' He pointed that out himself, in a letter to his sister Frances in 1859. But it was not a lesson which he really took to heart. Questioning whether Milton had ever read the Greek tragedians, he wrote to his nephew, 'Though Milton was an excellent scholar after the fashion of his time, Aeschylus was, I suspect, a little beyond him.' For anyone who knows anything about Milton – on whom Macaulay wrote such an excellent essay – this is a most ridiculous piece of patronage. He substantiates it by a generalisation which is quite possibly true, but which fails to take account of Milton's unique linguistic accomplishments. 'You cannot conceive how much the faculties for reading the Greek writers have increased within the last two hundred years.' Milton read Plato fluently when he was twelve. Macaulay still found him a struggle in his thirties. But Macaulay lived in the nineteenth century, so he must have been cleverer than someone who lived in the seventeenth century. Onward and upward!

It is a little melancholy to read Macaulay's smug Whiggish judgement of the world today, for we stand amid the smouldering ruins of a system which he thought was everlasting. In India, he was quite confident that, by imposing a system of education on the whole subcontinent, they would all be converted to the Reform Bill and the Church of England, to parsing Caesar's *Gallic Wars* and building railways, and revering the House of Lords. At home, he was sunnily confident that men like Lord Palmerston or Lord Holland would be raised up in each generation to govern the grateful populace; and that the Church, while not abandoning the evangelical piety of the Clapham Sect of which his father Zachary had belonged, would grow more reasonable, tolerant and latitudinarian. Puseyites were a terrific laugh. And the Gorham judgement of 1850 was a matter which Macaulay was confident would be of no consequence at all. 'No man eminent in learning or station will be among the seceders,' he pronounced to his sister. In fact, it made Manning become a Roman Catholic, and began the process by which the Church of England as known to Sydney Smith evaporated as though it had never been; in which the Puseyites were triumphant; and in which the Archbishop of Canterbury could stand in his cathedral church, his voice raised in prayer with a Polish Pope and a black female Pentecostalist. These are things which Macaulay would have thought impossible.

On the other hand, when one considers Macaulay not as a judge of his own times but as a phenomenon, we may have cause to revise our picture of the much-maligned 'Whig view of history'. Consider his breakfasts with Tom Campbell ('the argument "it is but the third hour of the day", however forcible when used by St. Peter, was by no means decisive as to Tom Campbell's society'); his dinners with Sydney Smith, with Thackeray, with Palmerston; or his evenings in Albany, settling down to re-read Plato, or Milman's six volumes of ecclesiastical history. Was it so very foolish of him to suppose that this was the most glorious age of history? If one had been lucky enough to belong to the same set as Macaulay, one would surely think that things had never been better since Adam ate the apple. And with hindsight we can see not only that he belonged to one of the most stimulating societies in history, but also that all the things he most valued have declined steadily since the date of his death in 1859.

Our century cannot compete. But one little advantage it possesses over the last is this: we have been able to read the complete letters of Macaulay, rather than the tantalising snippets recorded in Trevelyan's *Life*. They were edited by Thomas Pinney and published in six volumes by the Cambridge University Press, each volume receiving a higher chorus of praise from the reviewers. The trouble is that, although Macaulay's letters make a perfect bedtime book, the edition of six volumes is too weighty for the average *table de chevet*. Professor Pinney has now made good that disadvantage of producing a splendid one-volume selected edition.* It does not seem cheap,

---

* *The Selected Letters of Thomas Babington Macaulay*, edited by Thomas Pinney (1983).

until you reckon that you will want to re-read it at least twenty times as often as a novel which could be obtained for a third of the price.

*Spectator*, 29 January 1983

# A Verse Life of Queen Victoria

*Happy and Glorious* was the title given to Laurence Housman's forty-seven plays. Collected in one volume they made up a life of Queen Victoria (the best, perhaps, till that of Cecil Woodham-Smith). Happy and glorious is what they were, these scenes imagined from the monarch's life, with E. H. Shepherd drawings for each play. Astonishingly, Housman's plays were banned: it took him more than twenty years before the licence came from the Lord Chamberlain, allowing some of them to be performed. They made a very perfect wireless play. Since then, the life of Queen Victoria has been rehearsed by twenty pens or more. Jean Plaidy, in five volumes, told the tale, while Lady Longford managed it in one. The public's appetite can't be appeased. The great Queen's letters to the Crown Princess (which Roger Fulford edited so well) come out in frequent volumes year by year. And now (for fashion's word is surely out) Christopher Tower's *Victoria the Good*:* a play, in *verse* of Queen Victoria's life, repeating each familiar mythic scene, from Lehzen's kisses to the old Queen's death (coloured, in Tower's verse, by Strachey's prose).

Over six hundred pages, bound in cloth; over a dozen handsome coloured plates, depicting eras of the Monarch's life. How could Lord Weidenfeld, one asks oneself, sell such a book for £9.95? Viewed merely as an object (paper, cloth) at twice the price the volume would be cheap. And no review could fail to sing the praise of Mr. Tower's patient plodding task: six hundred pages, all of them in verse!

Except for fairies, and Lord Tennyson, the characters don't have to speak in rhyme. Yet, if they had, the play might have been neater: a poet's often helped by rhyme and metre; should inspiration flag or drama fail, he can think of rhymes for 'Moonshine' or 'Disraeli'.

* *Victoria the Good,* Christopher Tower.

64

Strangely enough, in Queen Victoria's time, a verse life of Prince
Albert was essayed, made up of couplets, one of which ran thus:

> He took such care of etiquette,
> He even smoked a cigarette.

The rest, and the author's name, I don't recall.

But our poet has viewed with a frown the form that brought
Dryden renown: nor attempted the art of limericks which start
'There was a young man called John Brown'. No, Tower chose
instead a plain blank verse.

It is not hard to speak in blank verse lines (the rhythm's natural to
the English tongue), as Mrs. Siddons's utterances showed: 'Beef
cannot be too salt for me, my lord; I asked for porter and they
brought me beer.' Alas, one's bound to say that Mr. Tower has
neither Siddons's ear, nor Milton's voice. He is no master of pen-
tameters. The tone is flat, the scansion quite unsure, as when Lord
Melbourne, asked to dance, replies

> O, I am far too old and rickety
> To attempt that sort of thing with you, Madame.

('Madam' or Ma'am, but surely not 'Madame' is how Lord M.
would have addressed his Queen; and yet the scansion here demands
'Madame'.) Again, the poet writes such mouthfuls as

> But here where liberal attitudes prevail
> And authority is tolerant of
> Manifestations of ill discipline
> To the extent that people are aware
> That however insupportable . . .

. . . and on, like this, for line on boring line. This is reordered prose,
but hardly verse (the dullest civil servant's prose at that). It's better,
though, than his attempts at rhyme: the parody of Tennyson's
grotesque; the songs with which the lengthy drama ends (while
fairies dance about the dying Queen) defy description, they are all
so bad.

> Since never once was spurned or broken
> Never denied nor once forgot
> That elemental vow once spoken
> Here in this gladsome island grot.

And yet, one does not wish to mock or carp. The whole thing's madness makes one want to cheer: Lord Weidenfeld, for publishing a book, which hardly anyone will want to read; Arthur Barbosa, whose accomplished brush supplied delightful plates recapturing the wallpaper, the carpets, the trees, the soldiers' uniforms, the table-cloths, each tiny detail of Victoria's life.

To publisher and illustrator, then, all praise is due for work superbly done. But Mr. Tower deserves the higher praise. How many months or years it took to write, one hates to contemplate: but with what joy the poet probably fulfilled his task. It's very pointlessness inspires respect, like those who build cathedral replicas with used Swan Vestas and a tube of glue; or those who climb an unscaled mountain peak just to say they were first to reach the top.

This mountain was well-trodden, so we can't say of this play-wright that he has achieved 'Things unattempted yet in prose or rhyme'. But, even if the poem's not much good, it's something that he tried it on such scale.

Spectator, 27 March 1982

# The Triumph of Pio Yes-Yes

'Infallibility is the work of the Devil.' That was the view of Pope John XXII in 1324. In his bull *Qui quorundam* he rejected Franciscan suggestions that Popes were infallible on the sensible grounds that the doctrine would be a restriction of his sovereign powers. If his predecessors had been infallible, how could he reverse their decisions?

This conundrum must have weighed heavily on Pope Paul VI as he pushed through the reforms of the 1960s in the Roman Church. It is greatly to his credit that he allowed scholars free access to the Vatican archives. August Bernhard Hasler (a German Catholic) was one of many enquirers who were allowed to read, and to publish, material which a more cautious Pontiff would have wanted forgotten. The result is a fascinating book which Hasler published, in German, a year before his death in 1980. It now appears in an English translation,* and it is compulsively readable. It ends with an open letter to the present Pope, who has convinced himself that 'infallibility is . . . the key to the certainty with which the faith is confessed and proclaimed'; it asks him how the doctrine of infallibility can be justified on Biblical, traditional, or theological grounds. And, quite devastatingly, it tells the story of how the doctrine came to be promulgated at the First Vatican Council.

'Jesus has placed the Pope higher than the prophets, than the precursor John the Baptist, than the angels. Jesus has put the Pope on the same level as God.' These words were spoken by the founder of the Salesian order, St. John Bosco. Their veracity had been vouchsafed in a heavenly vision and he hastened to pass them on to Pope Pius IX. That Pontiff had been having very similar thoughts for a number of years. Further encouraged by Bosco's mystical insights, Pio Nono felt that the time was ripe, in 1869, for the

---

* *How the Pope Became Infallible*, A. B. Hasler (1982).

67

summoning of an ecumenical council to define the doctrine of Papal Infallibility.

'I have the Mother of God on my side,' the Pope averred. It was just as well, since he did not have on his side the bishops of France, Germany, Eastern Europe and America; and they, unlike their Celestial Patroness, had votes. One thousand and eighty-four men were entitled to vote in the Council. By the time the matter was finally put to the test, a mere four hundred and fifty-one gave full assent to the doctrine that the Pope was infallible. Eighty-four bishops voted against it; sixty-two assented, but only with reservations. The rest, nearly half the Council fathers, had either failed to attend the Council, or had left it early, like the saintly bishop of Montpellier, François Lecourtier, who threw his Council documents in the Tiber. 'An imposing minority,' he declared in exasperation, 'representing the faith of more than one hundred million Catholics, is crushed beneath the yoke of a restrictive agenda which contradicts conciliar traditions.' Others, almost able to tolerate the manner in which the infallibility matter was steamrollered through the Council deliberations, had been affronted by the unseemly wrangles which went on behind the scenes, and by the threats to withdraw money and privileges from poorer dioceses which did not vote the Pope's way.

Since 1870, the schismatic churches of Moscow and Constantinople, the renegade 'old Catholics' who broke away from the Roman Church at that date, as well as those of more heterodox obedience – Armenians, Copts, Anglicans and the rest – have cast doubt on the validity of the decree. The First Vatican Council was not, they claim, a true ecumenical council, since it restricted the freedom of its members. As such, it is not binding upon Christendom to accept its deliberations.

The Greek Melchite patriarch, Gregor Yussef, whose Church was in communion with Rome, was one of the most fervent opponents of infallibility, and a defender of the rights of the ancient patriarchates, of which Rome was but one. Pio Nono summoned him; when the ancient Yussef kissed the Pope's foot, Pius brought his heel down hard on the old man's neck and said, 'Gregor, you hard head, you.'

Others, primarily the French and German bishops, raised arguments from history. If previous Popes had been infallible, it was pointed out that they had taught heresy. Pope Liberius (A.D. 352–66) had been an Arian. Pope Virgilius (A.D. 537–55) had condemned the teachings of the Council of Chalcedon. Pope Boniface VIII (1294–1303) had taught that political, as well as religious, obedience to the Papacy was necessary to salvation.

None of these arguments carried any weight with Pius IX. The fiercer the opposition became, the more frequently he flew into childish tantrums. His (perfectly justified) sense that people were plotting against him led to the development of paranoid insecurity. He even ordered the confiscation of a brand of matches which was advertised as infallible (*fiammiferi infallibili*). But the disloyalty of his opponents was matched by the adulation of his Ultramontane supporters, who claimed that the Pope was 'the Word made flesh'. The Bishop of Geneva spoke of the threefold incarnation of the Son of God: in the Virgin's womb, in the Eucharist, and in the old man of the Vatican. No wonder that Pius began to act the part. In June 1870, as he was passing the church of Trinita dei Monti, the Pope approached a cripple who was lying in front of the crowd. The Pontiff was not uncertain of his powers. 'Rise up and walk!' he ordered. The paralytic, anxious to obey this celestial injunction, was helped to his feet, but collapsed again at once, to the disedification of the faithful who witnessed the scene.

As this story went the rounds, fears were naturally expressed about the Pope's sanity. There was his history of epilepsy. Now delusions of divinity were interspersed by outbursts of uncontrollable rage. There were particularly vitrolic public *contretemps* with Cardinal Guidi, believed to be the natural son of the infallible Pontiff. All this tittle-tattle was, however, an irrelevance. 'I am the Way, the Truth and the Life,' Pius replied to those who had expressed lingering doubts about the matter.

For all this, Hasler failed to convince me that Pio Nono was mad. In fact, having read this book, it is impossible not to admire him. He managed to persuade the representatives of the entire Roman Catholic world to assent to a proposition which most of them believed to be untrue. There are splendid illustrations, too. The photograph of Pius IX blessing his kneeling troops at the Campi di Annibale compares not unfavourably with pictures of John Paul II urging pacifism on the baying yobboes of Bellahouston.

Pius IX commands respect he won, even if the formulation of the doctrine of infallibility was, in the end, much modified. While not denying the view of the Bishop of Tulle, that 'when the Pope mediates it is God who thinks in him', the Council settled, in the event, for the idea that he was only actually infallible when speaking from a particular object of furniture in St. Peter's. Once this sacred doctrine had been proclaimed, the opponents diminished in number. The Croatian Bishop Joseph Georg Strossmayer stubbornly protested, 'Better to be exposed to every humiliation than to bend my knee to Baal, to arrogance incarnate.' Coercion worked more effectively on younger bishops, still in harness. German bishops who dissented from the doctrine lost their right to issue marriage dispensations, which meant that, within a few months, they were beleagured by hordes of angry couples, beseeching them to submit to the Holy Father. Other primates and prelates underwent conversions. Aided by the prayers of the Mother of God and of St. John Bosco, their minds became suddenly illumined. The primate of Hungary, for instance, supported by his bishops, had risen in the Council to say that the Hungarian people knew nothing of infallibility. Less than a year was to pass, however, before, taught by divine institution, he proclaimed in a pastoral letter that 'everyone in Hungary had always believed in infallibility'. It was not the last time in history that the unfortunate Hungarians had to swallow unpalatable doctrines wholesale.

*Spectator*, 3 March 1982

# Alfred Lord Tennyson

# I

## The Life

(*The Tennyson Album*, Andrew Wheatcroft; *Tennyson; the Unquiet Heart*, Robert Bernard Martin)

Who said that reading the novels of George Meredith was like 'wading through glue'? Or complained, when hearing a recording of his own voice, that it was like 'the squeak of a dying mouse'; or protested to a friend that he read aloud as if 'bees were about his mouth'? Tennyson. There is a vigour, and a humour, about his reported utterances which, if not lacking in his poetry, we do not associate with his name. 'Tennysonian' means, to most of us, a delicious melancholy music, 'red with spirited purple', like his own magnificent description of wine vats, but with a solemnity which is always in danger of being absurd. His most ardent admirers can see what prompted a harsh Victorian critic to say that the author of 'O darling room' deserved to be read only by schoolgirls and Oxford dons. Yet, the paradox is that Tennyson's own high estimation of himself is more justified than the cynicism of detractors. When he conceitedly said to a gathering at the Society of Authors, 'which of us will be alive in five hundred years time?' no one could seriously have doubted his claims to immortality.

Is there a biographical answer to the Tennysonian paradox? Tennyson himself, like so many authors, dreaded biographical attention but was wounded when he failed to get it: he paced the lanes around Farringford and Aldworth to scare off the sightseers, returning in a fury if there had been none to drive away. (When one of them, Oscar Browning, the social climber, had the temerity to approach the Bard in Freshwater Bay with the words 'I'm Browning,' Tennyson peered at him myopically and replied, 'No, you're not.') He was afraid that future biographies would 'rip him open like a pig' and in conversation he was cautious of intimacies. As early as the 1840s, meeting Frederick Robertson in Cheltenham, he said, 'I felt as if he had come to pluck out the heart of my mystery – so I talked to him about nothing but beer.'

This Garbo-like self-protectiveness is partly explained when we peruse the photographs of the poet and his family, which we can now do in Andrew Wheatcroft's delightful *The Tennyson Album*. No poet ever looked more like a great genius. How could he have lived up to his appearance? Sir John Betjeman, in his splendid introduction, says 'he was like a big friendly dog'. One knows what he means. But there is surely something more august, more alarmingly beautiful than canine about Tennyson's face? It is as if he knew that nothing could match the beautiful exterior. He spoke of beer because he was fearful that he had no mystery to pluck out; and, as a poet 'with no language but a cry', he dreaded having nothing much to say, while being able to say it so melodiously.

All this would have seemed a plausible enough theory until now, even with the very fully published material in Sir Charles Tennyson's portraits of his grandfather to confuse us. But Professor Robert Bernard Martin, with his new, magnificent biography, has changed our vision of Tennyson forever. This is the book of which Tennyson was so afraid when he spoke of being ripped open like a pig. Yet a pig was never ripped open with such delicacy, charity, wit or learning. It will stand as one of the great literary biographies of the century.

Professor Martin examines each piece of the Tennyson mythology and finds them to be, if not false, different from what we thought. Tennyson was not, for instance, disinherited by his grandfather, 'the old man of the wolds'. He got more or less as much from that will as the dreaded Tennyson d'Eyncourts. In 1835, when he was twenty-four, he probably had a capital of £6,000 and an income of something over £500. This did not prevent him from cadging £100 a year from an aunt and £300 from a friend; nor from thinking himself so poor that, even at the end of his life, when his royalties were enormous, he still accepted his Civil List pension, thereby depriving some author in genuine need. His stinginess was so extreme that his closest friends somehow assumed, in spite of the fact that he ran two country houses, that he was short of money. It was Gladstone's belief that Tennyson could not afford the appurtenances of nobility which delayed his elevation to the peerage.

The family reading of the *Maud* myth, similarly, has always suggested that it was poverty which delayed Tennyson's marriage to Emily Sellwood for nearly twenty years. He did not actually marry her until he was forty-one. Professor Martin is exquisitely convincing on the nature of Tennyson's matrimonial arrangements. But he makes it clear that at every stage it was Tennyson himself who delayed the marriage, for reasons, it would seem, of pure funk. Was he afraid of sex? Professor Martin delicately suggests that sex was really rather unimportant to Tennyson, and to his wife; and that, for all the stories of his senile squeezing of young women, there is no evidence that he was 'highly sexed'. Nor is Professor Martin inclined to suspect a hint of homosexuality in his profound attachment to Arthur Hallam (whose neurotic fears of insanity make the young Tennyson seem positively solid). In sex, marriage and every other aspect of life, Tennyson was quite extraordinarily lethargic. From his undergraduate days until he was forty he appears to have done almost nothing except smoke, drink rather heavily, and wonder whether he was suffering from fatal illnesses.

Perhaps the most dramatic of Professor Martin's discoveries is that Tennyson believed himself to be epileptic, a condition which had tormented his unfortunate father and more than one of his crazy siblings. In fact, if he had an identifiable illness it was probably gout (and hardly surprising since he drank at least a bottle of port a day). But before making this discovery, poor Tennyson put up with all manner of horrifying 'cures'. One of his diets involved taking no food but the juice of eighteen lemons for three days, which left his knees 'miserably imbecile'. And he was one of those many Victorians who were prepared to submit to hydropathy. His brother Horatio, a fellow patient, said 'it chiefly consists in a series of packings and unpackings. You are packed in a wet sheet two or three times a day and each time on coming out you are plunged into a cold bath, after which you have a wet bandage tightly bound around your waist; you are also occasionally thawed and dissolved in a dew being swathed in three or four blankets on the removal of which, greatly to your disgust, you are again plunged into stinging cold water.'

Contrary to the impression you could get from famous photographs like 'The Dirty Monk', Tennyson delighted in immersion. When he installed running hot water at Aldworth during the sixties, he had four or five baths a day and could think of no greater luxury than 'to sit in a hot bath and read about little birds'. But water was not the only cure he took for his melancholy. One of his friends was Dr. Matthew Allen, who ran a select lunatic asylum patronised by the Carlyles, Septimus ('the most morbid of the Tennysons') and, for a while, by the poet himself.

When he married Emily Sellwood, as he himself averred, 'the peace of God came into my heart'. It did not stop him getting bored, though; in old age, far from being satisfied with solitary country walks with his dogs and his thoughts, he craved sycophantic companionship and bright lights in London, abandoning his two houses for long stretches in order to inhabit a poky flat in Albert Mansions off Victoria Street. He longed for companionship but, as Professor Martin writes so touchingly, 'there can be few poets in the language who more consistently and successfully wrote about friendship, and there were probably equally few with whom it was more difficult to maintain untroubled relations over a long period. As a friend he was a born sprinter rather than a long-distance runner.' Coventry Patmore, Gladstone, Edward Fitzgerald were only a few of the men who fell foul of Tennyson at one stage or another. His touchiness is notorious, nowhere better demonstrated than in the story of his reading aloud to Jowett, Master of Balliol, who dared to say, 'I think I wouldn't publish that if I were you, Tennyson.' 'If it comes to that, Master,' answered the poet, 'the sherry you gave us at luncheon was beastly.'

As almost everyone's reaction to that anecdote shows, there remains something endearing about Tennyson's childish egotism. It is a great triumph of his new biography that Professor Martin has, unlike his subject, the patience of a long-distance runner. He has presented us with warts and all, but in a spirit of such warm charity that however damaging much of it is, his book enhances, rather than diminishes, the seriousness with which we regard Queen Victoria's Laureate.

*Spectator*, 8 November 1980

# Alfred Lord Tennyson

# II

## The Letters

'Break not, O woman's heart, but still endure!' Tennyson wrote to his Monarch. One imagines the shade of Prince Albert, like Bishop Proudie, jumping out of his chair at hearing the wife of his bosom called a woman; but one imagines wrongly. The night before he accepted the Laureateship (which he did after much indecision because someone had told him, 'if I became Poet Laureate I should always when I dined out be offered the liver-wing of a fowl'), Tennyson dreamed of Prince Albert kissing him, which made him think, 'very kind but very German'. When they were near neighbours on the Isle of Wight, the two men developed an easy, natural friendship and when the Queen was widowed, she turned to Tennyson almost as to a guru. Unlike our own Monarch, Queen Victoria felt free to make friends from widely-differing social worlds.

The offer of the Laureateship comes to Tennyson at the end of this first volume of letters*, in December 1850. He was forty-one. He had finally got round to marrying Emily Sellwood, though it was fourteen years since that patient girl had first fallen in love with him and he had 'murmured (like a hen in the sunshine) lines and half-lines of some poem'. He had just published *In Memoriam*. Otherwise, he had done very little with life. He had more or less avoided becoming a drug addict, the fate of his madder brothers. He had been the victim of depressions which almost gave the lie to his brother's assertion, 'I am Septimus: the most morbid of the Tennysons.' He had had a spell as a voluntary patient in a lunatic asylum. He had made occasional visits abroad. But for the most part, to judge from these letters, in the twenty years which elapsed after he

* *The Letters of Alfred Lord Tennyson, Volume I (1821–1850),* edited by Cecil Y. Lang and Edgar F. Shannon Jr.

came down from Cambridge, he mainly mooned about in London. He moved from one cheap lodging to the next; he worried (unnecessarily as it happened) about money; he drank and smoked far too much; he hung about in bars. This was the man that Queen Victoria chose not merely as her Laureate but as her close personal friend.

Even if the present Monarch is a discerning poetry-lover, would she be able to make friends with Tennyson if he were alive today? If not, it is not the Queen's fault. It is ours. We may be fouller-mouthed than the Victorians, and possibly less chaste. But we are unquestionably stuffier. For all our supposed fondness for royal walkabouts and films of the Duke of Edinburgh tinkering with the portable Bar-B-Q, we want the Royal Family to be unapproachably mysterious, the sort of people who need servants to go and buy their winegums. It is the contemporaries of Queen Elizabeth II, and not those of Queen Victoria, who would jump out of their chairs at hearing the wife of Prince Philip's bosom called a woman.

Perhaps, however, things are getting better. Tennyson's reputation has never been higher, since his death, than it is today. Prudes will always protect themselves against the knowledge of how stuffy they are by sniggering. Only puritans like dirty jokes. We no longer snigger at Tennyson. Taught by Bloomsbury to lark about when the teacher's back was turned, two generations of twentieth-century readers felt nervous in Tennyson's presence. Few people over the age of fifty approach his poetry without a foolish sense that they might laugh when they come upon lines like 'God made himself an awful rose of dawn' or 'My Willy 'ill rise up whole when the trumpet of judgment 'ill sound'. It does not occur to younger readers to laugh at these lines; they recognise Tennyson as the really great poet that he was.

He was much too idle to be a great letter writer. This volume calls itself *The Letters of Alfred Lord Tennyson* but a hundred and forty pages out of three hundred and forty-six are not by Tennyson at all. It is easy to see why. He did not bother to record great events of his life (few as they were), so that if the book is to have any narrative coherence, it is necessary to read other people's accounts of the death of Arthur Hallam or of Tennyson's own wedding. Some people will wonder whether it was worth printing such hastily scribbled notes as this: 'Dear Mrs. Dickens, I am leaving London today for the North: otherwise I should have been most happy to celebrate your boy's birthday with you. Kindest regards to Dickens.

Ever yours, A. Tennyson.' At least it was addressed to the wife of a famous man. There is less interest in 'My dear Keyser, I shall be very glad to see you next Tuesday. Ever yours, A. Tennyson.' (If you want to read that in manuscript, by the way, you must go to the University of Kentucky.) Others will regret that such a substantial amount of space at the beginning of the volume is given to the rather tedious letters written by other members of the Tennyson family.

But I did not regret this, because the contrast between the pompous verbiage of (say) his brother Frederick's letters and Tennyson's own is so very informative; 'You have probably heard this from other sources,' Frederick wrote, 'the sad death of our dear friend Hallam, and the consequent affliction into which our family, especially Emily, has been plunged.' It is the sort of letter of which Podsnap might have been proud. Tennyson would have been incapable of writing such flannel.

The striking thing about his letters is their language. It is a true test of a great poet that his voice is unlike any other's. Tennyson's distinctive tone is present from the very beginning. It was not learnt from anyone. At the age of twelve he was writing to an aunt, enthusing about *Samson Agonistes*. 'I think it is beautiful, particularly, "O dark, dark, dark, amid the blaze of Noon" ' – the line from Milton's poem that is most Tennysonian, and which he would have singled out at any period of his life. To another aunt, in his first year as an undergraduate, he writes, 'I am sitting Owl-like and solitary in my rooms (nothing between me and the stars but a stratum of tiles), the hoof of the steed, the roll of the wheel, the shouts of drunken Gown and drunken Town come up from below with a sea-like murmur.' No reader of his mature poetry, if presented with that sentence 'unseen', would have a moment's doubt about its authorship. There is always a vigour and directness about his speech, whether he is complaining about being marooned in quarantine off the Dutch coast ('good reasons have I to be sulky, John; as plenty as blackberries; I am bugbitten, flybitten, fleabitten, and hungerbitten') or whether he is remembering a silent, drunken evening with a friend ('looking smoky babies in each other's eyes') or witnessing the Solemn Exposition of the underwear of Our Lady at Aix-la-Chapelle ('Truly I must say that the Virgin wore marvellously foul linen').

*Spectator*, 13 March 1982

# Henry James in his Letters

## I

In these letters the Master still signs himself 'Henry James Jr.' If scarcely juvenlia – he is thirty-two when the volume opens – they reflect his apprenticeship as an author. In 1875, James had just published his first novel, *Roderick Hudson*, and was to some degree still finding his feet. More importantly, he was thinking of somewhere to put those feet when found; somewhere, that is, congenial to his art, a background against which the novelist's necessary obsession with, yet detachment from, the human race could best be fostered. Few cultivated Americans have omitted to give Paris a try, and this James did in 1875–76, the years in which this volume* opens.

He was a rising star, and knew it. While he was achieving great success with the serialisation of *The American*, Zola's current serial novel was suspended 'on account of protests from provincial subscribers against its indecency'. There is a splendid and revealing moment of self-congratulation when, taking his leave of Flaubert, Henry James met Zola coming up the staircase, 'looking pale and sombre, and I saluted him with the flourish natural to a contributor who has just been invited to make his novel last longer yet'. The young American triumphed, but he felt out of things, socially and aesthetically, with the French Realist school. 'I heard Emile Zola characterize his manner sometime since as *merde à la vanille*. I send you by post Zola's own last – *merde au naturel* – simply hideous.'

Morever, much as he loved Paris, he suffered from 'a long encroaching weariness with the French mind'. 'I was bored, the rest were in ecstasy,' is a characteristic comment, as it happens about a performance of Wagner at the Opera. The French seemed to James 'an awfully ugly and bilious little race'; and he tired of 'French

* *Letters of Henry James: Volume II, 1875–1883*, edited by Leon Edel.

eating, the messes, sauces, greases, &c. combined with the extreme predilection for the table, of the natives, male and female, who all look red and fat while they sit there'. He made few French friends during his Parisian year, though, after his usual manner, he had dinner companions enough. The author for whom he felt the closest affection was his fellow exile, Turgenev.

His rejection of Paris seems a far cry from the young men in *The Tragic Muse*, for whom the French way of life seems so intimately connected with an artistic vocation. Gazing at Notre Dame,

'How it straightens things out and blows away one's vapours – anything that's *done!*' said Nick; while his companion exclaimed, blandly and affectionately:

'The dear old thing!'

'The great point is to do something instead of standing muddling and questioning: and by Jove, it makes me want to!'

'Want to build a cathedral?' Nash enquired.

'Yes, just that.'

Henry James Jr., of course, wanted to build a cathedral, but France was not the place to do it. It is the letters after the move to 3, Bolton Street, Piccadilly, which thrillingly reflect the eventual engagement of his mind and art. Nick Dormer's feeling was James's own – 'The great point is to do something' – and it was this, mysteriously, which London allowed. Not merely were his Bolton Street apartments warm, 'a pleasure I never knew in Paris'; they were a place where he could get down to things: 'I didn't come here on a lark,' he wrote to Henry Adams, 'but to lead my usual quiet workaday life and I have limited myself to such entertainments as was consistent with this modest programme.'

As is notorious, this was on one level not the case. The new volume covers the legendary winter of 'the conquest of London', during which he dined out a hundred and seven times. His appetite for English social life being voracious, he met everyone there was to meet. As his addiction became more intense he became increasingly blasé, failing to get his 'kick' out of a day unless it were crammed to bursting with new people. 'There are several people here,' he wrote home to his mother from the splendours of Mentmore, 'but no one very important, save John Bright and Lord Northbrook, the last Liberal Viceroy of India. Millais the painter has been here for a part of the day and I took a walk with him this afternoon . . .' Not bad going, one would have thought; but by then James's social appetite was literally insatiable: not, as he himself believed, because he wanted more and more society (though he so obviously did) but because precisely at the moments when he was most obsessively involved, most anxious for the chimneypiece to be thick with invitations, he was able to be imaginatively detached.

Proust says that the artist who gives up an hour of work to converse with a friend 'sait qu'il sacrifie une réalité pour quelque chose qui n'existe pas'. James's obsession with England began with the fallacious view that 'here . . . everything is someone or something – represents something – has, in some degree or other, an historical identity'. Of course, this was no truer in England than anywhere else, and James passed with great delicacy and blandness through the next, almost paranoid stage of disillusionment, the sense that the English are deliberately keeping something back, concealing a secret that will not be extended to the foreigner.

It is this awkwardness – so grandly exploited in his great novels when it had ceased to be a matter of intimate concern to himself – which lay behind his composition, at the close of 1878, of An International Episode, a rather sharp novella in which a pert young American woman, Bessie Alden, rejects not merely Lord Lambeth's offer of marriage, but the whole system of values which she believes to be embodied by the British aristocracy. The story is not much read nowadays – it is one of his least successful creations, perhaps because of its conspicuous lack of detachment – and although the offence it caused some of his sillier hostesses was something he laughed off in his letters home, there is a shrillness in his attitude to the tale and its reception which is a trifle disconcerting. 'So long as one serves up Americans for their entertainment it is all right – but hands off the sacred natives!' It is the paranoia behind the story, however, which explains why in general terms the intense years of socialising did not destroy his art, but actually fed it: explains, indeed, how he found the energy for so many dinners and so much writing. Reviews, short novels, travel articles pour from his pen at this date. Perhaps paranoia is too strong a word for the infinitely slight humourlessness of the tale: but the frisson of disconcertment which it provoked lays bare, though he failed to understand it at the time, precisely why his muse required not the French cathedral which inspired Nick Dormer, but the Trollopian world of clubs and dinner parties: 'quelque chose qui n'existe pas'.

A conversation formative of An International Episode is related

80

by E. S. Nadal, at that time secretary to the American Embassy in London, a compatriot with whom James used to walk the streets late at night. 'Some lady of the middle class, whom he had lately visited in the country, had said to him, "That is true of the aristocracy, but in one's own class it is different," meaning, said James, "her class and mine". Rather than this, he preferred to be regarded as a foreigner.' He arrived, while being sure of the 'superiority of English culture and the English mind to the French', with the classic American snobbery about the English middle class. He ends with the discovery that the so-called class system is the very reason that foreigners can always feel as much at home as the natives; for it guarantees that each area of society feels excluded by the others: a state of things, however undesirable from the point of view of egalitarian altruism, which is ideal for the artist who requires isolation in a crowd. At the time of *An International Episode* James complained of 'the bother of being American'. By the end of this volume, he can cheerfully describe going through social routines 'somnambulistically, I am afraid'.

It was in this state of social somnambulism that his great art flourished, the disconcertment of the Innocent Abroad being externalised – and so pushed to the furthest borders of consciousness – in *A Portrait of a Lady*, completed in 1881. There is no evidence here of Henry James being, as Auden said a novelist should be, 'among the filthy too'. On the contrary, his art thrives on detachment, even though, to judge from these letters, there was a good deal of 'dully putting up' with all the meals, if not 'the wrongs of man'.

Yet, while somnambulating, he meets everyone. If for the purposes of his art, the person by his side at dinner '*n'existe pas*', there is much good gossip to relate to his family back in Massachusetts. 'One of my latest sensations was going one day to Lady Airlie's to hear Browning read his own poems – with the comfort of finding that, at least, if you don't understand them, he himself apparently understands them even less. He read them as if he hated them and would like to bite them to pieces.' Or, of the recently widowed John Cross, husband of George Eliot; 'He, poor fellow, is left very much lamenting; but my private impression is that if she had not died, she would have killed him. He could not keep up the intellectual pace – all Dante and Goethe, Cervantes and the Greek tragedians, as he said himself, as it was a cart-horse yoked to a racer.'

James was always rather homesick in this period. The great

proportion of the letters – skilfully selected and unobtrusively edited – are to his mother and father, or to his sister Alice, his perpetual thoughts of them contributing to the sense of disjointedness and detachment which went to create his masterpieces. 'I have retired from the glittering scene to meditate by my bedroom fire on the fleeting character of earthly possessions and to commune with my dearest Mammy.'

He did manage to return to America before his mother's death, though this came wholly unexpected, after an attack of asthma. By the end of that year, 1882, his father had died too. The loss of his mother afflicted him bitterly, and it was doubtless the experiences of intense suffering during the previous twelve months which enabled him to write his noble letter to Grace Norton in July 1883: 'Sorrow comes in great waves – no one can know that better than you – but it rolls over us, and though it may almost smother us, it leaves us on the spot and we know that if it is strong, we are stronger, inasmuch as it passes and we remain.'

The demise of his parents suggested a new chapter to his life: it cut off, effectively forever, his sense of belonging to America. Once bereavement had passed and been sublimated, the period begins in which his grand manner is fullest, his observation most acute. All the great novels from now on concern themselves with the parental relationship. 'Ever faithfully yours, Henry James', he wrote to his publisher Frederick Macmillan at the end of a letter in April 1883. 'Please, in any more announcements or advertising (of things of mine) direct the dropping of the *Jr*.'

*Times Literary Supplement*, 4 April 1980

# Henry James in his Letters

# II

Before saluting the Master, we must turn to Leon Edel, who, for as long as many of us can remember, has been His Master's Voice. This is the last volume of the *Letters of Henry James*,\* a huge, beautiful book to which I shall return even more often than to its three no less punctiliously edited predecessors.

It is hard to express one's admiration for Professor Edel, who, as well as achieving this monumental task, and presiding over almost every major Jamesian publication of modern times, has also written in his five-volume biography what might be seen as the greatest Jamesian novel of them all.

This volume begins in 1895 when James was still living in the Kensington flat, but takes him fairly swiftly to Lamb's House, Rye, which he describes as a 'high-door'd, brass-knockered *façade* to one's life'. It is the period of his most stupendously impressive work: *What Maisie Knew, The Awkward Age, The Ambassadors,* and *The Golden Bowl.*

The story ends, after journeys to Italy and France and two visits back to America (the first of these very extended, to grow into 'the American Scene'), with the return to London, the flat in Carlyle Mansions, the famous Sargent portrait and the adoption, after the outbreak of the First World War, of British nationality. Shortly before his death that least Jamesian of all monarchs, George V, bestowed upon him the Order of Merit.

Merit as a man, as a sentient human being, James certainly had. But you have to fight your way towards it, in the letters, through yards of verbose posturing. We all know what the London of the late 1890s was like. Dockers got paid less than sixpence an hour;

---

\* *Letters of Henry James: Volume IV, 1895–1916,* edited by Leon Edel.

children in Wapping and Holborn were hungry and barefoot; Jack the Ripper stalked the alleys and slums of Whitechapel.

It comes as something of a surprise, therefore, to learn, in a letter to Grace Norton, that 'of all the horrors of London almost the worst horror is the way it conspires against the evening book under the evening lamp. I don't "go out" – and yet, far too much of the time, I *am* out.'

There is clearly a paradox about finding in such a silly, socialising poseur a wisdom so deep that it is almost the secular equivalent of holiness; or to feel in his pages that James, almost more than any other practitioner, seemed to understand the mess and drama of life while remaining, as he signed himself to his brother, 'your hopelessly celibate even though sexagenarian Henry'.

Professor Edel has gone a long way, in his biography, towards plumbing this mystery. The letters allow us merely to bask in it. Two of the most pregnant events in the volume are the shaving off of the beard and the purchase of a typewriter. The former suggests, undoubtedly, a willingness to reveal more than that round, intelligent face to the world.

The frontispiece to the book is a charming picture of James on one of the flats at Rye with an obviously rich niece of Henry Adams. At first glance, it is old Mr. Verver and Maggie; but a second perusal confirms that it is the servants' outing: the stately old butler walking on the sands with the pertest of the chief parlourmaids.

This sense of James as a comic figure, developing within himself, is brought out in the many jokey references to the typewriter. 'I can only address you,' he said to one correspondent, 'through an embroidered veil of sound. The sound is that of the admirable and expensive machine that I have purchased for the purposes of bridging our silences.'

This is the machine on which all the great novels were composed (typed up by, among others, the admirable Theodora Bosanquet), and the more he dictated, the more opaque the veil of sound became. In his greatest achievement, *The Ambassadors*, some readers have found the veil all but impassable. And yet, by a great paradox it is the Jamesian novel which speaks out, most directly, its message of sympathy.

The novel's plot is pure P. G. Wodehouse; a man is dispatched by a fierce older woman across the Atlantic to disentangle a young ass from an unsuitable attachment. But the theme of the novel concerns the Ambassador – Lambert Strether – learning to set in order his own absence of experience and to focus his superabundance of sympathy. James himself is not Lambert Strether, but coming as it does half way through this volume of Letters, *The Ambassadors* seems to provide a commentary on the Master's life.

Certainly though he was, Strether-like, 'hopelessly celibate', James had a great breadth of acquaintance and tolerance, as all these letters show: letters to his dear brother William whose death in 1910 was such a grief, and (unthinkably for James in an earlier incarnation) to Stephen Crane's mistress Cora Taylor, a Sussex neighbour who formerly, in Florida, ran a brothel called Hotel de Dream. ('All thanks for the strange images' is his way of acknowledging Crane's photograph of Cora and himself eating doughnuts.)

There are letters here to A. C. Benson, whose father the Archbishop told James the story of *The Turn of the Screw*; to Edith Wharton, to 'darlingest and delightfullest old Hugh Walpole'; to Mrs. Humphrey Ward (who received a fascinating essay of four printed pages on the art of the novel which begins 'I shall be very brief'); to the inevitable Edmund Gosse and to Kipling, whose best man he was and whose work he much admired.

The most striking, though not the most interesting, letters in the volume are addressed to the young Norwegian sculptor with whom James fell in love during a visit to Rome in Spring, 1899. As our editor reminds us, James uses words to Anderson 'hitherto absent from his epistolary vocabulary – phallus, penis, bottom, *derrière*'.

But how characteristic that these references are all to features of the human form as *sculpted*. Although he could apostrophise Hendrik as 'dearest, dearest boy more tenderly embraced than I can say', it would not seem as though these embraces ever came to much off the page and in what might be vulgarly referred to as the flesh.

He wrote, however, after meeting Anderson with something like abandonment. When the sculptor's brother Andreas died, James penned an impassioned letter of condolence, and every reader of this volume will surely sit up and remember Strether's great conversation with Little Bilham when they come to these words: 'Let yourself go and live even as a lacerated mutilated lover, with your grief, your loss, your sore, unforgettable consciousness.'

It is that which, as an artist, James had been doing, for all those years of changing into stiff shirts and putting cards on silver trays and salvers; for all those dinners and house parties at which he was such a patient listener and spectator; never quite an absorbed European, and never quite willing to take the plunge and accept his own medicine of 'Live all you can'.

But he kept thereby, in his own extraordinary fashion, the sacred fount unsullied and achieved, with such rich understanding, comedy, flair and pathos, those monuments, those masterpieces. In an earlier phase of life, he had surely spoken through the hero of *The Tragic Muse* when he admitted, gazing at Notre Dame, that he wanted to build a cathedral. 'Just that.' By the conclusion of this volume of letters, the towers and buttresses of his achievement swoop up before our gaze into the sky.

*Sunday Telegraph*, 29 July 1984

# William Barnes

William Barnes provided the Victorians with a picture of the country as they wanted to see it.

> As young Jemmy the smith is gone down leane
> A-playen his shrill vaiced flute,
> An the miller's man
> Do zit down at his ease
> On the seat that is under the cluster o' trees
> Wi' his pipe an' his cider can . . .

Whether yokels have ever quite conducted themselves in this bucolic manner matters as little as whether the urban poor ever died with the touching deportment of little Jo the Crossing Sweeper. The nineteenth-century zest for innocence, which shows strong signs of reviving, both feeds upon and creates such pictures. Barnes was saluted by the high and the low for his dialect poetry.

> *Dans la langue de Dorsetshire*
> *Avec un goût exquis, avec un art divin,*
> *Vous avez rendu le naïf et la fin*
> *Qui nous captive dans Shakespeare . . .*

Prince Lucien Bonaparte found the same kind of 'primitive' beauty in Barnes that Renan found in the language and lore of the Bretons.

But it would be a mistake to suppose that Barnes was deliberately playing to the gallery, or 'acting up' as a bumpkin by choosing to write his eclogues and verses in the Dorsetshire dialect.

The Victorians got the same sort of delight from his scenes of rustic simplicity as they derived from the garish greens of meadowland painted by Arthur Hughes. We, soaked in Flora Thompson and dressed in Laura Ashley, probably feel even more inclination to romanticise the dear old Parson of Winterborne Came, with his outmoded clothes, his flowing beard, his thatched parsonage, and his ability to recapture the 'happy days when I wer young' in what we deem to be peasant speech.

But Barnes is a cannier, cleverer and altogether more mysterious figure than such an approach would allow. It is a noticeable characteristic of certain shy people that they are capable of speaking quite freely in 'funny voices'. Barnes had the same sort of fascination with language which we find in the life of J. R. R. Tolkien.

He wrote books about philology which drew on a knowledge of seventy-two different tongues. Like Tolkien half a century later, he had a horror of Gallicisms or Latinisms sullying the pure well of English undefiled. Envelopes had to be 'wrappers', consonants were 'clippings'.

He found a language to meet his own private emotional needs. For example, in the diary which chronicled his love for his wife Julia, he wrote in Italian. But when a son died in infancy, he could find no language for it; none at all. He scrubbed out reference to the boy from the family genealogy.

Since Barnes's best poetry drew on the memories and half memories of those 'happy days when I wer young', it was natural that he should have written it in the dialect of Dorsetshire villages. He liked the dialect as a language. He considered it was 'a broad and bold shape of the English language, as the Doric was of the Greek'.

It was not mere whimsy which made him write like that, as Alan Chedzoy shows us in his highly sympathetic biography. 'What is England,' Barnes asked, 'that she should be dear to me, but that she is the land that owns my county? Why should I love my county, but that it contains the village of my birth? Why should that village be hallowed in my mind, but that it holds the house of my childhood?'

These admirably sensible feelings provide the clue to Barnes's genius. He had a d'Urberville sort of background. The Barnses were 'downstarts'. Barnses had been granted land at Gillingham in Henry VIII's day, but by the time William was born in 1801 (or 1800 if Thomas Hardy is to be believed) they were little better than peasants in the Blackmore Vale. But Barnes went to school, and his natural genius showed itself as, in Scotland, Burns's had, and Hogg's. Barnes, however, was much surer of himself than either Burns or Hogg, much better able to look after himself. He did not depend on the patronage of friends, nor on the consolations of alcohol.

He worked himself up from being a rustic usher to being a very learned and highly respected schoolmaster. He signed on as a part-time mature student or 'ten-year man' at St. John's College, Cambridge, and, when he was past his fiftieth year, he took his degree there.

He was pious in a completely natural, uncomplicated way. At forty-seven he was ordained. At over sixty he got his first and only living, at Winterborne Came. By then, his beloved wife Julia was dead (*'Giorno d'orrore'* in the diary for 21 June, 1852) and his family was large.

The photographs of them all at Winterborne Came Rectory, taken a few years before his death at the age of eighty-five (the bonneted girls, the grandson in a sailor suit on a donkey, the lookalike son with shovel hat and even bushier beard), show a man completely at home, successfully so, in his own environment.

One longs so intensely to be in that photograph oneself that there is a grave danger of responding to Barnes merely as a curiosity, a consoling eccentric. He was more than that, he was a very considerable poet. He is the only poet in English (Ben Jonson and Auden both tried) who wrote completely successful eclogues. He has a perfect lyric ear.

There is a wonderful combination, as there is in Hardy, of comedy and sadness in his moods. Every poet has to find a 'voice'. When he wrote verse in the Queen's English, Barnes was invariably flaccid and dull. It was in dialect that he made such perfect music.

> Since I noo more do zee your feace,
>   Up steairs or down below
> I'll zit me in the lwonesomc pleace,
>   Where flat bough'd beech do grow.
> Below the beeches bough, my love,
>   Where you did never come
> An' I don't look to meet ye now,
>   As I do look at hwome.

*Sunday Telegraph*, 29 December 1985

# Six English Novelists

# David Lodge

David Lodge is a perfectionist. He is also a Professor of English Literature who has devoted much of his time, over the last twenty years, to teaching the young, and to writing somewhat impenetrable works of criticism. He is a believer in Structuralism. He is a Roman Catholic.

These hobbies and hobby horses take up time. But there must be many people who regret that he has not written more novels, and that the earlier ones are so difficult to obtain. *Changing Places* was the first of his novels that I read, in 1975. Subtitled *A Tale of Two Campuses*, it is an hilariously observant account of two dons swopping jobs for a year. Philip Swallow ('No one could award a delicate mark like B+/B+?+ with such confident aim, or justify it with such cogency and conviction') is a diffidently ineffectual English lecturer from Rummage University who flies off across the Atlantic for twelve months' sabbatical at Euphoric State. Meanwhile his opposite number, Morris Zapp, exchanges the easy sex life, the air-conditioned libraries, the busy professionalism of his native campus for a confusing year at a university in the English Midlands, not wholly dissimilar from Birmingham. The routine farce in which both men become involved is handled with magnificent deftness. All the details are so good. And perhaps most surprising of all is the extent to which Professor Lodge's satire is aimed precisely at areas of professional life which he is known to take seriously. He is himself an ultra-professional modern don who has happily embraced many of the new doctrines. Yet nobody has guyed them to more hilarious effect.

That is not wholly surprising, perhaps, for much of the best literary malice is directed against objects of an author's love. University life and the world of Eng. Lit. are exposed to the scalpel in *Changing Places*. In his most recent novel, *How Far Can You Go?* (1980), he examines what has happened over the last twenty years in the Roman Church.

*Changing Places* was constructed as a most formally artificial piece of fiction, experimenting with rather too many types of narrative technique. *How Far Can You Go?* was presented almost like a documentary. Narrated by Professor Lodge himself, who occasionally makes asides about his present avocation, his literary fads, his earlier novels, there can be no pretence here (as in almost all novels) that we might be fooled by his fictive devices. He even doodles with changing one of the character's names after she had already made an appearance in the story. 'Story' isn't quite right. The book simply follows the fortunes of ten Roman Catholics from young adulthood to middle age, and chronicles the way in which the Second Vatican Council changed their attitudes to faith and to sex. It is a highly readable book: even re-readable. But, as in *Changing Places*, one is struck by its moral ambivalence. Two Roman Catholics recommended me to read it when it first came out. One was a trendy priest who thought that it exposed the horrors which his co-religionists had suffered until the Liberal Revolution: 'You know, people *really did* believe those things,' he said to me, with reference to the Real Presence of Christ in the Mass, the possibility of some actions being sinful, the wickedness of contraception, the dangers of hell. Another papist reader of the book, however, equally enthusiastic, while regretting the moments of sexual explicitness, praised the merciless exposé of how completely things have gone to the dogs: here are heart-rending accounts of the sheer embarrassment of 'House masses', guitars, handshakes, liberation theology and intellectual muddle. When I read the book, I erred on the side of thinking it *must* have been written from a conservative point of view. But it was an error, as is shown by Professor Lodge's preface to *The British Museum is Falling Down*, an early novel, reissued lately, about the pains and comedy of Catholic married life before the invention of the Tablet (rather disappointing).

As all these examples show, David Lodge's imagination flourishes on institutional life. He likes to describe how individuals are affected by belonging to big organisations, like the Church or a modern university. So, we can be grateful that he is just old enough to have done National Service. It is twenty years since the first publication of *Ginger, You're Barmy*, but this will be the first chance which many readers have had to enjoy it. Compared to the other novels I have mentioned, it is the least mannered. It is carefully constructed, as one would expect. The narrative technique (borrowed from Graham Greene's *The Quiet American*) involves an initially confusing switch in time scale, some of the action belonging to the hero's first, some to his last, days in the Army. But there are no very obvious 'tricks' here: no chapters which suddenly turn into film scripts or newspaper reports; no parodies of other novelists (and Lodge is a most uncertain parodist); no sudden intrusions of Lodge's own voice quoting letters from fans, professorially reproducing their errors of grammar. This, on the contrary, is a straight comic novel in the high English manner, and it compares rather well with the Army tales of Jocelyn Brooke, Anthony Powell or Simon Raven.

Perhaps its comparative simplicity derived in part from a simplicity of attitude in the author. With universities and the Church of Rome, he evidently enjoys a relationship of love-hate. With the Army, the love element, if felt, has been cleverly eliminated. At the end of his hellish two years, the narrator, Jonathan Browne, reads a newspaper leader which says that 'Some substitute must be found which will have the same beneficial effects of character training as National Service.' 'Mentally I phrased a reply: I think it will be difficult to find a substitute which will inculcate bad habits, bad language, slothfulness, drunkenness and the amiable philosophy of "I'm all right Jack" as successfully as National Service.'

That is the unashamed viewpoint from which the yarn is told. Jonathan Browne and Mike Brady have been at London University together and get drafted into the Royal Armoured Corps. The difference of attitude between the two men is melodramatically drawn. Jonathan decides, in effect, to 'sit it out'. He hates the coarseness of atmosphere and the time devoted to blanco, boot-polish and square bashing, which could otherwise have been spent reading Empson's *Seven Types of Ambiguity*. Having a chip on his shoulder about social differences, he refuses to try for a commission, because he hates the blimpish toffs who, in his imagination, compose the officer class. But he does end up with quite a cushy job, and the rank of corporal.

Mike, a fiery Irish Catholic, reacts to it all less astutely. In particular, he is outraged by the cruelty of the corporal to a poor holy idiot called Percy Higgins, whose combination of childishness and misery leads to a horrifying accident. Brady takes his revenge: on the corporal, on the Army and, for blood will out, on the English. In the course of these adventures, Jonathan has stolen Mike's rather

95

agreeable girlfriend and at the end, though agnostics, they find themselves in the position of a typical Lodge married couple: the wife vaguely cheesed off; the husband struggling to compose fiction and at the same time to further his academic career; a baby, who has arrived in the world sooner than anyone hoped, 'sitting on his pot beside me as I write'.

David Lodge is a writer who not only takes views, but is interested in ideas. This is a pity, not merely because the views are sometimes unpalatable (reading this novel in 1982, for instance, I was unable to find the I.R.A. conscript a misguided but fundamentally lovable rogue; unable to feel pleasure that there was a Guinness waiting for him on the table when he came out of prison; unable, more generally, to respond to the notion that all officers or speakers of Received Standard were necessarily pompous twits) but because it is a waste of a novelist's energy to have ideas. All one remembers from good novels is the extent to which they have believably captured human character, or been able to describe emotions, places and things. One remembers the 'ideas' of really bad novels. David Lodge's novels are so re-readable, not because they are as clever as Roland Barthes but because they are as observant (at their best) as Kingsley Amis.

*Ginger, You're Barmy* did not entirely shake my rather wistful regret at being too young to have done National Service. But although I have missed this excellent opportunity of being toughened up and acquiring moral fibre at the state's expense, I feel I know *exactly* what it was like to do Basic Training. This novel has all the ring of complete authenticity: the way the men spoke, their fears of having their leave cut short, the tedium, the physical hardship, the mingling of horror and farce are all brilliantly evoked. There must be lots of other novels about National Service. But even if there are, this must be the best.

*Spectator*, 31 July 1982

# Iris Murdoch

'The chief requirement of the good life,' says James Tayper Payce in *The Bell*, 'is to live without any image of oneself.' Iris Murdoch, one suspects, has disciplined herself so to live. She has the face of a benignant and beautiful nun. Her features are at once placid, and sharply sympathetic. And, like a nun's, they do not age.

She laughs a lot and enjoys 'bad' jokes – elephant jokes, Polish jokes, or the story of the man who opened his fridge and found a rabbit reposing among the butter and sausages. 'Why are you resting there?' 'Because this is a Westinghouse,' said the rabbit. At the same time, she is passionately serious and her bright, penetrating eyes are often filled with sadness, either when she is discussing subjects about which she feels keenly (such as Ireland) or when singing (after a meal, perhaps, or in the back of the car) sentimental lyrics such as 'South of the border, down Mexico way'. Again, like many a nun, she combines an almost limitless delight in human society with a desire to be intensely private. 'I hope Iris wasn't bored,' I once said to her husband after a party, to be told, 'Iris never finds anyone boring.' At the same time, she guards her domestic privacy jealously, and her novels are full of nightmares in which unwanted intruders burst in upon happy hermit existences.

In 1982, Iris Murdoch gave the Gifford Lectures at the University of Edinburgh on the philosophy of religion. She has been, for most of her grown-up life, a professional philosopher, though it is some years since she held a teaching post at the university. Most contemporary philosophers have steered clear of discussing such important questions as theology; and many of their utterances seem to laymen (who expect 'philosophy' to give them 'ideas about life') to be little more than arid wordgames. Miss Murdoch enjoys these games herself when she is talking to fellow professionals, but she has also been bold enough to explore the great question of how to pursue the Good in a world which has very largely discarded belief in God.

While following these questions in her academic life, Iris Murdoch has, of course, also been one of the most popular and prolific novelists of the age. She once remarked to me that when she considered how few books E. M. Forster had written she felt like saying, 'Six novels? Come on, Forster, you can do better than that!' When Ian Fleming started to write, he was advised by William Plomer, 'Keep at it! Keep on writing. The secret of success is to write a lot.' Fleming passed the word on to Iris Murdoch when she began her career as a novelist some thirty years ago, and she has been faithful to it. 'What do you do when you get stuck?' I once asked her. 'I just keep on writing,' was her reply.

The result has been one of the most impressive catalogues of moral comedy in the English language. And one of her most recent books, *The Philosopher's Pupil*, is her most adventurously expansive, a veritable *Middlemarch de nos jours*. In the past many of Miss Murdoch's novels have depicted small and often enclosed groups of people, households which seem sufficient in themselves, and are all but impenetrable to the outside world. This is as true of Imbert Court in *The Bell* as it is of the mysterious priest's house (surrounded always by fog) in *The Time of the Angels*: or of the romantic retreat, part prison and part Shangri-La, of Mrs. Crean-Smith in *The Unicorn*. There is such a household in *The Philosopher's Pupil* where Rozanov, the sinister philosopher, immures his grand-daughter Hattie, whose destiny he wishes to control, and for whom he nurses a more than grandparental love. But this particular prisonhouse (unlike some of its predecessors in the Murdoch *oeuvre*) is burst open by the chaotic revellings of the townsfolk of Ennistone.

In this story, Miss Murdoch had depicted a whole imaginary town. It is a spa (hot waters gurgle, sometimes explosively, in its midst) and we can share the evident enjoyment with which she has mapped it out. We know all about its churches, pubs and shops. There are a dozen or so characters in the foreground (including the philosopher's pupil, an accidental man called George McCaffery whose will is thwarted perpetually by his old master until he takes violent and ultimately futile remedies). But the background is seething with dozens more whom we glimpse – businessmen, prostitutes, shopkeepers, old-age pensioners, children, parsons – going about their lives in the finest traditions of English provincial fiction. But there is nothing placidly Trollopian about Ennistone. Even the town itself, where the hot springs gush and the citizens gather round the baths, is too narrow a confine for the vast perspectives of this extraordinary narrative. We live, as one of the clergymen in Ennistone reminds us (he is a vaguely sinister but ultimately sympathetic homosexual Jewish convert called Father Bernard), in the Time of the Angels.

Father Bernard no longer believes in God. But he believes that the Principalities and Powers of Another World still interest themselves in our tiny global scene. And his beliefs seem to be justified. There are outsiders in Ennistone, who peer into the lives and hearts of the inhabitants, witness their pathetic and muddled love affairs, their sins and their crimes. Some of the onlookers are animals. (A fox is seen, bizarrely, sitting at the wheel of a Rolls-Royce.) Some of the onlookers are spacemen, (there is more than one sighting of a flying saucer). Some of the onlookers are illusory. What appears to be a frightening blonde apparition gazing down from a tree is really a wig, caught in its branches. And there is the narrator himself, the unnamed N, who sees and chronicles all, but, at the end, acknowledges 'the assistance of a certain lady'.

That lady's readers here divided, over the years, between those who think that her characters are fantastic, unbelievable, weird, improbable; and those who say that 'there really are people like that'. One hears similar discussions from time to time about Dickens. One side will maintain that they have known a Mrs. Gamp or an Arnold Baffin; another will claim that Quilp or the Word Child are just the products of the novelist's lurid imagination, as though characters in fiction were ever anything else. Such debates usually founder on a misunderstanding of what it is that novelists are up to. Quilp would not exist without Dickens, so that it is pointless to discuss whether there 'really are' such people. On the other hand, the cumulative effect of reading Dickens is to feel our understanding of human nature enriched and made more generous. Novelists are 'only' fantasists, illusionists, magicians. It is the alchemy of great novelists which transforms these illusions into reality. What begins with the most extreme frivolity – the enlistment of our interest in unreal people in an unreal setting – becomes thereby morally serious. Many of us who are older than the heroine of *Northanger Abbey* (old enough, perhaps, to know better) feel that our greatest moments of moral discovery have come, not when reading philosophers or theologians, nor when having 'real' experiences, but when sitting in a chair with a novel open in our hands.

*Northanger Abbey* is much to the point since Iris Murdoch's early novels owe much to the traditions of fiction enjoyed by Catherine Morland – to Mrs. Radcliffe, to Horace Walpole, to Monk Lewis. One way of grasping evil, in artistic terms, has been to project it into fantasy. The castles of Gothic fiction, peopled with spectres, madmen or monsters, or the monasteries inhabited by demi-devils and sexual perverts, all came into being in a world where intellectuals rather hoped that evil could be argued or educated out of existence. It is no accident that the generation who first imbibed Rousseau should have reacted in imaginative terms by creating artificial horrors, no accident that Frankenstein's monster grows out of Godwin's decent Jacobinism. Evil *exists* and when philosophers abolish theology, the imagination responds by creating its own hells, its own monsters. Iris Murdoch's early novels, which seem initially so surprisingly un-Sartrian for the author of the best short book on Sartre, may be part of a similar phenomenon.

Equally, she has drawn on formal modes of 'genre' fiction, where our picture of good and evil is stylised: the thriller and the crime novel. Simple murder stories are not being written nowadays by the great mistresses or masters (chiefly the former) of the genre. Figures like Ruth Rendell, P. D. James, or Patricia Highsmith are very different from the old 'whodunnit' authors in the Agatha Christie tradition. But the form of the unexplained death is a good one. Nor need it, as Miss Murdoch has shown, be ritualised into a simple whodunnit formula. If a book such as *The Time of the Angels* was a variation on the Gothic, then her next novel, *The Nice and the Good*, was a variation on the old-fashioned 'tec'. But it also marks a deepening in the Murdoch *oeuvre* of the seriousness and realism with which she confronts the actual effects of evil in the world.

A man called Radeechy is shot in the offices of a government department in Whitehall. It looks like suicide. A gun is by his right hand. But the man who is put on to investigate this suicide (not for the police, but for the purposes of a private departmental enquiry), John Ducane, remembers that Radeechy was left-handed. That means that either someone murdered him, or that someone came into the office after Radeechy shot himself and (for some reason) moved the gun.

This is classic detective-story stuff: Miss Murdoch, with her magnificent bardolatry, has the sense that Shakespeare was able to pick up and use any trashy literary convention – like the Revenge

100

Tragedy – which happened to be lying around and transform it into a great work of art. It is this, on a modest scale but with patently Shakespearean overtones, that *The Nice and the Good* does, or tries to do. John Ducane is two Shakespearian characters (both from the same play) rolled into one. He is the Duke in *Measure for Measure* – his name even suggests as much – in his role as judge and investigator in the case of the Radeechy suicide where he exercises Godlike control; and in the affairs of the heart, too, he tries to be God. He tells Mary to propose to old Willy (another of these sad old refugees in whom Miss Murdoch delights): he tells Richard Biranne, at the end, to be reconciled to his wife Paula. But this final reconciliation (unlike the first suggestion, it is a success) is something John feels he owes to whatever moral code hovers about in this Time of the Angels. Because, as well as being the Duke in *Measure for Measure*, he is also decidedly Angelo in the same play: *Duke* is the first part of his name; *Ane* echoes *Angelo*. He is often thought of by the others as a cold fish. He is presiding in judgement over Radeechy's suicide. He uncovers the fact that Radeechy, in the vaults of the Whitehall office, has been indulging in black magic. It further emerges that Radeechy was the victim of blackmail and had been his wife's murderer. Here in the vaults, where the ludicrous paraphernalia of black magic – dead birds, copes, chalices – surround him, John should be able to sense evil. His own muddled emotional life, in which he has been as cold-hearted as Angelo in *Measure for Measure*, is, for Ducane and for us, the world where evil is most palpably confronted. The parallel is not of course as close as all that.

Shakespeare himself is as unashamed of using 'the motiveless malignity' of his villains as a way of moving the plot forward – and in none of Miss Murdoch's novels is one more conscious of this than in *A Fairly Honourable Defeat*. Here we have Rupert and Hilda, happily married for twenty years or more, and Rupert's brother Simon, happily established in a homosexual ménage with the manly and taciturn Axel. For the first half of the book it looks as if these stable relationships are almost boringly unshakeable when compared with the chaotic goings on of Hilda's sister, Morgan, separated from her wonderfully seedy little husband, Tallis, and recently emerged from an unhappy love affair with Julius King, an American Jew and a famous biologist. What we have not been prepared for is that Julius is a villain in a full Shakespearian sense. The plot of the

101

second half of the book is *Much Ado About Nothing*, in which Beatrice and Benedick are made to believe they are each in love with other, and therefore actually *do* fall in love. But Miss Murdoch gives the plot a sinister touch. Lurking behind the screen in the Prince Regent Museum to watch the first encounter between Morgan and Rupert is not some benign figure from Shakespearian comedy, but Iago. *Why* does Julius want to break up Rupert's marriage with Hilda or poison Axel's relationship with Simon? We are never quite told, though, like John Ducane in *The Nice and the Good*, he is one of those Murdochian characters who want to play God. At the end of the book we discover that Julius had been in a Nazi concentration camp, but this does not explain the evil. *A Fairly Honourable Defeat* is a splendidly stylish story, perhaps too stylish for the macabre and terrible ending. But its moral is fairly clear, relating to discussions Marcus has had in *The Time of the Angels*, or Willy in *The Nice and the Good* or Miss Murdoch herself in her book, *The Sovereignty of Good*: that is, that without a unified sense of the Good – a metaphysical sense of all good being one in the way that Christian apologists used to describe it, and before them the Platonist philosophers – there is nothing to rescue the human race from moral anarchy. It ties in, too, with her sense, expressed in many of her novels, that we become good by imagining ourselves good. This is a lesson young Pierce finds hard to learn in *The Nice and the Good*. Niceness is easy enough. But it is not, metaphysically, enough to combat the powers of evil which muster their unseen array so readily in the wings whenever Miss Murdoch's characters walk the stage. Everyone in *A Fairly Honourable Defeat* (except Julius the Iago-like villain) is *nice*. But although Tallis asks every character in the book, 'Why is stealing wrong?' no one can tell him.

Since these novels were written, the formalism of Miss Murdoch's account of evil has in some measure broken down. For all her flirtation in early days with Continental existentialism or Kierkegaardian metaphysics or symbolism of a kind which we might look for in post-war Italian and German fiction, she remains fundamentally a realist. Her roots in the British empirical tradition show. She falls neither into the Tolstoyan pitfall of wishing to discard art in favour of preaching; nor into the Leavisite mistake (a mistake of taste, chiefly) of making art a substitute for religion.

There must be many explanations for the phenomenon, but the

simplest is that she obviously loves writing novels; the sheer enjoyment of the exercise is communicated time and again. In recent books, too, one has felt how closely linked are the pleasures of those of reading. Her favourite authors hover in the background as 'the Masters' are supposed to do at a seance. They do not inspire her to parody. Her style, her world, the whole feel of her books, are completely her own. But the Masters act as kindly midwives to her own purely distinctive art. *The Philosopher's Pupil* was brought to birth, I felt, by Dostoevsky. Not only is it the only modern novel I know to use with creative effect the narrative manner of *The Devils*, but in its presentations of spiritual evil and human vulnerability it was highly Dostoevskian. Similarly, though no one but Iris Murdoch could have written it, *The Sea, the Sea* is the story of a man reliving his entire past; it is the story of an obsessive love, a love which wants to make its object a prisoner. There is not much in common between Hartley and Albertine, but we feel Proust lending a helping hand to bring her to being. The most conscious example of the Master midwifing the Murdoch novel is *The Black Prince*, which is not only a love story and a murder story but also a celebration of two sides of Shakespeare's genius: the obsessive, inner author of the sonnets and *Hamlet*, and the fecund, overproductive, cynical Shakespeare who could churn out the plays with seeming effortlessness.

*The Good Apprentice* is, once more, Shakespearian, but we feel here not the tormented Shakespeare of the sonnets who guided the pen of Bradley Pearson so much as the benign, old, all-forgiving magician of the last romances. This is a novel in which a young man gives his friend a drug sandwich, and by this act of silly thoughtlessness, is responsible for his death. His easy good looks and casual hedonism quickly land him in a ghastly mess. His half-brother Stuart, on the other hand, is a virtuous young man who keeps himself unspotted from the world. His idea of life is simply to be good; he is dedicating himself to it. His self-righteousness is awful. It is the best justification I have ever read for Bertrand Russell's peculiar statement that he could not imagine a more repulsive or dangerous ambition than the desire to be good. It is not Russell's wisdom, however, which informs this book so much as the warm Christianity of Shakespeare; Christianity, of course, with a highly Murdochian flavour. Not a single character in this huge book believes in God. And yet they nearly all seem to believe in some kind of moral absolute, they are all preoccupied with the question of how

103

forgiveness is to be found. This is true even of worldlings like Harry Cuno, who hates the corruption and failure of his life and seeks his escape through erotic love. He is Stuart's father and views his 'desire to be good' rather quizzically. 'The fact about human nature is that things are indelible,' he says; 'religion is a lie because it pretends you can start again.'

Lack of religion, however, is equally a lie, if it pretends you don't need to. All the characters do start again in this book, whether they choose to or not. Some of the new starts may be said to represent moral progress (Harry's nice little mistress Midge goes back to her husband) while others (the innocent Ilona becomes a Soho stripper) are new starts in the false direction. But the main shape and pattern of the story is borrowed from the best story of all about new starts. The opening sentence of the novel is: 'I will arise and go to my father, and say unto him, Father, I have sinned against heaven and before thee, and am no more worthy to be called thy son.'

Edward, the boy who administered the drug sandwich to his friend, is the Prodigal Son. Stuart, his fascinatingly priggish sibling, is the 'older brother' of the parable. Insofar as the novel retains its parabolic flavour, it is in keeping with its fundamental atheism that there is no father, as in the original tale, gazing for his son afar off, and waiting to slay the fatted calf. Edward's father is lost. He has only a stepfather. Or does he? In his quest for forgiveness, or a cure from the nervous breakdown which follows the death of his friend, Edward goes in search of his true father, a once famous artist called Jesse Bertram who inhabits a curious architectural folly called Seegard. The vaguely Wagnerian name rightly conjures up a feeling that Gods and spirits inhabit the place. Edward is told to wait at the house for his father, and there he meets Jesse's wife, Mother May, with her two beautifully inscrutable daughters. Jesse, as it transpires, has been in the house all the time. We even discover, by the end of the story, that he has (in spite of Mother May's denials) been looking for his son afar off, that he has in his own fashion killed a fatted calf against Edward's arrival. The quiet rituals of this house are both attractive and spooky, sinister and benign; strongly reminiscent in atmosphere of the community in *The Bell*, a book with which this has much else in common.

Apart from anything else, one ought to stress that, although it is very long, this book is exciting in a way that the early Murdoch novels were exciting. It has all their verve and pace, their alarming sense that anything might happen, that strange reversals await the characters in every chapter. It is compulsive reading. I found myself reading it late into the night, and woken by the excitement of it, I continued to read at dawn. It is the sort of book which takes hold of you completely, and which makes the 'real life' going on around you momentarily unvivid. Any attempt to summarise the story of Iris Murdoch's novels conveys nothing of the way they feel when you are inside them. Quick summaries are a familiar trick of reviewers, who are often unkind to her and like to rehearse the rapid emotional all-change among the distinctively named and usually enormous *dramatis personae* of her books. Yet the mystery of it is something one of the characters here discerns in Proust: 'What a lot of pain there was all the way through. So how was it that the whole thing could vibrate with such a pure joy?' There are passages of raw, terrible emotion in this book which are so painful that you wish you had not read them. They are strung together in a fantastic plot of almost Gothic unseriousness. There are unforgettably weird scenes: a seance; the shriek of a poltergeist; a secret grave where, bare-footed, a beautiful girl pirouettes in the dew, watched furtively by her unseen brother who is partly in love with her; a large house with forbidden rooms and a secret tower; a marsh where mists descend and where footing is unsure, on whose edges lurk sinister figures called the 'tree men'; water, beneath which lies a dead old man with a ring on his finger, a ring which his son stoops to remove. These could be scenes from Malory or Spenser, and they co-exist beside wholly realistic, and frequently very funny depictions of London dinner parties and modern adultery.

Thomas McCaskerville, the prodigal son's analyst, is in many ways the most Shakespearian character in the book. Being another character like the Duke in *Measure for Measure*, he excercises power over all the most crucial characters in the drama; Prospero-like, he renounces his magic and gives up his psychiatric practice; but also, as in *The Winter's Tale*, the necessarily comic preoc-cupations of marital jealousy become the occasions of large, warm forgiveness which extends much further than the confines of the story which they inhabit.

I would say that this is the best of Iris Murdoch's novels. She does here things which she has done before, but she does them more stylishly than ever, with even more bigness of heart, and with passages of magnificent celebration of the beauties of the natural world.

# John Braine

John Braine died towards the end of 1986. He and I did not have much in common, except for the fact that we both tried to earn our livings by writing novels. When he died, I sat down to write something about him, and for the only time in my life suffered from a 'block'. One day this will lift. Meanwhile, here is an article which I wrote about him in 1982 for *Time and Tide*. I consider him to be one of the most underestimated writers of our time, as well as a friend whom I miss constantly.

\* \* \*

It is over twenty years now since John Braine published his pamphlet 'Goodbye to the Left', joined friends like Robert Conquest and Kingsley Amis for a regular growling session nicknamed the 'Fascist Beasts Luncheon Club' and began to express views on Vietnam, nuclear war, capital punishment and religion which prompted an old friend on the *New Statesman* to say that Braine's politics were somewhat to the right of Genghis Khan. He seems genial about it all today. 'As Colin Welch said when I told him this, if Genghis Khan had any politics, he was a collectivist.'

Braine's political epiphany began after a visit to the United States in 1964, and was first declared in a legendary exchange between himself and his former Labour Party and C.N.D. comrade, Donald Soper. 'You had the feeling in America that you could be anything you wanted to be. Everybody admired it if someone got on and was successful, particularly if they started from nothing. I rather felt in England there was always a spirit of envy. No one admired someone who had lifted himself up from the bottom and done extremely well for himself. In America there is a different spirit, a greater sort of freedom. In America, no matter who you are, you could be anything you wanted. That is when Soper is supposed to have said to me, "Ah, but what if you're black?" and I said, "Well, of course I'm not black, you silly bugger."'

You have to distinguish in Braine's utterances between things he says for effect and things which he obviously means with great passion. One of the secrets of his great success as a writer has been his ability to shock and amuse his public. *Room at the Top*, published in 1957, the novel with which Braine's name will always be associated, disgusted John Bayley in the *Spectator*, who complained of its 'wide-eyed coarseness'. But it was the coarseness which made the *Daily Express* serialise this novel by a totally unheard-of Yorkshireman, and which made the novel into a bestseller. Joe Lampton, the hero, was not so much an Angry Young Man as a Randy Young Man, whose moral attitude to sex, money and social advancement was an obvious projection of Braine's own fantasies.

Before the book was published (Braine was thirty-five at the time) its author had had his ups and downs. He was not born into poverty, but he must have felt the deadening tedium of lower middle-class provincial life which makes Joe Lampton exclaim, 'No more zombies'. After the Navy, he had qualified as a librarian, and then come up to London with the hope of earning his living as a hack writer in Grub Street. He had been taken on as a regular reviewer by the *New Statesman*, but he now claims, 'They never liked me. I wasn't bourgeois enough for them to accept me as an equal, nor working-class enough to patronise.' His health collapsed, he went back north to spend a year in a tuberculosis clinic, and then to resume life as a zombie in the library. But it was then that he wrote *Room at the Top* and was transported instantly to fame. There was no nonsense about money not changing his life: 'What I want to do is to drive through Bradford in a Rolls-Royce with two naked women on either side of me covered in jewels,' he said at the time.

In the event, he moved to Surrey, and set up a marital home in stockbrokerish places such as Woking and Godalming. Cynics say that his political lurch to the right happened when he had to start paying income tax for *Room at the Top*. But this isn't true. Following the lead of another Yorkshireman, whom he regards in many ways as his master, and of whom he wrote a biography – J. B. Priestley – he continued to regard himself as a man of the left. He was a keen supporter of C.N.D. He sat on the National Council for

Civil Liberties. He was a keen member of the United Nations Association. Gradually, however, his colleagues on these bodies came to depress him. They seemed vigilantly anxious to condemn right-wing tyrannies wherever they occurred, but noticeably silent about the left-wing tyrannies.

A seminal book for Braine, read at the time he went to America in 1964, was *The Suicide of the West* by James Burnham. It opened Braine's eyes to what he calls Block Thinking, or the liberal package deal. 'The curious thing is, a left-wing person says something to me about one issue, and I can tell them exactly what they'll think about abortion, about capital punishment, about flogging, about nuclear war and so on. Whereas non-lefties judge each issue on its merits, singly.'

He now regards himself, not as a Tory, but as a counter-revolutionary. 'It's not good enough simply not to be communist. A true communist doesn't fight fair. If it helps to advance the Party a communist can lie, steal, murder, torture . . . Well, if you have people like that, then the people on the other side who are fighting them have got to be equally ruthless.'

Ruthless would seem to colour many of his more dogmatic pronouncements about the way the world is going. The former C.N.D. enthusiast now says, 'You're just as dead if you're killed with high explosives as with a nuclear bomb. The nuclear bomb at least has the advantage of killing you quicker.' And Braine, as is notorious, vociferously advocates the return of capital punishment. 'What always strikes me as rather amusing is the number of lawyers who are against it. There's a very good reason for that. Once your client is topped there's no more money to come from him . . . But the figures have been cooked. In the Homicide Act of 1957 the definition of murder was changed. If you count as murders killings which would have been so accounted before the abolition of hanging, you realise that murders have increased fourfold. There were some two hundred murders a year in those days. Now there are something like nine hundred. As a deterrent, hanging *works*. The police always say in order to find out the number of murders, don't look at the figures, count the bodies.'

Braine means what he says about all this. ('In the end, it's the poorest people who suffer the most. Always. People living in hell-holes like Brixton and Tower Hamlets. They all want to restore hanging. And people have got a right to what they want.') But there is undoubtedly an element of ghoulish humour in him which enjoys dwelling on the shock value which attaches to discussion of the rope. He likes to recall that the public hangman, Harry Pierpoint, lived in Clayton, a rather bleak and windy suburb of Bradford. Harry kept hens, but he was so sensitive that his wife Annie always had to kill them. 'She was a very fat jolly woman and she'd say "Harry, O he's so soft-hearted. He cannot bear to wring a hen's neck; it makes him positively ill." They lived near the cemetery in Necropolis Road.' Was that, I asked, the same cemetery where the Yorkshire Ripper had found such happy employment? 'No, lad, that was Bingley. This was Bradford cemetery in Clayton. I remember my mother used to say if you pass by that cemetery and they were having a cremation, "Ee, there's a lovely smell like roast meat." Particularly on a cold day, it would make your mouth water. And then, my God, you'd realise what it was . . .'

John Braine's mother was an Irishwoman, and it is from that side of the family that he believes he has inherited his delight in exaggeration, strong speech and embellishment. It is also from her that he inherited his religion. He recalls the dark aisles, heavy with stale incense and candle smoke, of St. Patrick's church in Bradford, and the old women in black, kneeling there to tell their beads. 'I know what they went there for: to lay down their burdens. One bloody thing I'm sure they'd never want to go there for is to have a talk about the bloody miners' strike.'

Braine doesn't like the modern breed of churchman. 'It makes me wild, these buggers, they're taking away from people the one thing they have: that they can go to church and hear the message of love. They don't want to be told about the bloody Government or wages or unemployment. That's precisely what they've come to get away from. I don't know what it's like in St. Patrick's now. Probably all sorts of bloody things go on in it, and they've started serving fucking coffee.'

Fed up with the social gospel and 'appalling' figures such as Monsignor Bruce Kent, Braine has abandoned the habit of going to Mass. 'I will no doubt come back to it. I still say my prayers. Always a quick act of contrition. Pascal's gamble. It may be wrong, but if it's right and I haven't said my act of contrition I shall be very sorry for it, but by then it will be too late. And I always ask God for things I want.'

Does he get them?

'Generally, I do. Always at a time in life when I've needed money, money has come along. When I've thought, "O God, I don't know what I'm going to do next, I really am in desperate trouble now," then the Marines have arrived.'

A few years ago, John Braine suffered a personal crisis, and moved (surprisingly for someone who has castigated its inhabitants for the last twenty years) to Hampstead. He lives there modestly in a small flat, and feels that he has achieved something like serenity or happiness. Though he hates to admit it, he is mellowing.

Actually, there has always been an odd contrast between the harsh persona created for Braine by his enemies on the left, and the guiding intelligence of his novels which have, in my view, got much better since *Room at the Top*. Even Joe Lampton, though Braine tries to make him into a complete shit, has his moment of illumination at the end of the story, when he gazes down on the lights of an industrial town at night: 'There was no open country to be seen, not one acre where there wasn't a human being, two hundred thousand separate lonelinesses, two hundred thousand separate deaths.'

Subsequent Braine novels have all been full of a warm human sympathy. He writes unpretentiously, about recognisably real human beings, and that is why he continues to be popular with the readers. (He almost earned his full quota last year out of Public Lending Right.) Critics, misled by the utterances of Braine the Fascist Beast into thinking of him as a purely joke figure, have chosen to ignore his considerable achievement. Does this worry him? He refers me to one of his best recent novels.

'Tim, in *One and Last Love*, says that he had expected, as he got older, to get tougher. In fact what is happening to him is that he's losing layer after layer of skin. I've now reached the point where I hope I'm still reasonably tough-minded and realistic, but I can't read the papers because there's always something which literally makes me dissolve into tears.'

He views developments in modern fiction with dismay, particularly those which appear to trivialise the sufferings of children. He instances a modern short story by one of the 'best of young British writers' about a thirteen-year-old boy having intercourse with his nine-year-old sister – 'completely nasty'; or a story by another young writer in which sheep droppings are found in the vagina of a dead child – 'cruel and completely decadent'. He contrasts these stories

110

with the moment in Dostoevsky where Ivan Karamazov sees a general setting his dog on a small peasant boy, a moment when Ivan says he would like to hand back his entrance ticket to God.

The sheer ugliness of the modern scene often makes Braine want to hand back his entrance ticket. But he now feels a duty, as part of his vocation as a writer, to assert the possibility of maintaining human dignity amid all the squalor and the pain. A favourite quotation is from Alexei Tolstoy: 'Thrice bathed in blood, thrice washed in fire, thrice scoured with caustic, who so clear as we?'

Braine is not the lowbrow, blustering monster which caricature makes him out to be. In person, he is courteous and amusing. In his books, he keeps alive all that is best in the old-fashioned realist tradition, not only of English fiction, but of the novel in general. In fact, the writers he reads most, and whom he most admires, are largely Russian, French and American. He has catholic tastes, and quotations come readily to his lips from Hemingway, Scott Fitzgerald, Flaubert (pronounced uncompromisingly *anglice* as Floor-Bert) and Dostoevsky. I think that when the history of the twentieth-century novel comes to be written, it won't be entirely absurd to speak of Braine as a worthy successor to these writers.

At the moment he is writing a sequel to *One and Last Love* which is to be called *The Golden Years Return*. The hero, a novelist not unlike Braine himself, thinks of Hemingway's *The Snows of Kilimanjaro*. 'Do you remember? He is climbing towards the snows and thinking of all the experiences which he has been saving up to write. But now it's too late, because he's climbing toward the snow. Well, Tim thinks to himself that he's not saving things up any more. He is more fortunate than Hemingway's hero. He's got the time, and he's going to be totally different. It's going to be about somebody absolutely unlike himself in every way. In fact, what I've thought of more and more is Flaubert's *Un Coeur Simple*. Because what was behind writing that book for Flaubert was the challenge of describing someone utterly unlike himself, a simple person like those old women in black in St. Patrick's Church in Bradford that I was telling you about. "Oh God, John," said my agent to me the other day, "you're too bloody mellow. You're not abrasive any more." But I no longer want to be abrasive.'

111

# Barbara Pym

Conrad's Marlow, in *Chance*, expounds the idea that fiction and gossip spring from the same wells of curiosity in the human mind. 'Is it merely that we may amuse ourselves by gossiping about each other's affairs?' he is asked, replying, in characteristically sonorous vein, 'It would still be a very respectable provision if it were only for that end. But from that same provision of understanding there springs in us compassion, charity, indignation, the sense of solidarity; and, in minds of any largeness, an invitation to that indulgence which is next to affection.'

Too few modern novelists have displayed this gossipy curiosity about other people's lives; and it is this quality, above all, perhaps, which we will miss in the coming years, since the death of Barbara Pym. Why have all her novels survived so well, while others, more daring, or more recent, already seem jaded or unrealistic? They, and not Miss Pym, chronicled 'the sexual revolution'; poured out, in many confessional volumes, the details of marital collapse and promiscuous erotic adventure. Yet, in most such books, perhaps, neither author nor reader retained sufficiently the curiosity which is present in the really satisfying experience of fiction, the curiosity which sends us back again and again to *Excellent Women* and *A Glass of Blessings*. Barbara Pym was the chronicler of quiet lives. If her heroines were married, they were not unfaithful to their husbands, although they might take a shine to the curate; if they were unmarried, they usually remained so at the end of the story, eating solitary meals in their small houses or not particularly nice flats, and yet as real and as rounded as some of the best characters in nineteenth-century fiction.

Philip Larkin, among others, was responsible for the Pym revival a few years ago. He and Barbara Pym have much in common. Larkin, along with John Betjeman, is outstanding among modern poets for his generous sense of the oddness and bleakness of solitary lives: Betjeman's Eunice, with her poky cottage in Kent ('Keys with Mr. Groombridge, but nobody will take them') and her flat 'high in Onslow Gardens'; or Larkin's Mr. Bleaney, in his ghastly little rented room; these are lives which could bear the more leisurely and inquisitive glance which the medium of prose fiction allows. And it was this field which was explored so punctiliously and amusingly in the novels of Barbara Pym. *Think of being them!* That was her motto.

In her two most recent novels, *Quartet in Autumn* and *The Sweet Dove Died*, the poignancy and loneliness of her characters was as sharp as that of Mr. Bleaney; and their unloveliness, their inability to connect with one another was analysed with a depressing iciness. Brilliant as both books were, many of her admirers must have pined for the early hilarity of *Some Tame Gazelle*, set in a country village and centring on two curatolatrous, late middle-aged ladies: one who dotes on each new curate arriving in the parish and the other who has been quietly in love with wonderfully absurd Archdeacon Hoccleve ever since he was her undergraduate contemporary at Oxford. It was a book full of the rich dottiness of English village life; the world peeped at from behind chintz curtains; less Larkin and more Betjeman.

Now, posthumously, *A Few Green Leaves* has appeared. In tone and setting it goes back to the comic atmosphere of *Some Tame Gazelle*, but the realism is sharper, the underlying poignancy more carefully implied. Reading it, one gets the best of both the early and the late Pym manner; a full and distinctive taste of what her novels are like.

That taste is such a mild thing that it is almost impossible to describe. 'Not enough salt, or perhaps *no* salt, I thought, as I ate the macaroni. And not really enough cheese.' Mildred's reflection on Winifred Malory's cooking (*Excellent Women*) comes to mind. If one says that *A Few Green Leaves* is a beautifully written, very delicate comedy about a group of people living in a West Oxfordshire village, and that the two most exciting things which happen are a coffee morning and a Flower Festival, every Pym fan will go to their bookshop to buy it, unable to wait for the Public Library copy, and certain that they will want to read it half a dozen times. (I have ready found myself perusing it again after two readings.) But will someone who has not read Barbara Pym before think, from such an account, that the novel is worth starting? They will scarcely be encouraged by learning that the book is as unashamedly churchy as its predecessors. 'Daffodils on the altar at Quinquagesima,' muses Emma, the heroine, a rather plain young anthropologist who, by the end, has become rather sweet on the rector. Is this the stuff of which great fiction is made?

Perhaps not great fiction; but of very good fiction, yes. All the people in *A Few Green Leaves* are completely realistic: the sort of people we meet every day of our lives and never particularly notice; the sort of people, if we are true Pym fans, we are ourselves. By *noticing* them in such detail, Barbara Pym's art endows them with a significance which they could never possess in life, so that what sound – if they are described outside the context of the book – to be mild and uneventful moments really come over as quite strong.

In the third chapter, for instance, we glimpse Doctor Gellibrand (Doctor 'G') and Doctor Martin Shrubsole interviewing their patients during morning surgery. Nothing is really wrong with any of them. They are merely queuing up for the sake of something to do and in order that someone will give them some attention.

> Going out of the surgery, clutching her bit of paper, a prescription for *something* at least, Daphne felt that Martin, the 'new doctor' as he was called in the village, had done her good. He had listened, he had been sympathetic, and she felt decidedly better. Much better than she should have felt if she'd gone to Dr. G – *he* never even bothered to take your blood pressure.

Daphne Dagnall is the rector's sister. She is bored with being his housekeeper in the large, draughty parsonage. She dreams of livening up her existence by getting a dog. She also dreams of living in Greece, where she has had blissful summer holidays, failing to notice, as Miss Pym has done, the terrible quality of Greek food, the ugliness of modern Greek architecture, 'with a garage and hideous square white concrete buildings baking in the sun', and everywhere bright plastic bags. Someone (inevitably) even remembers glimpsing a priest carrying one. During the preparations for the Flower Festival

> Daphne realised that she hated flower-arranging altogether. Sometimes she hated the church too, wasn't sure that she believed any more, though of course one didn't talk about that kind of thing.

In the end, Daphne does escape her life of servitude, and she buys a dog, but she is no happier. The friend that she elects to live with is

114

much bossier than she remembered and she has to make do, not with a villa in Greece, but with a house on the outskirts of Birmingham.

Daphne is only one of many characters in the book who comes to life under Barbara Pym's deft and unobtrusive investigation. There is Adam Prince, a former clergyman who doubted the validity of his orders, went over to Rome and became a food journalist. The 'most remarkable sole nantua', he recalls, was eaten not in a restaurant, but in a clergy house (cooked by Wilf Bason in *A Glass of Blessings*). There is Beatrix, Emma's mother, who is an English don at Oxford and her well-evoked, tiresome friend. There is Terry Skate, the golden-haired boy who appears at the rectory one morning too late for coffee and has to be given a glass of sherry. 'My friend and I have taken over this florists, you see – of course we have lots of regular orders for floral displays, not to mention weddings and funerals, you name it, we do it – but we've never done a mausoleum before.' There is Mrs. Dyer, who cleans at the rectory. There is Magdalen Raven, Dr. Shrubsole's mother-in-law, who has come to live with the young family, and finds herself being put on a strict diet, none of her favourite farinaceous foods; and being left to babysit rather more often than she had reckoned on.

Piffling stuff, it may be thought; but Emily Eden and Charlotte M. Yonge would not have thought so; nor would Jane Austen or George Eliot. The scene in which the Shrubsoles have the rector to supper, hoping to persuade him to move out of his rectory because they want a larger house, is worthy of the creator of Mrs. John Dashwood:

> 'I expect you miss your sister,' Magdalen said at last, 'being by yourself in that big house.' Tom looked surprised, for that aspect of Daphne's going had not occurred to him. It seemed rather a suburban concept, his being by himself in a big house. 'Have you ever thought of moving to somewhere smaller?' Avice asked.
>
> 'Well, no. It *is* the rectory after all, and I suppose as I'm the rector I'm expected to live in it.'
>
> 'I believe some clergy *are* getting smaller houses, even having them specially built for them,' Avice went on. 'The wives find it so difficult to manage in these great rambling old places.'
>
> 'Really?' said Tom politely. 'That hadn't occurred to me. Having no wife I suppose I'm out of touch.'

In exchanges of this kind, one recognises something more than mere 'talent'. Nor is the novel, as my random selections might suggest, a wholly disconnected series of sketches or 'scenes from clerical life'. For, woven throughout the book, and touching almost all the large cast of characters, is the shadow of the tomb and the fear of death. At the big house on the edge of the village, there is a mausoleum falling into disrepair, and the frequent returns to this theme and this spot, while smacking of nothing so portentous as symbolism, keep the story very neatly together. The rector himself is obsessed by old burial customs, and by the fact that in the old days one had to be buried in wool. '"Nowadays, of course, it wouldn't apply – one was probably buried in some man-made fibre – Acrilan, Courtelle, Terylene or nylon."'

How good a novelist Barbara Pym was, by absolute standards, perhaps only the coming decades will allow us to decide. Many enjoyable re-readings lie ahead. Some people have compared her with Jane Austen, a comparison few writers could survive. But very good indeed she certainly was. And the entry Sir Walter Scott made in his *Journal*, having read *Pride and Prejudice* for the third time, is not entirely inapposite:

> That . . . lady had a talent for describing the involvements and feelings and characters of ordinary life which is to me the most wonderful I ever met with: . . . the exquisite touch which renders ordinary commonplace things and characters interesting from the truth of the description and the sentiment . . . What a pity such a gifted creature died so early.

\* \* \*

Bárbara Pym died with Stoic quietness in January 1980. A few months later, Macmillan published her last novel, *A Few Green Leaves*, and her many admirers must have finished it with the intensely sad feeling that there would never be another. Like me, they must have re-read it slowly, any number of times, savouring each delicately painted scene, each quiet life, in the Oxfordshire village which she depicted. Her genius was wholly distinctive. People likened her to Jane Austen, but the comparison ignores Barbara Pym's total absence of malice. Few novelists' eyes have ever observed the lonely ludicrousness of human existence more acutely than she did. But there is nothing shrill about her, and nothing unkind. She always sees the pathos, as well as the absurdity, of her familiar cast of selfish librarians and anthropologists, ineffectual

116

clergymen, food-conscious homosexuals and single ladies trying to keep up vestiges of the decorum which had marked their fathers' parsonages in genteeler days.

Now, to be heralded with delight, a tenth novel, *An Unsuitable Attachment*, has been published; and none of her fans will be disappointed in it. Philip Larkin has written a sensitive (and very restrained) introduction which explains why we have waited until now for its appearance.

This was the seventh novel which she completed. Her previous six had established a following, though she probably never made much money out of them, either for herself or for her publishers, Jonathan Cape. They were serialised on *Woman's Hour* during the 1950s and were popular in the vanished days of Boot's lending library. They were not of a wholly even quality. The first, *Some Tame Gazelle*, is much the most hilarious and unrestrained; *No Fond Return of Love*, the sixth, is by far the feeblest. But there was no doubt of her merits or of her modest popularity.

Then, in February 1963, she sent off *An Unsuitable Attachment* to Cape. Since Larkin tells the tale, the date seems all too miserably appropriate, when one remembers from his poem 'Annus Mirabilis' what 'began' in that year, 'Between the end of the Chatterly ban/ And the Beatles' first L.P.'.

It is a novel set in a high church parish in an unfashionable district in North London. 'We dare not ask for the grace of humility, but perhaps we don't need to when it is so often thrust upon us, thought Sophia, beating together eggs and sugar for a sponge cake, knowing that her cake would not rise as high as Sister Dew's.' This was hardly the sort of sentence to cheer up a pushy young publisher on the make in 1963.

Mr. Maschler, now the Chairman of Cape (television viewers might conceivably recall his recent apologia for the wholly meretricious and nonsensical *Holy Blood and Holy Grail* best-seller) was at that stage Literary Adviser to the firm. *An Unsuitable Attachment* was sent off to two readers, William Plomer and Daniel George. Their reports were in one case 'extremely negative' and in the other 'fairly negative'. Clearly Cape faced a problem. They could have found any number of ways out of it. They were not bound to take any notice of these (to me incomprehensible) judgements. They might have recognised that Barbara Pym was a novelist of the very top rank who had a devoted (and growing) band of

117

admirers. *An Unsuitable Attachment* was perhaps not as perfect as *Excellent Women* or *A Glass of Blessings*; and it unquestionably needed editing. (This has been unobtrusively done, in the present, published edition, which I compared with the typescript in the Bodleian Library.) Cape could, if they really felt that the book was unworthy of Miss Pym, have asked her to call, they could have explained that, while they were glad to have her on their list, they believed that, in her own interests, the book should not be published or that it should be altered. Instead, they waited three months, made no suggestion that she should visit them, gave her not so much as lunch, and posted the manuscript back to her with a curt refusal letter. She wrote to Philip Larkin telling him the story. 'I write this calmly enough, but I really was and am very upset about it and think they have treated me very badly. Of course it may be that this book is much *worse* than my others, though they didn't say so, giving their reason for rejecting it as their fear that with the present cost of book production etc. etc. they doubted whether they could sell enough copies to make a profit.'

Mr. Maschler now denies that Cape rejected the book on these grounds. 'Neither then nor at any time since has this company rejected a manuscript for commercial reasons,' he says. His words contrast oddly with the letter Miss Pym received at the time, but she has her reward. Her name will be remembered for as long as the English novel is read, and we need not sling mud at this Maschler, who is probably more of a fool than a knave.

It is a shocking tale, nevertheless. For, as everyone knows, Barbara Pym, who bravely wrote a few more novels in spite of this ill-mannered and needlessly callous treatment, remained unpublished for fifteen years; and the revival of her fortunes might never have happened in her lifetime had it not been for the coincidence that Philip Larkin and David Cecil both named her, in a symposium in the *T.L.S.* in 1977, as the most underrated writer of the century (the only living writer to be mentioned by more than one contributor). As a result, she was at last acclaimed for the genius that she was. Three novels were published by the admirable Macmillan, and now, two years after her death, we can at last enjoy *An Unsuitable Attachment*.

It is a book which is well up to her usual standard and rich not only in all the familiar Pym ingredients, but also in quite a few familiar characters too. We meet Everard Bone again (from

*Excellent Women*); Wilf Bason (*A Glass of Blessings*) is alluded to by a friend called Eric who is running rather a nice restaurant in South Kensington; Esther Clovis from *Less than Angels* appears at a dowdy little party; and there is even a glorious moment in a restaurant in Rome when Harriet Bede, curatolatrous spinster of *Some Tame Gazelle*, turns up with a wet young man in tow called Father Branche and tries to persuade the waiter to bring her hot milk: '"*latte* – hot," she hesitated for the Italian word, "*bolente*", she brought it out at last'.

But since I cannot write at the length which the book deserves, I will single out two features of it which struck me.

'"Those great red signs you sometimes see in London – TAKE COURAGE – have you ever noticed them?" "Yes," said Ianthe, "I believe it's a kind of beer – but how many people must have been strengthened and comforted by seeing that message shining out into the night."' The characters with whom Miss Pym was at home all need this quality of quiet courage. Ianthe, who is a rather too seemly spinster of thirty-five in love with an unsuitable younger man, is shocked when a neighbour quotes approvingly Matthew Arnold's lines about there being really neither 'joy nor love nor light'. '"I don't think one should feel like that about life," said Ianthe.' Nor, evidently, did her creator. Unlike most heroines of early Pym novels, Ianthe does eventually solemnise her 'unsuitable attachment' at the altar of St. Basil's. But not before she has had the silent misery of letting 'love sweep over her like a kind of illness'. Most people in Barbara Pym's novels do not get what they desire out of life. The grace of humility was thrust on Sophia because her sponge cakes did not rise as high as Sister Dew's. They all have to Take Courage whether they like it or not. 'Oh, this coming back to an empty house, Rupert thought, when he had seen her safely to the door. People – though perhaps it was only women – seemed to make so much of it. As if life itself were not as empty as the house one was coming back to.'

In this world where human relationships are so often muted or unsatisfactory, food bulks large. That is the second feature of *An Unsuitable Attachment* which I would single out for special praise. 'Rock salmon – that had a noble sound to it,' muses the vicar at the beginning of the book outside a fish and chip shop, 'though he believed it was actually inferior to real salmon.' Food, often of a very ordinary kind, fills the consciousness of every character in the

119

book: ranging from Mervyn Cantrell's exquisite little snacks in the library to Penelope's idea for eking out some warmed-up stew: '"Add a few more vegetables, some carrots, or a tin of peas, and a bouillon cube – or even just water – and serve rather a lot of potatoes with it."' There are Italian restaurants lovingly described; harvest suppers with lots of sausage rolls; and a romantic high tea of buck rarebit, at the Humming Bird, 'a little restaurant near Westminster Abbey, run by gentlewomen'. Mistaking the identity of the donor of an oxtail nearly breaks young Penelope's heart, while Father Anstruther pines for the parish parties of the old days: '"Fairies," he murmured, "who *was* it now who used to make such deliciously light fairies?"' There is something almost appropriate about Father Branche's absurd misapplication of a quotation when he has drunk too much at Ianthe and John's wedding: '"'Imparadised in one another's arms' as Milton put it," Basil went on, "or encasseroled perhaps" – the bay leaf resting on the *boeuf bourgignon.*'

Father Branche eventually '" got a church" of his own – St. Barbara-in-the-Precinct – a very old, almost moribund church'. When Ianthe tries to get into it, she finds it is locked. And now St. Barbara-in-the-Precinct is shut forever, and Miss Pym will write no more. It would probably do her reputation no good if her few unfinished novels were published. But there is a sizeable collection of short stories in typesetting in the Bodleian Library, and we must all hope that her literary executor and Macmillan can allow the world to read them. It will be a bit like eating Penelope's watery stew, or finishing up yesterday's cold spam out of Ianthe's tin. But beggars can't be choosers.

*Times Literary Supplement*, 15 January 1977
*Spectator*, 20 February 1982

# C. P. Snow

Twenty years have passed since F. R. Leavis published his notoriously vituperative reflections on C. P. Snow in the pages of the *Spectator*. 'The judgement I have to come out with is that not only is he not a genius; he is intellectually as undistinguished as it is possible to be . . . Snow is, of course, a – no, I can't say that, he isn't: Snow thinks of himself as a novelist . . . As a novelist he doesn't exist; he doesn't begin to exist. The nonentity is apparent on every page of his fictions.'

To our mild generation, the stuttering prose of the crazed sage of Bulstrode Gardens has some of the belligerent attraction of Milton's pamphlets, ranting in a long-forgotten controversy with some seventeenth-century ecclesiastical buffoon. But, as a piece of literary judgement it is surely impossible to fault. To wade through Snow's *Strangers and Brothers* sequence today is to have the eerie experience of reading *A Dance to the Music of Time* narrated by Widmerpool. Snow's brother has now written a memoir of the novelist,* confirming on every page that this impression is the right one. The biographer writes of Snow's 'consuming ambition to get ahead'.

At the age of twenty, shortly after completing a B.Sc. as an external student of London University, Snow (Percy Snow in those days) was pacing the streets of Leicester with a school friend and exclaimed, 'I'd like to be known as Snow of Leicester . . . then Snow of England . . . finally just Snow.'

In this scheme of self-advancement, academic promotion and the simultaneous practice of letters provided very serviceable ladders. He went to Cambridge, did a Ph.D. in molecular physics, got made a fellow of Christ's and started to write novels in his distinctively wooden idiom. (It often puzzled him in later life that he was not

* *Stranger and Brother: a Portrait of C. P. Snow*, Philip Snow.

121

more popular in France. 'His style: . . . when translated faithfully into French, he believed, as did others, that it resembled a Civil Service minute.' He, not Leavis, said it.) The war provided a further leg-up in the world as a civil servant. 'They have co-opted me on to the Physics panel of the Royal Society which is the body that advises the Ministry of Labour, ultimately the Service scientific departments.'

When the war ended, he found that the 'corridors of power' ('a cliché. But I console myself with the reflection that if a man hasn't the right to his own cliché, who has?') suited him better than being a don, and he remained in London, pursuing a number of sordid love affairs, writing books, and ultimately marrying a very good novelist, Pamela Hansford Johnson. Thereafter, he was known as Charles. Like many grotesquely ugly men, he was reassuringly attractive to women, retaining a constant mistress and having a number of casual affairs throughout his married life. His assiduous cultivation of 'important' friends, his vacuous atheism, and his ability to claim 'humble' origins all served him well, for in 1964 Harold Wilson elevated him to the peerage and made him a Minister of Technology. He was the sort that men ennoble. When choosing his heraldic device, he selected the appropriate Widmerpudlian motto, *Aut Inveniam Viam aut Faciam*: I will either find a way or make one.

At this date I was still a child and happened to inhabit, for part of the year, the same Midland suburb as Snow's brother, who was a school bursar. One would sometimes glimpse the famous novelist waddling along the pavement, his gross features crowned with a Homburg, seeming like an embodiment of the world, the flesh and Devil rolled into one flabby form. Since putting away childish things, I am inclined to a much kinder view. Snow as a writer had no ear for dialogue; no narrative gifts at all; and sadly little of that gossipy curiosity about distinctiveness which all natural novelists possess. But, writing feeble yarns, whatever Savonarola Leavis preached, is not a sin, and if people enjoy Snow's books, why shouldn't they? As a public man, Snow was scarcely decorative or interesting, but once again, the mad Doctor surely painted him blacker than he really was.

As a private man, unless you were unlucky enough to be involved with him sexually, Snow's callous self-absorption seems to have done nobody much harm. As a brother, he could obviously be kind and companionable. There is something touching about the appendix to Snow Minor's book, which lists what Lord Widmerpool had to show for all that committee work, all that dining out, all that self-advertisement, all that huffing and puffing: thirty-one honorary doctorates (D. Humane Letters, Akron University, Ohio); the odd lectureship; presidency of the British Migraine Association. He had hoped for the O.M. and the Nobel Prize for Literature. His biographer adds loyally, 'I myself always hoped that the Royal Society would elect him a Fellow for his coordinating interpretative work for science, and it always seemed odd that he was never offered the Chancellorship of any of the new universities.'

C. P. Snow died, predictably, of a perforated gastric ulcer. The best anecdote in this engagingly written memoir shows the famous novelist at the table. When he had completed his long sequence, the most his publisher, Harold Macmillan, could find to say about it was, 'You have done fine work as others have done before you,' a remark worthy of the Squid in *A. J. Wentworth B.A.* Nevertheless, Supermac took Snow out for a celebratory luncheon. 'They went to the Ritz, Macmillan's favourite place. "Charles, what will you have? You can have anything you like, on or off the menu." Charles cheered up. " 'I'll have a poached egg on toast." Macmillan looked bemused. "No," said Charles, "I'll change my mind if I may." Macmillan looked encouraged. "I'll have two poached eggs on toast, please." And that was that. Macmillan had caviare, roast beef, a pudding, and cheese.'

*Spectator*, 16 October 1982

# Ivy Compton-Burnett

The last scene that Ivy Compton-Burnett ever created was not in the pages of her novels, but in the much more curious fiction which surrounded her person. She left a highly elaborate will, directing that almost every item of furniture from the notorious flat in Braemar Mansions be left to a separate friend or luminary from the London literary world. There was an inspired malice in the choice that determined which particular looking-glass or *objet* was left to which 'friend' and it was further decreed that they should collect their trophy immediately after the funeral at Putney Vale crematorium. Thus Ivy Compton-Burnett guaranteed that even if they did not (as she had done herself several times during her last months) slither to their downfall on her sparse linoleum, they would, while clutching their bequest (in most cases a looking-glass) be sure to jostle one another in the corridors and impede one another's ascent and descent of the stairs. In this way, the final Braemar Gathering (as, among members of the circle, they were known) almost resembled one of those modernistic theatrical productions in which the actors themselves work as stage hands and dismantle the scenery on stage at the end of the final act.

What sort of drama was it that had been enacted? 'All Russians are brutal,' Miss Compton-Burnett once remarked to her friend and fellow-novelist Elizabeth Taylor, 'except Chekhov. People dislike his plays as they are all about nothing. *I* like them very much.' People might say the same of the Compton-Burnett *oeuvre*, though they would be wrong. If anything, too much happens – incest, human sacrifice and suicide all tripped easily from her melodramatic pen – in the novels. But she was absolutely determined that nothing much should happen in her talk or in her life. There are many versions of the legendary occasion on which the editor of the *Times Literary Supplement* arranged for the Duchess of Buccleuch to meet the famous novelist. The Duchess was neither the first nor the last to discover that Miss Compton-Burnett had nothing to talk about except her window-box and her refrigerator. When she was reproached afterwards she shrugged and complained, 'I wish people would *tell* me when they want me to be literary.'

She was, of course, more literary than such stony encounters would suggest. She did read a certain amount, and she kept up with, while eschewing, the latest fashions in fiction and critical taste. But in spite of the fact that her conversation amused her friends as much as her lack of it intimidated her mere acquaintances, there is not much in the later life of Ivy Compton-Burnett for a biographer to make interesting: rather less, it might be thought, than there is in the lives of the characters of Chekhov. 'My life was over when I was four. I wonder how many people can say that,' remarks Fabian Clare in *The Present and the Past*. If that was not entirely true of Ivy Compton-Burnett, she certainly liked to live as if experience was 'over'.

'People in life,' she once remarked, 'hardly seem definite enough to appear in print.' It could never be said of her, who drew the outlines of her own mannerisms and eccentricity with such attention (the donning of the pork-pie hat and mackintosh to water the window-boxes; the striding across the park, complete with all the stage props of umbrella and hair-net, to have her daily greedy feast of buns at Buzzards in Oxford Street) that she was *indistinct*. But it could be said that she inhabited, like the saint in the poem, a world without event. You can make a funny essay out of Compton-Burnett anecdotes. You can tell again the tale of Frankie Birrel (or, if you prefer, Philip Toynbee, for the same story is told of him) coming to dinner with Miss Compton-Burnett and Miss Jourdain, somewhat drunk, and waking up in the small hours to find his face in a plate of cold soup, the ladies having eaten their dinner and gone to bed without attempting to wake him or dislodge him. You can imagine, while Miss Jourdain's friends talked about books or furniture and her mousy little companion passed the radishes or the watercress or the home-made gingerbread, that she was dreaming up the plots and exchanges of her frenziedly arch novels. 'Spotless dullness is what Andrew and I are good at,' as the heroine of *Brothers and Sisters* remarks. But it would take considerable imaginative panache to make all this into a book. Luckily for us, this is precisely the panache which Hilary Spurling possesses in such rich abundance. She has made one of the most fascinating of modern biographies out of what must have been one of the most boring of all modern lives.

What gave Mrs. Spurling's first volume *Ivy When Young* its thrilling plausibility is that she, like George Painter in his biography of Proust, managed to show conclusively that the nature of the novelist's subject is the very opposite of what we are meant to expect. Ivy Compton-Burnett can certainly be seen, and to some extent saw herself, as a 'Freudian' novelist. Freud's picture of human memory coloured the vision of all his generation, and of succeeding generations – although, comparing him with other, roughly contemporaneous figures, we can see that like many insights of genius it came partly from himself and partly from something that was in the air at the time. Freud's 'parapraxis' is obviously comparable to the effects, in the memory bank of Proust's narrator, of an uneven paving stone or *madeleine* dipped in weak tea, but no one would dream of saying that Proust 'got the idea' of *À la recherche du temps perdu* from Freud.

Anthony Powell, the novelist who has most successfully avoided imitating Proust by constructing a *Recherche* in which the narrator has no inner life at all (and hence, properly speaking, no memory), has said that Ivy Compton-Burnett 'embodied in herself a quite unmodified pre-1914 personality', a remark which would surely have delighted her; and Hilary Spurling continues in her second volume, *Secrets of a Woman's Heart,*\* to expose the relentlessly *voulu* nature of the Compton-Burnett cult of the past.

The cataclysm, long before this volume begins (with the publication of *Pastors and Masters* in 1925) has already happened. The hellish past had been put behind her; probably, one suspects, as so often with pain, completely forgotten. Just as her skirt lengths, her diction, her hairnet and her sense of humour were 'unmodified pre-1914', so she substituted fiction for memory. She had, for instance, or so she would have wanted us to believe, been in love with her brother Noel. One of the greatest 'blows' (hidden in the irrecoverable past of pre-memory) was his decision to marry, and another was his death in the Trenches, which led to the unsuccessful suicide attempt of his wife. Ivy (who was to suffer the suicide of two of her own sisters) apparently nursed her brother Noel's wife for a

---

\* *Secrets of a Woman's Heart: the Later Life of I. Compton-Burnett 1920–1969,* Hilary Spurling.

year through the 'nervous breakdown' which followed his death. Out of this experience, Mrs. Spurling shows, grew the scene of Josephine nursing Gabriel's wife in *More Women than Men*: the half-murderous impulse which leads her to put the patient in an icy draught, and the guilt and self-disgust which follow upon her death.

But where Mrs. Spurling really shines is in showing that this is not, in fact, a *memory* at all. The scene is lifted, directly, from that haunting and much-neglected masterpiece of Somerville and Ross, *The Real Charlotte*. The heroine, Charlotte Mullen, does precisely what Josephine does in *More Women than Men*. Most of Ivy Compton-Burnett's early reviewers, Mrs. Spurling informs us, noted that she lifted her plots wholesale from such trashy late-Victorian works as *East Lynne*, *The Wide, Wide World* or *Irene Iddesleigh* (due for a reprint?) and then imposed these plots upon her own 'experience'. The word demands quotation marks, for even so painstaking an investigator as Mrs. Spurling cannot sort out what 'really happened' in Ivy's past from what she thought happened or wanted to have happened. 'Ivy When Young' might have gone through hell, but the dowdy, guzzling witch of Braemar Mansions, prosing ceaselessly on about refrigerators or the difficulty of getting servants, made her artistic reputation out of shaping other hells which owe their power to their Wildean lack of reality. Like her own invention, Terence Calderon in *Elders and Betters*, she 'on second glance presented a normal appearance'. The rhetorical trick in the Compton-Burnett *oeuvre* is not to allow us a second glance, so that, as in a play by Wilde, we are so delighted by the verbal displays that we do not pause to consider the reality or otherwise of the mouthpiece who is giving them utterance. 'We shall feel this house is our own when we have planted memories in it,' says Benjamin in the same novel. The words might have been written up in letters of gold over the portals of Braemar Mansions.

The family which she chose to recreate in book after book – the intense, unhappy, sadistic mothers and elder sisters, the ineffectual clergyman and schoolmasters, the languid young cousins ('"Well, a man is a man," said Mr. Bigwell. "That is rather sweeping," said Oliver, "I am not."' – *Two Worlds and their Ways*), all inhabit the nightmare which she herself has painstakingly brought into existence. The fact that strangers at Braemar Gatherings sometimes had difficulty in distinguishing Miss Compton-Burnett from the more aggrieved or etiolated governesses of her own stories only empha-

127

sises how completely the habits of distortion, affectation and creation were ingrained in her. One is struck repeatedly in the novels by the fact that all the grown-ups are infantile whereas all the children are parodies of nineteenth-century *gravitas*, like Mr. Bultitude of *Vice Versa* imprisoned by magic in his son's Eton Collar and school uniform. The children, moreover, are much sager, and much more cynical, observers of depravity, like the Clare children at the beginning of *The Present and the Past* who watch the hens pecking the sick one to death. '"Perhaps it is because they are anxious," said Megan, looking at the hens in the hope of discerning this feeling.'

Mrs. Spurling reveals, a trifle mercilessly, that if there *were* any 'models' for the unpleasant Compton-Burnett 'families' they were to be found not so much in the recesses of her memory as in the figures she collected or created at her famous teaparties. But much more than any model from life, the books themselves are unremittingly, archly, artificial, bookish and 'made'. As one very perceptive reader of *More Women than Men* observed when it was published, 'Oscar Wilde is not so much borrowed from as contributed to.' Or, as Ivy herself admitted in Spurling's first volume, 'I do not claim that the children in my books, any more than their elders, resemble the actual creatures of real life.'

If Wilde (contributed to or borrowed from) seems to hover about like one of the more disconcerting maiden aunts in her novels, and if one of the eventually tiring things about her fantasy life is its tendency to relapse into epigrams, it is the less genial figure of Samuel Butler who was Ivy's greatest inspiration or fairy godfather. Butler himself is another figure who can be easily associated – and not only in time – with Freud. *The Way of All Flesh* is a vulgarian version of Freud's world view, like the *Introductory Lectures on Psychoanalysis* written for *Punch*: as it were, *Oedipus Simplex*. There can be no doubt that Butler hit the spot for many late-Victorian readers, in just the way that F. Anstey did, by constructing a drama in which the whole comedy depends on our shared hatred, not simply of Mr. Pontifex, but of all fathers everywhere; and, come to that, all families. In her copy of Samuel Butler's *Notebooks*, given her in 1919 by Margaret Jourdain, Ivy Compton-Burnett underlined the phrase 'a long living deathbed, so to speak of stagnation and nonentity' and added 'I am a living witniss of this crushing lifless stagnation of the spirit' (*sic*).

128

The most impressive thing about Ivy Compton-Burnett, as revealed in Spurling's pages, is her unerring instinct to preserve this 'lifeless stagnation' against all comers. After the dazzling success of *Brothers and Sisters*, we learn that there were attempts by the 'literary world' to 'take her up'. Leonard Woolf, who had earlier turned down one of her books on the rather attractive grounds that 'she couldn't even write', sent her invitations. Her instinct was to avoid Bloomsbury and the bright lights, and to 'remain on her sofa most of the day writing with a pencil in a notebook'.

Even if nothing odd will do long and it should transpire that Ivy Compton-Burnett's highly idiosyncratic and recognisable creations do not last, Mrs. Spurling has guaranteed that their author will live on as a tragi-comic figure in her own right. This is a biography which will satisfy even those who enjoy the Compton-Burnett books less wholeheartedly than Mrs. Spurling does. There is a good anecdote on almost every page, and welcome and memorable exchanges with Rose Macaulay, Lettice Cooper, Robert Liddell, Elizabeth Taylor (the novelist, not the actress), Francis King, Kay Dick and others. Ivy's companion, for the greater part of her writing life, was the (in her day famous) historian of furniture Margaret Jourdain, and there is added comedy in the fact that the majority of distinguished callers at their flat, in the early days, regarded Ivy with distaste. Margaret herself pretended not to read the novels or to think them 'rubbish'. All this, too, was an invaluable aid in creating the right background of dullness against which the exchanges and violent melodramas of her fiction could be surreptitiously embroidered. The effect of the whole story is more uncanny than anything Ivy Compton-Burnett ever dreamed up in her pages.

There is strong feeling in the electrically charged 'atmospheres' and sharp intakes of breath among that fascinating category of person designated by Elizabeth Bowen 'old-fashioned lesbians of the highest sort'. One of the dons at Oxford labelled the novelist 'poison Ivy' and it is not altogether difficult to see why. This donnish background itself provides a fascinating subplot to Ivy's middle years, for Miss Jourdain's sister, Miss Nelly Jourdain, was the most notorious college Principal of modern times.

Miss Jourdain's precipitate dismissal of Miss Ady as the history fellow of St. Hugh's College, Oxford, was an affair which, as the saying goes, blew up in Miss Jourdain's face. At that date, St. Hugh's depended upon other colleges to supply its students with tuition. All the dons in the University sided with the wronged Miss Ady and withdrew their teaching until she was reinstated. Finally, in the last disgrace of all, Miss Ady received the support of the Chancellor of the University, Lord Curzon, and the disgraced Nelly Jourdain died suddenly. Margaret and Ivy believed she had been murdered. The whole incident reveals the extraordinary extent to which life, even at one remove from a powerful artistic imagination, follows the patterns decreed by novelists.

You might have thought, given her very unhappy experience of dons, that poor poison Ivy would have given them a wide berth as she grew older. Moreover, it might have been guessed, by someone who knew that Ivy was deeply fond of her companion, that she would have felt inconsolable when Margaret Jourdain died. So indeed she did. Nevertheless, after Margaret's death, Ivy wrote a letter to the Principal of Somerville College, asking her if she could be supplied with 'some don who is retiring, and does not want living expenses on a large scale' who could share the flat with her in Braemar Mansions. It was a pathetic letter, and she withdrew the request almost as soon as she had made it. Of course it reveals how lonely she was, and what a muddle her grief had thrown her into. But it also shows an absolutely extraordinary arbitrariness in her attitude to selecting human companionship. Many people would take more trouble about choosing a new cat. The letter asking for a new maiden lady with whom to share her highly distinctive mode of life revealed momentarily that flash of inspired callousness, that combination of boldness and total indifference, which were the breeding ground for her finest moments of fiction.

*Times Literary Supplement*, 29 May 1982

# Sketches for Portraits

# L.B.J.

The scrawny, insensitive features of Lyndon Baines Johnson were a waking nightmare for the gentle, Spock-reared young Americans of the 1960s. As they chanted the lyrics of the pre-Christian Dylan, and held hands, and destroyed their draftcards, caricatures of L.B.J.'s vast ears and deepset eyes brooded over their sit-ins, love-ins and sleep-ins. That was merely an historical accident. Had he not been assassinated, it would have been the crooked, potato-faced President Kennedy whom the Western world held responsible for the death of thirty thousand American servicemen in the napalm-infested jungles of Vietnam. And we would all have been chanting, *Hey, hey, J.F.K., how many kids have you killed today?*

Yet, even with Johnson in charge, things would seem very different if the Stars and Stripes now flew confidently over Saigon. A minority of pacifists would have continued to express horror at the way in which the war was conducted. But most American consciences would have been salved by an all-out victory. In that event, Johnson would probably have died a much-loved national institution, scarcely distinguishable from John Wayne as he rode home into Apache country with a Stetson on his head, the white man triumphant over the reds or the redskins. As it happened, however, the Americans were ignominiously defeated. They were shown up in south-east Asia, not merely as bestial, but as incompetent. L.B.J. must be the scapegoat on which they unload their guilt. And Robert A. Caro, a brilliant biographer and a Pulitzer prizewinner, has devoted the last seven years to chronicling the story of this coarse-grained Texan nonentity who, to judge from the first* of three volumes, never read a book, never had an interesting thought, and never said a memorable thing in the first thirty-two years of his life.

Why, then, does Mr. Caro devote eight hundred and eighty-two

---

* *The Years of Lyndon Johnson: the Path to Power*, Robert A. Caro (1983).

pages to telling us that Lyndon Johnson rose from poverty and obscurity in the hill country of Texas to being a successful Congressman; and from being a Congressman to being a failed candidate for the U.S. Senate in 1941? If Volume I is the length of *War and Peace* (a novel which Lady Bird Johnson has read twice), the subsequent tomes will presumably be even bigger.

Part of the explanation is that Mr. Caro is merely following the prolix conventions of American biography. But another reason is more lugubrious. He is intent to reveal what the majority of middle-aged Americans surely long to be told, that there was not a single moment in the course of their bogeyman's life when his ruthless aggression, his craven dishonesty, and his vulgarity of mind were not blatantly apparent. It is not a whole nation, still less a whole administration, who have the blood on their hands. The monster responsible leapt, fully formed in all his bloodthirsty ambition, out of his cradle in Johnson City in 1908.

The details of his turpitude are thick on every page. As a child, his table manners were so vile that his father would leave the table in a rage. Mrs. Johnson would sob as Lyndon tormented her by cramming huge spoonfuls into his mouth 'with loud slurping noises'. When his father lost all his money, and his seat in the Texas Congress, little Lyndon stopped speaking to him. Meanwhile, he tortured his siblings, and swindled his younger brother, Sam Houston Johnson Jnr., into buying a bicycle which was so big that only L.B.J. could ride it. When punished, he would become hysterical and, horror of horrors, he was whipped. During adolescence, he was a hooligan, whose chief delight was in stealing cars and attaching sticks of dynamite to trees in order to terrify the local farmers.

When he finally got into south-west Texas Teachers' College, San Marcos (he had initially funked going there for fear that, tinpot though it was, he would not be clever enough for it), he was most unpopular with his fellow students. And yet, for all his unpopularity (they called him M.B., the Master of Bullshit) he had an inexplicable power over his contemporaries. He was an adept at flattering the teachers and, vile phrase, 'brown-nosing'. He was a compulsive liar. Arrayed in clothes bought at Woolworths, he claimed they were purchased at the most expensive store in Austin. By cajolery, threats, blackmail and lies, he managed to get himself elected as President of the Student Council. He delighted in cruel practical jokes. He once told a simple-minded fellow student that the best cure for acne was the direct application of cow-dung to the afflicted areas; and he laughed as this foolish youth smeared the stuff on to his face with a trowel.

L.B.J.'s cruel obsession with ordure was again apparent when he had managed to wheedle himself a job as Congressional Secretary in Washington. Underlings would be compelled to take down letters from L.B.J., rasped out as he sat in all his satanic pride on the lavatory.

Shall I go on, as Milton's chaste lady asks, or have I said enough? As Congressional Secretary to Richard Mifflin Kleberg, Johnson showed administrative flair, both in his ability to dominate men and his willingness to buy votes for his master. (They paid Mexican Americans five dollars a vote in 1934.) He further advanced his career by battening on to the legendary Congressman Sam Rayburn and by marrying a rich heiress, Lady Bird Taylor. He proposed to her on their first 'date' and married her in a hurry. But within a few weeks, he was treating her abominably, and shouting orders at his nervous young bride. 'Lady Bird, go get me another piece of pie.' 'I will in just a minute, Lyndon.' '*Get me another piece of pie.*'

Before long, Rayburn, one of the many father-figures whom L.B.J. sought out in his pursuit of power, had secured his protégé a job organising the National Youth administration in Texas. This was a scheme for creating jobs (part of Franklin D. Roosevelt's New Deal) for the young unemployed. L.B.J. was good at it. He created thirty thousand new jobs within the state of Texas within a few years. His success in this field is yet more evidence, in Caro's eyes, of L.B.J.'s essential ruthlessness. Before long, aged twenty-eight, he was offered the managership of the State Railroad Commission, but he turned it down. He wanted more pie.

By spending a lot of money (but whose? Lady Bird's?) he got himself elected as a Congressman. As he crept up in the world, he began to cultivate Charles Marsh, the rich newspaper proprietor and Marsh's mistress Alice Glass. At their palatial house, Longlea (designed as a replica of a house Alice had seen and liked in Sussex, England), L.B.J. started to meet influential people like Walter Lippmann, Henry Wallace and Helen Fuller. A friend recalling those days said, 'Every time I looked at Lyndon, I saw a Uriah Heep from Texas.' He had soon purloined a large slice of Marsh's money, while secretly paying court to his mistress. L.B.J.'s love affair with Alice Glass was perhaps the only episode, Caro believes, that 'ran counter to his personal ambition'. Unfortunately, we know little of it, since Alice Glass destroyed all her private papers in 1967. She did not want her grand-daughter to know she had ever been associated with the man 'responsible for Vietnam'.

Onward and upward, L.B.J.'s gift for brown-nosing, his zest for money-making, made him ideally qualified to squeeze dollars out of Texan oil magnates for the cause of Franklin D. Roosevelt; and by the time he felt rich enough himself to stand for the Senate, L.B.J. was a firm Roosevelt man. To everyone's surprise, he was defeated in his first attempt by Governor 'Pappy' O'Daniel. Then came Pearl Harbour, and the volume peters out, leaving our hero's career somewhat in suspense. Caro does, however, manage to tell us that after Roosevelt's death, L.B.J. quickly switched his allegiance and 'before the paint had faded on the billboards proclaiming his loyalty to Franklin D., Lyndon B. had turned against him'.

One cannot quarrel with a man when he is practising his religious observances. Mr. Caro has spent seven years smearing L.B.J. with filfth; not in the fun-loving spirit which made Johnson himself urge a (surely *very* foolish?) coeval to paste cowpats on to his acne, but with all the solemnity of a hierophant, expiating the guilt of a nation and heaping it on to one man.

One of L.B.J.'s life-long colleagues and aides, Thomas G. Corcoran, ('Tommy the Cork') asserts that L.B.J. was 'the best Congressman for a district that *ever was*'. Caro himself cannot conceal that Johnson was an efficient and, on the whole, benign administrator, who, in his private dealings, exerted extraordinary charm, particularly over those older than himself. He was a good raconteur and his stories were full of a pathetic understanding of the lives of the poor in the hill country of Texas. In his political campaigns, his father, Sam Johnson, spoke enthusiastically on L.B.J.'s behalf.

And yet, for Mr. Caro, all this evidence is damaging. We might think that a man who had himself known poverty and who helped to create thirty thousand jobs for the unemployed in his own district was a human benefactor. But since Caro's L.B.J. had no principles, we have to conclude it was done *purely* to attract attention in Washington. We might think that the man who charmed so many people was, simply, charming; but it suits our druidic purposes better to call that 'brown-nosing'. We might think that a man who was once surprised embracing his father, and who asked him to speak at his own rallies, was not wholly devoid of filial affection.

136

But on the other hand you might just think he was a screwed-up Freudian case, who exploited his father's local popularity to win himself votes.

Caro's L.B.J. was consumed from his earliest years with a desire to be President of the United States. He first declared his ambition when he was twelve years old. It was repeated at frequent junctures, usually when he was in a bad temper. It is clearly recalled by a pupil of his, when L.B.J., aged twenty, did some teaching practice at a school on the Mexican border, that he thrashed a boy and told the awe-struck class, 'You are looking at a future President of the United States.'

How well did this witness know English? How do we know that any of this book is true? Evidently, L.B.J. was highly ambitious, and in a curiously single-minded way. His desire from early years was to be a politician, and he never pursued any other profession. Anyone going into politics presumably wants to get to the top. But only when they get there do their childish dreams take on any significance. The famous photograph of the infant Harold Wilson on the steps of Number Ten would hardly be very interesting if Sir Harold had remained as a don at Oxford. Most family albums contain such pictures, but since Cousin Derek did not become Prime Minister, there is no interest in seeing his infant form outside that residence. Similarly, most loud-mouthed roughs from Texas might well exclaim that they intend to be President, to rule the world, to pilot Concorde or buy up the moon. Memory would only heighten their boasts if they were to be subsequently successful.

And there is obviously a lot of 'heightening' in Mr. Caro's book. When you peruse the one hundred and twenty pages or so of explanatory matter, notes etc. at the end of the volume, it becomes apparent that Mr. Caro has relied heavily on what is called 'oral history'. That is another name for tittle-tattle. Every child who ever got its ears boxed by L.B.J.; every woman who was, or was not, 'insulted' by him in his adolescent cups; every fellow student who sucked up to teacher less cunningly than he; every jealous Congressional secretary less efficient or less clever than the Texan whizzkid have drooled their hard-luck stories into Mr. Caro's tape-recorder. Alice Glass, once in love with Johnson, cannot have been the only person who decided, in 1967, that she did not want her grandchildren to know that she had been associated with the man 'responsible for Vietnam'.

No one would pretend that the young L.B.J. was particularly nice; nor even that he was the sort of man you would have in the house. But a biography which relies heavily on 'oral history' and on the malicious, self-protective reflections of septuagenarian, bourbon-sodden minds, needs to be treated with circumspection. Not all the stories in this book can possibly be true. Even if the witnesses were honest, no memory which stretches back forty or fifty years can escape inexactitude. On the other hand, where eyewitnesses contest Mr. Caro's assertions, he admits that he relies more strongly on his own hunch than on the testimony of those closest to Johnson.

So, Mr. Caro believes an account which recalls L.B.J.'s ears getting distinctly larger during the first of his Congressional campaigns. But when his closest associates deny that L.B.J. tried to 'manipulate them', this is just evidence of how manipulative he was; so manipulative, they didn't know he was doing it.

It is not surprising that Lady Bird Johnson, having initially cooperated with Mr. Caro, 'abruptly and totally ceased' to have anything to do with him when she discovered his line of approach. It is a great pity. For she alone, one suspects, would be able to answer the mystery which Caro has not plumbed. How did the penniless Congressional Secretary manage to become so rich, so fast, in the early 1930s? Before he met Charles Marsh, the money had started to accumulate. Was it all from Lady Bird? Probably only she knows.

*Spectator*, 5 February 1983

# C.S. Lewis

In a diary entry for 21 January 1934, C.S. Lewis's brother records that he had read Moffat's translation of the epistle to the Romans, 'and found it very difficult. After the very fine passage at the end of Ch. VII describing the struggle against sin, *before* receiving Christ, he goes on with Ch. VIII apparently on the assumption that to become a Christian is to be relieved from all temptation to sin. What the whole episode boils down to in fact is, that if to be a Christian means, as St. Paul apparently says, to be free from any and every sinful desire, it is to be doubted if many, even of the Saints, have been Christians. Then again there is the fearful stumbling block of predestination – does St. Paul in fact say that certain people are pre-destined to salvation, and that it doesn't matter what they do? And if he says so, is he right? J. [i.e. C. S. Lewis himself] has been reading this epistle with a commentary, but could get no help from it' (*Brothers and Friends*, p. 141).

This passage occurs some two and a half years after W.H. Lewis had returned to the Christian faith. As he put it (on 13 May 1931 after he had resolved to return to the practice of receiving Holy Communion) 'with me the wheel has now made the full revolution – indifference, scepticism, atheism, agnosticism, and back again to Christianity'. This conversion of Lewis's brother appears to have happened during his summer leave at the Kiln's, Headington. It was five months after Captain Lewis (as he was then) had resumed the habit of receiving the Sacrament that the two brothers made their momentous visit to Whipsnade Zoo, and (on 1 October 1931) C.S. Lewis could write to his friend, Arthur Greeves, 'I have just passed on from believing in God to definitely believing in Christ – in Christianity' (*They Stand Together*, p. 425).

I started with the chronologically later quotation (the Lewis brothers' attitude to *Romans*) to emphasise the difficulty, at the outset, of analysing a Christian conversion. St. Paul's own conversion is the classic example of the man who suddenly turns to Christ. And Lewis himself, in his autobiography, employs language which makes it unambiguously clear that he believed himself to have been confronted with no less ambiguity than St. Paul, and by the same God, and by the same Christ. But at first – very notably – he was unaware of Christ specifically, and was merely aware that he had encountered God:

> You must picture me alone in that room at Magdalen night after night, feeling, whenever my mind lifted even for a second from my work, the steady unrelenting approach of Him whom I so earnestly desired not to meet. That which I greatly feared had at last come upon me. In the Trinity Term of 1929 I gave in, and admitted that God was God, and knelt and prayed: perhaps, that night, the most dejected and reluctant convert in all England (*Surprised by Joy*, p. 182).

But as he goes on to say almost immediately in his autobiography, 'The conversion was purely to Theism, pure and simple, not to Christianity.' It was the visit to Whipsnade which, some two years later, affected the final conversion.

I begin at the end, however, in order to make it clear what the conversion was *not*. It was evidently not a conversion which involved an immediate consciousness of the presence of Christ. And it was not a conversion which seemed to involve an immediate consciousness of the forgiveness of sin. It is particularly remarkable that when, as a fully established Christian, Lewis came to read Paul's epistle to the Romans in detail, he 'could get no help from it'. For the experience of sudden and dramatic conversion to belief in God is most commonly felt among Christians for whom the epistle is the key New Testament document. The conversion of Wesley, for example, as expounded in his *Journals*, is really little more than a living commentary on the eighth chapter of *Romans*. And the same could be said of the conversion of Luther. Whether or not the believer subsequently comes to climb over what W.H. Lewis called 'the fearful stumbling block of predestination', there is usually, accompanying such conversions, a profound and sublime egoism. I do not mean that in a perjorative sense. I mean that the convert feels, as John Henry Newman did when he experienced such a conversion, 'that there are two, and only luminously self-evident beings in the universe, myself and my creator'. The convert in such cases finds that his own personal sense of forgiveness is an essential part of the

140

experience: the conversion comes as a package — the strange and inescapable sense of an encounter, the unexplained (inexplicable?) sense that this encounter was with Christ; and the conviction that Christ would heal, had healed the convert from all his guilt, and all his sin. With Lewis, the certain encounter with God was separated by two years before he came to accept that Christ was God.

The Whipsnade drive itself took place in the side-car of Warnie's motorcycle on 28 September 1931.

> When we set out, I did not believe that Jesus Christ is the son of God, and when we reached the zoo I did. Yet I had not exactly spent the journey in thought. Nor in great emotion. 'Emotional' is perhaps the last word we can apply to some of the most important events. It was more like when a man, after long sleep, still lying motionless in bed, becomes aware that he is now awake (*Surprised by Joy*, p. 189).

There have been plenty of sceptics reading these words who have drawn attention to their oddity. There is, apart from anything else, the rather weird conjunction of Whipsnade Zoo and the high doctrine of Our Lord's Incarnation. Moreoever, when we read Warnie's account of the day in the diary, the only subject on Jack's mind appears to be his dream of 'adding a pet bear to our private menagerie, which he intends to christen "Bultitude" — a capital name'. In other words, amid all the kafuffle which W. H. Lewis somewhat mercilessly describes of a day out with Mrs. Moore and her daughter and her dog, the Lewis Brothers had been talking, as was their wont, of the childhood dreams and games of Boxen, that magic world at the boxroom at the end of the landing where they played together as children. Nothing here, the sceptic would want to say, to suggest that a revelation, an epiphany, had occurred. Lewis's silence in the course of their walk, however, is entirely consistent with his later manner of describing the thing. It was, in the last analysis, a matter of letting things fall into place, as the motorbike glided along at a fairly stately fifteen m.p.h. beneath the boughs of autumn and a bright sky (*Brothers and Friends*, p. 87).

It is interesting that Lewis did not attempt to articulate what was passing through his mind that day when, years later, he wrote the matter up in *Surprised by Joy*. This cannot have been because he thought the matter too nebulous, too numinous, still less too vague, to be alluded to in some sort of language, however inadequate. It must have been because when he published his autobiography, he did not wish to embarrass his friends Hugo Dyson and J.R.R. Tolkien by revealing details of his private conversations with them. But, as we now know, it was such a conversation a few days before the Whipsnade trip which, in his letters to his friend Arthur Greeves, Lewis recounts these conversations in some detail, details which more or less match Tolkien's poem on the subject, *Mythopoeia* (see Humphrey Carpenter: *J.R.R. Tolkien,* p. 147). What has held him back from accepting Christianity was 'the whole doctrine of redemption: in what sense the life and death of Christ "saved" or "opened salvation" to the world'. He found himself incapable of believing that 'someone else, whoever he was two thousand years ago, could help us here and now, except insofar as his example helped us'. And he sees that the example of Christ, though important, is not central to Christianity, where 'you keep on getting something quite different and very mysterious expressed in those phrases I have so often ridiculed – "propitiation", "sacrifice", "the blood of the Lamb" – expressions which I could only interpret in senses that seemed to me either silly or shocking'.

Dyson and Tolkien, in the memorable walk round Addison's Walk during the night of 22 September 1931 told Lewis that if he came across sacrifice and propitiation in other mythologies, he did not mind it at all. 'The reason was that in Pagan stories I was prepared to feel the myth as profound and suggestive of meanings beyond my grasp even tho' I could not say, in cold prose, "what it meant". Now the story of Christ is simply a true myth: a myth working on us in the same way as the others, but with this tremendous difference that *it really happened.*'

There can be no doubt that this conversation between the three friends was one of the most momentous of Lewis's life; and, in terms of his *oeuvre*, it is absolutely crucial. Even after an experience of God so direct that he felt himself invaded, compelled, by the Hound of Heaven, Lewis could not submit to the central tenets of Christianity, 'the whole doctrine of redemption'. It would seem as though he found the doctrine notionally, intellectually incomprehensible and historically improbable. He did not believe that the condition of the human race was materially and radically affected by the life and death of Jesus Christ.

Now, the book in which this doctrine of the redemption is most explicitly expounded is St. Paul's epistle to the Romans. It is not the only book of the New Testament where it is expounded, and no one would say that St. Paul's *manner* of expounding it was the only way. But the epistle is the first great work of organised, or semi-organised systematic theology. It is also one of the most lyrical expressions of Christian belief that, once we have accepted that the law cannot save us and self-improvement cannot save us, we can live a new life through grace, and that nothing in life or death can separate us from the love of God in Christ. 'Jack has been reading this epistle but could get no help from it.'

It would be absurd to build too much on one stray sentence in W.H. Lewis's diary. No one but a fool ever thought they *understood* the Christian doctrine of the atonement. But C.S. Lewis was not the sort of Christian who thought that you could approach the faith with a sort of shopping trolley, merely taking bits from the shelves which you happened to find 'helpful'. The fact that he got no help from the epistle to the Romans three years after he had had the experience of Christian conversion would indicate how difficult that conversion was, from an intellectual point of view, how much work and what sort of work he put in after his epiphany in the Daudelspiel of October 1931. He could see, both before and after his formal acceptance of Christian theology, that the redemption of the world by Christ was the essence of the Gospel. But he obviously found it completely impossible to focus on this redemption in the Pauline manner. This is not to say that he was approaching the whole matter in a purely 'intellectual' spirit. He was not like those various Thomist converts of the 1920s or 30s who almost made a boast of having no personal religion, and who accepted the Catholic doctrine of atonement as a Thing – almost, if not entirely, external to themselves. His post-Christian writing abounds with the very opposite approach to the doctrine of atonement, and redemption. While finding it privately impossible to understand St. Paul's geography, his analysis of the cosmos, Lewis entirely accepted the personal implications of Christ as Saviour.

> Put right out of your head the idea that these (e.g. having the mind of Christ, or putting on Christ) are only fancy ways of saying that Christians are to read what Christ said and try to carry it out – as a man may read what Plato or Marx said and try to carry it out. They mean something much more than that. They mean that a real person, Christ, here and now, in that very room where you're saying your prayers, is doing things to you. It's not a question of a good man who died two thousand years ago. It's a living Man, still as much a Man as you, and

still as much God as He was when He created the world, really coming and interfering with your very self; killing the old natural self in you and replacing it with the kind of self He has . . . (*Beyond Personality*, p. 38).

It is impossible to doubt that Lewis was a man who was through and through engaged in this drama of self-transformation, self-immolation. This 'putting on Christ' which forms so important a part in his writings was the great business of his life. It is hardly perhaps necessary to emphasise this purely biographical fact, but Lewis was not only a great Christian apologist, but also a great Christian. This 'putting on' of Christ was a costly thing, and the cost was borne secretly. Those who saw only a loud-voiced, hectoring, rather coarse public man saw nothing at all of Lewis. We all know the caricatures of the man put about by those who disliked him, and I am not claiming that he had no faults. But he did try to practise, and very largely succeeded in practising, what he preached. His works on the spiritual life such as *The Screwtape Letters* and *Letters to Malcolm chiefly on Prayer* are rooted in actuality. And it is an actuality which, as we have now discovered from the evidence of his biographers, and from his brother's diary, was filled with pain of the most trivial, grinding and everyday kind. I emphasise these things because what I want to say about Lewis's theological position might appear to imply that he affected Christian attitudes, if not for fun, at least because he liked the feel of them. That he was 'trying them on for size'.

And there is an argument which, if put by a Devil's advocate, could go something like this. Lewis was a determined, and self-confessed attitudiniser. He spent his entire life in Oxford setting himself up against groups of dons he disliked – scientists, logical positivists, 'moderns' of various kinds. And when he was translated to Cambridge, he advertised himself, in a highly self-conscious manner, as a 'dinosaur', who embodied all the values and beliefs of the 'old world'. Putting it at its most base, we could say that he cherished the sheer annoyance value of claiming that he did not believe in the modern, so-called scientific world outlook, he did not believe in Darwin, he didn't believe in Freud, but that he did believe in the New Testament. Notice, the Devil's advocate will say, how, in his critical writings, Lewis likes to strike attitudes. He likes to be the one man whose reading tastes are so voracious, and whose sympathies are so broad, that he can enjoy Lydgate's *Fall of Princes* or the works of Thomas Usk. Notice, in his enthusiasm for science fiction, how he likes to show off about the extent of his imagination, his ability to transcend the imaginative limitations of materialism. Isn't it inevitable that such a man would fasten on to traditional Christianity, which had been pretty largely discredited and torn to shreds by Biblical scholars and others by the beginning of the 1930s, and proclaim, as the ultimate boast of how olde worlde and imaginative he was, that he could swallow the whole ridiculous pack of lies – Virgin Birth, Miracles, Atonement, Redemption, Heaven and Hell? And then, says the Screwtape of our imagining, look at how the conversion, so-called, came to pass. On the one hand, it was all part of Lewis's desire to be one of the boys, his longing to think the same thoughts as Tolkien and Dyson. On the other hand, look at the *way* they presented the faith to him. They presented it as a *myth*, and then went on to say (and it was three a.m. notice, and we aren't told how much they'd been drinking) that it just happened to be a myth that was true. In real life, when he actually came to read the New Testament, he found he got no help from actual Christian doctrines. It was only by affecting Christian doctrines that he *thought* he believed them, and persuaded others to do the same. Notice, in W.H. Lewis's diaries, how even his brother got fed up with 'Jack' on walking holidays in Ireland, pretending he believed in the fairies. He made a positive virtue of make-believe but make-believe isn't the same as believe. Doesn't he even admit it himself time and again? For instance, when he talks about saying the *Our Father*, he writes 'Do you now see what these words mean? They mean quite frankly that you are putting yourself in the place of a *son* of God. To put it bluntly you are dressing up as a Christ. If you like, you're pretending.'

Now in answering the Devil's advocate, I think we go a long way towards discovering why C.S. Lewis was and remains so important a figure in twentieth-century Christianity. For, as my final example showed, he is bold enough to confront this matter head on. The place where he does so most vividly, to my mind, (but there are many other examples to choose from) is in *The Silver Chair* where the two children, Jill and Eustace, with Prince Rilian and Puddle-glum the marshwiggle, are imprisoned in the sunless Underland by the Queen of that place who is, of course, a witch. She asserts, until the weary brains of the children very nearly assent to the assertion, that 'there is no other world but mine'. She accepts the existence of

145

her little lamp, but she laughs to scorn the idea that there is such a thing as the sun. She believes that there are cats, but she mocks at their belief in lions.

> You have seen lamps, and so you imagined a bigger and better lamp and called it the *sun*. You've seen cats, and now you want a bigger and better cat, and it's to be called a *lion*. Well, 'tis a pretty make believe, though, to say truth, it would suit you all better if you were younger. And look how you can put nothing in your make-believe world without copying it from the real world, this world of mine, which is the only world. But . . . put away these childish tricks. I have work for you all in the real world. There is no Narnia, no Overworld, no sky, no sun, no Aslan . . .

It does not take much perception to see in the witch's speech the pure distillation of modern secular belief. Versions of the speech are heard every day on the lips not only of atheist philosophers, but also of modern churchmen, politicians, and public benefactors of all kinds who seem convinced that this world is the only world. Equally, we can be sure that Lewis speaks through Puddleglum, the pessimistic, rather gloomy marshwiggle, when he makes his heroic reply to the witch:

> 'One word, Ma'am,' he said, coming back from the fire, limping because of the pain. 'One word. All you've been saying is quite right, I shouldn't wonder. I'm a chap who always likes to know the worst and then put the best face I can on it. So I won't deny any of what you said. But there's one thing more to be said, even so. Suppose we have only dreamed, or made up, all those things — trees and grass and sun and moon and stars and Aslan himself. Suppose we have. Then all I can say is that, in that case, the made-up things seem a good deal more important that the real ones. Suppose this black pit of a kingdom of yours *is* the only world. Well, it strikes me as a pretty poor one. And that's a funny thing when you come to think of it. We're just babies making up a game, if you're right. But four babies playing a game can make a play-world which licks your real world hollow. That's why I'm going to stand by the play-world. I'm on Aslan's side, even if there isn't any Aslan to lead it. I'm going to live as like a Narnian as I can even if there isn't any Narnia. So, thanking you kindly for our supper, and if these two gentlemen and the young lady are ready, we're leaving your court at once and setting out in the dark to spend our lives looking for Overland.'

In the writings of an 'existentialist Christian', such a speech would almost certainly stand by itself. And it is one of the most moving things that Lewis ever wrote. But it is very decidedly only

146

the beginning of his credo and not the whole of it. As he walked round Addison's Walk with Tolkien and Dyson, and as he went along the road to Whipsnade a few days later, Lewis was, we may believe, making the giant leap of faith which enabled him to say that 'I'm going to live as like a Narnian as I can even if there isn't any Narnia'. But the point about such a leap is that it brings with it the conviction, the discovery that there is such a place as Narnia. Puddleglum does not go off gloomily into the dark, not knowing. His words have power to show up the witch for what she really is, a snake like Keats's Lamia. Her transformation into her 'true' state is instantaneous. And by the gesture of faith, combined with the heroism and fighting which follows, the spell is broken, before Jill and Eustace leave the bright world of Narnia for the hateful walls of Experiment House, and the cruel taunting of 'Spotty' Sorner, Big Bannister, and the two loathsome Garrett twins.

The Narnia books are Lewis's most accessible and, I would say, his most eloquent exploration of what we could call his Christian Platonism, his sense that this world is but a shadow of another, and that the 'reality' of which we are already partakers, and for which we are destined in eternity, far outshines the temporal nonsense of whatever Experiment House we happen to inhabit. The Professor, Digory, makes this overt point about Narnia at the beginning and end of the whole series. Digory is more rigid and more sternly logical than Puddleglum, for he is in a position to have experienced for himself, and to have seen in others, the comings and goings between our own world and the world beyond the Wardrobe. He notes at once that if Lucy has not been to Narnia, as she claims that she has, she must be lying, or mad, or telling the truth. Her whole demeanour and character make it impossible to believe that she is a liar or a lunatic. We must believe therefore that she is telling the truth. So too, we may assume, Lewis felt about Christian 'visitants' from the heavenly realms, those who had at least glimpsed the blue remembered hills of the heavenly country-heroes from the past such as Dante or George Macdonald; friends of the present such as Charles Williams. If they did not behave like lunatics, what reason did one have for supposing that they were liars? But the full extent of this Platonism is spelt out by Digory towards the close of *The Last Battle*.

'When Aslan said you could never go back to Narnia, he meant the Narnia you were thinking of. But that was not the real Narnia. That had a beginning and an end. It was only a shadow copy of the real Narnia which has always been here and will always be here: just as our own world, England and all, is only a shadow or copy of something in Aslan's real world. You need not mourn over Narnia, Lucy. All of the old Narnia that mattered, all the dear creatures, have been drawn into the real Narnia through the Door. And of course it is different: as different as a real thing is from a shadow or as waking life is from a dream.' His speech stirred everyone like a trumpet as he spoke these words: but when he added under his breath, 'It's all in Plato, all in Plato: Bless me, what do they teach them in these schools!' the older ones laughed. It was so exactly the sort of thing they had heard him say long ago in the other world when his beard was grey instead of golden . . . (*The Last Battle*, p. 154).

Those within the Christian tradition might be surprised, once they dwelt upon the matter, by the extent to which Lewis draws on purely non-Christian sources for some of his finest apologetics. ('It's all in Plato.') And while not for a second doubting his orthodoxy, I confess to being puzzled that Lewis is most wildly popular these days among those Christians for whom the drama of redemption is, if one could put it so crudely, a cut and dried event. I am constantly struck in Lewis's Christian writings, as in Dante's, by the sheer size of the redemptive drama. It isn't all the epistle to the Romans. It isn't even – and this is boldness bordering on blasphemy – it isn't even all Calvary. In the Narnia books, the Calvary event happens only in the first book of seven, and there are many other workings out of Aslan's Deeper Magic from before the Dawn of Time. For Lewis, the process of personal sanctification, and his own specific evangelisation of the world, involved a putting on of Christ, and a rediscovery of Christ in all corners of the created universe, in all crannies of the imagination. With his frolicking fauns and satyrs, his talking beasts, his revived Platonism, we seem almost to be reading again another imaginative harrowing of the Inferno. But the great big belief which Lewis stands for is the absolute reality of the supernatural world. He spells it all out in his XXIInd letter to Malcolm when he describes his quarrel with the demythologisers. They think 'the ship must be lightened if she is to keep afloat. It follows then that the most mischievous people in the world are those who, like myself, proclaim that Christianity essentially involves the supernatural . . .' It is in this letter that, Puddleglum-like, he looks back over his life since he made that leap of faith and can say, 'You know why my withers are quite unwrung by the fear that I was bribed – that I was lured into Christianity by the hope of everlasting life. I believed in God before I believed in Heaven. And even now, even if . . . His voice, unmistakably His, said to me, "They have misled you. I can do nothing of that sort for you. My long struggle with the blind forces is nearly over. I die, children. The story is ending . . ." Would that be the moment for changing sides? Would not you and I take the Viking way: The Giants and the Trolls win, let us die on the right side, with Father Odin.'

In fact, however, he believes that there is a Heaven and that, purified and chastened, we will go to it; that there is a God, glimpsed now, and seen then, face to face. 'Don't run away with the idea that when I speak of the resurrection of the body I mean merely that the blessed dead will have excellent memories of their sensuous experiences on earth. I mean it the other way round: that memory as we now know is a dim foretaste, a mirage, even, of a power which the soul, or rather Christ in the soul (He "went to prepare a place for us") will exercise hereafter. It need no longer be intermittent. Above all it need no longer be private to the soul in which it occurs. I can now communicate to you the vanished fields of my boyhood – they are building estates today – only imperfectly by words. Perhaps the day is coming when I can take you for a walk through them.'

Lewis baffles those who have no taste for his writings by his total and rather overwhelming consistency. Whether we are reading his voluminous scholarly and critical works, or his works of theology, or his science fiction novels, or his children's stories there is the same voice, the same set of convictions, the same disarming readability, the same smack of something which can only be described as greatness. There is nothing petty about him.

One word from the Devil's advocate, though. I once heard an Oxford philosopher on why he disliked Lewis. The philosopher was an atheist, and he objected to the fact that, for all his famous reputation for the fisticuffs of debate in the Socratic Club and elsewhere, Lewis always refused to meet the logical positivists. He would not debate with those who considered religious language to be simply without meaning. He would not debate with those who, by implication, thought it was 'meaningless' to use words not merely such as 'God', but also such as 'beauty' or 'love'. There was no point in merely discussing the cat with the Queen of Underland if

149

she persistently refused to believe that the syllables *Li-on* could, in any circumstances, have any meaning.

There are Christians who share this disquiet about Lewis's refusal to 'take on' the logical positivists. They consider him an indifferent philosopher ('the problem of pain is quite bad enough without Jack making it worse', as one of his Christian contemporaries once said to me) and his refusal to meet the chief philosophical objection to religion in his day smacks of cowardice.

I think this charge is not only unfair, but irrelevant. And it is irrelevant strangely enough (which is why I mention it) in precisely the way that his inability to get on with St. Paul is irrelevant. Although the Christianising of C.S. Lewis's intellect unquestionably involved time, and many an act of will, his theological position differed from so many of his contemporaries not on a purely notional level, but on one of experience. And although the experience was obviously an extremely quiet and nebulous one, it obviously *was* an experience, and we are forced to make the same decisions about it as Peter, Susan and Edmund are forced to make when Lucy calmly tells them that there is another world beyond the Wardrobe Door.

Lucy, I say, and not Edmund. He, you remember, accompanies her on her first visit to Narnia, but is bewitched by magic Turkish delight. So he says, with 'a very superior look as if he were far older than Lucy . . . "Oh yes, Lucy and I have been playing-pretending that all her story about a country in a wardrobe is true. Just for fun, of course. There's nothing there really."' The very fact that Lewis was 'unhelped' by the epistle to the Romans helps to authenticate, for me, the reality of his conversion. A sceptic, or even a liberal Christian, approaching the matter in a purely cerebral and externalised way would say something like this: 'If you are going to become a Christian, you have got to come to terms with what Christianity *is*. You have got to read the New Testament and accept it, and make it your own.' Lewis would not have quarrelled with that, but I think in those early days of his conversion, he was in a very strange position. When Paul was converted he tells us, or rather the Galatians, 'neither went I up to Jerusalem to them which were apostles before me, but I went to Arabia'. He didn't have to get his information about Christ from Peter. He had had an experience of Christ which, afterwards, he found to tally with the broad Christian body but which was his own. Lewis, converted some

150

nineteen hundred years later, was in a very similar position vis à vis Paul. He did not need to authenticate his experience of conversion by checking it with the epistle to the Romans. On the contrary. Although later, in humility, he would absorb and expound the books of the New Testament, he was, at first, in the strange position of being able to say, 'Well, He may have appeared so to St. Paul, but He did not appear so to me. I have not so known Christ.' That he had known, and did know Christ was, I do not doubt, the most 'real' experience of Lewis's life. It was the reality of the experience which confirmed for him the reality of the doctrine, and not the other way about. When I say 'reality', I am not presuming to judge Lewis's sincerity, still less am I presuming to erect any kind of 'proof' from the experience of Lewis in the sidecar for the reality he came to see and believe. But he was involved, after the experience, in living out, writing out, and speaking out his belief in the actual, palpable and empirical reality of the supenatural.

Not long ago, after I had written in a newspaper something rather slighting about a modernist clergyman, I received a letter from another clergyman. He liked what I had said, as he thought, on the positive side. He liked my rather feeble expressions of faith in Christianity. But, he said, I was wrong to pour scorn on Christian modernism. And the reasons he gave were as follows: the scientists really *have* changed our picture of the world, and there is absolutely no arguing with their conclusions. There is no possibility in believing any longer, for instance, that Christ ascended into heaven as is described in the New Testament, because we know, as St. Luke did not know, that heaven is not a place just above the clouds into which you can penetrate by vertical take off from a Galilean hillside . . . The letter was not a full one, but I dare say the clergyman would have gone on to think that there was no possibility that a man could walk on water, or change water into wine, or multiply loaves and fishes. And probably, it was very unlikely that he could rise from the dead. Probably, such an outlook would also believe that the psychoanalysts had made completely inappropriate any discussion of guilt or personal responsibility for our unresolved anger or our sexual natures. Such an attitude is not held for reprehensible reasons. It is held out of respect for the truth. And the former atheist in Lewis respected this. But he could see that behind such an attitude lay the unsubstantiated assumption that the supernatural world did not really exist. Or the less rational assumption that the supernatural world had once existed but did so no longer. Or the yet odder idea that it existed just for the time of the New Testament but had since suspended operations.

Lewis's enmity to this pseudo-scientific attitude was absolute. And I say pseudo-scientific, because of course 'science' or 'natural philosophy' does not have anything to say, and never has had anything to say about the supernatural. No one was better aware than the author of *The Discarded Image* that our picture of the cosmos had changed; that our picture of the human body had changed; that our picture of the human psyche had changed, not once but many times since antiquity. But Lewis the poet and Lewis the science-fiction writer could see that everything was much less simple than the anti-supernaturalists presupposed. Of course, you could put a man in a sky rocket and launch him from Mount Olivet or anywhere else and he would not penetrate heaven. But what Lewis knew, and these anti-supernaturalists did not know, was that a man could go to heaven and back in the sidecar of his brother's motorcycle. In his fiction, more than in his expository works, he explores innumerable ways in which one world could overlap or interpenetrate with another; or in which time might work at different levels on different spheres – so that you might go to Narnia for years and return to earth to find that you had been absent for only a few minutes. The opponents of Lewis, within and without the Church, felt that there were certain given 'facts' by which even religious truth must be judged, modified and, if necessary, discarded. Lewis, on the other hand, felt that in this strange life it was unscientific, and downright dangerous, to take anything for granted, and that these 'facts' were not necessarily true. His starting point, however, is the absolute reality of the supernatural world; the certainty that, however memory might trick him, or however sceptical his colleagues or his audiences might be, he had to cling to the perceptions he had been granted at that early stage of the journey. The result was the steady outpouring, for thirty years, of letters, articles, novels, essays, and poems, almost every one of which is touched by the view that this life is a mere preparation for its later stages beyond the grave, that all good things in this life are mere foreshadowings of things in heaven. Moreover the significance of worldly events and activities – such as, for example, what passes for important news in the newspapers – or the truth of scientific discoveries are to be assessed, measured or ignored by the standards of eternity.

152

The effect of reading Lewis therefore becomes cumulatively disturbing, for it is not in the end possible to go on regarding him, as he begged his Cambridge audience to regard him, as a mere fossil, a mere relic of the way people thought and believed in the old days. The authority of his writing derives from its truth, if he has any authority at all.

I am not suggesting that in order to appreciate Lewis you have to swallow him whole, or that he was not capable of gross oversimplifications, slapdash use of analogy, or that his vision of human nature was not sometimes extremely crude. I am not saying that you can get nothing from his fiction or his literary criticism if you don't share his outlook, because thousands of people who are not, and never will be, Christian believers have enjoyed Narnia, and benefited from *The Allegory of Love* or what must be the best and most entertaining work of literary scholarship ever written, *English Literature in the Sixteenth Century Excluding Drama*. But it is an unusual Lewis fan who does not admit – if he or she is honest – that part of the attraction of Lewis's writing is something quite unliterary, something infinitely bigger than literature. It is the challenge which it presents of another world. The reality by which he judges our own shadowy world is not a reality made up by Lewis. Many of Lewis's readers would echo what he says of George Macdonald; 'how hard I had tried not to see that the true name of the quality which first met me in his books is Holiness' (*The Great Divorce*, p. 60). You will remember in *The Great Divorce*, Macdonald plays the role of a sort of Virgil to Lewis's Dante in his journey from the outskirts of heaven towards its brighter regions. And as they go, they speak, and Lewis asks ' "Then those people are right who say that Heaven and Hell are only states of mind?" "Hush," he [Macdonald] said sternly, "do not blaspheme. Hell is a state of mind – ye never said a truer word. And every state of mind, left to itself, every shutting up of the creature within the dungeon of its own mind is, in the end, Hell. But Heaven is not a state of mind. Heaven is reality itself. All that is fully real is heavenly. For all that can be shaken will be shaken, and only the unshakeable remains." '

Address given to the C.S. Lewis Society, 14 May 1985

153

# Rainer Maria Rilke

Rainer Maria Rilke (1875–1926) is a gift to a biographer. First, there is the quite extraordinary psychological background. His mother, a devout Roman Catholic, who did not get on with his father, insisted that the child Rilke be dressed as a girl.

Not content with this, she also made him adopt a high piping voice and the name of 'Sophie'. When she called out 'Sophie, Sophie!' he had to appear in his female guise and report on all the naughty things which 'her' brother René – that is, Rilke himself – had been doing during the day. They would then settle down to prayers of the utmost familiarity in tone, calling on the Blessed Virgin as 'Heavenly Mummy!'

Shortly after this phase, Rilke's mother eloped with her lover, and his father insisted that he be 'toughened up' at a military academy. 'Sophie' was given a short back and sides and put in uniform at the Military College, Mahrish-Weisskirchen. No wonder that in grown-up life Rilke attended the International Psychoanalytical Congresses with such close interest.

Then again, he is a gift to a biographer because his life spans so many different countries and seems to take in so many of the other great geniuses of the age. He was born in Prague of a German-speaking family, and his youth was spent in Bohemia and Austria.

Though he did more than anyone this century to enrich and adorn the German language, he was really a citizen of no country. After his infatuation, brief love affair and life-long emotional dependence on the formidable Lou Andreas Salomé (fourteen years his senior; in her youth, she had resisted the advances of Nietzsche) he became acquainted with the whole of Europe.

She took him to Russia (where she was born) where he met Tolstoy, Leonid Pasternak et al. Subsequently, he went to Paris, where he became Auguste Rodin's secretary and the friend of the whole literary circle surrounding Gide.

And then began the extraordinary *mouvementé* (in all sense of the word) existence, when Rilke moved about from Switzerland to Italy, and back again to France, collecting a string of mistresses, and a wife whom he subsequently divorced.

The love life of Rilke is so extraordinary that it would itself explain the interest of biographers. Lou decided that he was really bisexual (which might explain the rather unpleasant phallic poems he wrote at the beginning of the First World War) and urged him to undergo psychoanalysis. Very wisely, he always resisted, knowing that an artist with too much self-knowledge can easily smother his daemon.

Whatever the reason (and the simple ones must be right, that he had enormous charm and stunning good looks), women simply queued up to be jilted by him. Each was richer or more beautiful that the last, and none of them seemed to bear him the slightest ill will when the affair was over. It was always accepted that a great genius had to put his work first.

In the famous thought which occurred to him when surveying the art of Rodin, '*Du mußt dein Leben ändern*' ('You must change your life'), the word *Leben* could easily have been changed for *Liebe* (love). By the end, one modern critic has rightly remarked, Rilke's narcissism 'amounted to a kind of hermaphroditic self-sufficiency'.

As if none of this were enough, Rilke, with Yeats, is one of the very greatest lyric poets of the twentieth century, and one of the most self-dedicated artists.

When Lou took him to Russia, he made the mistake of praising the beauty of the Orthodox liturgy to Tolstoy, who urged him not to countenance such superstitions. In fact, it made a profound impression on Rilke, as did the monkish icon painters, who inspired his 'Visions of Christ'.

Rilke was not a Christian (his mother's antics had seen to that), and he put into the mouth of the Orthodox monks the idea that God needed to be created by the artist.

> What will you do, God, when I am dead? . . .
> You lose your meaning when I am no more.

Reading Donald Prater's new life of Rilke,* I was particularly

---

* *A Ringing Glass* (1986).

struck by the absurdity of this, as of nearly all Rilke's ideas. Mr. Prater does not quote the poetry in its intoxicating and incantatory original, and in bare English one sees what rubbish most of it is. For example, when the First World War broke out, Rilke wished that he did not speak German, and felt that the whole language had been tainted by the bullying tactics of the Kaiser. He enlisted most unwillingly in 1916. This did not stop him writing ludicrous (and offensive) invocations to the god of War.

For many people, reading Rilke is a substitute for religion. (As Magda von Hattingberg, the 'Benvenuta' of his poems said: 'For me he is a voice from God . . . but he is not a man.') His remarkable letters have been edited in a multi-volume German edition, and there are innumerable biographical studies of him.

In recent years, in English, we have had the translation of Wolfgang Leppmann's highly readable biography and a good short study by J. F. Hendry, as well as a fascinating biography of Lou Andreas Salomé by Angela Livingstone, which throws a lot of light on Rilke. Mr. Prater's solid book will be an admirable companion to all these others.

It aims to give a purely biographical picture and, while drawing heavily on the letters and quoting from the poems (in not altogether successful renderings into English verse), it presents a picture of Rilke the man, rather than the sage or the artist. From the opening pages, we feel that Mr. Prater is admirably in control, and is going to stand no nonsense from his subject.

For no obvious reason, he largely pooh-poohs the notion that Rilke had a bizarre or unhappy childhood, and implies that the military academy was not as unhappy as Rilke claimed. Rilke used to claim that he was only allowed by his mother to play with other children once a year. In Mr. Prater's version this becomes merely, 'he remained rather a lonely mother's boy'.

The whole story of the love affairs and the famous artistic 'crisis' are told with common sense and good humour, and there is enormous poignancy in Mr. Prater's delicate handling of Rilke's lingering death from leukaemia.

*Sunday Telegraph*, 16 March 1986

# Arthur Ransome

Few Englishmen saw more of the Russian Revolution than the Petrograd correspondent of the *Daily News* in 1917. He played chess with Lenin. He was almost a friend of Trotsky. A thirty-four-year-old Rugbeian man of letters, he had come to Russia chiefly to escape a catastrophically unhappy marriage. If he was biased in Lenin's favour it was perhaps because he had fallen in love with a Bolshevik girl called Evgenia Petrovna Shelepina.

His life between 1917 and 1918 was a series of adventures. He sent back a stream of reports to his paper; he acted as unofficial go-between between the Foreign Office and the Bolsheviks; he was accused by MI6 of sedition (when they asked his politics, he replied 'fishing') and he had a hair-raising time getting his mistress to safety in Scandinavia.

If he was slow to recognise the barbarism of the Cheka, it was less because of political prejudice than because his imagination was still fixed in the English Lake District. 'Revolts may come, revolts may go,' he wrote, 'but brats go on forever. And I would like to do a perfectly stunning brat book.'

The reporter was Arthur Ransome. Those who enjoy his essentially mild adventure stories of the English outdoors will initially be surprised by Hugh Brogan's* revelations about Ransome the man. But the surprise evaporates as the predominantly miserable tale unfolds.

Adventures for the Swallows are, after all, things which go on inside their heads. Occasionally, hazardous or frightening things happen to them, as 'We Didn't Mean to Go to the Sea'. But the essence is that very ordinary middle-class people are transformed, through children's fantasy, into enemies and pirates. T.H. White harshly viewed Ransome as 'a good, simple second-ranker'. The

* *The Life of Arthur Ransome*, Hugh Brogan (1984).

cleverness of Mr. Brogan's biography is to plot the workings of an imagination which, second-rank if it were, has given very harmless delight to readers for nearly fifty years.

Ransome was conspicuous, as a writer, for the soundness of his instincts. Many another second-ranker would have dissipated his imagination in novels drawn from 'experience'. It was Ransome's genius (like another very different ornament of the old Cape list, Barbara Pym) to cash in on his non-experience. He could have attempted a Strindbergian tragedy about his marriage or tried to be an English Pasternak. He wisely stuck to English children having fun in boats.

He was the son of a professor at Leeds. From earliest years he conceived the desire to be a writer, and for the first decade of this century hung about in bohemian London picking up hackwork.

He wrote a good critical study of Oscar Wilde and was sued (painfully but unsuccessfully) by Lord Alfred Douglas. He married a frightful woman called Ivy Walker (a surname later given to the Swallows) who bore him his only child. The divorce was long and acrimonious.

Going to Russia to escape Ivy, he got entangled with the formidable Evgenia Petrovna, who was his consort until he died. He hardly ever saw his daughter again. Ivy Ransome brought up Tabitha to believe that if Dor-Dor took her boating it would be with the intention of drowning her. On the appearance of *Swallows and Amazons* the child wrote a hurtful letter to its author saying that she had been unable to struggle beyond chapter twelve.

The wonder is, from Mr. Brogan's enthralling account, that Ransome ever got down to writing *Swallows and Amazons* at all. He was forty-five before he began it, having wasted ten years on the *Manchester Guardian* after the First War. (When in Cairo he got Malcolm Muggeridge a job on the paper and, ever a loyal *Guardian* man, he was horrified by the merciless excoriation of such figures as Kingsley Martin and C.P. Scott in Mugg's novel *Picture Palace*.)

Eventually, Ransome gave up foreign journalism, crippled by an ulcer, and wrote a column called 'Rod and Line'. But even when these distractions had been laid aside, and he began his famous books, he had to tolerate the persistent and jealous discouragement of his wife.

Mr. Brogan charitably says that 'one cannot help warming to Genia'. Perhaps, after Ivy, Ransome was tough enough for anything. But it cannot have been much fun to write book after book (he was very unsure of his skills, and read them all aloud to her) only to have them belittled in a heavy Russian accent.

Not that Ransome sounds a wholly amiable figure. The ulcer did not do much for his temper, and you had only to mention to him Russia (everyone got it wrong except himself) or caravans in the Lake District for him to fly into apoplectic rage.

Discouraged by Genia's abuse, he gave up writing, and devoted the last twenty-five years of his life (he died in 1967) to quarrels and fishing. He became furiously jealous of the little friends who had initially inspired him to write *Swallows and Amazons*, resenting that they had any part in the story. It was all the work of that perfectly stunning brat himself.

None of this matters. Mr. Brogan has done his work well. But all it shows is that writers like Ransome do not really have lives. Anything which is interesting about them goes into their stories, usually so transformed that it is hidden even from themselves. The rest – the money, the illnesses, the marriages – are just the chaff which the imagination has discarded. It does not diminish our gratitude for *Swallows and Amazons*.

*Sunday Telegraph*, 22 January 1984

# Cecil Beaton

Two of the more widespread delusions of the twentieth century are the belief that the camera does not lie and the belief that photography is an art form. The life of a distinguished photographer is bound to throw both delusions into comically sharp relief. For the photographer depends for his bread and butter (or in this case for his pearls and caviare) on the lies which his camera will tell. When makeup, lighting and all the artifical paraphernalia of the studio cannot be forced to tell sufficiently whopping lies, sitter and photographer alike must take to the brush. There are hilarious accounts in this book of Princess Louise, Duchess of Argyle, not allowing any of Beaton's portraits out of her hands until they had been 'touched up', and of Clementine Churchill having hysterics because he had failed sufficiently to disguise the black bags under her eyes.

To my bloodshot, baggy eye the portraits of Cecil Beaton (or Malice in Wonderland as Cocteau called him) have something almost invariably bogus about them. This book* confirms that hunch, with a thousand little vignettes of our twentieth-century Vanity Fair. We see Churchill, half-sloshed and babyfaced, steeling himself to assume the 'indomitable' bulldog look while Beaton fiddles with light meters and lenses. The teenage Princess Margaret, raddled and ashen, having been up at a nightclub until 5.30 a.m., is arrayed in a white Hartnell dress, studded with sequins. Lighting did the rest. Reading this book is like being on the other side of a looking-glass, and seeing the great and the famous assuming their masks of display, painting on their beauty, agonisingly peering at the warts and pimples and lumps of which their features are composed and hoping that dear Cecil can do something to disguise them. This he ever obligingly did, which is why his sitters applauded

* *Cecil Beaton*, Hugo Vickers (1985).

him so warmly and believed him to be not only a charming companion, but also a great artist.

The absurdity of using the word 'art' in this connection becomes clear when you realise that you could train for fifty years and still be unable to paint a single brushstroke as good as Tintoretto's or Rembrandt's. With a fortnight's training and a good Rolleiflex *any* of us, let us be candid, could take snapshots every bit as good as Cecil Beaton's famous 'portraits'. If he was an 'artist' it certainly did not show itself in his feeble little drawings, nor in his paintings, which even his admiring, not to say sycophantic, biographer cannot pretend to praise. The biographer, Hugo Vickers, began to admire Beaton when he first saw *My Fair Lady*. Certainly Beaton designed some very amusing hats for that show, and on and off, throughout a busy life, he had a passionate interest in the theatre (he even wrote some execrable plays). When he designed Noël Coward's play *Quadrille*, the playwright concluded that Cecil's 'sets were a bit over elaborate', and few except the more dogged devotees of the gin-and-ostrich-feathers school of thirties rococo would question this judgement as a general reflection on Beaton's aesthetic mode. Whether as a powdered boy at Harrow, plastering 'red stuff' on to his ruby lips, or as an old man doting upon the features of Mick Jagger, Cecil Beaton had no fear of the obvious and no fear of overdoing things in his quest for the beautiful. We read, for instance, that when he made friends with Mr. Stephen Tennant in 1927, 'My dressing gown caught his eye and he nearly went mad with the joy of it.' Not content to wear a ravishing dressing gown, we discover that he also, on this memorable occasion, 'wore a flimsy pair of speckled pyjamas which completely went with the room'.

This is hardly the voice of an aesthete. They are more the mincing tones of a man some women might ring up if they were uncertain of their own taste in lampshades. Can we imagine Ruskin or William Morris speaking of pyjamas which 'went with' a room? The fact that we can't might make us wish to dismiss Cecil Beaton, as Virginia Woolf did, as 'a mere catamite'. (Mrs. Woolf, incidentally, was the only person apart from Queen Mary who ever refused to be photographed by Beaton.) A shorter and more objective biography might have persuaded us that Mrs. Woolf was being rather harsh. But after five hundred and ninety pages of Hugo Vickers's prose one sees the force of her invective all too vividly. It simply does not *do* to inform us, on his penultimate page, that 'as a diarist he [Beaton] will be increasingly important'. Important to whom, and why? Beaton was not observant enough to be a great diarist. He seldom noted down conversations or the opinions and appearance of his contemporaries. His diaries are a snobbish, flabbily written and prolix exercise in self-analysis of a not very searching kind.

Even the much vaunted so-called love affair with Garbo is curiously unreal in Beaton's own accounts of it. One says 'even' but one should perhaps say 'especially', for one can see that Garbo and he were made for each other, both essentially candyfloss creations (though from different sides of the camera) of the photographic mirage which our parents' generation took for the truth. 'A woman is a delicate object,' she told him. 'You have to be careful and not abuse her. The tissues are so easily damaged.' The physical details of the bedchamber are not without a certain ribald farce. We read of Beaton making 'elaborate ablutions before going to bed', or of evenings when he was 'tired with my cold and Greta was also feeling ill as it was the time of the month when she is indisposed'.

Evidently there was genuine attraction between the pair, though predictably enough there seem to have been few occasions when the legendary beauty was actually pleased by the attentions of her swain. 'I'd been so rough and now was gentle and the desired result had been achieved.' Although when the affair ended he cried in the taxi ('It was a wonder the driver did not notice in his mirror that he was driving a lunatick [sic] middle-aged man that was convulsed in childlike tears and sobs'), it would seem as though a certain relief was felt on both sides. Beaton, who was never work shy, could plunge back into the role which destiny had appointed for him. His flattery of the rich, and of the Royal Family in particular, was based on a vision of sorts. He genuinely wanted them all to look as they did in his photographs. Seeing the Queen Mother in old age he asked himself 'what matter if her upturned nose is not specially delicate in its modelling nor the teeth as pearly as they used to be?'

At Heath Mount Preparatory School at the age of eight Beaton first encountered his life-long enemy Evelyn Waugh, who recalled later that 'our persecution went no further than sticking pins into him'. Many readers of this far-too-long biography will wish themselves back in a time machine so that they could stick pins into Beaton; or applaud the moment when, at the age of seventy, he was punched in the face by Robert Heber-Percy. Others will feel tempted to apply to Beaton his own censure of Katherine Hepburn: 'she is a rotten ingrained viper'. But I closed the book merely feeling that he was rather silly, and a little bit sad.

*Harpers and Queen*, August 1985

# Bernard Walke

Dostoevsky believed that it was only through beauty that the world would be redeemed. English Puritans have always believed the precise opposite. Not merely have they feared and hated beauty. They have extolled and worshipped ugliness. The iconoclasm and philistinism of the present is descended directly from a system which thought it was virtuous to throw Rubens altarpieces into the River Thames and smash medieval stained glass. The ruin and destruction of English towns in our day, parallel to the destruction of churches in the sixteenth and seventeenth centuries, has come about partly through folly, partly through greed, but largely because the English regard ugliness as a virtue.

An acquaintance of mine once sat on a committee to decide the fate of a row of dilapidated Georgian houses in Oxford. The committee assumed from the outset that these pretty old buildings should be demolished, and were simply anxious to fill their place with erections of the most hideously incongruous design. A lone voice spoke up. Could not the houses be retained? No, he was answered, the survey had made it clear that they were structurally unsound. Well, then, since the old houses looked very much more beautiful than any of the new designs, could they not reproduce the old houses as accurately as possible? A hush fell on the room. It was as though a man had opened a packet of bacon sandwiches in a synagogue. And then came the revealing remark, from a pompous young don: 'I regard that as a very *immoral* suggestion.' It was a clear case of beauty being equal, in the English mind, with wickedness.

The ritualist movement in the Church of England was one of the bravest and most sustained attacks on the notion that ugliness is a good thing. As those old High Churchmen donned their maniples and birettas, and filled their churches with flickering lamps and madonnas, and all the treasures which Mr. Bartlett or the Society of

164

St. Peter and St. Paul could furnish, they met of course with fierce theological objection. 'R.C., what does it mean? Real Catholic. A.C., what does it mean? Amateur Catholic,' as an Austrian Anglican clergyman of the 1920s firmly preached. Protestants within the Establishment Church regarded the advances of the ritualists with horror; papists regarded them with contempt. It was, a revealing phrase, *mere aestheticism.*

There can have been few Anglo-Catholic clergymen who were *merely* aesthetes, if by that is meant men who loved the ritual or music of the Church while disbelieving its doctrines. They were all, however, aesthetes in a more important sense. In many of the vilest slums of our inner cities in late Victorian and early twentieth-century days, Anglo-Catholic churches were the only things of beauty in the lives of the poor. Frequently, they were places of great beauty, and without their beauty they could not have brought so many lives into touch with the saving mystery. They are almost the strongest example in our century of Dostoevsky's dictum that the world would be saved through beauty.

Those of us who feast on stories and memories of the ritualists will have heard of Bernard Walke, and of his book *Twenty Years at St. Hilary.** It is a wonderful book, but for years it has been impossible to get hold of. Last year, however, saw the launch of a new paperback series called The Cornish Library. As well as classics like the novels of Quiller-Couch and the autobiographies of A.L. Rowse, the publisher's are being bold enough to issue books with a 'minority interest', such as the memoirs of this obscure country parson, who died in Mevagissey in 1940.

Older readers, even if they do not have a hankering to read about ecclesiastical controversies, will probably remember the name of Bernard Walke as a broadcaster. As early as 1926, if you had a crystal set and a pair of headphones, you could tune into *Bethlehem*, a Christmas play which the B.B.C. broadcast from the church of St. Hilary in Walke's tiny parish in West Cornwall. It was broadcast annually for a decade. Walke wrote it, and it was performed by his congregation in their distinctive Cornish tones, in part an anticipation of the Dorothy L. Sayers style of religious radiodrama, and in part a genuine throwback to the medieval mystery plays. St. Hilary's therefore became known to a huge audi-

* Reprinted in 1982.

ence. Other plays were broadcast from there. *The Eve of All Souls* became a regular feature on 1 November; and so, to Lord Reith's eternal credit, did the broadcasting of Benediction of the Blessed Sacrament.

Bernard Walke, then, was in many ways rather a 'successful' clergyman. He had built up a remote and tiny church into something of a national shrine. He was a close friend of many of the most interesting writers and artists of his day. Compton Mackenzie, Walter de la Mare and George Bernard Shaw all stayed in the Walkes' parsonage. He was married to a painter, Annie Walke, and with fellow artists Roger Fry and Laura Knight she helped to adorn and beautify the church with murals. But *Twenty Years at St. Hilary* is the story of a broken-hearted man. He wrote it in a tuberculosis sanitorium five years before he died; and in its minor way, it is one of the most sorrowful testaments ever penned.

Not that the whole book is depressing. The first twenty-two chapters chronicle, as its title implies, a score of years in a remote Cornish parish. Neither Walke nor his wife were natives, and although they came to love St. Hilary, they always knew that they were strangers there. In the sixteenth century, the Cornish had objected to Cranmer's prayerbook on the grounds that it was like 'a Christmas play' and they had begged for 'the return of the simple service of the Mass'. Bernard Walke found them, three hundred and fifty years later, happy with an ill-rendered Morning Prayer and baffled by his desire to restore the old Mass which they regarded as 'theatrical'. But, very slowly, they accepted him, and his wife, and his friends. The book is full of delightful anecdotes, about donkeys, about country superstitions, and about neighbouring eccentrics. Walke was a clergyman somewhat in the 'Mass and Maypoles' tradition; he was a pacifist during the First World War; he attempted to organise a form of guild socialism among the Cornish tinminers (totally unsuccessfully). He was a good and gifted man, and the memoirs of his country parish seem as though they deserve a place on our shelf somewhere between Conrad Noel and Hawker of Morwenstowe.

It is only when the horrifying final chapter has been read that one recognises *Twenty Years at St. Hilary* as something very different. Walke, like so many ritualist priests, found himself involved in a dispute with the Chancellor of the diocese over the exact legality of some of the ornaments in his church. These disputes seem farcical to

us now. It seems perfectly appropriate that the only religious question to trouble P.G. Wodehouse's curates is whether bishops will
allow incense and/or orphreys on chasubles. The ritualists concerned often enjoyed baiting their bishop, but the prosecutions
could be painful affairs. In Walke's case, he refused to attend the
court. 'As a citizen I regretted having to place myself in conflict with
the law of the land, but as a Catholic priest I felt bound to defend to
the best of my ability the rights of the Church.' The Chancellor, who
was a reasonable man, visited Walke and begged him to attend.
Walke refused. Their conversation took place at St. Hilary's as they
were walking round the church, and they came to the altar of St.
Joan of Arc; 'I hope you won't burn me as they did Joan,' Walke
remarked with prophetic whimsy.

In fact, he ignored all the proceedings which were being taken
against him, and spent more and more of his time riding about his
parish on horseback, or on one of his donkeys. Then, on 10 August
1932, a woman rushed into his stable, just as he was saddling a
horse, and said, 'They've come, Father, and Captain Hope [the
church warden] is locked up with them.'

The few remaining pages of the book are among the most chilling-
ly sad that I have ever read. 'They', of course, were a busload of
hired thugs from Plymouth. By the time Walke had forced his way
into the church, accompanied by an old man and a boy, there was
nothing he could do except bargain with the looters who eventually
allowed him to remove the Holy Sacrament from the building.

> I might shut my eyes, but I still saw men standing on the holy altar,
> hacking at the reredos or carrying away the image of Our Lady. I could
> not close my ears to the sounds of hammering which now filled the
> church.
>
> I have not yet escaped from scenes I witnessed that day and possibly
> never shall: whenever I enter an old country church and see the signs of
> destruction wrought there in the sixteenth century, I can hear the sounds
> of hammering and the crash of falling images. The men working this
> havoc have in my imagination the same faces as those who invaded St.
> Hilary that morning in August. The old church, quiet and peaceful when
> I entered, is filled with the phantoms I have conjured up. I see them
> tearing down the figure of Christ upon the Rood and casting out the
> Mother from the House of her Son . . .

Bernard Walke was destroyed by this experience. He suffered what
some would call a nervous breakdown and others would call a

broken heart. His church was never properly restored. The bishop shoved in a Protestant incumbent after Walke's departure and St. Hilary has, by many accounts, a sinister and unhappy atmosphere when visited today.

But the memories remain; and they could not have been published at a more apposite moment. Many of the old theological conflicts which divided Christendom in Bernard Walke's day seem to have been swept under the carpet. Anglican bishops rarely, if ever, upbraid their clergy for Romish practices; the Pope himself, far from dismissing the Anglican claims to Catholicity, appears to embrace them. We might be so baffled by much of 'ecumenism' that we ignore one of the most sinister features of modern Christianity. While the Pope says, in effect, that there was no need for Newman or Manning to have left the Church of England; and while the Protestants, with their 'agreed statements' on the eucharist, appear to believe that Ridley and Latimer died for mistaken principles, we have all witnessed something much more immediate and worrying: it is the deliberate uglification of Christendom. I do not understand many of the theological arguments and agreements of the present day. But we have all seen and heard horrors to match the terrible day when Father Walke saw his church wrecked by vandals. During the 1970s, the vandals were hard at work in most churches in France, tearing down altars, smashing images, burning missals and vestments. Roman Catholics in England have been more conservative, but also more fortunate, for they possessed fewer beautiful things to destroy. A certain, silly type of Anglo-Catholic has always believed that the way to make the Established Church kosher was to follow slavishly everything done by the R.C.s. Thus, by a paradox, the vandalistic effects of the Second Vatican Council have been more strongly felt in established churches in this country than in recusant ones. How many lovely baroque High Mass sets moulder in Anglican sacristies while the celebrant (sorry, President) wears hideous floppy linen vestments? How many splendid altars have been discarded?

We should look to the rock from which we are hewn. The Protestant martyrs, and the Papist ones, suffered for theological principle. The ritualists suffered for the sake of beauty. The Church of England, while it sings from its ugly modern hymn and service books, and arrays its holy tables in frontals of fluorescent tweed, should pause and consider its ritualist heroes. Is it on the side of

Father Walke, or on the side of the vandals who wrecked St. Hilary's church? It is the only denomination in this country with a large number of beautiful buildings. It has beautiful liturgical and musical traditions. It should not be imitating the stumbling ugliness of other Christian rites. It should be unashamedly beautiful. For it is only through beauty that the world will be redeemed.

*Spectator*, 8 January 1983

# The Gloomy Dean

Dean Inge's distaste for music is notorious. 'If I believed that I shall listen through all eternity to the seraphim blowing their loud uplifted trumpets,' he wrote in his diary, 'it would almost deter me from the practice of virtue.' For twenty-three years, he was the Dean of St. Paul's and had to suffer what he called 'the dreary and interminable musical services'. Another diary entry reads: 'Use not vain repetitions. For ten minutes today the choir repeated the words "I wrestle and pray". Are we quite sure that the Deity enjoys being serenaded?'

Whether there be music in heaven, we do not know. One thing is certain. There could be no more shocking purgatory for William Ralph Inge than to return to earth today, thirty-one years after his death aged ninety-four, and to discover that he had been almost completely forgotten.

In his day, he was much the most famous clergyman in the Church of England. He achieved eminence in three fields: as a scholar, becoming Lady Margaret Professor of Divinity at Cambridge in 1907; as a churchman, being Dean of St. Pauls from 1911 to 1934, (always, I have thought, the nicest job in the Church); and thirdly, he was a much sought-after public man, both as a speaker and as a journalist. 'I began my career as a pillar of the Church,' he said, 'and ended it as a column in the *Evening Standard*.' His journalism reached an enormous audience. His collected journalistic pieces, *Lay Thoughts of a Dean*, sold well over seventy thousand copies. Now, you can pick them up for almost nothing in any second-hand bookshop, usually on the rain-spattered shelves outside labelled 10p. The large majority of Englishmen, for whose parents Inge's name was as familiar in their mouths as household words, are not aware that he existed. Where his memory survives, it does so patchily. Some people are dimly aware that he was in favour of eugenics, which sounds to them a bit like the social engineering favoured by the Nazis. One comes across amusing references to him in the works of Shaw and G. K. Chesterton. When I protested to P. J. Kavanagh, the compiler of a recent Chesterton anthology, that he had included a not very good onslaught on Inge by Chesterton, that kindly Catholic poet replied, 'Oh, wasn't he one of those atheists like your Bishop of Durham?' Kavanagh admitted that he had never read a word that Inge wrote, but that in his Catholic boyhood he had been taught to abominate Inge as an advocate of contraception.

So, first, perhaps, as a little act of reparation to get him out of purgatory (if he is there) I should remind you of who he was. He was born in 1860, in an isolated parish in the North Riding of Yorkshire, Crayke, of which his father was the vicar. Crayke is an appropriate enough place for him to have been born, since he sounded like a corncrake, his rasping voice becoming steadily less euphonious as his deafness (which afflicted him from early manhood) increased. I expect that if we knew the full story of Inge's inner life, the first thirteen years would be very important. He was educated entirely at home, and hardly ever strayed from the village in his early boyhood. I suspect that, like William Wordsworth, he had the makings in him of a nature mystic, and that had he been brought up in another environment, or another place, or another time, he might never have gravitated towards the Church, still less towards the career of a clergyman. His grandfather and father were both clergymen. His grandfather had been a friend of Pusey and a contemporary of Manning and Newman, neither of whom he had much liked. The religion of the home was Tractarian. It was High Churchmanship of the 1840s. Here is his own description of it.

There was no ritual; I do not think my grandfather ever wore a cassock. We were taught to fast in Lent – not, however, by abstaining from meat, but by drinking sugarless tea and eating rice pudding, which we hated. The verbal inspiration of the Bible was almost as much insisted on as among the Evangelicals, and the Sunday was a slightly mitigated Puritan sabbath. Theatre-going was not exactly sinful, but in fact we never went there. Novel-reading was allowed, but chiefly the classics, like Walter Scott. New novels, with 'yellow backs', were severely frowned upon. Above all, the slightest concession to liberalism in theology was denounced with unqualified indignation. The names of Colenso, Stanley, Jowett, and Arnold were mentioned with horror. 'Low Churchmen', as the Evangelicals were called, were spoken of with pitying tolerance, except when they interfered with the Tractarians; but a 'Broad

Churchman', we were given to understand, was absolutely outside the pale.

It was a Broad Churchman that he was to become, but in various crucially important ways this Tractarian upbringing always formed a part of his nature, both in the discipline of his personal life and in the rigour of his religious and philosophical enquiries. One easily forgets them, but it is a mistake to do so.

Before long, the extraordinarily remote, old-fashioned, Charlotte Mary Yonge-ish way of life came to an end. His father came south, and was eventually to become Provost of Worcester College Oxford. In 1885 Dr. Inge (*père*) was offered the Bishopric of Salisbury by the Prime Minister. Lord Salisbury told the Queen that the Provost of Worcester declined this honour 'most resolutely – in terms which would be unnecessarily strong if he had been asked to go to Sierra Leone'. W.R. Inge himself went to Eton in 1874 where he was much bullied, and then to King's College, Cambridge. These were years of hard work and great academic triumph: 'mainly', as he said himself, 'a record of scholarships and prizes'. The Porson, the Bell, the Craven scholarships; Firsts in both parts of the Classical tripos; Chancellor's medallist. But, as he unwillingly avows in his short memoir, they were years of acute misery for Inge. Partly, no doubt, these miseries were caused by overwork, and by the fact that his three or four closest friends at Eton were not only acutely jealous of his successes (as he was of theirs) but also plagued with melancholia. Two of them committed suicide in later life, and a third, A. C. Benson, the famously neurotic Master of Magdalene College, Cambridge, had long spells of mental collapse.

> My miseries, which were mainly hypochondriacal, began before I was seven years old, so it is not necessary to call in the unpleasant Doctor Freud

Inge tells us. But he admits in the next sentence:

> I could say with Tennyson, 'From the time of my marriage the peace of God descended upon my life'; and I have no doubt that when a man suffers from these troubles and the *acedia* to which they lead, the blessed realisation that he loves and is loved is the best of all remedies . . .

and this reflection might well make us, with or without reference to the unpleasant Doctor, think that the depressions were sexually related.

My father, who had the placid and healthy temperament of a family of athletes, could only say, 'Remember good Bishop Hackett's motto "Serve God and be cheerful!"' Alas! How could I be, with a legion of Devils waiting for me in my unoccupied moments?

Nervous depression, as he called it, plagued Inge throughout boyhood and early manhood, stealing from him any chance of pleasure in his prodigious academic successes and prizes. Nor were his spirits lifted by four years as a master at his old school. He was much too aloof to have been a good schoolmaster. After four years of it he was made deacon in the college chapel at King's by the saintly Bishop King of Lincoln. And in the same year he became Fellow and Tutor at Hertford College Oxford.

There seems to be a sort of inevitability about his following in his father's footsteps, and perhaps there was. But, when we compare him with his contemporary Arthur Benson, we realise that Inge did not have to be a clergyman. Benson, son of the Archbishop of Canterbury, dragged out his sad life as a schoolmaster and don, appeasing the agony of his mental breakdowns and his hopeless emotional attachments with a torrent of words, leaving behind him one of the most copious diaries in the English language and volume after published volume of vapid reflexions on life, which in their day enjoyed a great vogue. Inge's tongue, too, was the pen of a ready writer, but his mind was infinitely more searching, and his temperament more religious. The mind and the temperament were in conflict. The conflict was to be sharpened by his contemplating the religious controversies of the day, but above all, by his arrival in Oxford and encountering another fellow of Hertford, Hastings Rashdall.

'What is the seat of authority in religion? Historically, there have been four; an institution, a book, the inner light and human reason.' Young men of Inge's generation, particularly young Anglicans, were peculiarly obsessed by the institution and by the book. And the problems had begun with the book. Tractarians of his father's temper believed implicitly in the divine inspiration of every word of Holy Scripture, a belief which was utterly shaken by the advance of science, and the dissemination of modern Biblical criticism. Figures such as Inge's new colleague Hastings Rashdall, an extreme liberal, had more or less abandoned any belief whatever in the divine inspiration of Scripture, since some of the narratives in the Old Testament were plainly unhistorical and self-contradictory. But

173

where did this leave the Anglican's grounds for belief? The crisis of belief in the Bible is inextricable from the crisis of belief in the Church as an institution. In the Catholic and Tractarian traditions this led to a division of the ways, which Inge chronicles in some of his *Outspoken Essays* – 'On Bishop Gore and the Church of England', 'On Roman Catholic Modernism' and 'Cardinal Newman' in particular. The one way is the path of absolute conservatism. It was exemplified in the English Church by Dr. Pusey and his disciple Liddon, and in the Roman Church by the Papacy itself. This was to condemn, outright, any attempt to question in any particular the historicity or scientific accuracy of the Scriptures. Such an attitude led, inevitably, in the Roman Church, to the growth of Modernism. Inge was deeply read in the works of Modernists such as Loisy and Tyrrell who believed (as we know now, incidentally, quite wrongly) that all the Gospels were extremely late. They further thought that Jesus was a sort of doomed prophet, preaching a pathetic Messianic kingdom which never came to pass. 'The conditions of his burial,' Loisy wrote, were 'such as would make it quite impossible to recognise the corpse after a few days even if anyone looked for it.' None of the disciples saw Jesus buried. The Resurrection was something dreamed up long after the event, as were all the other so-called miraculous elements in the Gospels.

'It seems hardly credible,' Inge wrote, 'that such views should be propounded by Catholic priests, who claim to remain in the Catholic Church, to repeat her creeds, minister at her altars, and share her faith.' But what he found most exceptionable in the Modernists was their belief in the institutional Church. It was a cardinal belief of Loisy's that Christianity *is* the Church. We can know nothing for certain about the origins of Christianity except what the Church teaches us and, therefore, the only future for Christianity, albeit a purged and steadily evolving creed quite unlike that of its Founder, is in the institution.

Coming back to England, and its Church, Inge found in what might be called the Liberal Catholic school a watered down version of the same contradictions. The person who best and most intelligently represented this point of view was Charles Gore. Gore believed much more than Loisy and Co., but was not his position, logically, very much the same? When he came to be a Bishop, Gore insisted that his clergy subscribed to the thirty-nine articles and to the Creeds. 'The Bishop himself has affirmed his personal belief that some narratives in the Old Testament are probably not historical. It may fairly be asked on what principle he is prepared to evade the plain sense and intention of a doctrinal test in two cases while stigmatising as morally flagitious any attempts to do the same in a third.' These words were written long after Inge's ordination, but they represent the sort of problems which were facing him at that date.

For in his encounter with Hastings Rashdall, he came across, in nightly post-prandial conversations, a mind who had utterly absorbed all the Modernist scepticism, while having no interest in, let alone belief in, Christian institutionalism. The Catholic Modernists shared with scholars such as the great German historian of dogma, Harnack, the belief that Christ's preaching on earth had been of a purely moral character. 'The Kingdom of God' which Jesus preached was one in which the principle of retaliation would be replaced with that of forgiveness; in which licence would give place to chastity, and avarice to holy poverty. Pathetically doomed as Jesus was Himself, His words and moral teachings have somehow or another survived, in spite of all the buzzing fanaticism of St. Paul, the arcane philosophical arguments of the Greek Fathers, the bullying of the Latin Fathers, the shocking skulduggery of General Councils, the wickedness of Popes and the excuses and superstitions of generations of unlettered Christendom. Thus (in caricatured form) is Rashdall's and Harnack's vision of Christianity. It was one which enjoyed great vogue at the time. When we read Canon Scott Holland's essay on Tolstoy, for instance, composed at about this date, we discover that the Russian's enormous popularity and fame in England rested entirely on his belief that he had rescued these words of Christ from the maw of the superstitious Church; and that hundreds of thousands of Englishmen had read such books as *The Kingdom of God is Within You* while being only dimly aware that its author had written a novel – *Peace and War*, as Henry James called it.

Night after night in Hertford, when the other fellows retired, they would leave Inge and Rashdall talking, and sometimes the two men would not get into bed before three a.m. No one was much aware of what they were arguing about, though Inge in later years felt that they were both holding on to Faith itself by very slender threads. He himself delayed his ordination to the priesthood for four years,

175

evidently because of religious doubts. He could see the difficulties over the interpretation of Scripture; he felt the impossibility of embracing a purely institutional faith. But he could not subscribe to Rashdall's view that Christianity was moralism; all or nothing. I like to think of those painful conversations. Rashdall emerged from them as still a Modernist and a moralist, but it was more than a desire for preferment (he died as Dean of Carlisle) which enabled him eventually to subscribe to the orthodoxies. Inge's line was very different. It was not, at that period, unique. It had much in common with that of Baron von Hügel. But it was, in the context of Oxford, completely original.

In 1899, he astonished his undergraduate pupils by becoming the Bampton lecturer. They had thought of him primarily as a philosopher, with particular interest in the neo-Platonism of Plotinus, and as a classical scholar. Clearly, none of his religious concerns ever came out in conversation or tutorials. And the lectures which he delivered from the pulpit of St. Mary's revealed a whole side of Inge which had been kept hidden by that aloof, deaf, rather harsh exterior.

The lectures were printed under the title *Christian Mysticism*, a book which was of seminal importance in the religious history of our century, and which at the same time reveals the man who wrote it. I know of no better book on the subject. I cannot hope to summarise it here, for the subject of the book is really the Christian experience of God, from New Testament times down to the present. Throughout his life, Inge distrusted, in his fellow Modernists, the divorce between the Christ of faith, and the Christ of history. At the same time, the intellectual impasse which he suffered in his own person, and which caused such a crisis of faith in the Christian churches at the close of the nineteenth century, finds a release in his return to the broad mystical tradition of Christian Platonism. His sweep is very large. It begins with St. John and St. Paul. It takes in the Christian Platonists of Alexandria, the writings of the Pseudo-Dionysus, St. Augustine, medievals such as Eckhardt and Julian of Norwich, Teresa of Avila and John of the Cross, the Cambridge Platonists, William Law, and the nature mysticism of Wordsworth. But it is very far from being a dry historical survey. It is in the experience of prayer that the Christian tradition survives:

> The inner light can only testify to spiritual truths. It always speaks in the present tense; it cannot guarantee any historical event, past or future. It

176

cannot guarantee either the Gospel history or a future judgment. It can tell us that Christ is risen, and that He is alive for ever more, but not that He rose again on the third day . . . If anyone finds this inadequate, he may be invited to explain what higher degree of certainty is within our reach.

But the witness of the mystics is strong, and Inge makes out an imaginative case for wishing to include them in any consideration of the general religious debate. The Catholic Modernists were in danger of abandoning all credence in the historic Christ and clinging to an embodiment of Christian values in a mere institution. The institution was often fallible and frequently disgusting. The book was not all that Christians had thought it to have been. But Christianity is more than merely an institution or merely a book.

> The principle *Cuique in sua arte credendum est* applies to those who have been eminent for personal holiness as much as to the leaders in any other branch of excellence. Even in dealing with arts which are akin to each other, we do not invite poets to judge of music or sculptors of architecture. We need not then be disturbed if we occasionally find men illustrious in other fields who are as insensible to religion as to poetry. Our reverence for the character and genius of Charles Darwin need not lead us to lay aside either our Shakespeare or our New Testament. The men whom we naturally turn to as our best authorities in spiritual matters are those who seem to have been endowed with an *anima naturaliter Christiana* and who have devoted their whole lives to the service of God and the imitation of Christ.

It was this realism which saved Inge from the path of absolute scepticism, for he was compelled to recognise that the majority of mystics whom he studied were manifestly sane, manifestly speaking the truth, and also curiously consistent (though so different in race, temperament and generation) in the religion which they prayed and believed.

As a footnote to *Christian Mysticism*, I should like to quote the final sentence of an essay he wrote fifteen years later on St. Paul: 'St. Paul understood what most Christians never realise, namely that the Gospel of Christ is not *a* religion, but religion itself, in its most universal and deepest significance.' It is a saying which repays any amount of reflection and meditation, and it is one which coloured the whole of Inge's outlook. *Christian Mysticism* marks the end of the great crisis in his life. It is the outcome of profound, hard thinking, and in it, he has not found the answer to all the questions

177

which troubled him. As his life progressed, these troubles grew less acute, and he no longer wrestled with the problems. He never really came to terms with the Church. That is to say, he was quite sure that Jesus Christ had not intended to found a theorocracy or a papacy, but the exact connection between Jesus Christ and the Church militant here on earth is always a little hazy in Inge's writings. Likewise, his problems over the authenticity or plausibility of the New Testament as historical record fade into the background in his writings over the next forty years. In many particulars, he would appear, in his diary, to remain a sceptic. But the Tory public man sometimes leads him to a greater gentleness with tender consciences than does the Christian enquirer. Hearing the famously heretical J. M. Thompson preach at St. Margaret's Westminster in 1912, for example, he observed:

> He was very outspoken, denying the Virgin Birth and the Resurrection without any circumlocution. I have no doubt that Christianity must cease to depend on belief in miraculous interventions in the order of nature, but I question the wisdom and propriety of such utterances in the pulpit . . . Traditionalists have a deep sense of loyalty which deserves respect.

This, as far as we can tell, remains Inge's position for the next half century, but in the remaining time, I want to consider him as a public man. *Christian Mysticism* has revealed his profound fascination with Plotinus, and it was to this non-Christian neo-Platonist that he was always meaning to devote his unimpeded scholarly attentions. But his career kept interrupting the *magnum opus*. In 1905, most inappropriately, he was given the living of All Saint's, Ennismore Gardens, in London, and in the same year he got married to Kitty Spooner, niece of the famous Warden of New College. It was a blissfully happy marriage, and there were five children. It is a sign of how things have changed, but when Inge confessed that he was an advocate of at least *discussing* birth control, the entire bench of bishops denounced him. He calmly consulted *Who's Who* and noted that of the forty diocesan bishops, one had five children, two others had four each and the remaining thirty-seven only twenty-eight among them. 'When my advice is asked by a young couple,' he said, 'I say let two children be born and afterwards do what you think best for them and for yourselves. As I have had five children myself I cannot be accused of advocating what has been rather absurdly called race suicide.'

Two years after his attempts to be a parish priest, Inge was given the Lady Margaret Chair of Divinity at Cambridge and he settled down in a nice house in Trumpington Street with his pretty wife. He assumed he would be there for life, but after only four years Asquith, the Prime Minister, offered him the Deanery of St. Paul's. 'I was much disposed to decline, knowing that no power on earth could turn me into an ecclesiastic, and being rather afraid of what I had been told of the tone of the Chapter at that time.' But, of course, he accepted.

There was no humbug in his dread of the ecclesiastical world. He genuinely loathed many of the things which a Dean might be supposed or hoped to enjoy. Contemplating the lengthy choral services of the cathedral he wondered, 'how I can reconcile with my conscience so criminal a waste of time?' and resolved to take books in to read during the services. When someone once asked him if he was interested in liturgy he replied, 'No. Neither do I collect postage stamps.' The spirit of the Chapter was predominantly High Church (what he called Anglo-Catholic), and the appointment was a grief to his old mother, who clung to her Tractarian beliefs and could never reconcile herself to her son's Broad Churchmanship. 'My mother never really forgave me,' he wrote, 'for not being an Anglo-Catholic.'

The *Diary of a Dean*, which is an amusing bedside book, is a catalogue of vigorous social activity. He was rather a snob, and he liked dining out and finding himself next to Duchesses, Prime Ministers, famous authors. He became a friend of George Bernard Shaw, Lord Haldane, Margot Asquith, and an acquaintance of anyone who was anyone. He seems to have been incapable of refusing a speaking engagement. He preached in every English cathedral except Southwell. He travelled abroad, he gave every conceivable course in lectures in British universities – the Hulsean lectures, the Gifford lectures, the Jowett lectures, the Warburton lectures. 'A great crowd; many turned away,' appears again and again in his diary. 'I preached the University sermon at Cambridge, and again at Jesus College. I was well advertised; the *Granta* said, "The Dean of Deans is coming to preach. Those who cannot come early had better bring their hassocks, for they will find no other seat in the church." It was so.'

Those who heard him at this period have told me that they can't remember why on earth they crowded so uncomfortably to listen to him. He had no particular oratorical skills, reading every word of his sermons from very thin pieces of typing paper which were scattered one by one at the base of the pulpit as he had finished with them. He never looked up, and his voice was rasping and uninspiring. But he had become a phenomenon, a character, a cult. He was what people call 'outspoken' and his views were always delivered in a crisp, usually rather satirical style which amused people. He was a man of views, and the Beaverbrook press took him up, greatly enriching him by giving him a regular column in the *Evening Standard*.

Politically, the Dean was a diehard Tory, whose views, when read today, make the utterances of Messrs. Auberon Waugh and Enoch Powell (both I would suspect students and admirers of his manner) seem rather wishy-washy. In a paranoid moment in the diaries, he writes with some glee about his 'enemies'. 'There is G. K. Chesterton, who certainly hates me, and is reported to have said that one of his reasons for becoming a Papist was that he could not remain in the same church as the Dean of St. Paul's. I retaliated in my diary by hoping that the public would soon get tired of the elephantine capers of an obese mountebank.'

On the question of capital punishment, he believed that the principle of retribution, and an eye for an eye, was incompatible with Christianity, so that he could not advocate hanging all murderers. For the same reason, he was a pacifist. However, he believed the state had the right to take life (he had St. Paul on his side). 'If it is fairly certain that a criminal is irreclaimable, that he must be, as long as he lives, a pest and a danger to his fellow citizens, it is right that he should be removed.' Inge advocated a humane execution in a lethal chamber immediately after trial. On the question of divorce, he thought that the Church should be flexible. Christ was not 'legislating even for the Church, since there was no Church to legislate for', in Inge's belief. The state, however, should be tougher. 'I should like to see adultery made a criminal offence, as it was by the Mosaic law and in many other ancient codes . . .' 'Nothing poisons the life of a country more surely than anything which threatens the security, the confidence and the purity of home life.' He saw nothing un-Christian 'in saving money in moderation, and I believe that from the social point of view that is the best use we can make of a small surplus. It is plain, for example, that if I give five pounds to the unemployed I am preventing someone else from earning that five pounds. It is not easy to be charitable without doing as much harm as good.' He was suspicious of democracy – 'Inefficiency and wastefulness are almost inseparable from this type of government' – and hankered after the more ordered ways before universal franchise came in during the nineteenth century. 'Power is always abused, and always will be.' And he liked to quote Mandell Creighton: 'Socialism will only be possible when we are all perfect, and then it will not be necessary.' On votes for women, he had this to say. 'The effect of the new extension of the franchise will be to depress still further the average intelligence of the electorate, and to make our political system still more unmanageable; but there is something to be said for carrying an absurdity to its logical conclusion. It may bring the next political experiment nearer, though what is to be I cannot even imagine. It can hardly be a change for the worse.'

It was writing of this sort which won him the nickname 'the Gloomy Dean'. He predicted that if women ever did hold high political office in this country, we should not necessarily like it. 'When women do air their political views, we observe that they tend to be either diehard Conservatives or rabid Socialists. During the [First] War it was usually the women who wished to exterminate everyone who had had the misfortune to be born between the Rhine and the Vistula. Women, as a rule, have no leaning to compromise; moderation is a quality which they do not value.'

Who is to say whether history has proved Inge right or wrong in this area? It is interesting to note, however, that he gloomily regarded the ordination of women to the priesthood as an inevitability, and one to which he had no particular objection.

The thing which gave rise to the greatest bouts of gloom in the reflections of the Gloomy Dean was the decline in numbers of the intelligent middle class compared with the rest of the population. 'The only high birth rates now are among slum-dwellers and the feeble-minded,' he noted despondently, as though the two were inevitably synonymous. 'Christopher Dawson, who as a Roman Catholic condemns the practice [of birth control] gives us a harrowing picture of England and Scotland overrun by Irish, the United States by Mexicans and negroes, France by Italians (who, however, are not undesirable citizens) and Senegalese. To which the answer is that these intruders should be kept out.'

But, of course, keeping the intruders out was only a partial solution to the problem.

181

'It is not true,' he wrote, 'to say that I dislike the British working man. Individually, I have always found him a very good fellow . . . Shakespeare's Bottom the Weaver is a type which we all recognise. But I maintain that the politicians are corrupting his citizenship by their pampering and pauperising legislation . . . A country which depends for its existence on its export trade can hardly expect to be a working man's paradise . . . Political power has been transferred to the masses and they naturally wish to transfer the power to their own pockets. A man may surely point out the dangers and injustice of a policy of confiscation without being an enemy of the working man.'

The answer lay in eugenics. Defined crudely, this was the theory (advocates of it called it a science) that only the desirable elements in society should be allowed to breed. One of its earliest advocates in England was a friend of Inge's, Sir Francis Galton, 'one of the best and wisest men whom I have known personally'. It is easy to see what attracted Inge to the science. In his boyhood and youth at Eton and Cambridge, he had been surrounded by clever, talented people who came from enormous upper middle-class Victorian families, like the Bensons. It is a curious fact that few of these people ever married themselves, or produced large families. Those who did marry and produce sons were to see them killed in the Trenches during the First World War. Who was to rebuild the world after the destruction of that war? The world had watched what had happened after the Bolshevik Revolution in Russia, and men of Inge's temper did not want the same to happen in Western Europe. The proliferation of the poor and the uneducated, and the devastation of the cultivated middle and upper classes made it all too probable that some such revolution would take place in England. One has only to read contemporary accounts of the General Strike in 1926 to see that. But even if it did not have dire political consequences, a Platonist like Inge would have wanted to ask what quality of life people were living. Here is a typical piece of eugenic apologetics:

The abnormal fertility of the feeble-minded, which leads to the multi-plication of the worst social types, is a sinister fact which quite justifies legislative precautions. The descendants of one mental and moral imbecile have often supplied scores of inmates to prisons, workhouses, and penitentiaries. The inheritance of unusual ability is equally well-established, though the laws which determine it seem to act irregularly. The record of such families as the Darwins, Coleridges, Wordsworths, Pollocks, is enough to silence scepticism.

182

Before we allow scepticism its voice – for scepticism about the eugenic theory cannot and will not be silenced – we should quote one other passage of Inge, lest we believe that he has left Christianity behind altogether.

> It seems to me strange that Christians should not be eugenists. Christianity aims at saving the soul – the personality, the nature of man, not his environment. In direct opposition to Marxian socialism, we are taught that from within, out of the heart of man, comes all that can exalt or defile him. For the Christian, as for the eugenist the test of a country is the quality of the men it turns out . . . Our Lord gives us some admirable eugenic precepts. 'Do men gather grapes of thorns, or figs or thistles? A corrupt tree cannot bring forth good fruit, neither can a good tree bring forth evil fruit. Every tree which bringeth not forth good fruit is hewn down and cast into the fire . . .' We know that such mental defect, disease, vice and crime, might be prevented if obviously undesirable parents could be prevented from adding to the population. We also know what injury is being done by the present policy of taxing out of existence those families which have proved that they possess the qualities which society has hitherto thought deserving of honour.

It may be that I do injury to Inge by devoting such attention to his eugenic theories. His own great work, he would have said, was his book on Plotinus, given as the Hulsean lectures, and why am I not concentrating on that? But the eugenic theory is all of a piece with Inge the man, Inge the scholar, and Inge the religious enquirer. Inge the man detested the twentieth century and wanted to populate it once more with the large, well-read Victorian families whom he had known at school and university. Who shall blame him? It is impossible to read the memoirs of that period without recognising that there were indeed 'giants of the earth in those days'. Speaking purely personally, if I could choose between eating hamburgers and tomato ketchup while watching Bruce Forsyth on television and, let us say, spending an afternoon in the household of Archbishop Benson, I would have no difficulty whatsoever in reaching my decision. I feel this more acutely, in a way, than Inge could. At least he had known fifty tranquil years before the outbreak of the First World War. And he could have no conception, even dying in 1954, of the degradation and ruination which was to come upon England in the latter half of the twentieth century: a degradation which is partly due to the fact that cultivated, civilised people are in an ever decreasing minority in our world.

183

Inge the scholar was primarily a Platonist, who believed in cultivating the purity of the inner man, and who had absorbed almost wholesale the authoritarianism of *The Republic*. People say that Plato's politics are fascist, but that really is silly. For men of Inge's generation (who were horrified by the barbarism of the fascists as they had been by the barbarism of the Bolsheviks) the authoritarianism of Plato's republic would have been no better or worse than the authoritarianism of the Headmaster of Eton in his own small domain. A deep objection to the eugenic theory is its political naïvety. Doubtless it might be splendid if the country were governed by the committee of the Athenaeum, but we never have been and never will be. Not long after Inge and Galton had decided how desirable it would be to regulate the births of a populace, Europeans were able to see such a policy in action. You cannot decree who gives birth and who remains sterile unless you have absolute power. And men with absolute power are seldom scrupulous. They are still searching up and down South America for some of the 'doctors' who shared Galton's cranky beliefs about blood and inheritance and who had human guinea pigs, in the Nazi prison camps, on which to experiment.

But in the end, the question is a religious one, as has been shown by the rather analogous debate in our own day about experiments on human embryos.

Inge expressed a lifelong belief in the Incarnation, but many Christians would find this hard to reconcile with the eugenic principle. The idea that Our Lord's corrupt tree, cut down and cast into the fire, is a defective human being is grotesquely at variance with the Gospel, which tells us of an itinerant who, though fully capable, from childhood, of holding his own with the eminent scholars and ecclesiastics of his day, shunned their company for the sake of 'these little ones'. One gets the feeling – if it is possible to say this without profanity – that Inge believed in the Incarnation, but that he really believed that Jesus had become an honorary member of the Athenaeum. The fact that the New Testament is full of the 'worst social types', as Inge would have them, completely passes him by. And this is not just for reasons of snobbery, but stems from deep theological causes. His theological position seems at first glance a very attractive one: soft-pedal belief, don't worry about any bits of the Bible which fail to give you spiritual uplift, sit lightly to your membership of the institutional Church. When questioned in public about whether you really believe that God became flesh in the womb of the Virgin Mary, or whether there was actually an empty tomb in the Garden of the Resurrection, try to suggest that these are not the important things. The important thing is prayer, and mystery and purity of heart.

I do not criticise Inge, or belittle him. Who am I to do so? He was an honest man, a good man and a clever man, and his position is intellectually respectable. He was much more Christian in his emphasis and in his theology than I have made him sound. He knew, much of the time, that he had not got the balance right between those four things, the book, the institution, the inner light, and reason. Perhaps it is a balance which can't be got right. I certainly do not want to end on a note of criticism. One of the very good things about making friends with the dead is how much easier it is, with them, not to take sides. Had I been my age in 1925, I would probably have viewed Dean Inge with abomination. I would have been (or suspect that I would have been) an extreme Anglo-Catholic socialist. I would hardly have regarded Inge as a Christian at all. I would have hated him as a Tory who thought that the slum-dwellers of Hoxton and Stepney should be eliminated and, as a Low Church liberal Protestant, who thought the work of priests in those quarters was at best a superstitious folly, at worst an exercise in sedition. I would have had to concede that in practical matters (restoration work on the dome, for example) he was a perfectly competent Dean, but that his liturgical views were deplorable. (Once, I think a service of thanksgiving after the First World War, Inge consented to have a cope put round his shoulders. Seeing him thus arrayed the Archbishop of Canterbury expressed surprise: '*On souffre pour être beau*,' was the reply.)

Coming to him thirty years after his death, these things merely amuse me. The fact that I do not share all his prejudices does not stop me loving them. To me, the most beautiful noise in the world is a cathedral choir singing Evensong. 'Music hath charms to soothe the savage beast,' he scratched furiously in his diary. 'It has the opposite effect on me who am not a savage.' I admire him as a prosewriter and as a humourist. In that rather dotty way which happens when one befriends the dead, I like his family life, his devotion to Kitty and the children, his desolation when two of his children, and finally his wife die. If I have made him sound a hard character, I would commend you to the appendices to *Diary of a*

*Dean* in which he writes about his boy Richard, who was a priest killed in the R.A.F. during the war, and about his wife. Finally, though, and most important, I revere Inge as a religious thinker. The fact that he probably got a lot wrong is hardly a reason not to take him seriously. We all get things wrong. There have been times when I have been rescued from unbelief by reading Inge. Nor is it merely the thought that if so cynical and gloomy and naturally sceptical a figure could be a Christian, might not I? It is his positive affirmation of the validity of religious experience. In the end, the Bible and the Church can be what they like, or what anyone would like to make of them, and still have absolutely no effect upon our own inner lives. The test of true religion in Christ's teaching was what happened when we retire into our own inner chambers and are still. The writings of Inge draw us back to that inner chamber. 'Religion,' he wrote, 'can only be understood from the inside. What are called "evidences" will not help us much; but when the mystic tells us what he has seen, we may believe him.' It is for this insight, and the development of this insight through many magnificent books, that I feel much gratitude to the Dean of Deans. And because he makes me laugh.

Address given to the Ambrose Society, 1 April 1985

# Philip Larkin

## 1. Larkin's England

Since all things change and, with a few exceptions (dentists, sound recordings), get worse, there will always be room, you would have thought, for elegiac poets. The poplars are felled, Ha'nacker Hill is in desolation, and they're in business. So you would have thought. Obviousness was no handicap for the old elegists. But, paradoxically, in the last twenty or thirty years, elegy has become the hardest thing of all to write. Change and decay have reached such exaggerated proportions that it has been hard to find a tone of voice in which it is acceptable to talk about them. Everyone sympathises with Betjeman's fulminations on the subject, but his justifiable horror has not always produced his best verse.

To get the feel of what has been lost in the last thirty years, I find myself turning back again and again to Larkin. It isn't so much his attitude, though in 'Homage to a Government' and 'Naturally the Foundation Will Bear Your Expenses' he has been bold enough to express a diffident, semi-despondent patriotism. It is his eye, and his delicacy, and his impeccable lyric gift which bring his world alive.

Certainly, Larkin's England is a sad sort of place, whether glimpsed through bedroom curtains ('Groping back to bed after a piss') or train windows ('An Odeon went past, a cooling tower') from the moment of dawn when

> In locked up offices all the uncaring
> Intricate rented world begins to rouse

to the sad hour when

> all the salesmen have gone back to Leeds
> Leaving full ashtrays in the Conference Room.

'Life is first boredom, then fear.' His glimpse of the 'wax-fleshed out-

187

patients' in the park, or of Mr. Bleaney in his horrible 'rented box' would seem to confirm this bleak creed. Like the vandals in 'Sunny Prestatyn', Larkin has spent the last thirty years defacing any notion that it might be otherwise. The assurances of 'An Arundel Tomb' are only based on tentative 'almost-instinct' and can't be reached without the realisation that 'Time has transfigured them into untruth'.

'Self's the man', of course. Long ago, in 'Wild Oats', the girl in specs had come to the conclusion that he

> was too selfish, withdrawn
> And easily bored to love.
> Well, useful to get that learnt.

Having learnt the lesson, he has thrown himself vigorously into the part. He has opted for

> my in-tray,
> My loaf-haired secretary,
> My shall-I-keep-the-call-in Sir . . .

offering the reading public a version of himself which works all day and gets half drunk at night. Slumped in his chair drinking his 'three goes of gin' with 'a ten ounce tonic', he largely resents the idea of being invited out,

> Holding a glass of washing-sherry, canted
> Over to catch the drivel of some bitch
> Who's reading nothing but *Which*.

And, lest anyone should have missed the point, he offers this advice:

> Man hands on misery to man,
>   It deepens like a coastal shelf.
> Get out as early as you can,
>   And don't have any kids yourself.

And it is when you reach this point that you might start answering back. Why sit reading this when we could be reading something less doggedly miserable?

For anyone who has caught the habit, though, it is not a matter of whether we should, but why we *do* go back to Larkin again and again and find something which actually belies much of the foul-mouthed Movement casualness and self-deprecation. Without any kind of false solemnity, someone forever surprising 'a hunger in himself to be more serious' will find it answered in Larkin.

Reading *High Windows* makes you sorry you barged in; there seem to be 'Keep Off The Grass' notices all over the place and, as with Hardy and Housman, fairly insistent reminders not to make the mistake of thinking the poet is 'nice' or wanting him to be your intimate. Yet, as with Housman and Hardy (the Belloc, too, of 'On with my coat and out into the night'), it all springs from an absolute certainty of lyric purpose, an unerring touch. If it were not such an un-Larkinian concept, you would be tempted to call it good taste. So many bad lyric poets have wanted to spill the beans, bore us with their depressions and love affairs. 'Ambulances', 'Home Is So Sad', 'Livings', these are matchlessly accomplished outward-gazing elegies. No poet has ever conveyed the still sad music of humanity in quite Larkin's perfect tone.

> I listen to money singing. It's like looking down
>    From long french windows at a provincial town,
> The slums, the canal, the churches ornate and mad
>    In the evening sun. It is intensely sad.

Any old poet can say that 'we mortal millions live alone'. Larkin's poems of isolation and lament not only convey aloneness, but are infused with a sympathetic sense of sad, separate lives, dotted all over the landscape of an almost-ruined England.

In two of his most brilliant muted set-pieces – 'The Whitsun Weddings' and 'Show Saturday' – human beings are not alone, but placed in an odd and arbitrary confluence. In the first poem of the dozen married couples all clambering aboard the train at different stations down the line,

>                                    none
>    Thought of the others they would never meet
>    Or how their lives would all contain this hour . . .

At the end of the agricultural show in the second poem, there is an analogous dispersal, when all ('mugfaced middle-aged wives/ Glaring at jellies,' and the rest) who have been there go

>    Back now, all of them, to their local lives:
>    To names on vans, and business calendars
>    Hung up in kitchens . . .

No absurd claims are made. But the dispersal would be almost absolute without Larkin's almost priestly remembrance of the col-

189

lective experience, and his longing that the memory of it all should stay in all those separate minds 'hidden there like strength'. Achieving this rather big effect without being remotely grandiose or pompous is an extraordinary accomplishment. And without the consistent self-deprecation which he has laid upon himself, it would not really be possible.

It isn't all gin and grumbling. Beneath the pathos, the inconsolable loneliness, the relentless ugliness of modern life, Nature offers an encouraging reproach. 'The Trees' is one of the most hopeful poems in our language, its beauty springing from the kind of unmannered simplicity which all the best lyrics have had since the Middle Ages:

> Yet still the unresting castles thresh
> In fullgrown thickness every May.
> Last year is dead, they seem to say,
> Begin afresh afresh afresh.

*Poetry Review*, 7 June 1982

## 2. Larkin as critic

Poets sounding off about literature are nearly always portentous or boring, if Matthew Arnold, T. S. Eliot and W. H. Auden were anything to go by. We need have no such fear about the occasional essays of Philip Larkin.

'Life's so flat that you can see your own tombstone at the other end,' he quotes with approval, though without saying who wrote it. Was it Logan Pearsall Smith? Anyone presented with the sentiment 'blind' would guess that it was said by the Eeyore of the Brynmor Jones Library himself.

> Nowadays you can live by being a poet. A lot of people do it: it means a blend of giving readings and lecturings and spending a year at a university as poet in resident or something. But I couldn't bear that: it would depress me very much. I don't want to go around pretending to be me.

The voice is unmistakable. But the poet who describes himself, admittedly on the imagined lips of an American, as 'one of those old-type *natural* fouled-up guys' obviously enjoys pretending to be himself very much indeed. As he said in his speech as chairman of the Booker Prize judges, 'If you tell a novelist, "Life's not like that," he has to do something about it. The poet simply replies, "No, but *I* am."'

He would not have chosen to recycle the first seventy-five pages of *Required Writing*\* if, like a contemporary novelist, he was trying to live 'without an image of the self'. Put together, the pages constitute a casual autobiography. There is the childhood ('Oh, I've completely forgotten it') in a comfortable house in Coventry ('Bourgeois certainly, but neither *haut* nor *petit*'). There is the agony of having a stammer at school ('Really classes were just me sitting there with bated breath dreading lest I should be called on to say something'); Oxford, and the friendship of Bruce Montgomery and Kingsley Amis; the failure (twice) to get into the Civil Service.

There is the desire to become a novelist ('I'd had visions of myself writing five hundred words a day for six months, shoving the result off to a printer and going to live on the Côte d'Azur uninterrupted except for the correction of proofs') and the acceptance, instead, of a crummy job in a public library in Shropshire.

There is the obtaining of qualification, the library work at Belfast, Leicester and Hull. 'You get medals and prizes and honorary this-and-thats, but if you turned round and said, "Right, if I'm so good, give me an index-linked permanent income equal to what I get for being an undistinguished university administrator" – well, reason would remount its throne pretty quickly.'

Yes, Larkin likes 'pretending to be himself', but in an introspective rather than a show-off way. At several points he reveals that he keeps a diary. I would not be surprised if readers in a hundred years' time enjoy him as we enjoy A. C. Benson.† One of the best autobiographical pieces, 'Early Days at Leicester', has the flavour of Barbara Pym. 'At lunchtime we went to a small restaurant on the London Road called the Tatler: I believe it is still there.'

The two interviews make good reading. 'Until I grew up I thought I hated everybody, but when I grew up I realised it was just children I didn't like;' or, 'I feel very much the need to be on the periphery of things.'

His questioners, some woman from *The Observer* and an arty

\* *Required Writing: Miscellaneous Pieces 1955–1982*, Philip Larkin.
† I still hope this, in spite of the fact that the executors of his will are said to have fed Larkin's diary into the office shredder in the Brynmor Jones Library.

American, have set up the questions to make Larkin's provincialism seem ludicrous. Here is a man, these cosmopolitans hoot incredulously, who hardly ever goes out in the evening, doesn't like abroad, prefers Dick Francis to 'serious fiction' and has never even heard of Borges.

What they do not seem to realise is that these are sentiments to which every bosom returns an echo. In an essay on Louis Armstrong, he wrote, 'When, after a severe bout of emphysema, the trumpet could not longer maintain even "the straight lead" Louis so advocated, his singing – perfectly pitched, perfectly timed – could bring tears to the eyes.' The same, *mutatis mutandis*, could be said of Larkin's writing now that his poetry appears to have stopped.

He is a punctilious, honest critic. He prefers good clear writing to pretentious eyewash; he prefers tunes to discordant wailing; and he prefers home to abroad. Unlike the majority of critics, he is clear-sighted enough to say so.

He likes Anthony Powell's early novels better than *A Dance to the Music of Time*. He likes A. E. Housman, of course, and Stevie Smith, whose poems 'speak with the authority of sadness'. He has a perhaps surprising taste for Montherlant. And he is at his best as a critic when describing the genius of John Betjeman and of Barbara Pym.

Many of the more memorable passages in the book, however, are not the curmudgeonly jokes (good as they are), nor the irrefutable common sense of the critical judgements, but Louis, as it were, the trumpet abandoned, bringing tears to our eyes with his voice. Take this evocation of the Victorian age as seen through the eyes of Lord Tennyson.

> There are the emerald-green landscapes, the dewy roses, the pearly-toothed children; the melancholy maidens, the heavy gardens; the peasants, at once comic and pathetic, bob and curtsy. Then there is the teashop orientalism, the cardboard classicism, the sawdust Arthurianism. There are railways and geology. The silliness and sentimentality are excruciating. We see the flash of moral indignation, and hear the rumble of received opinion: the smoke of double-think drifts obscuringly across the scene. Then suddenly we are brought up by a sharp voice speaking of doubt; there is a vision of Fen country on a winter evening; something robust and chuckling digs us in the ribs; finally we hear the assertive trumpeters of imperial patriotism and historic endurance.

'What oft was thought but ne'er so well expressed' used to be a definition of poetry. In this poet's case, it is a good way of describing his prose.

*Sunday Telegraph*, 20 November 1983

# 3.  An Obituary

There are many ways of judging poets. One sure test of their personal appeal is how many lines of their poetry you can remember. Not only can I remember a lot of Larkin, I found that it has sunk very deep, and become part of my private language. This is true both of his funny stuff —

> My wife and I have asked a crowd of craps
> To come and waste their time and ours . . .

and also the jokey sadness of

> What else can I answer,
> When the lights come on at four
> At the end of another year?
> Give me your arm, old toad,
> Help me down Cemetery Road.

or the tenderness of 'The Arundel Tomb' or the sheer bleak despair of 'Dockery and Son' or 'Aubade'. One will never forget such poems, and perhaps the reason Larkin made such a great name from so small an *oeuvre* was that he so exactly caught the mood of so many of us. One of the symptoms of the decline of our society is that we distrust fine expressions and rhetoric. Since the death of Yeats, there has been no poet who could *quite* manage a high style. Larkin found the perfect voice for expressing our worst fears.

All the other papers will have articles explaining why he was such a good poet, and trying to 'place' him in the History of Eng. Lit. I am not competent to do that, nor to praise his achievements as a librarian. Doubtless at some later date I might be able to fathom out what *happened*: why he stopped being able to write. Did the poetry dry up because of his relentlessly negative view of things? Or was it much more a technical matter? He often described the dawning of poems to me. He said that it was like music in the head, always accompanied by a sense of excitement and exhilaration. 'I went to

193

the doctor and said it's years since I heard a bird sing. He said, "That's not surprising. You've gone deaf."' The silencing of the inner music was even more crushing than the deafness.

In his writings, and in the various profiles, interviews and so on, Larkin was always represented as a crushingly sad man. ('Oh!' he exclaimed late one night, 'I hate being fat, I hate being deaf, I hate not being able to write any more, I hate having a stammer! You can't imagine how much I hate it!') Doubtless he was sad. I remember his saying to me that he really believed the last four lines of 'Dockery and Son', and that he was prouder of having written them than of anything else he'd done.

But it was not sad being with him. For someone who made such a thing of his social awkwardness, he actually had great conversational gifts, and although he tried to make himself sound like a cynical old brute, he actually had great tenderness and sympathy. His friendships often started with his taking the initiative, and once formed they were a great source of mutual pleasure. To say that he had a sense of humour would be to imply that he sometimes said things which it was safe to take wholly seriously. ('I know how to stop unemployment. Stop unemployment pay.') His pessimism, and the Toryism which was its concomitant, were tinged with irony. One often laughed at things he said, not because they were preposterous, but because of how they were expressed. 'But I really mean it,' he would have to add, having reduced his company to laughter by some confession of distaste for the young or the left.

When Betjeman died, it was natural that Mrs. Thatcher should offer him the Laureateship. Not only was he fervently patriotic, and filled with a sense of place; his tone of voice was untranslatably English. Given the fact that the poetry had stopped, however, it was not surprising that he said no. 'I never want to see my name in the papers again,' he said after the speculation about whether he would succeed Betjeman, adding, with characteristic candour, '(not quite true)'. Now that one knows how short a time he had to live, it is hard not to wish that Larkin had accepted the Laureateship, just for a year. I even had a superstition then – which is still stronger now – that he would have been able to write verse to order; that, as it were, Mrs. Thatcher would have been able to succeed where the muses failed.

Larkin had an absolute conviction that death was nothing but extinction. It was a fact which filled him with terror and gloom.

Religion was completely unable to console him. In the last year of his life he read through the Bible from cover to cover. He had a large lectern-size Bible and he read it while he was dressing. When he had finished it, I asked him what he thought. 'Amazing to think anyone once believed it was true,' was his only comment. Yet many of his closest friends were religious, and he shared the wistfulness of one of his favourite poets, Thomas Hardy, about his inability to believe. Needless to say, I hope that he is now blinking his eyes on the edge of paradise, perhaps responding as when I urged him to try out an exotic high church not far from his house in Hull: 'I finally attended Evensong at St. Stephen's – I say finally because after meeting Mr. B. [the vicar] I've had it in mind to do so. I'm far from being a church-taster, so I suppose it was just curiosity. However I was much impressed. The congregation numbered seven, but the service was as splendid as if there had been seventy. Of course I was pretty lost – "no church-goer he" – but I tried to be devout, and really quite enjoyed it.'

Meanwhile, for his friends, there is a dreadful silence. He was not looking foward to old age. He hated the modern world. He had been ill. So perhaps one ought to be glad 'for his sake' that he is gone. But with him has gone one of the most distinctive sensibilities of the age. He was right, in some famous lines, to suggest that 1963 was 'much too late' for him. He seemed like a living embodiment of something which had died out in the fifties – a world of intelligent provincials who had their suits made for them, and distrusted London and foreigners in almost equal doses. Not long ago, I lent him the diaries of Major Warren Lewis, and in his description of what he liked about them, he seemed to encapsulate something of himself: 'a bygone bachelor world – sticks in the varnished hall stand, lodgings, walking tours, pubs, discomfort – women as nuisances – books, irritation. And of course tremendous inarticulate love.'

*Spectator*, 7 December 1985

# J. R. R. Tolkien

J. R. R. Tolkien's genius was all of a piece. In his academic career and in his personal life and in his art, he was the same man. This sounds like a platitude, but it is in fact highly unusual. Eminent scholars are, more often than not, bored with their subjects. And there is often so complete a division between the 'writing persona' and the 'real self' of an author that the task of biography becomes necessarily offensive. None of this applies to Tolkien. That is what gives his mythologies their power. Plenty of people have disliked them, or been jealous of their commercial success; but no one, with justice, could ever have thought them whimsical or posing. They sprang naturally out of his apprehension of the real world, as we can now perceive by reading this remarkable selection of letters.*

Perhaps his first and greatest love was language, for its own sake. He speaks, in a letter to W. H. Auden, of 'the acute pleasure derived from a language for its own sake, not only free from being useful but free even from being the "vehicle of a literature"'. That was why he loved Gothic, which has no literature. And so it was as a child that he gazed with fascination at coaltrucks on the railway line in Birmingham, labelled with Welsh names. It was as if the words alone had the power to transport him to a different time and plane; just as in old age, during a seaside holiday he enjoys the very names of Sidmouth shopkeepers 'such as Frisby, Trump and Potbury'.

In many obvious senses he was not at home in the modern, materialist world. When he writes with frustration of living at 99, Holywell (in Oxford), he is speaking of more than noisy traffic: 'This charming house has become uninhabitable – unsleepable-in, unworkable-in, rocked, racked with noise, and drenched with fumes. Such is modern life. Mordor in our midst.' But not merely did he feel displaced in 'this polluted country of which a growing

* *The Letters of J. R. R. Tolkien: a selection*, edited by Humphrey Carpenter with the assistance of Christopher Tolkien (1981).

proportion of the inhabitants are maniacs'. In the human body itself, he felt a stranger. After an unpleasant session with a doctor in old age he wrote to his son, 'We (or at least I) know far too little about the complicated machine we inhabit.'

With good Augustinian, not to say Platonic, precedent, Tolkien's sense of the present world's futility, folly and unreality stemmed from his lively faith in a world beyond: and this other world was, primarily, the heaven of conventional Catholicism. So, to his son Christopher, posted to South Africa during the war, he can write, 'Remember your guardian angel. Not a plump lady with swan-wings! . . . But God is . . . behind us, supporting, nourishing (as being creatures). The bright point of power where that life-line, that spiritual umbilical cord touches: there is our angel, facing two ways, to God behind us in the direction we cannot see, and to us . . .'

When, years later, this umbilical cord was loosened and his correspondent lost a sense of this other world, it was an enormous grief to Tolkien: 'When I think of my mother's death . . . worn out with persecution, poverty, and largely consequent disease, in the effort to hand on to us small boys the Faith, and remember the tiny bedroom she shared with us in rented rooms in a postman's cottage in Rednal, where she died alone, too ill for viaticum, I find it very hard and bitter when my children stray away from the Church.' In the same letter he writes, '*in hac urbe lux solemnis* has seemed to me steadily true'.

Yet its truth was best apprehended, in his distinctive imagination, when transformed into story and mythology. His love of language suggested much of the myth's substance. In the case of the *ents*, for example, the majestic walking trees of his story, 'as usually with me they grew rather out of their name than the other way about. I always felt that something ought to be done about the peculiar Anglo-Saxon word *ent* for a "giant" or a mighty person of long ago – to whom all old works are ascribed.' He was not content to leave the *ents* as they appear on the pages of *Beowulf*, shadowy, unknown figures of an almost forgotten past. A natural storyteller, Tolkien invested them with shapes, voices and habits of his own creation. Many of his fellow medievalists have found *The Lord of the Rings* perpetually irritating for this reason. Any student of Anglo-Saxon knows that an *ent* is not a walking tree: it is some sort of giant, perhaps a nickname for the Romans. But in the imaginations of the millions, in their Gandalf T-shirts, the *ent* has taken leave of its Anglo-Saxon origins and become something other. So the dons would argue; and they could choose countless other examples of names from the Edda, or medieval Welsh, or from Anglo-Saxon verse and riddles where Tolkien took up an old name and transformed it for his own storytelling purposes.

The objectors fail to recognise the wholeness of Tolkien's imaginative sweep. The tales were not one part of his life, written in 'time off' from academic or family pursuits. They are an expression of his whole experience of life. This is what the *Letters* make so fascinatingly clear. At the beginning, in an undergraduate letter to his future wife, he reports that he has 'done some touches to my nonsense fairy language'; but the importance of this invented grammar had not yet dawned on him; he can still apologise for it as 'such a mad hobby'. Almost no letters of the intervening twenty years are included in this volume; perhaps they do not exist; perhaps they are too personal for publication. But by the late 1930s, when Tolkien had returned to Oxford as Rawlinson and Bosworth Professor, all the strands of his life had become enmeshed in their inevitable pattern: the love of philosophy; the sense of the Church as the one city in which *lux solemnis* shines on in a dark world; the poignant and increasingly strong sense that 'Men are essentially mortal and must not try to become "immortal" in the Flesh'. Thus the divisions between his imagined world and the world of all of us grow shadowy. 'I am historically minded,' he protests to one correspondent. 'Middle Earth is not an imaginary world . . . The theatre of my tale is this earth, the one in which we now live.' This is not whimsy. The letters reveal innumerable glimpses of how it was, in his own life, literally true. This is particularly true of the letters written in old age. To a son who has enjoyed a holiday in Switzerland he writes, 'The hobbit's [Bilbo's] journey from Rivendell to the other side of the Misty Mountains, including the glissade down the slithering stones into the pine woods, is based on my adventures in 1911.' To another son, he writes more solemnly on the subject of his wife's gravestone, inscribed simply with her name and the word *Lúthien*. 'I never called Edith *Lúthien*, but she was the source of the story that in time became the chief part of the *Silmarillion*. It was first conceived in a small woodland glade filled with hemlocks at Roos in Yorkshire (where I was for a brief time in command of the Humber Garrison in 1917, and she was able to live with me for a while). In those days her hair was raven, her skin clear, her eyes brighter than you have seen them, and she could sing – and *dance*.

But the story has gone crooked and I am left, and *I* cannot plead before the inexorable Mandos.'

None of the letters show more movingly how much his inner mythologising and his outer storytelling were at one. The reader begins to see why he protested to R. W. Burchfield, the reviser of the *Oxford English Dictionary*, against his etymology of the word 'hobbit': 'invented by J. R. R. Tolkien'. He was not sure that the word *had* been invented. It was almost no surprise in 1956 when he received a letter from a 'real person' called Mr. Sam Gamgee, of Tooting. 'He could not have chosen a more hobbit-*sounding* place, could he? – though un-Shirelike, I fear, in reality.'

These letters, then, are primarily interesting because they reveal more of the mind which created *The Lord of the Rings*. There are extended epistles to admirers or publishers, giving commentary on the great tale and answering points of difficulty with donnish precision. The letter to Milton Waldman of Collins, trying to persuade him to publish *The Silmarillion* simultaneously with *The Lord of the Rings*, goes on for seventeen printed pages.

But it must be stressed that these are very good letters in themselves, quite apart from their relevance to hobbit-lore. There are good gossipy vignettes of Oxford: C. S. Lewis downing three pints of beer before lunch and insisting that he was 'going short for Lent'; or Frank Pakenham, yelling from the dress circle of the New Theatre during a quiet moment of Gielgud's *Hamlet*, 'A very fine performance, and I'm enjoying it very much, but cut out the swearwords'! There are letters which reveal Tolkien as a wise counsellor, a kind friend, an admirable father. The best, and most moving, are those written to his son Christopher during the war, sent out with installments of *The Lord of the Rings* as the tale grew. In perhaps the most impressive of all, he recounts a sermon by Father Douglas Carter on the raising of Jairus's daughter. The sermon moved Tolkien so much because it captured what he called the 'eucatastrophe' of that story: 'the sudden happy turn in a story which pierces you with a joy that brings tears'. The Resurrection is the great 'eucatastrophe'. 'Of course I do not mean that the Gospels tell what is *only* a fairy-story; but I do mean very strongly that they do tell a fairy-story: the greatest. Man the storyteller would have been redeemed in a manner consonant with his nature: by a moving story.'

*Spectator*, 12 September 1981

# Anthony Crosland

Anthony Crosland was married to Susan Barnes, a practised journalist who specialised in 'profiles' and biography. When he died, having been Foreign Secretary for less than ten months, it was inevitable that she should write the story of his life. She has taken the obvious risk of writing a completely personal account and has produced a book* which many will consider indiscreet and tasteless. That is what makes it so readable. The bizarre collection of people who composed Harold Wilson's various Cabinets have already been paraded before us in the diaries of Dick Crossman and Barbara Castle. Here they are again, making us consider once more why, in democracies, the scum should so inevitably rise to the top. But this narrative also gives us intimate glimpses of a Cabinet Minister's amorous and domestic life, set against the background of his quarrels and alliances with the clowns who were set in authority over us during the 1960s and 1970s.

Crosland was the son of a high-ranking civil servant. He had a prosperous upbringing in north London. He was educated at a private school in Highgate (described here as a 'public school') and, during the war, he served in the Royal Welsh Fusiliers before taking up a place at Trinity College, Oxford. The only notably unusual feature of this otherwise conventional middle-class background was the religion of his parents, who adhered to the sect known as the Exclusive Brethren. Once, when he found his future wife reading *Father and Son* (Gosse shared a similarly eccentric religious parentage) Crosland exploded with rage: 'Why don't you mind your own bloody business?' He was loath to recall the Brethren. The secularism of his mind, and his free alcoholic and sexual indulgence were alike reactions against the puritanical rigours of the Meeting House at Highgate.

* *Tony Crosland*, Susan Crosland (1982).

200

Crosland did well at Trinity, became a don, taught politics and economics and gathered the store of notions which were to be fed into his various books, of which *The Future of Socialism* is the best known. From his arrival in the House of Commons in 1950, he was a close friend and disciple of Hugh Gaitskell. The chief political fascination of this biography is the light it casts upon the so-called Gaitskellites in the Labour Party during the last fifteen years. It shows, for instance, that Roy Jenkins and his henchmen – particularly William Rodgers and David Owen – were all set to form a breakaway party as early as March 1976, when Jenkins was defeated in the leadership contest which followed Wilson's sudden resignation. By then, the Gaitskellites had formed into two quite distinct groups: the Jenkinsites who (by the standards of the rest of the party) had ceased to be socialists at all; and those, like Crosland, Hattersley and Healey, who wanted to hang on to their jobs and felt capable of concocting an ideological socialism which was distinct from the loony left wing.

Both these groups (by then hardly on speaking terms – even the wives cut one another) invoked Gaitskell's name to hallow their position. His early death somehow served to disguise the more foolish or dangerous aspects of his political creed. Is the same thing likely to happen to Anthony Crosland? In the terms of *1066 and All That*, was Crosland A Good or A Bad Thing?

On a personal level, this biography makes a strong case for his being A Good Thing. It is written by someone who loved him, who divorced her husband in order to marry him, who was in awe of his cleverness and charmed by the characteristics which she knew were irritating to the rest of the world: the arrogant irascibility, the drunken bossiness, the inverted snobbery which made him refuse to wear 'correct' dress on 'official' occasions. She knows that not everyone will be charmed by her glimpses of Crosland at home – making love, shaving, watching *Match of the Day*, smoking cheroots and bellowing down the telephone. But everyone will see that it is written from the heart and praise the honesty and courage of her portrait.

On the public level, one is bound to say that he will leave little trace. Obviously, in terms of what he stood for, he was A Bad Thing. He held five offices of state. After brief service in George Brown's ill-starred Department of Economic Affairs, Crosland became Secretary of State for Education in January 1965. 'If it is the last thing I do, I'm going to destroy every fucking grammar school in England,' he remarked at the time. As it turned out, the last things he did were in the Foreign Office – bungling the Cod War and trusting in Henry Kissinger to get us out of the Rhodesian crisis. Crosland, like the Americans, was completely hoodwinked by Ian Smith. He said that when he died, *Fish* and *Rhodesia* would be written on his heart.

Anyone can make mistakes. If Crosland had not wrecked the British educational system and made an ass of his government in Africa, some other man would have done precisely the same. He was never (to judge from his widow's account) a very conscientious, nor enthusiastic, minister of the Crown, and that is greatly to his credit. One feels at frequent intervals throughout this book that he was too nice to be mixed up with the crowd he was in with.

In general political terms, however, Crosland's brand of socialism is already extinct. In the leadership contest in 1976 (in which Callaghan ultimately beat Foot and Jenkins), Crosland decided (he did not need much prompting) to 'throw his hat into the ring'. He calculated how many votes he would 'find not too bad': '10–15 would be a disaster; 15–20 very bad' . . . 'anything over 35 sensational'. In the event, 17 M.P.s voted for him. He had only stood because he wanted to be Chancellor of the Exchequer. Instead, Callaghan made him Foreign Secretary, a post for which he had no preparation or qualifications.

By then, the Labour Party was hopelessly split. On the one hand, there were the true socialists, prepared, for the time being, to shove in Worzel Gummidge as a figurehead for their aspirations. On the other hand, there were the disillusioned Jenkinsites, already preparing for the Great Divorce. A decade earlier, Crosland had contemplated the divisions in the party and given utterance to the most ludicrous hyperbole in this book: 'Harold knows best. Harold is a bastard, but he is a genius. He's like Odysseus. Odysseus was a bastard, but he managed to steer the ship between Scylla and Charybdis.' Whether one now considers the Party to have crashed on a rock or to have floundered in a whirlpool, there is manifestly no political future for Crosland's brand of socialism.

His mistake, perhaps, consisted in believing that political power was vested largely in the Parliamentary Party at Westminster. The Conservatives do not suffer from this delusion. Nor does the former Viscount Stansgate, who was a pupil of Crosland's at Oxford and known to him as 'Jimmy'. He emerges from this book as an amusing friend and neighbour of the Croslands, giving to ringing up at odd hours, putting on funny voices and pretending to be a Post Office engineer. After Labour's electoral defeat in 1970, Tony Benn was not in the least cast down; he saw himself as 'a left-wing answer to Enoch Powell. "Enoch has had more effect on the country than either party," said Benn, adding that he himself intended making a major speech every three months.'

Susan Crosland asked her husband if he thought Tony Benn would succeed in his Messianic ideals. Perhaps Crosland never spoke more truly than when he replied 'Over my dead body'.

*Spectator*, 12 June 1982

# Lionel Brett

Anyone familiar with Abingdon before it was vandalised by modern architects will remember one of the most beautiful river towns in northern Europe. Now it is the familiar nightmare of traffic signs and new buildings all the wrong height and wrong colour. Still, you might say, if you lived in the Thames Valley, Abingdon is a good deal better than the centre of Maidenhead, a dull but pleasant old town which has been almost wholly destroyed in the past twenty-five years.

But, then again, you might say you would rather do your shopping in Maidenhead, bits of which survive, than be blown about the windswept Guildhall Square in Portsmouth, where chunks of copper coloured glass (1976) rise in staggered tiers about you, catching the reflection of the glue sniffers and the 'precinct'.

Who on earth, we sometimes ask ourselves, is responsible for such ghastliness? And this delightful book* provides us, in these three cases, with the very surprising answer.

It is the 4th Viscount Esher, grandson of the promiscuously homosexual 2nd Viscount and nephew of Doll Brett, that eccentric girl who knew D. H. Lawrence in Mexico, but who failed to consummate her union with the priest of love. It is, in other words, the architect Lionel Brett.

No one looking at Lord Esher's work over the past forty years would suppose him a monster. We might deduce that he was, as he says here, a young man who once drank a dry martini with the Modernist architect Chemayeff 'in his elegant apartment in Bayswater' and who was a 'paid up member of the Modern Movement'. We might even, if we were rather unkind, suspect that the architect of the new buildings at Exeter College, Oxford, which so completely spoil Broad Street, was a man who saw nothing wrong with dullness.

* *Our Selves Unknown: an Autobiography*, Lionel Brett (1985).

'"I love dull books," my father would say,' observes our author in a characteristically name-clustered sentence, 'and I was and remain in sympathy with Noel Blakiston's announcement on some country Sunday (according to Molly MacCarthy), "I think I'll walk by myself, it's duller."' Perhaps Exeter College is an unfair example of Lord Esher's work to choose, for as he himself admits, with beguiling honesty, 'some of our stuff looked pusillanimous and dull'.

In such a setting, however, it has no *right* to look dull. It is seventy-five yards from Wren's Sheldonian Theatre. It is bang opposite Trinity. If the architect sees how awful it looks now, why didn't he see it when it was still on the drawing board?

He grew up in a beautiful Georgian house in Watlington, the clever, sensitive child of a Henry James heroine sort of American, and the 3rd Viscount. He had all the usual experiences for a child of this class, and they are here described with elegance. He hated the brutality of Summerfields (particularly the occasion when a Dutch boy was set upon and scalped in the ha-ha).

At Eton, he admired the bravery of a boy called A. J. Ayer who protested against being beaten by the Library, and he made friends with a boy called Jo Grimond. He belonged to that generation of Etonian aesthetes who enjoyed the poetry of Robert Bridges.

As an undergraduate at Oxford he saw Rachmaninov perform on the stage of the Town Hall; he lunched with Lindemann and Harrod; he dined with Betjeman, Bowra and Crossman; he made friends with Cuffy's girls on Boar's Hill; he felt vaguely pacifist; but like the man in the poem, 'when there was a war, he went'.

He married a beautiful wife and their relationship is touchingly described, both in quotations from their diaries and in reminiscence. He became the father of a number of children to whom he is obviously devoted, and who are all strikingly good-looking, as the photographs show.

In all respects, then, it would seem that Lord Esher is a perfectly sane, lovable man, whose heart is in the right place, who is of high intelligence, and who gazes on the world – whether it is the world at war, or the passing seasons – in prose which will be a source of admiration, even envy, for all his readers.

With what delightful self-deprecation he describes such bizarre episodes in his life as standing as Liberal candidate for South Oxfordshire in the 'khaki' election, or presiding over the unpleasant student unrest at the Royal College of Art, of which he was Rector during the seventies. When he is looking at a tree, or a cloud, or a woman, he seems to be looking at what Wordsworth called 'the world of all of us'.

But here is the puzzle. An entirely different vision takes over when he is looking at buildings. He describes his nasty little Wimpey houses in Hatfield (1956: how tawdry they look now) as 'miniature twentieth-century versions of Lansdown Crescent'. Any non-architect reader of these words will realise at once that Lord Esher is no longer looking at the 'world of all of us'. Some crazed vision has taken possession of him. Think of what he wanted to do in the Cadogan estate in the mid-1960s:

> The long dull stretch of Sloane Street itself we would split into three, with two business ends and a residential centre piece, the latter achieved by bridging the street with buildings at the top and bottom ends of Cadogan Place. Under these bridge buildings you would enter a unified and noble space on the scale of the Palais Royal.

How can he have thought, for one moment, that the slabs and blocks and litter-strewn wastes which would have resulted would have resembled, even remotely, the Palais Royal? Now, he is modest enough to concede that it would not have been such a good idea after all.

I notice that his normally delightful prose (touches of Ruskin, a bit of Anthony Powell) frequently descends into jargon and planners' cliché when he is describing these schemes of his.

*Our Selves Unknown* gives no real answer to the mystery, except for a magical one. At his christening, we are informed, a bad fairy (not, I hope, the 2nd Viscount) gave him two fatal gifts; 'a compulsion to succeed and a longing to be liked'. The longing to be liked has produced a charming and even a beautiful book. It is impossible, having read it, *not* to like its author. But the compulsion to succeed has littered the south of England with many a dreary tribute to that glass of dry Martini in Chermayeff's 'elegant apartment'.

*Sunday Telegraph*, 3 February 1985

# A Fabulous Griffin

Broadly speaking, we divide journalists into two categories; those who find things out, and those who comment upon things. The first category is much larger than the second. The first category, of discoverers, would include almost anyone we read in the newspapers: from the cub reporter describing a local flower show to the man who unearths the corruption of an American President; from the reporter who describes the present state of things in Manila or Moscow to the anonymous court correspondent who tells us the colour size and dimension of the hat worn yesterday by the Queen Mother. The second category contains the sages, the wiseacres. These men never find anything out. But if we already believe (having heard the radio or read the front page of the paper) that we know 'the news', it may very well be that it is this second category of journalist whom we value more. They are the commentators. They never need to stray from their typewriters or their bar stools. All they need to do is comment upon what we sometimes take to be the facts unearthed by the other journalists.

Many people, looking at the two Chesterton brothers, and their outstanding brilliance as journalists in the first decades of this century, would find no difficulty in placing Cecil in the first of these categories, and Gilbert in the second. It was Cecil, for instance, who, with Hilaire Belloc on *The Eye Witness*, found out about the notorious skulduggery of Lloyd George, the Master of Elibank and the others in the matter of the Marconi shares. It was Cecil who would be relied upon to have found out the 'true story' behind the conventionally delivered tale on the front page of the other papers. It was his friendship with Cecil Chesterton, surely, which led to that lifetime habit of Belloc's (if he were in the country and you were visiting him from London) of asking 'What is the news?' He meant, what has somebody found out? What is being kept secret? It is the journalistic habit of mind behind the great phrase *I Think We Should Be Told*.

Cecil's much more amiable brother Gilbert, on the other hand, was surely a supremely obvious case of the journalist who fell into the second category. Possibly no one in this century – possibly no one in the history of the English language – has poured out such a stream of delightful comments upon the world through the medium of popular journalism. There has never been anyone in his league; reliably amusing, reliably opinionated and quirky, he could fashion his essays and thoughts into delightful shapes for almost any occasion or purpose. And if that did not make him a rarity – an editor's dream – one has to add that although his characteristic mode is to differ from the intellectuals and political thinkers of his day, to point out the wrong-headedness and absurdity of most of what passes for thought through the brains of clever men, there is never a breath of malice or satire in anything he said or wrote. To be devastating without malice – to be funny without whimsy or coyness – surely these are great qualities of an essayist. And in the whole bulk of Chesterton's work – as a critic, as an apologist for Distributism, as a political commentator, as an anecdotalist – we find abundant evidence of his skills as a columnist.

But it is not simply the desire to be paradoxical which makes me dissatisfied with these divisions and categorisations. For I would say firmly that if the division has to be made between discoverers and commentators – between men who told us what was really the news, and between those who told us what to think about it – I would be more inclined to place Gilbert Chesterton in the first category, not the second.

One of the most interesting pieces of news that Chesterton ever discovered was to be found on the front page of *The Times* in May 1874, and it was that he had been born. As he was to write later: 'Children are grateful when Santa Claus puts in their stockings gifts of toys or sweets. Could I not be grateful to Santa Claus when he put in my stockings the gift of two miraculous legs? We thank people for birthday presents of cigars and slippers. Can I thank no one for the birthday present of birth?'

Chesterton has told us – most notably in *Orthodoxy*, and in his *Autobiography*, as well as in what is I suppose his greatest work, *The Everlasting Man* – how, from this first surprising and extraordinary experience (of being born) he flirted with the various ideological possibilities on offer to a young man in the 1890s. Though always deeply moral, there was much in *La Décadence* which appealed to

208

his nature – its sensuous love of words for their own sake, its rich enjoyment of colour, its quest for romance in the dullness and grubbiness of commercial, late nineteenth-century England. Equally, and as an offshoot of the Aesthetic Movement, there was much which appealed to the innately religious nature of Chesterton in such organisations as the Order of the Golden Dawn. Similarly, his compassion and his common sense were appalled by the economic injustices of the time, by the plight of the poor. So it should come as no surprise to learn that he flirted with a form of Christian socialism, nor that, at the time of the Boer War, or in the early days of his friendship with Belloc, Chesterton should have been attracted to the radical wing of the Liberal Party. 'As much as I ever did,' he wrote in 1908 when his head had cleared, 'I believe in Liberalism. But there was a rosy time of innocence when I believed in Liberals.'

Through all this ideological pilgrimage, Chesterton moved, not as an amateur philosopher, who was deciding for the sake of effect to change his pose, but with the excitement of a young investigative journalist who was finding something out. Six years before he died, scientists discovered a new exciting planet that no one knew very much about, and they called it Pluto. Chesterton's achievement as a writer was that fifty-five years before the discovery of Pluto, he discovered an absolutely fascinating planet called Earth, and he discovered that what most of the so-called experts and wiseacres had told us about it was not true.

Chesterton's excitement at the extraordinariness of the ordinary is the beginning of his great scoop.

> The sun rises every morning. I do not rise every morning: but the variation is due not to my activity, but to my inaction. Now, to put the matter in a popular phrase, it might be true that the sun rises regularly because he never gets tired of rising. His routine might be due, not to a lifelessness, but to a rush of life. The thing I mean can be seen, for instance, in children, when they find some game or joke that they specifically enjoy. A child kicks his legs rhythmically through excess, not absence of life. Because children have abounding vitality, because they are in spirit fierce and free, therefore they want things repeated and unchanged. They always say, 'Do it again'; and the grown-up person does it again until he is nearly dead. For grown-up persons are not strong enough to exult in monotony. But perhaps God is strong enough to exult in monotony. It is possible that God says every morning 'Do it again' to the moon. It may be not automatic necessity that makes all daisies alike: it may be that God makes every daisy separately, but has never got tired

209

of making them. It may be that He has the eternal appetite of infancy: for we have sinned and grown old and our Father is younger than we . . .

Since G. K. Chesterton died, we have all learnt rather more than the scientists of his generation and age knew about the universe, and its simple extraordinariness has eluded, as Chesterton said it always would, the strictures and simplicities of grown-up scientific categorisation. We now know that atoms themselves are charged with energy. Victorian scientists thought that stones were lifeless. We know that stones pulsate with as much life as tigers. Almost all the scientific absolutism which went on in Chesterton's lifetime has been shown to be false, almost all that categorisation of the universe as if it were manageable, or explicable.

Chesterton recalls in his autobiography going to a dinner at *The Clarion*, one of the many defunct papers of his youth edited by Mr. Robert Blatchford. Chesterton had just published *Orthodoxy*, and it was from the position of Christian orthodoxy that he argued in public debate with old Blatchford who was an atheist, a socialist and a materialist. After his exchange with Blatchford Chesterton sat down next to

> one of those very refined and rather academic gentlemen from Cambridge who seemed to form so considerable a section of the rugged stalwarts of Labour. There was a cloud on his brow, as if he were beginning to be puzzled about something; and he said suddenly, with abrupt civility, 'Excuse me asking, Mr. Chesterton, of course I shall quite understand if you prefer not to answer, and I shan't think any the worse of it, you know, even if it's true. But I suppose I'm right in thinking you don't really *believe* in those things you're defending against Blatchford.' His cold and refined face did not move a visible muscle; and yet I knew in some fashion it had completely altered. 'Oh, you *do*,' he said, 'I beg your pardon. Thank you . . .' and he went on eating . . . But I was sure that for the rest of the evening, despite his calm, he felt as if he were sitting next to a fabulous griffin . . .

But while thousands of his fellow countrymen were turning away from the Apostle's Creed and finding more of interest and of gratification in the *News Chronicle* or the *Morning Post*, Chesterton was able to shock them back into the discovery that the Apostle's Creed was news: very good news, and very much truer news than one was likely to read in the newspapers.

It was his conviction in the simple and literal truth of Christianity which colours everything that he wrote. When you first kindly asked me to address you, there were so many aspects of Chesterton's writing and life which I should like to have saluted. I should like to have spoken about his crime fiction. A fascinating evening could be spent (not fascinating because of the eloquence of the speaker, but fascinating because of the contents of the subject before him) considering Chesterton's political and economic ideas. One could spin out several hilarious evenings doing nothing except repeat Chesterton's jokes, or rouse one's listeners by recitations of his poetry. I could equally have spoken of Chesterton as one of the most percipient literary critics. But in all these things, there would have been an everlasting return to the subject of Chesterton's religion. For I do not know many other writers whose religion colours everything they wrote in the manner or degree that this is true for Chesterton. Nor, as my far from conclusive list of his range as a writer demonstrates, was Chesterton always banging the same drum or playing the same tunes. Far from it. But behind it all there is the hard and simple conviction that the teachings of the Christian Church were quite literally true.

If it is partly this fact – that he believed in the Church – which added to the flavour of excitement, the tone of breathless astonishment when he came to write about religion itself. For he knew that 'the Christian Church was a living teacher not a dead one . . .'

> Plato has told you a truth, but Plato is dead. Shakespeare has startled you with an image; but Shakespeare will not startle you with any more. But imagine what it would be to live with such men still living, to know that Plato might break out with an original lecture tomorrow, or that at any moment Shakespeare might shatter everything with a single song. The man who lives in contact with what he believes to be a living Church is a man always expecting to meet Plato and Shakespeare tomorrow at breakfast.

This was an insight into Catholicism which he had formed while being a reasonably lethargic member of the Church of England. But he develops it in *The Everlasting Man*, some twenty years later, with his insight that 'The Faith is not a survival. It is not as if the Druids had managed somehow to survive somewhere for two thousand years . . . It has not survived; it has returned again and again in this western world of rapid change and institutions perpetually perishing . . . The Church in the West was not in a world where things

211

were too old to die; but in one in which they were always young enough to get killed.'

This insight into the perpetually youthful nature of the living Church (of God saying 'Do it again') might well have surprised as many Catholics as Protestants when he wrote it in 1928. For at the period when Chesterton became a Roman Catholic, there were many people who believed that the Church was not a divinely revivified and everlastingly young, living body but something much more like a monolithic druidic survival. In fact, I believe, it was the extent to which the Church of England *was* something of a druidic survival which made Chesterton so unenthusiastic a member of it. And it was the extent to which it appeared to have lost hold on a sense of the truth, the literal truth, of the Christian Gospel, which made him want to leave it. We all remember his feelings about the row which blew up after the First War about the memorial to the slain in Beaconsfield, and the feeling, which disturbed him so much, of a *concession* being made when the committee allowed the memorial to be a crucifix. 'And if anyone wants to know my feelings about a point on which I touch rarely and with reluctance: the relation of the Church I left to the Church I joined, there is the answer as compact and concrete as a stone image. I do not want to be in a religion in which I am *allowed* to have a crucifix, I feel the same about the much more controversial question of the honour paid to the Blessed Virgin. If people do not like that cult, they are quite right not to be Catholics. But in people who are Catholics I want the idea not only liked but loved and loved ardently and above all proudly proclaimed . . .'

Now the point of all this, the thing on which it all hinges, is not a matter of taste, but a matter of fact. I do not think Chesterton would have minded remaining a member of a Church many of whose bishops suspected Catholics of idolatry in their attitude to the Blessed Virgin if he did not know perfectly well that there were also bishops in that Church who did not believe in her virginity. Similarly, in the matter of crucifixes; if all the Anglican authorities feared was a revival of idolatry, or a growth of profanity, Chesterton might have stayed where he was. But he knew perfectly well that there were figures such as Barnes of Birmingham and Hensley Henson of Durham, not to mention his friend Dean Inge of St. Paul's, who did not really believe what the Apostle's Creed taught about that figure on the crucifix. They did not really believe, as

212

Chesterton really believed, that the whole of human history, the whole of the human condition had been fundamentally and actually altered by the Incarnation, Passion, Death and Resurrection of Christ.

I consider his description of Easter not merely one of the finest passages of his prose, but also one of the best statements of Christian theology to be found in the English language.

> They took the body down from the cross and one of the few rich men among the first Christians obtained permission to bury it in a rock tomb in his garden; the Romans setting a military guard lest there should be some riot and attempt to recover the body. There was once more a natural symbolism in these natural proceedings; it was well that the tomb should be sealed with all the secrecy of ancient eastern sepulture and guarded by the authority of the Caesars. For in that second cavern the whole of that great and glorious humanity which we call antiquity was gathered up and covered over, and in that place it was buried. It was the end of a very great thing called human history; the history that was merely human. The mythologies and the philosophies were buried there, the gods and the heroes and the sages. In the great Roman phrase they had lived. But as they could only live, so they could only die; and they were dead.
>
> On the third day the friends of Christ coming at daybreak to the place found the grave empty and the stone rolled away. In varying ways they realised the new wonder; but they hardly realised that the world had died in the night. What they were looking at was the first day of a new creation, with a new heaven and a new earth; and in a semblance of the gardener God walked again in the garden, in the cool not of the evening but the dawn.

Although he wrote these words at the very crown of his career as a writer, we may be certain that he had believed them for well over half his life. He believed that we were living in a new age, and that everything was coloured by that dawn in the garden of the resurrection: our relationship to one another as political entities in society; our relationship to the natural world; our relationship to our past, and to our future. It sounds like a scoop which is very nearly two thousand years late, and which had already been 'blown' long before, to readers in Rome, Colossae and Ephesus. But, as the very word 'Gospel' indicates, it always does remain news, and its implications are new for each succeeding generation, managing to blind itself with different varieties of claptrap. In each generation, therefore, the Christian reaction against claptrap will be different.

213

Chesterton himself saw this as the function of the saint. 'The saint is a medicine because he is an antidote. He will generally be found restoring the world to sanity by exaggerating whatever the world neglects, which is by no means the same element in every age.'

The remark comes, as you will recognise, towards the beginning of his masterly little book about St. Thomas Aquinas. For Chesterton, the saint is one who comes fully into his or her own during an age which is completely at variance with the manner in which they lived or thought. In England, therefore, it was during the materialistic age of Queen Victorian that St. Francis of Assisi enjoyed greatest popularity. 'In a world that was too stolid, Christianity returned in the form of a vagabond.' Similarly, he saw that in the post-First War decades of Dada and Surrealism, of fascism and communism, of the triumph, that is, of irrationality, there was a resurgence of need for the saint who was most logical: Aquinas. My guess would be that in this very idea, of the Christian light shining most brightly where the contrast to it is strongest, we discover some of the reasons why Chesterton has endured in this twentieth century which seems so much at variance with many of the things he believed in and stood for. It may well be, in these terms, that Chesterton has not yet had his hour and that there will arise a new generation even more out of tune with his sanity than our own, who will be led back to the knowledge of Chesterton, which it needs.

I thought of him not long ago when I was seated in a train and surveying the majestic heights and the storm-filled sky and the windswept trees of the landscape outside the windows. It was unquestionably one of the most romantic views in England, yet I was in a county which is a byword for dullness and suburban absence of poetry. I am speaking of Surrey.

It was one of those old-fashioned trains with a corridor and a child with his mother, who had just got on at Gatwick airport, was struggling along with his luggage. When he saw the compartment in which I was sitting with a number of grown-up people, he exclaimed, 'What a funny room!' And all these so-called grown-ups laughed at him in a way which was somehow unpleasant. The boy turned on his heels and went in search of a compartment to himself, and I did not blame him. Once you looked at it, of course, the compartment was a very funny room indeed. It was the room which was funny, not his remark. But the grown-ups had almost certainly

214

lost their sense of humour with their vision, had laughed at the child and not at the room.

Chesterton had no difficulty in being able to keep alive within himself the child's simplicity of vision which can see things as they are, and not as the dulled eyes of habit makes us see them. He made the point himself very vigorously when he was analysing the poetry of Browning. 'To present a matter in a grotesque manner does certainly tend to touch the nerve of surprise and thus to draw attention to the intrinsically miraculous character of the object itself. It is difficult to give examples of the proper use of grotesqueness without becoming too grotesque. But we should all agree that if St. Paul's Cathedral were suddenly presented to us upside down we should, for the moment, be more surprised at it, look at it more than we have done all the centuries during which it has rested on its foundations. Now it is the supreme function of the philosopher of the grotesque to make the world stand on its head that the people may look at it.'

Many people think of G. K. Chesterton as a philospher of the grotesque and doubtless he felt tempted to become one himself. But in spite of sorties into grotesquerie in his fiction, he was in fact the reverse of grotesque. He was a realist. It is only the environment in which he worked, that of materialist, agnostic England in the first three decades of this twentieth century, which might make him appear to be fantastical: a fabulous griffin. As I say, I had this thought in a funny room looking out over the romance which is Surrey, and I knew that not far across the hills in that lovely stretch of country my old friend John Stewart Collis lay buried in Abinger churchyard. Collis remains a much-neglected writer, but he shared with Chesterton this wonderful ability to make you see that the world we inhabit is a truly remarkable and astonishing place; not at all to be taken for granted. You get the flavour of Collis's work in his assertion that when we are children we think there is something magical about getting a rabbit out of a hat; but there is really something much more magical about getting a rabbit out of a rabbit.

Shortly before he died, I went to see Collis and we both knew, I suppose, that we were talking to one another for the last time. He had been lolling on his bed in a grey tracksuit, feeling fairly ropey, but he got up at the mention of Chesterton and stared out of his bedroom window across the rolling fields. 'People,' he said in his

215

angry Irish voice, 'people make out that Chesterton was only interested in weaving paradoxes and that they were mere figures of
speech. But they weren't figures of speech at *all*. For the longer you
look at the world, the more you realise that the truth is the precise
opposite of what most people suppose it to be.'

I agree with Collis's words, and I know that does not commit me
to a belief in the infallibility of Chesterton. Sometimes he doodled
with words, sometimes he made false political judgements, sometimes he exaggerated, sometimes he predicted things which were
simply wrong. Moreover, sad to say, the political and economic
system which he developed as a result of Belloc's inspiration, that of
Distributism, never got off the ground and is never likely to.

But I do think the majority of what he wrote was right because it
was right-headed and true because he understood the ultimate
truths. And the manifestation which makes me surest of this is in his
humour. 'I do not like seriousness,' he wrote in one of his best essays,
'I think it is irreligious. Or, if you prefer the phrase, it is the fashion of
all false religions.' In the same essay, he talks of religions which
worship animals and of the modern habit of taking animals too
seriously. Hence in a large measure I suspect the slight bee he had in
his bonnet about the absurdity of vegetarianism: 'I am quite prepared
to love a rhinoceros, with reasonable precautions: he is, doubtless, a
delightful father to the young rhinoceros. But I will not promise not
to laugh at a rhinoceros. I will not worship the beast with the little
horn. I will not adore the Golden Calf; still less will I adore the fatted
calf. On the contrary I will eat him. There is some sort of joke about
eating an animal, or even about an animal eating you. Let us hope we
will perceive it the proper amount, if it ever occurs.'

When I quoted his idea that saints are antidotes to a poison, it was
chiefly of his humour that I was thinking, for his humour grew
directly out of his religious beliefs. It is, generally speaking, those
who do not believe in religion who think of it as a purely solemn
subject, whereas those who do are able to see that religion, while
having many humorous outward signs, is also, in its essence, the
source of all humour. For nothing emphasises as much as religion
the supremely comic divergence between our vision of ourselves
and the reality, between our aspirations and our actual achievements. These things, for an irreligious person, are sources of tragedy
– but for a religious person, even failure itself can be funny. By a
similar token, an unbeliever would think it improper to talk about

religion in a pub,* whereas for Chesterton who believed in a God who chose to be born in a pub, the matter would seem entirely appropriate.

Chesterton then, in his humour, reveals his religious stance most fully and delightfully to a noseless generation who failed to sniff out the riches of God's world: there was one thing (you remember) 'that was too great for God to show us when He walked upon our earth; and I have sometimes fancied [wrote Chesterton] it was His mirth'. It was his sense of the mirth of God which was Chesterton's greatest scoop. He thought we should be told, and this makes Chesterton such a wholesome antidote to the humourlessness of our age, to our sad and solemn contemporaries who haven't got no noses . . .

> They haven't got no noses,
> The Fallen sons of Eve;
> Even the smell of roses
> Is not what they supposes
> But more than mind discloses
> And more than men believe.
>
> The brilliant smell of water,
> The brave smell of a stone,
> The smell of dew and thunder,
> The old bones buried under
> Are things in which they blunder
> And err if left alone.
>
> The wind from winter forests,
> The scent of scentless flowers,
> The breath of bride's adorning,
> The smell of snare and warning,
> The smell of Sunday morning
> God gave to us for ours.
>
> And Quoodle here discloses
> All things that Quoodle can.
> They haven't got no noses,
> They haven't got no noses,
> And goodness only knowses
> The Noselessness of Man.

Address given to the G. K. Chesterton Society, 17 September 1984

* This talk was given in The Devereux, off The Strand.

# Montague Summers

Montague Summers died in Richmond on 10 August 1948, aged sixty-nine. As he had requested, they placed him in his coffin dressed in soutane, amice, alb, girdle and violet Mass vestments. Also buried with him in the Richmond cemetery were his biretta, his ivory crucifix, his rosary, his much-thumbed breviary and the coat which had belonged to his (deceased) dog Tango. The rites were performed hugger-mugger by a Roman Catholic priest in the presence of only a handful of people.

Buried too were a multitude of 'secrets' of his own invention. This was a man who was reported to have seen the Devil. When asked if the Prince of Darkness really had a goat's head, horns and a forked tail, he replied in his high-pitched, lisping voice, 'No *tail*, my dear'. Rumours of Satanism, sexual perversion and skulduggery hovered about him all his adult life. But he was more justly famous as a prodigiously learned and prolific man of letters; an authority on the Restoration Drama and the Gothic Novel; and a leading influence on the English theatre during the 1920s and 1930s.

These things are made clear by the all too brief memoir of Summers by J. Jerome (1965), to which Sybil Thorndyke wrote a loving introduction; and they deserve remembering. He is too often thought of merely as a dabbler in the occult (for his book *The Vampire in Europe*, for instance, he claimed to have made first-hand investigations) and as a disturbingly accomplished pornographer. When he died he had just completed a volume of autobiography and for some reason we have had to wait till now to see it in print.* Very welcome it is.

Summers was born into a prosperous banker's family in Bristol, one of several brothers and sisters. This volume begins with early memories of his father's library at Tellisford House, Clifton Down, where, at least,

---

* *The Galanty Show*, Montague Summers (1980).

we could be quiet and in peace, of a winter afternoon chair-croodled over a blazing fire; on a July day in the embowerment of soft-cushioned window-seat with a vista of green lawn below, a grass plot in the centre of which a young laughing Triton scattered from his wreathed horn crystal drops of water that sparkled and diamonded in the sunlight as they disported and comminuted over a surface of the rock-girt pond where swam – an eternal fascination to watch – the great fat lazy goldfish, Chinese carp we called them, the lotus-eaters of the pool.

The library was well-equipped and it was here that day after day Summers imbibed an immense store of idiosyncratic and haphazard learning. The passage just quoted, saccharine by the austere standards of later decades, prepares one for his boyhood tastes. He liked the Renaissance Latin poets better than the classical and considered Mrs. Henry Wood an altogether better read than George Eliot. His father was evidently a cultivated man, but his tastes were rigidly wholesome. *Don Juan* was kept locked away in a cupboard with the brandy decanters; and it was suggested when the young 'Monty' was discovered reading *Tom Jones* that he lock that away also in case his sister should find it lying about the house.

> It was fatal to hesitate in the library and to say, 'I want something light to read, just a novel.' The answer inevitably came, 'Read one of Trollope's, my boy.' At last I made reply one fine day, 'I've read all Trollope's.' Of course I had not; but I thought I might score. No such thing. The answer came pat, 'Read them over again then. They will bear reading two or three times.' A sentiment with which I cannot agree.

Trollope had regularly played whist with Summers's father at the Garrick Club when the old gentleman was up in London. Summers believed it was Trollope's business acumen which his father admired rather than any literary quality. For the boy, W. Harrison Ainsworth and 'Monk' Lewis were in every way superior; and *John Inglesant* brought comfort which 'few other books (save those that are of divine inspiration) can give'.

Summers also had a passion for plays. Like Chesterton, his favourite toy as a growing child was his puppet theatre, and from an early age he began to collect old plays in Bristol bookshops; he was also familiar with Wycherley, Otway and Congreve at a date when most of their work had been practically forgotten by the cultivated world.

219

Summers's delight in seeing himself as an anachronism is well illustrated by a story he tells of his schooldays at Clifton, where he went as a dayboy in the 1890s. His English master – the brother of a future Prime Minister – was teaching the boys *The Rape of the Lock*.

> We came to the party at ombre in the third canto. 'You will have mainly to rely on the notes for this,' Asquith warned us. 'I do not know how to play ombre, and I don't suppose there are twenty people today who could teach us . . . We shall get the outline of the game more or less. You may be sure the examiner won't ask you to play a game of cards.' And looking round with a smile, he continued, 'Do any of you here play ombre, by any chance?' A rhetorical question obviously. The form laughed. I put up my hand. Asquith said, 'Well, what is it?' 'I play ombre, sir.'

After he left Clifton, Montague Summers went up to Trinity College, Oxford, where he read Greats and eventually got a Fourth. Temperamental differences between himself and his father had become more acutely obvious by this stage in his career. His father was a no-nonsense Low Churchman; the young Summers delighted in the ritualistic worship of All Saints', Clifton, and had even, horror of horrors, nipped in now and again to the Roman Catholic pro-cathedral. His fascination with old drama was undiminished, too, with all the danger it involved of being exposed to the scabrous language and practices of a more dissolute age. A college friend of those days recalls how things came to a head during one long vacation when Summers *père*, purple with rage, came into the library, tossed down a book and spluttered, 'Is this filthy thing yours?' It was *The Ballad of Reading Gaol*.

> Monty picked up the book, closed it carefully, reverently pressing the strained and damaged covers together, and in a very gentle voice replied, 'Yeth, Father' – of course he could pronounce an 's' as clearly as the next man, but, because he wanted to annoy and knew that it teased, he would often adopt a ridiculous lisp – 'Yeth, Father! I have read all the workth of the Mathter.'

It will come as no surprise to those acquainted with the byways of ecclesiastical history to learn that Montague Summers's chosen profession was sought in the Church. He attended Lichfield Theological College from 1903 to 1905, eight years before Alfred Hope Patten, the restorer of the cult of Our Lady of Walsingham, entered the same establishment. Summers was a devout and popular seminarian, who burnt joss sticks in his room and wore purple socks during Lent. A friend described him as 'always an interesting, entertaining and, I think, gay is the right word, companion'. He was made deacon by Dr. Forrest Browne, the Bishop of Bristol in 1908. For some reason, he served his title in the diocese of Bath and Wells, but he soon went for his second curacy to a suburban church in Bitton, Bristol, where the vicar was an eccentric man called Canon Ellacombe, who had been ordained in 1847. Summers showed a friend the tombstone in the churchyard over the grave of the vicar's wife, who had died many years before. Under her name and the dates of her birth and death were inscribed Canon Ellacombe's name, with the date of his birth and an exactly predicted date of his death. On that very day, a few years later, the old man died in his sleep. (Similar stories were told of Burton, author of *The Anatomy of Melancholy*; whether they 'suggested' the story of Canon Ellacombe one cannot be sure.)

Summers's career as a curate came to an abrupt end in 1909 when he and another clergyman were prosecuted on a charge of pederasty. The other clergyman was condemned and Summers was acquitted, but he nevertheless felt he had to leave the parish; a few months later he was received into the Roman Church at St. Joseph's, Kingswood (Bristol). On 9 September 1910, at the age of thirty-one, he entered the seminary of Wonersh, near Guildford, with a view to becoming a priest of the Latin rite. For some reason, this little adventure lasted even less long than his career in the Church of England. He received the tonsure – and probably minor orders – from the Roman Catholic bishop of Southwark on 28 December 1910; but after that date his exact ecclesiastical status becomes clouded with uncertainty. Some believe that he was raised to the Roman diaconate; it has even been said that he was once seen acting as deacon at a High Mass in the Roman pro-cathedral in Clifton. It is certain that he *was* subsequently raised to the priesthood, but how or when will probably never be known.

The likeliest explanation is that he was priested by an *episcopus vagans*, Ulric Vernon Herford. This holy man, otherwise known as Mar Jacobus, was the Bishop of Mercia and of Middlesex, the administrator of the Metropolitan See of India and Ceylon and of the Syro-Chaldean Church and of the Patriarchate of Babylon and the East; he was also the founder of something called the Evangelical Catholic Communion.

Herford was certainly a bishop in as full, historic and apostolic sense as the Pope himself, a fact no Catholic theologian has ever questioned; but his following was somewhat smaller. His pro-cathedral was a small red-brick building in Percy Street, off the Iffley Road in Oxford; and if Summers was ordained in England it was probably here that it happened. As was so often the case with men who were ordained in this canonically heterodox manner, Summers almost certainly got himself conditionally reordained in Italy, whether by a Roman bishop on the sly, or by another *episcopus vagans*, we shall never know. Possibly he was even raised to the purple. During his five years of adult life in Oxford – 1929–34 – he frequently entertained at his house, 43, Broad Street, wearing full canonicals for dinner: a purple stock; black cassock; a wide black silk cincture with a purple fringe at least a foot deep; and large silver buckles on his patent leather shoes. It is easy enough to sneer at all this sort of thing; and there are plenty of people belonging to larger sects who have been eager to decry such uncanonical procedure. On balance, the record seems to have been that Summers was a devout man. His breviary was recited daily. At least one devotee – the Hon. Mrs. Greville-Nugent, for whom he said Mass in her private oratory in Hove – regarded him as a saint. And if not a saint, he was, for all their unwillingness to accept him, a devout and regular worshipper at Roman Catholic conventicles. Father Arthur Tooth, that great Anglican saint (imprisoned for wearing the maniple), was charitable enough to recognise Summers's merits and allowed him to take part, fully vested, in the annual Corpus Christi procession at Woodside Convent, Croydon.

Alas, much as one would like to hear Summers's own account of all these things, the volume of ecclesiastical reminiscences which he intended to compose was never written; and the present memoir is limited almost exclusively to his literary reflections.

He does not give much of himself away, except his opinions. Everyone who knows Oxford will lament with him the demolition of the houses at the end of Broad Street, his own among them, 'in order to erect that superfluous monstrosity, the New Bodleian, a memorial of a silly woman's vacant and resultless vacuity'. In literary matters, for all his adulation of the Spooky, the Occult, and the Popish, he is perhaps most outspoken in his criticism of people one would have expected him to admire. He had no time for Aleister Crowley, 'one quarter conjuror and three quarters charlatan and whole common publicist'. He did not, although he liked Yeats personally, join the Order of the Golden Dawn. Ronald Knox doubtless had his temperament under more melancholy control than did Summers, but one would have thought them, from this distance of time, to have had much in common: both brilliant men with a priestly vocation, but with no desire to do anything with their lives except doodle in the trivial byways of literature.

Yet Summers complains at the way that Evelyn Waugh can 'overgush with praise of the literary graces of Monsignor Ronald Knox'; and, when one thinks about it, Summers really seems the more solid figure of the two. Similarly, it may come as a shock for some readers to hear him dismissing Graham Greene in these terms: 'To my mind, *Brighton Rock* lacks sincerity and rings untrue. Whence I conclude that Mr. Graham Greene is not a competent writer.'

The memoirs dart about from one subject to another: ghosts and witchcraft; the salon of Emerald, Lady Cunard, who was one of his greatest admirers; the friendship of Saki and Edmund Gosse. Behind all these memories is hidden the sheer labour and plod of his achievement. *Nulla Dies Sine Linea*, he quotes as the motto of his friend Stewart Mason Ellis. It might have been his own. Before his emergence on the scene, for instance, the Gothic Novel was all but forgotten. His *The Gothic Quest* and *Gothic Bibliography* were pioneer works in what is now regarded as an important literary field. Until his encouragement of the society known as The Phoenix – the purpose of which was to promote the performance of forgotten dramatists – almost no one in England had read and no one had seen such works as *The Country Wife*. His studies, *The Restoration Theatre* and *The Playhouse of Pepys*, have perhaps dated and been superseded: but they are works of phenomenal liveliness and fullness and erudition. In addition, he produced the Nonesuch editions of the complete works of Wycherley, Otway, Dryden and Congreve, and helped prepare John Hayward's edition of the Earl of Rochester.

The admirably learned *Bibliography of the Works of Montague Summers* (1964) by Timothy d'Arch Smith gives a full account of his labours. All this was, as is shown by the modesty of his autobiographical writing, lightly borne. And one captures in the pages of *The Galanty Show* (overwritten though the purple passages unquestionably are) much of what made him a celebrated and amusing conversationalist. One rather assumes that with so many books and so many literary and theatrical preoccupations, and so many famous friends, here were careers enough for two lives. The memoir conceals the fact that for much of his adult life he was a schoolmaster. Among other posts, he was an assistant master in the Junior School of the Central School of Arts and Crafts in Holborn. Then, in 1922, he became senior English master at Brockley County School in south-east London. The boys called him 'Wiggy', for reasons which are obvious if one looks at his photograph: a pudgy, clever face, framed with thick curls which cling to the side of his head like earmuffs. He was a successful schoolmaster, much loved and respected by his pupils. He was obviously one of those extra-ordinary men who managed to read widely, write enormously, and still have time and energy left for a full-time professional occupation.

It was his own hair, of course, not a wig. That seems right. As with so many men of religious genius, it is impossible to distinguish in Summers the phoney and the real thing. For all his affectations, he was his own man. Pederast he may have been, pornographer he certainly was. To this day, if you order up some of his books from the Bodleian Library, they can only be read under supervision; then some blushing library assistant locks the volumes away in a cup-board in his office, just as Summers's father all those years ago, locked away *Don Juan* in the Library at Tellisford House. How much that would have pleased him.

*Times Literary Supplement*, 30 October 1977

# The Lost Leader

It so happened that, just before I opened the second volume of Nicholas Mosley's life of his father,* I had been re-reading my favourite novel about a political fanatic. Born of a diabolically unpleasant aristocratic line, Redgauntlet has channelled many of his more disagreeable congenital characteristics into political fervour. For him, there is an answer to everything. He despises the English not merely because he is a Jacobite and a Scot, but because of their combination of intellectual woolliness with moral smugness. Darsie Latimer, our young hero, tried to suggest that 'an Englishman's best privilege' is freedom. He receives the crushingly absurd reply (true fanatics always love to generalise), 'The privilege of free action belongs to no mortal.'

Darsie Latimer, of course, does not realise it at the time, but he is Redgauntlet's son. Scott's novel is therefore partly a political adventure story about a man who fails to see that his obsolete political creed was doomed to failure from its birth. It is also the story of a young man coming to terms with his monstrous father, and finding that there is something to love and admire even in his doggedness. There are few more heroic moments in literature than when, parting from his son on the shore, old Redgauntlet says that the doom has departed from his house, 'since its present representative has adhered to the winning side. I am convinced that he will not change it, should it in turn become the losing one.'

Within hours of wiping away a manly tear at this scene, I was in Holloway Prison in 1943. A young British Army officer has smuggled a bottle of brandy and some gramophone records into the cell. A meal has just been enjoyed, cooked by the prisoner's wife, who shares his apartments. There have been aubergines cultivated by the prisoner himself on his own allotment, and *fraises du bois*.

* *Beyond the Pale: Sir Oswald Mosley 1933–1980*, Nicholas Mosley (1983).

And now, his earnest and religious young son wants to discuss Nietzsche. Kirsten Flagstad shrieks the airs of Wagner's Isolde on 'the gram', as they call it; and the older man tries to explain to the younger why Nietzsche valued the unlikeable quality of *Härte*, hardness or cruelty. Lest he missed the point Sir Oswald Mosley wrote to his son about it as soon as the conversation was over. 'Re *Härte*, the old boy would probably reply – "No beauty nor nobility in *Härte*, agreed; but what have men (majority) done to Beauty and Nobility – destroyed the one and persecuted the other. What then is the answer of the emerging *Ubermensch* to this situation except *Härte*?"'

The ludicrously Wodehousian phrase 'the old boy' to describe the sinister Teutonic philosopher is a tiny indication of the vast dichotomy which lay at the heart of Oswald Mosley's mystery. *Beyond the Pale* makes no attempt to displace Robert Skidelsky's straight account of that extraordinary political career. Nor, like his first volume, *Rules of the Game*, does it make any attempt to view Oswald Mosley dispassionately. It is not the story which we already know of Mosley's public life, but the story of Nicholas Mosley's relationship with his father. He moved from a position of absolute hero worship, and toeing of the Party Line, to a feeling, after his father's imprisonment, of intimacy and love. Throughout the thirties, Oswald Mosley had been so taken up with politics and social life that there had not been much time for conversation with his stammering and hopelessly neurotic first-born son. In prison, there was a flowering of the rarest and most awkwardly managed form of love, that of a son for his father. In time, of course, Nicholas Mosley saw the limitations of Nietzsche, and came to see, in Christianity, qualities stronger than *Härte*. Through the influence of an Anglican monk, a brilliant spiritual director as well as a pacifist of the extreme left (Father Raymond Raynes C.R.) he threw off the fascist yoke, and of course, in so doing, was estranged from his father. He writes of his father's political procilvities as though they were a species of addiction like alcoholism. A couple of years after the war, for instance, Nicholas Mosley drove his father and stepmother to a pub in the East End for a Party reunion. 'My father had been the joking family father in the back of the car; now he became urgent, with his chin up, striding.'

It might be said that the whole book revolves around this contrast, and Nicholas Mosley's puzzlement at it. In more glorious

226

days, 1939, Sir Oswald had filled the Earl's Court stadium and held twenty thousand people in thrall with his magnetic rant. After the two-hour harangue, he repaired to his mother's flat for dinner. 'Suddenly he put his head round the door so that he was like a clown popping his head through the curtain; he looked mock penitent. Someone said "You promised!" He came into the room and gave himself a pat on the behind and said "Naughty!" This was a reference to a promise he had given to my Aunt Baba that in his speech he would say nothing unpleasant about her friend Lord Halifax!'

The scene dissolves into English laughter, and Mosley *fils* is left gazing upon it, as upon the whole of his father's life, with chilled puzzlement. He evolves the theory that there was a complete split and division in what another author has described as 'a life of contrasts'. The fanatic, for instance, poured £100,000 of his own money into the movement, and made hypnotic speeches in which he denounced the usurers and international financiers who were bleeding our economy. But the clever country gentleman, who was the other side of this split personality, easily recouped the £100,000 by wise speculation on the Stock Exchange. Nicholas Mosley implies that the reason few members of the British Union formed part of the Leader's social circle was that there was a complete dichotomy between the smiling, clever, family man, and the raving, blackshirt revolutionary. It may have been so. But then, his mother and both his wives were fervent Party activists and few supporters of the B.U.F. would have been the sort 'one would have in the house'. The mystery, at the end of two volumes, remains a mystery, of how anyone with any sense of humour at all (Sir Oswald's was clearly strong) could have arrayed himself in his ridiculous uniform, spewed out nonsense to crowds of roughnecks, and expected the English electorate to take him seriously. Nicholas Mosley, as the mixed-up but ultimately loving son of this most arresting figure, was the last person in the world to be able to give a dispassionate answer to these things. As the professional novelist that he is, he has presented the most rivetingly credible story, and it is only at the end that one finds its credibility spurious. Surely Sir Oswald Mosley *ought* to remain incomprehensible.

One thing which does emerge from this book is how fatally Sir Oswald failed to understand the British temperament and the British people. From 1934 onwards, he could have been studying

Pont's cartoons of the British Character. They would have done him very much more good than his slavish desire to ape foreigners. It was this, I am sure, which people hated about him, more than any of the specific items of his political programme.

All political slogans rebound upon themselves, few more so than the British Union's unexceptionable *Mind Britain's Business!* at the time of the Abyssinian crisis. At the beginning of the war, Mosley was accused of having accepted money from a foreign power. The novelist Henry Williamson, an ardent fascist, said that he and thousands like him would have withdrawn support from the movement had these rumours been true. Mosley denied the rumours hotly, but pointed out that the *Daily Herald* had received over £75,000 of Russian money during the 1920s. Alas, Mosley was lying. As his son has now established (photostats of the documents are here reproduced) the B.U.F. received something like £60,000 per annum between 1933 and 1935 from the Italian Government. Mussolini only withdrew his support when he discovered that Mosley had formed an alliance with Hitler, then out of favour with the *Duce*.

In this, Mussolini failed to grasp a fundamental fact about Mosley's class and nationality at this period, that is, he was wholly the victim of the fatal Victorian pro-Germanism which to the modern taste seems so extraordinary. The image of Sir Oswald sitting in his prison cell during the war, reading Goethe and Nietzsche and playing Wagner on 'the gram' is pathetically absurd. Mosley liked to represent himself as a rebel to his class and culture but almost any reasonably cultivated Victorian or Edwardian gentleman would have chosen the same books and gramophone records for his prison cell. The English governing class, in spite of anti-Hun propaganda which they allowed to circulate in the vulgar press during the First World War, continued to love the Germans. This was the chief reason for their refusal to re-arm, during the 1930s, until it was nearly too late. When they did so, they were able to tell themselves that they were not fighting their beloved Germany, but having a crusade against the Nazis.

But when, since a brief expeditionary Elizabethan fiasco in the Low Countries much discouraged by the government of the day, has Great Britain ever fought an ideological war? Chamberlain declared war on Hitler because he was tangled up in treaties from which he would dearly have loved to extricate himself. Mosley was not alone in pointing this out, but he did so from a curious vantage point. His own pro-Germanism made of the British Union something which in all its trivial forms aped the barbaric bullyboys of the S.S. The Teutonic paramilitary ideal had been tried before in England, and once naturalised, it had been gloriously successful. One of Mosley's closest advisers, Major-General J. F. C. Fuller, pointed out to him that 'Every great movement starts off in a minority of *one* – e.g. The Salvation Army or even the Boy Scouts.' (The Major-General, who emerges from Nicholas Mosley's account like one of the battier eccentrics of Anthony Powell's imagination, was an enthusiast for Aleister Crowley, and had a scheme for imprisoning all the Jews in the world on Madagascar.) Mad as Fuller was, his examples of Baden-Powell and 'General' Booth showed that the English could absorb the paramilitary. With postman's uniforms and brass bands and the music of Arne and Parry, Mosley might have captured many more hearts. Instead, he had to have jackboots, hysterical ranting, street violence ('One must keep the boys happy' was how he justified this to his son), the ceaseless playing of the *Horst Wessel Lied* and slapstick challenges to 'international finance', made not to the family broker who was keeping his portfolio booming, but to the poverty-stricken inhabitants of the East End. The unquestioned folly of all this was sparked off directly by his Edwardian love of the Germans, which had nothing to do with any of the excellent features of his political programme: nothing to do with his Distributist economic principles; nothing to do with his contempt for the ineptitude and humbug of Parliamentary politics; nothing to do with his spiritual and intuitive patriotism. The fact that his more unpleasant followers, like William Joyce, endeavoured to make themselves exactly like Hitlerites of the coarsest grain would have been reason enough to expel them from the B.U.F. if Mosley had really meant the slogan *Mind Britain's Business!* But the more Germanic he became, the less he could be redeemed by humour.

One of the most splendid things about Nicholas Mosley's account is the faith he has come to place in the redemptive power of laughter. He says he has attempted to create an attitude 'by which the darkness in people (there is always darkness) might be made to seem not so much evil as somewhat ridiculous: evil may thus be exorcised: ridiculousness becomes life giving'. Unfortunately, fatally, Oswald Mosley's humour and his politics were kept in quite separate compartments. When Mosley had appendicitis in 1936, Magda Goebbels (who was to arrange their wedding) wrote to Diana Guinness, 'I sincerely hope that the Leader very quickly recovers.' The idea that any individual could be referred to, in private correspondence, as 'the Leader' is hilariously untranslatable into an English context. Having read Lady Mosley's own ironical account of things in *A Life of Contrasts*, and now this story by her stepson, one finds it so extraordinary that any English person could have used the language of fascism seriously that one falls back on the unpleasant thought that it was all a Gargantuan and rather evil 'Mitford tease'.

One feels this particularly in the embarrassing tone which Mosley allowed his followers to adopt when writing of the Jews. Again, as well as being humourless, it is simply un-English to rant against 'submen with prehensile toes' or 'hairy troglodytes who crept out of the ghettoes of Germany to seek sanctuary in the British Museum'.

The tone of General Fuller, William Joyce and the rest was not merely disgusting, expressing what few people thought and no English person would say. It was also foolish, since it lost the British Union its most valued patron, Lord Rothermere, who could not afford to antagonise Jewish advertisers. As it happens, though fascism by its very nature distorts the truth, one can readily believe Lady Mosley's repeated assertion that her husband was the least anti-semitic man she has ever known. The remark takes on a different colouring when one remembers some of the men she *has* known (her father, Dr. Goebbels, and Hitler himself) but there is no reason to doubt it, any more than one questions the testimony, quoted by Nicholas Mosley, of Sir Oswald's black gamekeeper: that in his employer's company alone did he feel no self-consciousness about race.

Lady Mosley, incidentally, emerges from this book extremely well, even from the end note which announces that 'she has asked that it should be made clear that she is not associated in any way with these memoirs, and that she strongly disapproves of many of my interpretations and of the publication of private letters'. Presumably she disapproves of the general public being told that, even after his second marriage, Sir Oswald continued his occasional love affair with 'Baba', sister of his first wife and married to his friend 'Fruity' Metcalfe. She would also have reason to disapprove of the unnecessary malice which prompted Nicholas Mosley to reproduce conversations he allegedly had with his father 'about Mummy and Diana. He used to say, as if he were making a special point of this, of course his second marriage was very good, but his first mariage had been perfect.' This is a perfectly understandable remark for a father to a son. Even had he loved his second wife more, he would not have said so to the boy. In any case, how can such things be judged? But the reproduction of the exchange, indeed the entire publication, is yet another trial to Lady Mosley's steely courage.

'There was a story of how my father and she had been driving once on a mountain road in France and he had had to back the car to turn it and he asked her to look out of the window and tell him when to stop; when the back wheels were half over the precipice, she had murmured, "Vaguely wo".'

In terms of his political aspirations, there is no record of her murmuring 'vaguely wo'. It was she who introduced Sir Oswald to Hitler, after her sister Unity had been entranced by the sight of him in his 'sweet mackintosh' in the Osteria Bavaria restaurant in Munich. She told Nicholas Mosley that her encounter with the Führer had 'ruined my life. And I think it ruined your father's.' That realisation did not prevent her from exhibiting her wedding present from the Führer (signed photograph in frame) well after the beginning of the war. Today, no less than her husband, Lady Mosley is 'beyond the pale'. Radio interviewers, for example, subject her to abusive and insulting questions which would be unthinkable in addressing anyone else. The hounding of the Mosleys since 1940, their imprisonment without trial, and the subsequent concealment of all the evidence relating to that imprisonment, make shaming reading. Normally, all documents are made public after thirty years; but the Attorney-General has decreed that no one must know the truth about Mosley's imprisonment for a hundred years.

As someone asked in another context, which was the face that launched a thousand ships: Sir Oswald Mosley or Sir Stafford Cripps? Doubtless, they wish to suppress the names of English politicians who were sympathetic to Mosley. Perhaps Nicholas Mosley is right in his suggestion that Attlee, Greenwood and the others, who could not forgive Mosley's defection from the Labour Party, would only consent to serve in Churchill's Cabinet on condition that the Leader was locked up. More fundamentally, I believe it had to do with the English feelings of love-hate for Romantics. By making him a martyr, they cast Mosley in the Romantic role, compelling him to suffer as Byron and Oscar Wilde, for different types of Romanticism, had suffered. One of Nicholas Mosley's girlfriends had a father who exclaimed, '"I would rather shake hands with Oscar Wilde than with Oswald Mosley." I told my father this story: I imagined, somewhat naively, that he would laugh, as he laughed about so many of the attitudes struck against him by a crazy world. But he said, "Does her father think I'm a bugger?" Pathetically, he did not quite *see* that he was "beyond the pale".'

Like Wilde, Mosley plunged from martyrdom into squalor. His son only allows us the briefest glimpse of him in old age in Le Temple de la Gloire, drinking pink champagne with his grandchildren, and trying to dissuade them of the truths of Christianity. The unforgettable image which this powerful novelist plants in our minds is twenty-one years earlier, when his father was fighting the election as the Union Movement candidate for North Kensington, in 1959. As a young man in his twenties, when he had left the Conservative Party and stood as an independent, Oswald Mosley still retained his Harrow seat with a majority of over seven thousand. As an old man, 'with his grey hair and grey suit' he lost his deposit, getting less than three thousand of a total of 34,912 votes. 'There was Dad on top of a van again and bellowing.' That 'again' has the painful confessional ring of a child who thought his parent cured of alcoholism, but had come home to find the old man pouring gin into a tooth mug. 'There he was roaring on about such things as black men being able to live on tins of cat food, and teenage girls being kept in attics.' The scene is electrifyingly embarrassing. It led to the great estrangement between the father and his eldest son which colours the shame and pathos of the whole book. The geniality of Sir Oswald at the end is explained, in his view, by the notion that the good side of his nature never wanted the fascist revolution to take place at all; in fact, felt hearty relief at its failure. At the beginning of *Beyond the Pale*, Sir Oswald seems like John Bayley's definition of a Shakespearean tragic hero in 'his unsuitability for the role'. At the end, he seems to have the comic pathos of an old man in Terence Rattigan who creeps off to the slums for cheap thrills.

Nicholas Mosley's account is a devastatingly brilliant story in the unreliable tradition of Gosse's *Father and Son*. He is the *ne plus ultra* example of the boarding-school phenomenon of embarrassment at one's parents' weird appearance or behaviour. Though written by a man of sixty, this book has all the fresh awkwardness of adolescent agony. And in the end, there is dogged filial pride mingled with heartbroken regret that Sir Oswald Mosley forfeited his claim to be thought of as a gentleman. He was not, after all, Redgauntlet, but something rather shabbier.

*Spectator*, 29 October 1983

# British Satire

# Peter Simple

Many people in the darkest days of the 1940s were thankful to the humorists (Pont, I.T.M.A., the Crazy Gang, etc.) for keeping their pecker up. As the lady said, 'the only good fing abart the Blitz is ow it tikes yer moind orf the war'. Later in the century, however, and especially in the Wilson-Heath era of unhappy memory, it was the humorists themselves who were doing the fighting. They were 'the Few' for my generation. They alone seemed able to puncture all the ridiculous cant of politics. And Peter Simple led the van. By looking forward to the day in 2020 when the country was ruled by the Royal Socialist Party with King Norman (heir apparent: Prince Barry of South Wales) and Queen Doreen, one almost feels that Peter Simple is responsible for it not quite happening. Now, as soon as some prize ass in lawnsleeves gets up and starts talking about the miners' strike, we all immediately recognise him as Dr. Spaceley-Trellis, go-ahead Bishop of Bevindon, and he seems less horrible than absurd. Only those who sit spellbound in the Beria Memorial Hall will fail to be amused by 'Mrs. Dutt-Pauker, the Hampstead thinker, chairman of Deck-chairmen against Racism and many other organisations', as yet again she denounces South Africa.

A very un-Peter-Simplish writer once began a poem with the words, 'Look, we have come through!' In spite of Mr. Scargill and the I.R.A., many people in England also echo the words, very cautiously, as they stare back over their shoulders at the Wilson-Heath era which we have moved away from. The changes of the time were horrible. England became coarser and uglier. But the left failed to establish dominance. The foamingly fanatical left-wing fringe moved in to take over the Labour Party and rendered it politically impotent. And among intelligent people it no longer became necessary to pretend that one subscribed to all the vacuities of the Liberal package deal. This was certainly not due to any skill on the part of right-wing politicians who in our generation have been feebler, thank God, than at any stage of history. Nor was it due to the 'serious' right-wing intellectuals of the *Salisbury Review* stamp, most of whom are as repugnant as their lefty counterparts. But it is due largely, I believe, to the humorists who have made us realise that we do not need to take any posturing bore seriously merely because she or he is claiming moral superiority over us.

So long live Peter Simple, who has helped to render paper tigresses such as Dame Judith Hart and Mrs. Barbara Castle into toothless hags who, in their judgements of the world, merely seem to echo the self-righteous pronouncements of Mrs. Dutt-Pauker. The hallmark of Peter Simple's humour is black pessimism, for he knows that there is little or no distinction between his darkest fantasies and the condition of the real world. But his vision is always tempered by a ridiculous childish whimsicality which gives it its particular charm. It has more in common with Beachcomber than with more modern satirists. In the latest selection from his column, for instance, I was delighted to renew my acquaintance with Saint Oick who was 'of course, the well-known hermit who lived with several anchoresses in a wall-to-wall carpeted hermitage in what was then a dense forest but is now occupied by St. Oick's Crescent, Oickwell Road, and other suburban streets . . .' Equally, I rejoiced to meet again all my old favourites: Dr. Heinz Kiosk, the social psychologist ('We are all guilty'); Neville Dreadberg, the playwright; and J. Bonington Jagworth, the beastliest roadhog of them all, accompanied, one need hardly add, by the Rev. John Goodwheel, the 'Apostle of the Motorways'.

But what of another character? What of Peter Simple himself? His fantasy world is wholly distinctive, and yet I have always found it impossible to reconstruct the personality of the man behind it. Meeting him was a surprise, for, in spite of the underlying melancholy of the column, I think I had expected the whimsy to predominate. In appearance, Michael Wharton recalls the Beachcomber, perhaps even the Belloc era of journalism, girt about as he is with black fustian and dark tie. There is laughter in his eyes, but something like affliction plays across his features as he talks in a low, quiet voice, which while lacking an 'accent', is recognisably that of a Yorkshireman. The two subjects about which he discoursed when I first met him were the legendary history of Britain – King Arthur and so on – and Belloc's attitude to the Jews. I was surprised to be told that Peter Simple's mother was a Yorkshirewoman, but that his father was the son of a German-Jewish emigré who had come to Bradford in the 1860s, and that as a young man, Peter Simple, alias Michael Wharton, was called Michael Nathan.

Some of the story which he then unfolded has been published in this remarkable autobiography.* It is deadpan, brief, modest, elegant and (I found) extremely moving. Now that I have read it more than once, it occurs to me that much of Peter Simple's brilliance derives from a sense that England is a strange place, not to say a foreign land. Although both his parents were thoroughly acclimatised, Wharton grew up as a social outsider. His father had cut loose from the Jewish wool merchants of Bradford and devoted himself to a weird life, hill farming, gambling and generally embarrassing his children as much as he had embarrassed his parents. But I don't think this sense in his writing that Michael Wharton is a stranger and sojourner derives from his inheritance. It is surely an ingrained part of his own imaginative nature. As he says, 'It was not until I went to Oxford and so, as far as such a thing is possible, escaped from my family . . . that I realised how extremely odd they all were.' It was only later that he realised that everyone else was even odder.

He left Oxford, as he put it, 'under the statutory cloud', having thrown a Scotch egg at the dons on High Table, and also dismantled a sofa and thrown it out of the window of his college rooms. He has always been an amorous man, and by this stage he had a girl in tow, by whom he had a baby, and whom he at some stage married. Having shared his 'life of mingled torpor, drunkenness and general oddity' in London, she accompanied him to a small cottage in Westmorland, the idea being that he was to be a 'writer'. Some of this book's flavour can be tasted if I quote a paragraph relating to those days:

> On one evening, I stood in the winding stony lane which led from the main road to our cottage; the soft, suffused light of the sun going down, the smell of May blossom, the calling of birds, the rustle, almost imperceptible, of the trees and tall grasses by the wayside, filled me with serene delight. I leaned on my bicycle waiting for my wife to come from our cottage to meet me, and thought: supposing it were some girl I truly loved, as I loved with holy fervour this natural world spread about me on every side! That would have been a perfection of life in which the

* *The Missing Will*, Michael Wharton (1984).

erotic and the numinous, the human and the inhuman, would have been joined in an experience I have never known. Not having known it, have I ever lived?

It is surely not completely absurd to think this is almost as good as some of Prince Andrew's ruminations in *War and Peace*. What puts it in such a league is its devastating truthfulness. Ninety-five per cent of the human race would so *want* to have enjoyed a moment of perfect ecstasy on that golden evening in Westmorland that their memories would have tricked them into supposing that they *had* done so. Michael Wharton's knowledge that he has failed to have an experience is much more moving than a lot of bogus people's belief that they have had one.

It is almost impossible to write well about one's own emotional history, which is why, I suppose, most novels about love seem so much more plausible than most autobiographies. But *The Missing Will*, which is a classic of the genre, is a great exception.

We are not surprised that the outbreak of war finds him as 'a rather useless and idle subaltern', spending a couple of languid years in India. By the time he has returned to England at the end of the war, and then spent five years wondering how on earth to live, his marriage had foundered. He does not go into much detail about his career at this date, but there is mingled melancholy and hilarity in such throwaway sentences as this: 'Another job I was working on at the time was editing the Football Association Yearbook, published by a small firm which had been infiltrated, for reasons I could not discover, by Marxists.'

Still with the vague ambition of becoming a writer (he wrote a novel called *Sheldrake* which was not published until years later by 'a rich Jew called Anthony Blond'), he got a job with the B.B.C. in Manchester. No less than the Football Association the Corporation was crawling with Marxist coteries whom Wharton found uncongenial. The book ends in 1965. Things are not going well with his second marriage. ('My wife was hurt by my neglect and lack of love – or to be more accurate perhaps, my perverse inability or unwillingness to express it.') The world itself seems very dark. There was Suez, 'the preposterous conspiracy of England, France and the State of Israel, and the political humiliations that followed'. There was the experience of weeping over the wireless set at the news from Hungary. And in England, it looked as though there was going to be a triumph of the liberal consensus, which 'at its silliest, involved a belief in human perfectibility and paradise on earth'.

It was at this phase that Michael Wharton was staying with some friends and Colin Welch arrived from the *Telegraph* to say that he was on the lookout for a full-time contributor to the Peter Simple column. 'I made no particular response to this. It was good old Theodora (Fitzgibbon) who shouted, "Can't you see, you fathead? He's offering you a job."'

At this point the book ends, with Wharton arriving at his desk in the *Telegraph*, 'with one of the most appalling hangovers I have ever had in my life and without a single idea in my head'. This phrase is the only lie in an otherwise preternaturally truthful story, for the ideas have been pouring out of him ever since. And because the dark-suited septuagenarian humorist is obviously so different, in many ways, from the young man at the end of this book, we can hope that there will be a sequel to shed light on the transformation.

*Spectator*, 17 November 1984

# Two Talks on Satire

## I. Satire and the Novel

The question to which I wish to address myself is this: is the novel an appropriate vehicle for satire? In some ways it will strike you as a rather silly question, since, for a start, how do you define the novel? The novel is, surely, anything you wish to make it, an improbable adventure story, a game of words which is no story at all, a boxful of letters, a magical fantasy, a religious parable: *Kidnapped, Finnegans Wake, Clarissa, Phantastes* and *Perelandra* are all novels; they are books which in some moods or at some periods I have read with enjoyment and admiration. Likewise, the two-dimensional comedies of P.G. Wodehouse, constructed with such consummate skill (or the no less skilful one-and-an-half-dimensional murder stories of Agatha Christie), what are we to call them if they are not novels?

Nevertheless, for the purposes of this lecture, I shall take it for granted that the mainstream of great novels is that great tradition which takes as its subject 'this world which is the world of all of us', and the human condition within it: the tradition, moreover, which uses this strange portmanteau, this extraordinary accident in the history of literature which we call the novel as a vehicle for concentrating on human character; the great tradition, that is to say, which embraces Sir Walter Scott, Charles Dickens, Honoré de Balzac, Flaubert, Tolstoy, Turgenev and Dosteovsky. These are the mountains in which the Trollopes, the Arnold Bennetts, the Barbara Pyms and the Jane Austens are the foothills. This tradition has not eschewed satire, but on the whole the satirical elements in novels of these giants are either, as in Dostoevsky's case, too large to be regarded as satirical, or, as in the case of Dickens, which we shall have to examine, they are subsumed in some *sui generis* comedy of the author's own particular making.

Before trying to expound what I mean, let me allude briefly to a curious phenomenon about what one might regard as the classics of satirical fiction in English. What do *Gulliver's Travels, Erewhon, News from Nowhere* or *Animal Farm* have in common? They are all, very conspicuously, fantasies. And a high proportion of them are either set in fantastical and imagined lands, or they are put, like Orwell's *Animal Farm*, in a fantastical setting where, for example, animals can talk. Nobody who knew anything about the history of the twentieth century could read *Animal Farm* and be in the slightest doubt what it was about. It is precisely because it is written so simply, and because it never strays beyond its claim to be a story about horses and pigs that its satire is so devastating. One does not have to have been alive at the time of the Nazi-Soviet pact to feel the appalling force of that last paragraph:

> Twelve voices were shouting in anger, and they were all alike. No questions now, what had happened to the faces of the pigs. The creatures outside looked from pig to man, and from man to pig, and from pig to man again: but already it was impossible to say which was which.

The lines derive their force from their parabolic remoteness. Compare them, on the level of art, on the level of satire, with the lack of success of *Nineteen Eighty-Four*. Admittedly the book was written when Orwell was dying, and his powers were failing. But the fundamental thing wrong with it is that it presupposes so many things about human nature and the world as we know it to be, as well as about the future, that its powerfulness as satire is by now almost dead — as dead, in a very different way, as the novels of Thomas Love Peacock.

To a twentieth-century reader, the novels of Peacock summon up a world as agreeable as it is possible to imagine. We are almost invariably in a house built in the early neo-Gothic manner. From the library windows, we see a view of hills and of water. The more energetic members of the houseparty are out airing their dogs and their obsessions with phrenology, micthyology, landscape gardening, metaphysics or hydrostatics; above all, they are working up an appetite. The lazier members of the household are indoors, snoozing over a bottle of Madeira and a morroccobound volume of the Welsh triads or of Homer, their slumbers sweetened by the sounds coming from the music room, where a rich and beautiful young woman, having completed her toilet and her Tasso, rehearses an air with which to entertain the gentleman after a very early dinner.

'Since Eve ate apples,' as Peacock's great contemporary observed, 'much depends on dinner.' The obese conservative parsons, the cranky young poets and philosophers, the crabbed political economists have returned from their walks and the Symposium can begin. A good soup, plenty of freshwater fish, fowl, a magnificent saddle of mutton, well-peppered, and pudding. 'The vast globe of plum pudding, the true image of the earth, flattened at the poles.' Salivation, as much as laughter, is an inevitable consequence of turning Peacock's pages. The title of his last novel, *Gryll Grange*, suggests endless gastronomic extravagance; it begins with a colloquy about Palestine soup and it ends with the popping of champagne corks.

The air of patrician indolence given off by his novels is sometimes hard to reconcile with the fact that, throughout a long and varied life, Peacock was what we should call a man of the left, and it is difficult to resist the impression, from the novels, that his radicalism sprang more from a taste for grotesque and wildly expressed views (his best friend in youth was Shelley) than from any profound intellectual commitment. The ideas in the books, as they fly fantastically about – the utilitarianism of Mr. Crochet, the Malthusianism of Mr. Fax – seem as arbitrary and peculiar as the names of the characters themselves; ideas about politics and society seem to be given no more weight than observations about the correct rules for ombre or discussions about the Bald Venus.

But such a reading of Peacock springs only from our ignorance of the intellectual issues which concerned him in his lifetime. The notions seem fusty – on a much higher level, but to much the same degree that the Victorian jokes in *Punch* seem to us fusty – because they allude to forgotten controversies. For an average reader, nearly all Peacock's contemporary allusiveness (and it was dense and varied) is lost. Occasionally we can play the crude game of 'identifying' the characters. Mr. Eavesdrop is Leigh Hunt, Skythrop Glowry is Shelley. Or we can play the slier game of linking Peacock's grotesques with our own contemporaries. Those who refuse to buy oranges or pork pies or sherry because these products come from particular countries are clearly throwbacks to the figure of Mr. Forester in *Melincourt*, whose anti-saccharine league disdains sugar reaped by slave labour.

But for the real Peacock lover this is less than satisfactory. We

244

now know, because of scholars who have been patient enough to wade through the periodical literature of the day, that nearly all the weirdest cranks in Peacock's *galère* are not, in fact, products of his imagination, but thinly disguised versions of people and issues of his own day. We read Peacock, therefore, in a manner which, however legitimate it may be, is wildly different from the spirit in which his books were composed. A 1911 Rolls-Royce must have seemed in 1911 like the height of modernity and *chic*. Our enjoyment of a ride in such a car today would be very different from the enjoyment of our grandfathers, for whom the motorcar was new.

Peacock and Orwell both turn out, by my slightly arbitrary definition, to be satirists before they are novelists. In the 'mainstream' or 'great tradition' sense, they are not, in fact, novelists at all. The satirist, notice, is only able to create something perennial and abiding by means of fable or fantasy. As we shall probably discover in my next lecture, about the uses of satire in journalism, the world is too anxious to parody the parodist, to behave in a manner whose absurdity outreaches the imagination of the most scathing satirist, for the satirical novel ever to 'do long' unless it is of the most general application. There are whole streams of novels – Mallock's *New Republic*, Belloc's political novels, H. G. Wells's *The New Machiavelli* – which belong to this category. Reading them, we always feel that we are savouring a curiosity rather than a work of literature. The satire is probably biting. But it has its teeth wedged in a victim whose flesh has long since vanished away.

Two contemporary English novelists who exemplify some of the problems which I feel in this regard are David Lodge and Malcolm Bradbury. And if I were forced to distinguish between them – not an exercise which all their critics force upon themselves; indeed, they are often spoken of as if they were two heads on one body – I should say that Bradbury is much more easily identifiable as a satirist *tout court*, whereas Lodge is more complex, humane and, for me, a more richly comic writer. I am sure that this assembly of learned and dedicated men and women bears absolutely no resemblance to any of the academic conferences in David Lodge's novel *Small World*. A friend of mine, a teacher of English Literature from Warsaw, very much detested that novel and, at a British Council seminar in Cambridge during the summer of 1985, she berated Lodge with its shortcomings. To my kind, intelligent, serious friend, it was quite literally inconceivable that those who devoted their lives to the study of great literature could be as coarse and unspiritual as the people in Lodge's book. To me, unfortunately, it is all too possible to imagine that a great disparity exists between, let us say, the high Aristotelian ethics of *The Faerie Queene* and the lifestyle of modern Spenser scholars, though I daresay that the disparity in most cases is less Rabelaisian than in the imagination of Professor Lodge. The disparity which my friend from Warsaw found so horrifying is, after all, one of the points of comedy, even though it could be argued that Professor Lodge wears it all and bears it all with a shocking lightness. For the structuralists who attend all the conferences in his book, literature itself is little more than a game; and in terms of the book, those games are played out with about as much interest in 'real life' as, on a Chaucerian pilgrimage, is to be found in religion. That is to say, both a little and a lot. Professor Lodge has a strong sense that life's absurdity does not provide us with an excuse for thinking of it as nothing *but* an absurdity. Because people are funny, often hilarious, in their antics, it does not mean that in the end we devalue them. To this degree, the comparison with Chaucer, which Lodge himself invites by his opening sentence, is wholly apt. As with Chaucer, we feel ourselves in the presence of a writer who loves playing with literary forms, and who takes a detached, fundamentally comic view of human existence; but the basis of the comedy is the high disparity which exists between our terrestrial follies and our eternal destiny. I never feel this to be the case with Professor Bradbury whose brilliant satire of English academic life, *The History Man*, is more doggedly worldly and more relentlessly ideological than anything Lodge has ever written. As a novel, in the end, it can't satisfy because the villain/hero is triumphant; and that, one assumes, is Malcolm Bradbury's point. If it were a comic novel in the Lodge manner we might expect Howard Kirk, the dreadful and villainous History Man, to get his comeuppance. In the event, by something like an inner ideological logic, we find that Howard Kirk even wins round the author, as the older critics used to imagine that Milton, in writing *Paradise Lost*, was, in spite of himself, on the side of the Devil. So, in the end, we judge *The History Man* on non-literary grounds. English academics who themselves resemble Howard Kirk usually dismiss the book as piffle, because they do not like to admit its truth. Those who see its truth dislike its lack of charity, which is another way of saying that it's good satire but bad fiction. In spite of my friend from Poland, I think one judges the comedies of David Lodge less by their absolute truthfulness than by stylistic and literary criteria: does the story work on its own terms or on its own level? It would not matter all that much if it turned out that David Lodge had actually invented academic conferences and seminars, if it were to transpire that they were in fact a product of his own arch imagination. His comedy is self-referential, and his books are not really any more satires on the university system than P. G. Wodehouse's comedies are satires on the English landed class; whereas *The History Man*, I believe, is pure satire. It refers to a world outside itself, a world which exists. If it fails to hit a particular mark, then its failure is total. We judge it by the standards which we would apply to history and to journalism, and not by the standards which we would apply to poetry.

Once in a blue moon, however, someone writes a brilliant novel in which these divisions and categories are broken, a book which is *both* a crazily humorous world in its own right (as, say, P. G. Wodehouse's was) *and* which makes a devastating comment on the world of affairs, the world of all of us. It would be wrong, if understandable, if the whole of this seminar were devoted to the study of Evelyn Waugh, so I do no more than allude to the fact that *Scoop* is such a book. The newspaper empire of Lord Copper and the absurdities of London's Fleet Street, as depicted by Waugh in this novel, are perennially and absolutely true; so true, indeed, that now one judges newspapermen in terms of *Scoop* and not the other way around. In more sense than one, Oscar Wilde was right to say that life imitates art. Another, and more monumental example, is the depiction of the English Law in *Bleak House* by Charles Dickens. It is fashionable to think that novelists create self-sufficient worlds, worlds of their own imagination; and of no novelist is this truer than Dickens, where the idiosyncrasies of human character, nomenclature, posture and habit are so readily distinctive. Surely Dickens is supremely the example of what I was describing earlier in relation to David Lodge and P. G. Wodehouse: the case of a comic writer whose works are entirely enjoyable in themselves and who could be enjoyed even if the world they depicted did not exist, or existed in a form completely different to their description.

Such a view, frequently held in relation to Dickens, would seek to emphasise that Dickens actually fails as a satirist. And it is as a satirist, partly, that he comes before us in *Bleak House*. Consider the satire on professional philanthropers and do-gooders in the figures of Mrs. Jellyby and Mrs. Pardiggle, who shamefully neglect their own domestic duties for the sake of their schemes to collect money for Africa. When Esther first encounters them, she asks who these young ladies might be.

> 'These young ladies,' said Mrs. Pardiggle, with great volubility after the first salutations, 'are my five boys. You may have seen their names in a printed subscription list (perhaps more than one) in the possession of our esteemed friend Mr. Jarndyce. Egbert, my eldest (twelve) is the boy who sent out his pocket-money, to the amount of five-and-threepence, to the Tockahoopo Indians. Oswald, my second (five and a half) is the child who contributed two-and-ninepence to the Great National Smithers Testimonial. Francis, my third (nine) one-and-sixpence-halfpenny; Felix, my fourth (seven) eightpence to the Superannuated Widows; Alfred, (my youngest, five) has voluntarily enrolled himself in the Infant Bonds of Joy, and is pledged never, through life, to use tobacco in any form.'
>
> We had never seen such dissatisfied children. It was not merely that they were weazened and shrivelled—though they were certainly that, too – but they looked absolutely ferocious. At the mention of the Tocka-hoopo Indians I could really have supposed Egbert to be one of the most baleful members of that tribe, he gave me such a savage frown . . .
>
> Chapter VIII, *Bleak House*

Since the world has gone so much Mrs. Pardiggle's way in the last hundred years, we are almost frightened to admit that this is satire. We prefer it to be grotesquerie for its own sake. The very word *charity*, which is a sacred word in its early connotations in English, and almost by definition a private word, has been appropriated and spoilt forever by Mrs. Pardiggles and Mrs. Jellybys. So strong is their hold, that we no longer dare to ask ourselves whether their demands are truly charitable at all.

Dickens, like all the very great novelists, celebrates the beauty of privacy, the inviolable importance of the individual life, threatened all the time in post-industrialised society by one sort or another of busybody, and by systems. The law is the perfect butt of his satire because it is in itself so highly grotesque, and because it does actually make people go mad. From the beginning of *Bleak House* as the fog swirls around Lincoln's Inn and Chancery Lane, almost, it would seem, emanating from the Lord Chancellor itself, the absurdity and the hatefulness of the law are held before us with unambiguous gusto, exemplified by the interminable lawsuit of Jarndyce and Jarndyce. 'Scores of persons have deliriously found themselves made parties in Jarndyce and Jarndyce, without knowing how or why; whole families have inherited legendary hatreds with the suit. The little plaintiff, or defendant, who was promised a new rocking-horse when Jarndyce should be settled, has grown up, possessed himself of a real horse, and trotted away into the other world . . .'

Figures like Miss Flite, driven mad by some case, and hovering about the corridors and galleries of the law courts, clutching her documents and expecting a judgement shortly, and living in squalor above a law-stationer's shop with her caged birds, are what we call 'Dickensian' when we want to convey that Dickens has a lurid capacity for invention. Just as little Jo the crossing-sweeper, who dies so heart-rendingly reciting the Lord's Prayer, is often used as an example of Dickens's 'sentimentality': 'sentimentality' and 'grotesquerie' in both cases being words that we can use to distance ourselves from the truth of Dickens. I think that Dickens is that very rare thing, a satirist who is also humane; a satirist, in fact, so devastating on occasion that even today we cannot bear the truth which he depicts. True, they have cleaned up Chancery Lane; they have given Miss Flite an old-age pension; there are no muddy crossings for Jo to sweep now; having been to a comprehensive school he still knows nuffink about nuffink, but the possibilities perhaps exist for him to lead a less wretched existence than his Victorian forebear. But the fog around the Lord Chancellor and Lincoln's Inn is just as thick, and the law is just as absurd and as cruel and as unjust as it was in Dickens's day. We can hardly doubt that it was his familiarity with Dickens which emboldened Tolstoy, in *Resurrection*, to describe the trial of Maslova with such devastating and angry truthfulness.

This moral self-confidence is something which we most conspicuously lack these days in England. Anthony Trollope, in his *Autobiography*, makes the not altogether believable claim that the moral purpose had been uppermost in his mind when he was writing all his novels:

There are many who would laugh at the idea of a novelist teaching either virtue or nobility – those, for instance, who regard the reading of novels as a sin, and those also who think it to be simply an idle pastime. They look upon the tellers of stories as among the tribe of those who pander to the wicked pleasures of a wicked world. I have regarded my art from so different a point of view that I have ever thought of myself as a preacher of sermons, and my pulpit as one which I could make both salutory and agreeable to my audience. I do believe that no girl has risen from reading of my pages less modest than she was before, and that some may have learned from them that modesty is a charm well worth preserving. I think that no youth has been taught that in falseness and flashness is to be found the round to manliness; but some may perhaps have learned from me that it is to be found in truth and a high but gentle spirit. Such are the lessons I have striven to teach . . .

There is a slight air of humbug about all this; that is, a modern reader inevitably feels there to be. But Dickens would probably have said the same. And Tolstoy, to use an extreme example, came to feel that it was his duty to be nothing but a moralist and gave up writing novels altogether.

Nowadays, we are struck by the fact that nineteenth-century novelists, even when they were not primarily moralistic, had to adopt moralistic attitudes; just as we, by contrast, if we do have moral designs on our readers, feel it is decent to conceal them. It is hard for us to absorb the idea that *Barchester Towers* or *He Knew He was Right* are simple stories of right and wrong, designed not merely not to bring a blush to the face, but also to put right thoughts into the mind of a young person. We would want to say that great novels are so much more than moral tracts, and that if they do teach lessons, or have morals, they are morals and lessons as complex as life itself. Such a view, towards which I incline myself, would wish to say that Trollope is a much better moralist and a much better novelist than his *Autobiography* would allow. His extraordinary power is to make us see how ordinary, decent, young men can get into awful situations, such as being in love with two women at once (as in *Is He Popenjoy?*). His art shows how innocents can be made to see that their way of life is based on corruption (as in *The Warden*) or how crudely comic characters become so fully understood and sympathised with that even monsters such as Mrs. Proudie can become in *The Last Chronicle of Barchester* a figure of something like tragedy. Turning back to Dickens, I would extend this. In Dickens, there is a passionate and vitriolic fury with injustice, as well as a wildly satirical sense not only of the craziness of human institutions, but also the absurdity of individual human beings. But there is also, always, in Dickens, a wonderfully celebratory quality. He loves people being themselves. He hates the law in

*Bleak House*; but at the same time, no writer has ever evoked it with such obsessive love: lunatic barristers with their ludicrous locutions; wigs, gowns, bands, sealing-wax, dust, high desks, scratching pens are all in the highest degree fascinating to Dickens; and if this is true of objects, it is a thousand times truer of human beings. He inveighs against the Lords, Ladies and Gentlemen, the Right Reverends and the Wrong Reverends, and in a way delights in them.

'I shouldn't call myself a satirist,' the poet Philip Larkin once said in an interview. 'To be a satirist, you have to know better than everyone else, and I've never done that.' Another poet, W. H. Auden, writing about what he considered the novelist's vocation, said that he must

> Become the whole of boredom, subject to
> Vulgar complaints like love, among the Just
>   Be just, among the Filthy, filthy too,
>
> And in his own weak person, if he can,
>   Dully put up with all the wrongs of man.

These two sayings, taken together, would suggest that for the truly humane novelist, knowall satire such as Pope wrote about the Dunces would be too destructive for a novelist to absorb. A novelist, even (or especially) a comic novelist, must love his creations while finding them absurd.

There is another tradition which I mention here in connection with the novel because I think it to be relevant. It is the English religious tradition. Christianity is the synthesis of two extraordinary contradictions. So is Judaism, as a matter of fact, but Christianity believes the synthesis to have occurred as a matter of recorded history, and not merely to be a theological notion. The two contradictions are these. On the one hand, the human is woefully fallible. There exist a whole series of moral absolutes, a whole lot of perfections which throw our imperfection into a grotesquely shaming light. There is a law, and we live condemned by it. On the other hand, it is asserted that human individuals are infinitely precious, made in the image of God. But unlike Milton's ruined archangels, fallen mortals are both imperfect, and redeemed. Their imperfection is not condoned. It has been condemned on a cosmic scale, but the penalty for that imperfection is paid. Hence, now, the fact that truth is so often to be discerned in paradox, that the weak things of the world confound the mighty, and that strength is made perfect in weakness. Wisdom cannot be found until failure and depravity are recognised. But our failure and depravity are not the only truths that can be told about us. Love is to the loveless shown they might lovelier be.

Satire as a form tends to the condemnatory; to an expression of the truth, in theological terms, of our condemnation under the law; whereas the novel, it may be thought, delights in human beings as they are, and thrives on all our weaknesses and imperfections. In either case, one sees the influence of the tradition at work even in writers who have long ago left behind a formal adherence to their culture's creeds. Nevertheless it has to be said that there is no accident in the fact that comedy, most richly understood, in English Literature, has nearly always been the work of religious believers. In much that we regard as destructive satire there is in fact a celebratory element; where there is not, there tends to be an aridity which is alien to our feelings of decency. The synthesis of which we have been speaking was achieved by revealing the unfathomable costliness of the saying, 'Judge not, that ye be not judged': which is another way of saying, 'Forgive them, for they know not what they do.'

Perhaps the novelist does not have to enact, as Auden's poem implies, an incarnation. Perhaps he does not have to become the whole of anything. Perhaps the truth is that no truth can ever be told in its totality in a work of literature: and that partial truth is what satire is so supremely well-equipped to tell us. Any attempts on its part to be decent or to see the other point of view would destroy it. This is where the satirist and the novelist become incompatible companions, perhaps. Think of what a very good novel one could have on Swift's young nymph going to bed. I do not know that we should like her any more in a novel than we do in a poem. I am not making the sentimental assertion that the novel is always kind, but in order for her to live on the page, she would have to undergo some sort of change, and it is on this level of change that what I see as the humanity of the novelist, his essential humanity, comes into focus.

Certainly, I have found this to be true in my own experience. I have seldom written novels with a purely satirical purpose, although I suppose that some of my stories, palely loitering in the Dickensian tradition, have satirical strains within them. The novel where I came closest to having a satirical purpose was *Scandal*, a book published some years ago. Writers differ in their degrees of self-awareness. I am seldom fully conscious of what I am up to when I am writing a work of fiction, but I think that my motives as I began to prepare the material for my tale were among other things satirical. But it was these other things which I think destroyed the satirical edge of the thing.

My book tells the story of a high-ranking politician, a diligent Parliamentarian, who could, conceivably, one day become the Prime Minister. Unfortunately, he is foolish enough, as a high-ranking public man in a country with a free press, to think that it is safe to lead a private life of a bizarre sexual character. Of course, in our cruel world, private peccadilloes seldom remain private for long. Before long, Mr. Derek Blore's absurd little visits to a private address in Hackney are known to the government of a foreign power, and without very much difficulty (photographs are produced) Mr. Blore is enlisted, as a senior Cabinet Minister, to spy against Her Majesty's Government. In return for this favour, the young people who have been embarrassing him will be murdered.

Since all the ingredients in the story are immediately recognisable to any student of the British political scene in the last twenty-five years, it might be supposed that I had a strongly satirical purpose in writing *Scandal*. All the more wildly implausible elements in the plot were merely toned-down versions of things which we have all been able to read in the newspapers.

But the wonderful thing about a newspaper story is that it is short, and flat, and wonderfully unreal; ditto a short newsfilm on T.V. It takes very little to turn them into satire, pure and simple. The difficulty for many of our contemporary satirists, indeed, is to find anything which will match the absurdity of what is actually going on in the world, or the means by which the newspapers or T.V. choose to depict what is going on. We could not invent politicians who were less impressive than the ones we have in fact. Ditto nearly all the great men and women of the world – the actors and actresses, the so-called 'sports personalities', the crowned and uncrowned dignitaries. And this is not an accident. It springs from the fact that there is an inherent absurdity in wishing to put ourselves forward, or wishing to be considered above others. Hence the self projected by those who desire to be publicly impressive will always be the least impressive self and not the most impressive. Hence, in public men and women, the extraordinary grotesqueries of character, the paradoxes which so delight the satirists: the judges behaving unlaw-

253

fully, the bishops who do not believe in their religion, the economists incapable of simple arithmetic, the semi-literate great writers, the buffoonery of sages.

The trouble, from a novelist's point of view, is that the novel does not concern itself with public men or public faces. It is concerned much more with the self whom we meet when the arclights are switched off, when the front door closes. Mr. Derek Blore, my villainous politician in *Scandal*, is about as awful a character as I have ever depicted, and yet . . . In a novelist, there is always that fateful 'and yet'. It is not that I ended up liking him, or pitying him. But I did end up asking, 'Why should good hours of sunlight be wasted on the judgement seat by those who, presently, will take their turn in the dock?' The wise saw comes from the unwisest of sources: Baron Corvo. But that in itself probably tells us something.

## II. Satire in contemporary journalism

There is a tradition of organised rudeness in England, which is extremely hard to explain to a foreign observer. It is particularly hard to translate because extremes of rudeness can imply quite opposite things about the relations between the insulter and the insulted. On the whole it is true in England that if you are rude about a man, it implies a level of intimacy with him. If you enter a room in England which is full of men who know each other well, the likelihood is that they will be insulting each other, though with smiles on their faces. The banter may be real, or unreal, or a bit of both. But rudeness on this level is a signal of friendship. Englishmen are rude to their friends and polite to strangers or to enemies. To your best friend, with a smile on your face, you might say that he is a lousy writer, a bad cook, a dangerous driver, a hopeless shot, a boring speaker, even though you think that he is quite proficient in all these areas. To a stranger whom you consider to be of indifferent accomplishment, you might well be fulsome in your praise. So, then, is it safe to say that when you express yourself insultingly in English, you actually mean it benignly? Not in the least. Sometimes, particularly in the political sphere, insults really are meant as insults. Praise can even, on occasions, be meant as praise (though it is usually safe to assume that praise is insulting in English).

My introduction to this topsy-turvy condition of things came at an English boarding school. Where else? At the end of each term, we were full of excitement because we were about to go home and join our families. For a whole term, we had been living together, morning, noon and night, and seeing very much more of our teachers than would be usual at a day school. Feelings ran high, feelings of irritation and animosity, in particular. The last meal of the term would be called a 'house supper'. There were perhaps fifty boys in a boarding house, with a housemaster to look after us, and several tutors and their wives. They would all attend this supper, and afterwards there would be entertainments which we called 'skits'. Some of these entertainments might have had some extrinsic merit. But it was not as drama that they were judged. They were an opportunity for us to be as rude as we liked, as rude as we possibly could be, to our teachers and to the unpopular boys in the house. To call the level of humour scabrous is to understate. No level of bad taste was too low to plummet. Some of the imitations were quite funny. Sometimes they were extremely cruel. Anything was thought to be fair game, ranging from comments on the ugliness of masters' wives, to speculation about the unsatisfactory nature of their conjugal relations.

I remember well the demeanour of the boys and of their teachers on these occasions. As a boy, I would sometimes be so overexcited that I could hardly breathe, laughing, as all the other children were, in a wild, hysterical abandonment which felt as if it might kill me. And there, in the front row, sat the teachers, listening to the cruellest possible attacks upon themselves and their colleagues; attacks on their ignorance, low social origins (what horrid little snobs we were!), repulsive physical appearance or ridiculous mannerisms. There they sat in a row, only a few feet away from us, as we imitated them, lambasted them, insulted them. Most of them had their faces wreathed in an artificial grin to show that they were big enough to take a joke against themselves. Some occasionally adopted an humbuggical expression of distaste if a lady were grossly insulted. For the most part, I think, their smiles were not artificial. Many of them positively enjoyed not only the insults to their colleagues, but to themselves. The real insult was not to be mentioned at all. The next morning, as if nothing had happened, we said goodbye to them politely. And the next term, we would meet on the old terms, accepting these men as our masters, doing work for them, bowing beneath their chastisements, even respecting them for another ten or twelve weeks before once again their baldness, myopia, and probable sexual impotence were lampooned before an audience of hooting hyenas.

So, you ask, this means that underneath it all, you did not like your masters? No, it did not mean that. Some we liked, and some we disliked. But all were lampooned – except, as I say, those who were beneath lampooning.

Let me give you two quite different examples, this time from programmes which have recently been popular on British television. One is a series of programmes entitled *Yes, Minister* which depicts the minister in charge of a government department as a conceited but almost unbelievably gullible and incompetent politician. The Yes, Minister of the title is highly ironic because it is what is always being said to him by his civil servant, Sir Humphrey, who in fact makes all the policies and all the important decisions which the hapless minister thinks he is making. This programme was so popular in England that a continuation of it was written called *Yes, Prime Minister*, in which the idiotic politician has gone on to become Prime Minister. He is as vain and ignorant as before, and the civil servants are as corrupt and as scheming. Taken as a serious portrayal of the way that government works in England, it is highly damaging. It suggests that extremely important issues – such as the defence of the realm or the management of the economy – are really decided behind the scenes not on their own merits, but for extraordinary reasons to do with the interdepartmental policies of the civil servants themselves. The politicians, who are really only interested in winning votes and keeping popular with the people, do not make the decisions, and do not really care about them.

This programme is, as I say, extremely popular. It is received to a roar of laughter from the audience in the studio theatre, and it is watched by several million delighted viewers. Presumably, these are people who are violently opposed to the Government, anxious for it to be scourged and overthrown, and for a new political system to be introduced? Not at all. The Prime Minister herself is so fond of the programme that she has even recorded a short episode of it, herself playing the part of herself. Does this mean that people laugh at the programme because they are safe in the knowledge that it is all untrue? No. Most of the people who laugh at it think that the picture of things which it paints is roughly true. Or, if it isn't true, that it expresses in an exaggerated form some kind of truth about British civil servants. The truer people think it is, the more it makes them laugh.

Another television programme which is extremely popular in England at the moment is called *Spitting Image*. It is a puppet show, shown late on a Sunday evening at sporadic intervals. The puppets represent figures who have been in the news in the previous week, favourites being the Prime Minister and her Cabinet, and the Queen with her family. The Queen is often represented at the breakfast table, peering at a copy of one of the more vulgar newspapers over her half-moon specs, and making comments about the sex life of one member or another of the Royal Family. Other royal personages are represented as swigging from gin bottles, having undignified fights with their in-laws, or indulging in conversations of mind-boggling sexual crudity. The Cabinet, meanwhile, is represented as a collection of cringing buffoons, grovelling before the bullying Mrs. Thatcher, who is usually dressed like a strict school prefect in a rather old-fashioned girl's story. Not only do all her senior Cabinet colleagues fawn upon her and fear her. They are often depicted in the most ignominious postures – for example, quite gratuitously vomiting in the middle of a conversation.

In part, the crudity and violence of *Spitting Image* is inspired by the cleverness, but essential blandness of comedies like *Yes, Prime Minister*. If *Yes, Prime Minister* can be so easily institutionalised, so totally acceptable, that the *real* Prime Minister wishes to appear on it, the scriptwriters of *Spitting Image* seem to say, let us write something which is so rude, so tasteless, so completely offensive that nobody represented in this programme can possibly pretend to like it.

But, of course, they have failed. Several British Cabinet Ministers, rather than maintaining what one might call a dignified silence about the matter, have said that they watch the programme with enjoyment. I do not know how one determines the truth of any statement coming from the mouth of a politician, but I suspect these statements of being true. As with the school entertainments which I described to you earlier, the enjoyment can be on three levels: fake enjoyment, to show that they are jolly good sports; secondly, genuine delight that they are sufficiently in the swim to merit such attention; thirdly, malicious glee at the way in which their colleagues and rivals have been dealt with. But who can know?

In order to give a fuller picture of these programmes, it is perhaps necessary to explain whom they are popular *with*. As described to you, they probably sound faintly mad, but at the time, highly subversive. Only those, you might suppose, who are profoundly opposed to the British Monarchy, and perhaps actively seeking its overthrow, could bring themselves to sit in front of depictions of Her Majesty the Queen in such ignominious postures? Only revolutionaries, surely, could stomach such a blatant indictment of Mrs. Thatcher and her Cabinet? But this is not true. The morning after such programmes are shown in England, you will hear people speaking about the victims of the satire with the strange mixture of affection and revulsion with which English people discuss their teachers or their parents. Occasionally, people will think that the bad taste has gone too far. But in my experience, those who enjoy such programmes are very frequently highly conservative in temperament. They might very well say that it was unfair to have an ugly little doll on television pretending to be the Queen, and say something to the effect that she is not in a position to answer her critics back. They will nonetheless watch it, and laugh at it. And also, without any hypocrisy, they will also stand to attention during the ceremonial singing of 'God Save the Queen' and feel a lump in their throats when they see the real Queen riding past in a procession.

Forgive me if I appear to be throwing a lot of inchoate examples at you, without just yet drawing conclusions or even stating the direction in which I am travelling. I am trying to work out what, in modern England, satire *is* before I ask various fundamental political or aesthetic questions about it.

Let us turn away from television to the world of journalism. And here let me digress a little into the history of British journalism. Ever since newssheets were invented, there have been those who knew that what they contained was false, and those who believed that the majority of things said by statesmen, governments, bishops, pundits, experts, were false. These people have been inspired to start newssheets of their own, in order to tell the truth, the real truth. Such a man, for instance, was William Cobbett (1763–1835) the Tory turned radical who, in the paper he founded, *Cobbett's Political Register*, devoted himself to exposing abuses in the established order. His attacks, for example, on flogging and torture in the British Army led him to being imprisoned for two years. It was he who first began a serious attempt to report what was said during the debates in the House of Commons. (Hitherto, as when Samuel Johnson, in a previous generation, had a job reporting Parliamentary debates, this had simply been a branch of fiction.) All this has an obvious and fundamentally serious commitment to the truth, to the sense that people have a right to know what is going on in their own country; and that those who are in a position to tell the truth have a duty to tell the truth.

Cobbett has been the hero of many British journalists. I think of Hilaire Belloc, who was the Liberal M.P. for South Salford from 1906–1910, during the Campbell-Bannermann-Asquith period. His experience of political life persuaded him that the British party system was a sham, and that the majority of politicians were liars. He gave up his seat in the House (which he would have had small chance of retaining in another general election!) and founded a paper called *The Eye Witness*, devoted, much like *Cobbett's Political Register* one hundred years before, to telling the real truth about what was going on. Notoriously, Belloc, and his colleague on the paper, Cecil Chesterton, got into trouble when they revealed that British Cabinet Ministers had been urging the purchase of wireless cable, which was to stretch the length of the British Empire, from a company, the Marconi wireless company, in which they themselves held shares. The five gentlemen involved included a subsequent Prime Minister, David Lloyd George, and the man who was one day going to become the Viceroy of India, Sir Rufus Isaacs (later Lord Reading). Unfortunately, by clumsy journalism, and the rather hysterical anti-semitism of Cecil Chesterton, *The Eye Witness* bungled it, and one of the villains, Godfrey Isaacs, managed to get them on a libel charge, which destroyed the paper. It was to be resurrected as *The New Witness* and as *G. K.'s Weekly*, but it never quite recaptured the bite it had possessed in the days when, as *The Eye Witness*, Belloc had to do with it.

Hilaire Belloc, as well as being a serious political journalist, was also a prolific satirist. He wrote a whole series of political novels – *Mr. Clutterbuck's Election, A Change in the Cabinet, Pongo and the Bull* etc. which are very funny. He is a good example of the way that radical seriousness and purely anarchic humour can exist side by side in the same writer. And no well-brought-up English child is ignorant of his verses, such as 'Lord Lundy' or 'The Garden Party':

259

The Rich arrived in pairs
And also in Rolls-Royces;
They talked of their affairs
In loud and strident voices.

(The Husbands and the Wives
Of this select society
Lead independent lives
Of infinite variety.)

The Poor arrived in Fords,
Whose features they resembled,
They laughed to see so many Lords
And Ladies all assembled.

The People in Between
Looked underdone and harassed,
And out of place and mean,
And horribly embarrassed.

For the hoary social curse
Gets hoarier and hoarier,
And it stinks a trifle worse
    *Than in*
The days of Queen Victoria,

    *WHEN*
*They married and gave in marriage,*
*They danced at the County Ball,*
*And some of them kept a carriage.*

AND THE FLOOD DESTROYED THEM ALL.

In the course of writing Belloc's biography, I found myself wondering what sort of relation there was between his sense of humour and desire to find out the truth about human life and human society. How much connection was there between his verse and his politics? How much, in fact, was it his sense of humour that relieved his various political standpoints from boringness – of indeed, lunacy. At the beginning of his life, his sense that all was not as it seemed gave him a wonderfully refreshing and strong insight into the cant, humbug and hypocisy of the hour. Towards the end of his life, the sense that 'all was not as it seemed' had become a merely rather dotty paranoia. When visitors came down to visit him in the country, he would peer at them and ask, 'What is the news?,' often expecting bulletins on events which had taken place thirty, forty or even fifty years earlier.

Since *The Eye Witness*, there have been various papers (usually they have failed for want of cash) which have attempted, in the teeth of the British libel laws, to tell the truth about what politicians were really up to. One might mention in this connection a little paper in the 1930s called *The Week*, edited by Claud Cockburn which did for the so-called Cliveden set, and those Tory politicians who wished to follow a policy of appeasement with Hitler, what Belloc and Chesterton had tried to do for the Liberals swindling on their Marconi shares.

Cockburn was to resurface again in the 1960s as an influential contributor and indeed on occasion a guest editor of the satirical fortnightly magazine *Private Eye*. It was Cockburn who was largely responsible for establishing in the *Eye* (as its title had always inherently promised) an investigative slant. In the twenty-five years of its history, *Private Eye* has spilt the beans on many a dishonest businessman, corrupt politician, profane cleric, or shady diplomat. Things which our lords and masters would consider best kept concealed have been blazoned across its pages: the name of the head of MI5; the name of an archbishop's mistress; or a Prime Minister's. Hundreds of thousands of pounds have been spent by the little rag in libel costs; and the more it has been stung by such setbacks, the more people have bought it. Having started out as a tiny little paper, typed up by a small group of young men in a back room in Soho, it has now become a vastly profitable paper, selling a quarter of a million copies of each issue, ten times the quantity of 'serious' weekly papers such as the *Spectator* or the *New Statesman*.

Now, *Private Eye* is a curious ragbag of a paper, and it would be completely untrue to say that it owed its huge commercial success to its fearless political radicalism. Part of its success does, unquestionably, derive from the fact that it tells the truth – or has sometimes been able to tell the truth – about politicians. A notable incidence of this was its exposure of the then leader of the Liberal Party, Mr. Jeremy Thorpe, who at the time stood a very strong chance of getting a Cabinet office in some political coalition, or at the very least of enjoying a considerable career as a defender of decency and honour and all the things the Liberal Party is meant to stand for in British public life. Though acquitted of the charge of murder, Mr. Thorpe had arranged for the shooting of the dog of his homosexual

PENFRIENDS FROM PORLOCK

lover in order to frighten him off. The disclosure of such almost unthinkable scandals might conceivably have happened through some other type of newspaper, but I doubt it. The libel laws are so strong in England that a rich newspaper, whom the judiciary knows to be capable of paying enormous damages, would seldom risk such a story as the Thorpe scandal being untrue.

So, certainly, people do buy the *Eye* in the knowledge that though it is often full of wild and unsubstantiated malice, it does also tell the truth where other papers cannot or dare not. But it also sells, let it be said, because of the wild and unsubstantiated malice, which people also enjoy reading, and because of the low gossip which has no serious public consequences – such matters as whether this or that minor member of the Royal Family, for example, is having a clandestine love affair. For my part, I think that the vulgar, cruel and indefensible parts of *Private Eye* are paradoxically precisely the bits which are most defensible; their presence in the paper prevents it from developing that most frightful tone of self-righteousness, which so often afflicts political radicals. It is only sandwiched between a whole lot of smut and half-truths that we might read that a possible Prime Minister elect is a murderer. And that to me is quite right. Truth of this kind is best tasted as cheap and as low as possible – the peccadilloes of politicians being exposed in the same slightly uneven, faintly smudged print as the sexual vices of the theatrical profession or the inferior clergy.

In addition to the investigative journalism of *Private Eye*, there is a large part of the paper given over to purely comic intentions. For example, there is a very good-humoured column at the moment in the paper, which begins 'Dear Bill' and purports to be a letter written by Denis Thatcher, the husband of the Prime Minister, probably to Bill Deedes, former editor of the *Daily Telegraph*, but anyway to a boozing and golfing pal, about the previous week's events. The *Dear Bill* letters are as sunny and as self-sufficient as the fiction of P. G. Wodehouse. Everyone would love them, even if such figures as Mrs. Thatcher and her husband had never in fact existed; if the aim of satire is to cast down and destroy, the *Dear Bill* letters can hardly be thought of as satirical at all. As a result of their publication, Denis Thatcher is one of the best-loved men in England.

So much for a few of the things which are going on in England at the present time, and which could be loosely described as 'satire'. As

I said, I have deliberately given you unconnected and popular examples of the genre because, in the time that remains to me, I wish to discuss the implications of these things with you.

Let me tell you two possible objections to magazines like *Private Eye* or television programmes such as *Spitting Image*. The first is that they are seditious and damaging. A senior businessman once told me that he considered *Private Eye* to be a cancer in British society. When questioned more closely about what he meant it turned out that the magazine had once been involved in a libel case with one of his friends. But, he wanted to add, this was not all that he meant. He believed that a healthy society had to have confidence in itself. It could not afford cynicism. It could not tolerate insidiously influential people such as journalists persuading everyone to be cynical about their government, their country, about their very future. What was needed, he believed, was a spirit of loyalty, optimism and dedication. During the Second World War, when England was threatened by enemies without, the English had united against a common foe. Journalists did not snarl and mock at Winston Churchill. They had all revered and praised him for his good work that he was doing for his country.

England still faced enemies: economic enemies, even political enemies. What good was served by undermining everything by this constant carping? You can see how the argument went. It surely can't be healthy for a society in which the intelligent classes are all persuaded to have no confidence in those who are running the show.

This point of view begs many questions. For example, it is not completely true that no one criticised Winston Churchill during the Second World War. But in so far as the Ministry of Information or Propaganda in London was empowered to prosecute writers or journalists whom it considered seditious, the record is not a particularly happy one. The way in which P. G. Wodehouse, for example, was hounded for his completely harmless broadcasts, given in Germany during the war, does not reflect particularly well on the British Government of the day. And the Wodehouse case shows what a deep gulf there is in England between politicians and the rest of us. Those who object to the destructive power of satire in England can only do so from the point of view that politicians deserve to be protected from attack, however corrupt, dangerous or silly they may be. As far as I know, only politicians or would-be

263

politicians in England take this attitude, in addition to a few weak-headed hangers-on to one or another of the political parties. One of the striking features of *Private Eye* in recent years has been the popularity of the feature known as Auberon Waugh's Diary. He has given up writing it now, but for fourteen years he kept up a cascade of magnificently creative abuse, purely capricious, and very rarely straying into sentimentality or good taste. One of the unshakeable tenets of Auberon Waugh's creed is that anyone who wishes to be a politician is by definition a contempible sort of pervert. I think a great number of people in England respond to and agree with this point of view, regarding with virulent distaste anyone bossy enough, arrogant enough and boring enough to think that they should be arranging our lives for us.

But this gives rise to a second objection to the 'satire' which is being produced in England at the present time. The first objection to satire, you will remember, is that it is dangerous. It is not a position which I feel able to adopt, because I cannot see that there is any evidence for it. The second idea is that satire is not dangerous enough. Long ago, when the sales figures for *Private Eye* reached 35,000 per issue, that veteran satirist Malcolm Muggeridge deplored the obvious fact that 'the satirical mission must be failing' since 'if it was proper satire, people would be far too offended to buy it at all'.

This point of view is much more damaging and, I believe, much truer. We may laugh at Auberon Waugh's turns of phrase or particular expressions of prejudice. We may admire his consistent ability to expose the Emperor's new clothes, an ability which he has more decidedly than any other English journalist of the present day. But the shock value of what he writes is very superficial. Most of what he writes is an expression of what the generality of intelligent people in England feel but are too polite or too timid to say. Far from being offended by his Diary, the public soon discovered that, as Dr. Johnson said of the poetry of Gray, it was the expression of sentiments to which every bosom returns an echo. If this is true, and I believe it to be much truer than any foreigner could possibly conceive, then most expressions of 'satire' in England can be regarded from the political point of view either as luxuries or irrelevancies, depending upon point of view.

Muggeridge's phrase 'the satirical mission' implies that satire has an almost serious function which, because of its popularity, has been neutered. I do not know, historically, whether this is true, or whether in a secret way, satire has not since the eighteenth century always had an insidiously conservative tendency in English literature. Pope and Swift, no more than Evelyn or Auberon Waugh, are hardly to be mistaken for figures of the left in the political spectrum.

In the medieval Catholic Church, a radically dangerous new figure grew up – Francis of Assisi – who aimed at putting into practice the ideals and beliefs of Jesus Christ, the Church's founder. Horrified at this development, what did the Pope do? He did not burn St. Francis at the stake. That would have been guaranteed the continuation of his order as he himself wished it to continue. No. He forced Francis to join the Establishment. Jesus had taught that His followers should not have possessions. Francis took this quite literally, and lived a life of total poverty as a beggar. But in order to found a religious order, the Pope insisted that Francis should have buildings, and priories and churches and treasures and all the paraphernalia which he most abominated. Thus, by hugging his most dissident member to himself, Pope Innocent III managed to destroy the Franciscan ideal by institutionalising it.

I am not for a moment suggesting that the motley band of hacks, cartoonists, puppetmakers and clowns who produce satirical material in England today do so from any particular motive, still less from a religious motive. My only reason for raising the example of St. Francis is to show how establishments can deal with possible threats. One way is the way of repression. Another, equally effective, is the way of bland tolerance.

Modern England is such a very odd place that I would be loath to generalise about its attitude to satire. I would certainly be extremely loath to produce *Spitting Image, Yes, Minister* or *Private Eye* as democracy's finest flower; loath to be so smug as to suggest that they are examples of a free society, which dares to criticise itself. I am not sure that they have political significance on this level at all. I began by saying that there are two sorts of rudeness in English: the familiar bantering rudeness which people express about their friends, and the genuine rudeness which, much more rarely, people express about their enemies. But one can, after all, find the antics of one's fellow men extremely funny while not wishing to attack or destroy them or cast them down. In many ways, the funniest bits of *Private Eye* are the parodies of other newspaper stories, or the 'true stories' which are simply accounts of what is going on in the world.

265

It would be a callous man who did not recognise that human life in most of its manifestations is a sad business. But the relief provided by satire is that it chooses to ignore this and to concentrate on another, equally important truth: that for much of the time, human behaviour is extremely funny, funnier by far than any parodist or satirist could invent.

Papers given at the Seventh All-Turkey English Literature Seminar, Hacettepe University, Ankara, 2 April 1986

# Last Things

# Celestial Salem

Religion does funny things to the mind. When you think of the ceaseless misery caused to the human race by the very existence of Jerusalem, it seems odd that religious people should have chosen that town, of all others, to be their emblem of celestial peace. If I wanted to think of a place which seemed like an image of heaven, it might be Bruges on a warm October day, the tourists all departed, golden leaves falling on the canals, bells ringing out from Gothic towers as one sat in a restaurant eating oneself sick on *moules marinières*. Or perhaps one would choose the image of Babylon, as seen from some Hanging Garden. Or, for a more elegant afterlife, you could think of heaven as a perpetuation of the Pump Room at Bath, pretty waitresses bringing you doughnuts and hot chocolate throughout the ceaseless morning while the Angelic crones (or Dominations or Powers) who compose the Palm Court Trio saw away at 'The Lost Chord' or 'The Londonderry Air'.

But instead, time out of mind, men and women have thought of the Other Side in terms of Jerusalem. And perhaps it is partly because you cannot be indifferent to the place. Those who visit it invariably experience extremes of emotion, ranging from disappointment to ecstacy; from visions of divine love to excesses of outrageous anger. And for everyone who has set foot in that enchantingly beautiful hill town, there must be a million who, from their earliest childhood, have learnt its name, sung about it, been taught about it in the mosques and synagogues, in Welsh chapels called Sion and Salem, and (until the R.C.s went barmy) at Catholic altars where daily reference once was made to the bread and wine offered by the King priest Melchisidech. 'If I forget thee, O Jerusalem: let my right hand forget her cunning.' Anglican choirboys in ruff and surplice trill the line mindlessly with one eye on the *Beano*; but their little Jewish coevals are taught the words as a political reality.

269

In the introduction to this most remarkable anthology,* Graham Greene brings out the contradictions in this unique city, whose name has traditionally been understood to mean 'Vision of Peace'.

> Those who come to pray and go away to mock are seeking the wrong Jerusalem. They expect, I think, to find peace there, the peace of a church, even of a museum. But Jerusalem was founded by a warrrior-king, it was the death place of Christ who foretold He would not bring peace but a sword, and it was the legendary scene of the Ascension of Mohammed who was hardly a peacemaker!

But for Graham Greene, the most remarkable fact about Jerusalem, which has been the scene of so many wars, sieges, burnings and sackings, is that it has survived. 'Perhaps that is what has drawn Miron Grindea to make this anthology in celebration of its survival. He founded his magazine *Adam* in the midst of the greatest massacre the world has yet known and he has fought over forty years to keep it alive with some of the obstinacy of those old trees in the Garden of Gethsemane that are more ancient, so it is said, than Hadrian's Wall.'

The range, the good taste and good sense of the anthology must all be commended, though they will be no surprise to Mr. Grindea's too few admirers and subscribers. The book is divided into two parts. In the first, the passages chosen allude to the chief historical associations of the city: the building of Solomon's Temple; its destruction and rebuilding and destruction again; the coming of Our Lord who said He would destroy it and rebuild it as the Catholic Church in three days; the long mourning of the Jews in exile, who did not understand His words. Then there is the coming of the pilgrims: Christians scavenging for bits of the True Cross; Jews wailing at their wall; finally, Moslems, venerating the rock on which the promise was made to their forefather Abraham, and from which the Prophet Himself was carried to Heaven on the winged steed al-Borak. And then, because there were pilgrimages, there were quarrels and because there were Holy Places there were wars. And a heart-rending and embittering section of the anthology is devoted to the holy wars which have been fought in that place ever since the seventh century.

In the second part of the book, we confront the extraordinary

---

* *Jerusalem: The Holy City in Literature*, edited by Miron Grindea (1982).

potency of the image of Jerusalem in the religious and poetic imagination of the world. G. K. Chesterton is quoted as saying, 'I can understand a man who had only seen in the distance Jerusalem sitting on the hill going no further and keeping that vision forever.' It is the fact that so few people have got even so far as the hills outside the place which has enabled the splendid flood of divine ideas to flood the consciousness of three major world religions: 'Seeking Jerusalem, dear Native Land/Through our long exile on Babylon's strand'. No delight in the Hanging Gardens for Abelard.

In a wonderful passage, Bunyan says 'Blessed is he whose lot it will be to see this holy city descending and lighting upon the place that shall be prepared for her situation and rest. Then will be a golden world . . . It will be then always summer, always sunshine, always pleasant, green, fruitful and beautiful to the sons of God. "And Judah shall dwell forever and Jerusalem from Generation to Generation."' It is the same thought which St. Augustine had had, homesick for the city of God, and which led Blake to write his perfect quatrain:

> I will give you the end of a golden string,
> Only wind it into a ball,
> It will lead you in at Heaven's gate
> Built into Jerusalem's wall.

The wonder of the Heavenly Jerusalem becomes more poignant and more remarkable the more you contemplate the earthly one. A certain sect of devout Jews regard it as so much their happy home, name ever dear to them, that they will stone you if you try to ride a bicycle through their *quartier* on the Sabbath. Jews of less fanatical mien have nevertheless been taught to regard Jerusalem as their rightful possession and home, a sacred truth which has entitled them to invade a Jordanian city, full of Palestinian Arabs, and desecrate the skyline with hideous Germanic architecture. Meanwhile, in the calm centre of this earthly Salem, Franciscans still occasionally inflict G.B.H. on Armenians or Copts for stepping an inch out of line at the Sepulchre of Our Lord; as if to remind us, in a trivial way, that Christian barbarities in the Holy City have been just as bad, and as blasphemous, as anything that the Jews get up to now, or the Saracens got up to in the past. One of the passages in this anthology which will stay in my mind comes from Havelock Ellis: 'Had there been a lunatic asylum in the suburbs of Jerusalem,

271

Jesus Christ would infallibly have been shut up in it at the outset of his public career. That interview with Satan would alone have damned him, and everything that happened after could but have confirmed the diagnosis. The whole religious complexion of the modern world is due to the absence from Jerusalem of a lunatic asylum.' A city of the mad with no loony bin sounds like an idea of hell. But the more you think about it, people being what they are, you can see why it becomes their idea of heaven.

*Spectator*, 23 January 1982

# The Facts of Death

The medical profession does not exactly deny that we are all incurable. But such a denial is to be inferred from almost all its pronouncements. Its panicky little pamphlets about heart disease or cancer suggest that with a little bit more self-discipline, we might all be immortal. Terrifying statistics are thrown at us, comparing the numbers who smoke cigarettes, eat butter, or die on the roads. But these statistics are no more nor less terrifying than the regular columns at the back of *The Times* each morning. The condition from which we are all suffering has reached 'epidemic' numbers of which AIDS, lung cancer and alcoholic poisoning constitute only the tiniest proportion. Mortality, that is what we have inherited from our parents.

One of the most striking, if not eerie features of life in the late twentieth century is how cleverly we disguise this fact from ourselves. Ours is the century in which the largest number of people has died. Europe has been strewn with corpses. And yet, how seldom nowadays we see them. I know many people who have reached the age of forty or fifty without having seen a single dead body in the course of their lives. In earlier generations, this would have been quite unthinkable. Not only would they have been shown the dead bodies of their parents or grandparents, but almost certainly they would have seen neighbours' and friends'. In the old days, if you died in hospital, they brought the body home as a matter of course. Now what happens? It has become a matter of interest to me what will actually *happen* to my body when I die. Dying – the spell before we actually turn into a stiff – has become a fashionable area of concern. For this, very largely, we have to thank the hospice movement. Pioneers at such places as St. Christopher's Hospice, St. Joseph's Hospice and Michael Sobel House have created an atmosphere in which ordinary members of the nursing and medical professions in National Health hospitals can recognise the need to

273

prepare for death and find how this is best done. In Oxford, Mother Frances Dominica at Helen House has established a hospice for dying children, and rediscovered what was familiar to the Victorians, that children are often better at dying than grown-ups. All these are admirable institutions and developments. They concern themselves with preparing the families for a person's death and with relieving the patient of pain.

All well and good. But when I come to lie in my hospice, having, I hope, patched up old quarrels and made my peace with God, I shall still find it hard to envisage my body as a corpse. I know it will happen. This hand, writing this essay, will be stiff and waxy. My features, only half recognisable, will be stiff. What colour or vivacity my face possesses will have ebbed away.

And what will they do with it? That is the question which haunts me. That is the area in which we most successfully manage to conceal from ourselves. It is one thing to prepare ourselves emotionally and spiritually for the great unknown. It is another to entertain theories about the passage of the soul from this world to the next. But somewhere, on a pavement, in a shop, at the bottom of the stairs, or in a hospital bed, there it lies. The thing which once was me.

Dying in public is the worst thing that can happen. Our body is then taken to a morgue, usually supervised by some unfortunate police officer. A friend of mind who was a Special Police Constable fainted three times when she was first taken to the St. Pancras morgue, as a raw recruit, and instructed in the procedure. There were about twelve stiffs laid out around them, and about twelve members of the Force listening to their senior officer. If more than eight days have passed since the dead person saw a doctor, there will have to be a coroner's inquest, to which the police will be summoned as witnesses if the death happpened in a public place. But, before the complications of the inquest, there is the embarrassing question of the stiff itself, its clothes, its rings, its pocket book. Families not infrequently accuse the police of rifling corpses, so it is necessary to do a thorough search and inventory. 'Now, which one shall we choose?' said the police officer looking round the morgue. At that point, a new one was being brought in, and he was selected. He was a smartly dressed man of the professional class. That very morning, he had looked in the glass, selected his tie, buttoned his waistcoat with those very fingers. 'Wrist watches,' said the policeman picking up one of the stiff hands. 'Now, many men don't wear them on their wrist, but further up the arm, so you rip up the sleeve to the elbow, like so.' (One Special Constable feeling queasy.) 'Now rings.' (Fingering the waxy ring.) 'This one here's got a signet ring, and that's just the sort of thing we might be accused of pocketing. So that must be included in the inventory and placed in a plastic bag with the pocket book and the watch and the various other effects. Sometimes of course a ring doesn't come off the finger that easy. In which case you have to break the finger.' Crack! (Collapse of Sensitive Special Constable.)

Most of us will hope to meet the end in hospital. In my experience, doctors have very little to do with the different aspects of dying. It may be they who diagnose the patient's condition and do the clever operations. But dealing with a patient in his last hours, knowing what to do with the corpse, and having to tell the family are all left in the hands of nurses; very often girls of less than twenty years of age. I went to see a staff nurse at a moderately big teaching hospital, and she agreed to let me sit in her seminar for student nurses on the subject of dying and bereavement. She was a pretty, elfin woman of twenty-three called Melanie. Her audience, all female, was aged about eighteen. All of them discussed the subject without callousness or breeziness, or false sentimentality. I was impressed by the fact that Melanie's eyes filled with tears at several points during the hour. All the girls admitted to being profoundly shocked by their first glimpse of a dead body, not least when the bodies did not *look* very dead. Sometimes the colour, and even the expression, lingers in a face for several hours.

Although, or perhaps because, they are dealing with it all the time, the nurses seem unable to recognise that we are all, at varying degrees of speed, turning into corpses. 'With a normal patient, you can put your head round the door and make jokes and that,' said one big pretty girl. 'But not with a patient who's terminally ill.' Perhaps if she recognised that we are *all* terminally ill, she would not be able to do her job properly.

We impose a lot on these girls. An extremely common phenomenon among nurses is the feeling of irrational guilt when a patient dies. They are often much closer to a patient than the family in the last few weeks and days; and as well as developing a deep bond with them, they are also responsible for administering the drugs. In cases of hopeless injury or incurably advanced diseases the doses of

275

painkillers will be stepped up. A narcotic such as diamorphine will eventually kill the patient. Many of these girls revealed sensations of ill-founded guilt when they had been the last to administer the dose.

When the end is come, it is usually the nurse who has to tell the family. In two cases close to me, a distraught nurse at the other end of a telephone has said that the patient has 'slightly collapsed' when they were actually dead. 'I had a call the other day about a patient who'd died,' admitted one of these student nurses. 'I said, "Hold on a moment, I'll get Staff Nurse." They must have thought I was really stupid.' Melanie told her girls that they must prepare for these moments. They must have a set form of speech. And they must be able to tell families straight out that the patient is dead. Easier to say than do, I would think.

I was still ghoulishly interested in what actually happens when there is a death on the ward. First, the nurse pulls the curtain round the bed, and makes sure the patient is really dead. 'I try to straighten them up a bit,' Melanie said, 'in case the relatives want to see them; and then I ring the family at once and tell them. Then, when the relatives have been told, I would lay the patient out.' 'While they are still in the ward?' 'Yes. It would be wrong to say that I like this part of the job, but I feel it is a privilege. It is the last thing I can do for that particular patient, and I always feel great reverence while I am doing it . . . It's a dreadful moment when the porter comes and takes the patient off to the morgue.'

I left Melanie hoping that she or someone like her would be with me when I turn into a corpse. Once that stage has been reached, almost everybody is placed in the hands of an undertaker. I went to see a Mr. D. because he had handled the funeral of a friend of mine some years ago. He is a raven-haired, plump sort of man who does not look old enough to have been an undertaker for twenty-eight years. 'Do you really want to know all the grisly details?' he asked with a nervous grin and lit up a small cigar called a Hamlet. 'Well, yes please, Mr. D.'

If the death occurs at home, the undertaker arrives with a van to take away the corpse. Some firms use ambulances. Mr. D. uses a van. 'No,' he corrected me. 'It is *based* on a van.' He did not explain what this meant. Another undertaker I have asked says that they 'sometimes' zip the stiff into an airtight plastic container, as is customary in the United States. Smaller English firms would be content to cover the body with a sheet. Nothing is done to the body until it reaches the 'chapel of rest' in the back yard of the funeral directors.

'The basic procedure is to strip the body and wash it down. Then you dress it again.' Dead legs splay apart unless you tie them together. Orifices leak unless they are stuffed. The centre of a dead eye turns to liquid, giving the closed lids a curiously flat appearance. An eyeshade or a bit of cotton wool is usually stuffed under the eyelid to make the corpse look a little less dead.

A high proportion of families still ask to see the 'deceased', as Mr. D. invariably called the corpse. If the body is to be kept for any length of time or viewed, Mr. D. recommends embalming. 'Largely for reasons of hygiene. The body is decomposing from the moment it dies and well,' he puffs his Hamlet, 'there's a bit of a smell. People think when you embalm the deceased, its going back to the practices of ancient Egypt or something, but it's not like that at all. You make a small incision, not much more than an inch and a half in length and you drain off the fluid. Then you pump in the same amount of embalming fluid.' 'How much?' 'On average, there is one pint of liquid for every stone of body weight.'

One of the things many people find shocking when seeing the dead body of someone they loved is the absence of colour. The rosiest, jolliest looking man with a glass in his hand at the bar can turn, in a matter of hours, to the colour and texture of a cheap candle: waxy and white. Embalming fluid reduces the shock for mourners by restoring a little colour to the cheeks. Does Mr. D. advocate the use of makeup, as in American funeral parlours? He pauses; 'I usually add a little powder. Just to take the shine off.'

Opinions differ about how corpses should be arrayed. 'We don't talk about shrouds,' said Mr. D. 'We talk about gowns.' 'What's it like?' 'Well, it's more like a dressing gown worn over your shirt and tie, that kind of thing.' Some friends of mine were so horrified at their father being dressed, as they thought, like a cheap imitation of Noël Coward that they went to the trouble of taking off the 'gown' and dressing him up in one of his own tweed suits. Not easy to do, I should imagine. High Anglican priests are vested in the coffin, as for the altar. 'It's a difficult job,' I was told my one of them. 'You have to slit the alb down the back and wiggle the arms through. It needs at least two people to do it. It's much easier if you can keep the body upright and just pop the chasuble over its head.' The clever Jesuits, on the other hand, have an ingenious solution to this. They cut the

277

chasubles in half and lay them on top of their recumbent brethren. 'No one's going to look underneath,' the superior of one Jesuit house told me, 'and what the eye does not see, the heart doesn't grieve over.' He did not, candidly, look as if he was going to grieve very much over *any* part of his dead *confrère*'s anatomy.

All dressed up, and ready to go, the stiff will finally be disposed of. When my father died, the village joiner made the coffin, and friends carried him into the church. After the nicest funeral service I have ever attended, he was carried out a few yards into the churchyard and buried under the yew trees half a mile from the sea. Most of us won't be so lucky. Forty per cent go to municipal cemeteries, usually in the bleakest part of a town. Sixty per cent (and the number is rising all the time) will end up in the crem. The only metal in a coffin due to be cremated is in the screws and nails keeping the thing together. The handles are either wood or plastic with a metallic finish. The directors of crems are understandably cagey about the mythology which has grown up around them. We have all heard of stories of the corpse being taken out of the coffin, and the coffin resold. In most crems, this would be quite difficult, since the coffin glides down the chute directly into an individual oven ('cremator' as they are called in the trade). Everyone in the world seems to know someone who knew someone else who worked in a crem. We are all familiar with stories; stiffs sitting up in the coffins in the flames; inexperienced orderlies opening the oven doors and finding that the Loved One has not been quite cooked through. By that stage, when my turn comes, I shall be beyond caring. What continues to haunt me and to horrify me is the period between Melanie drawing the curtain around my bed and the crematorium parson pressing the button. Some people will tell you that it is stupid to be afraid of corpses. On the mercifully few occasions when I have seen the dead, it has not been *their* corpses that I have been afraid of. It has been my own.

*Spectator*, 2 November 1985

P9-BIQ-246

2 555 000 020349 Z

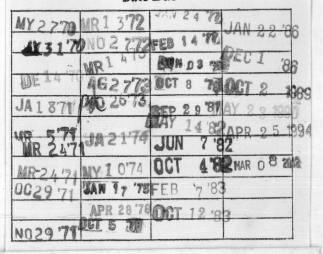

62414 PZ
3
Jackson J14we

We have always lived in the
castle

**Date Due**

| | | | |
|---|---|---|---|
| MY 27 70 | MR 1 3'72 | JAN 24 72 | JAN 22 '86 |
| JX 31 70 | NO 2 7 72 | FEB 14 72 | DEC 1 '86 |
| DE 14 70 | MR 1 4'73 | JUN D3 72 | |
| JA 18 71 | AG 27 73 | OCT 8 73 | OCT 2 1989 |
| | MO 26 73 | SEP 29 81 | MAY 2 9 100 |
| MR 5'71 | JA 21 74 | MAY 14 '82 | APR 25 1994 |
| MR 24 71 | | JUN 7 '82 | |
| MR 24 71 | MY 1 0'74 | OCT 4 82 | MAR 0 8 2012 |
| OC 29 '71 | JAN 17 '75 | FEB '7 '83 | |
| | APR 28 '78 | OCT 12 '83 | |
| NO 29 '71 | OCT 5 78 | | |

## CHABOT
## COLLEGE
## LIBRARY

25555 Hesperian Boulevard
Hayward, California 94545

 PRINTED IN U.S.A.

# WE HAVE ALWAYS LIVED IN THE CASTLE

**Also by Shirley Jackson**

# SHIRLEY JACKSON

## We Have Always Lived in the Castle

THE VIKING PRESS · NEW YORK

PS
3519
.A392
.W4

PZ
3
J14we

COPYRIGHT © 1962 BY SHIRLEY JACKSON
ALL RIGHTS RESERVED

PUBLISHED IN 1962 BY THE VIKING PRESS, INC.
625 MADISON AVENUE, NEW YORK, N.Y. 10022

PUBLISHED SIMULTANEOUSLY IN CANADA BY
THE MACMILLAN COMPANY OF CANADA LTD.

LIBRARY OF CONGRESS CATALOG CARD NUMBER: 62-17935
PRINTED IN THE U.S.A. BY THE COLONIAL PRESS INC.

EIGHTH PRINTING NOVEMBER 1968

FOR PASCAL COVICI

62414

# WE HAVE ALWAYS LIVED IN THE CASTLE

~~~~~~~~~~~~~~~~~~~~~~~~~~~~~~~~~~~~~~~~~~~~~~~

MY NAME IS MARY KATHERINE BLACKWOOD. I AM EIGHT-
een years old, and I live with my sister Constance. I have
often thought that with any luck at all I could have been
born a werewolf, because the two middle fingers on both
my hands are the same length, but I have had to be content with what I had. I dislike washing myself, and dogs,
and noise. I like my sister Constance, and Richard Plan-
tagenet, and *Amanita phalloides,* the death-cup mushroom. Everyone else in my family is dead.

The last time I glanced at the library books on the kitchen shelf they were more than five months overdue, and I wondered whether I would have chosen differently if I had known that these were the last books, the ones which would stand forever on our kitchen shelf. We rarely moved things; the Blackwoods were never much of a family for restlessness and stirring. We dealt with the small surface transient objects, the books and the flowers and the spoons, but underneath we had always a solid foundation of stable possessions. We always put things back where they belonged. We dusted and swept under tables and chairs and beds and pictures and rugs and lamps, but we left them where they were; the tortoise-shell toilet set on our mother's dressing table was never off place by so much as a fraction of an inch. Blackwoods had always lived in our house, and kept their things in order; as soon as a new Blackwood wife moved in, a place was found for her belongings, and so our house was built up with layers of Blackwood property weighting it, and keeping it steady against the world.

It was on a Friday in late April that I brought the library books into our house. Fridays and Tuesdays were terrible days, because I had to go into the village. Someone had to go to the library, and the grocery; Constance never went past her own garden, and Uncle Julian could not. Therefore it was not pride that took me into the village twice a week, or even stubbornness, but only the simple need for books and food. It may have been pride that brought me into Stella's for a cup of coffee before I started home; I told myself it was pride and would not

avoid going into Stella's no matter how much I wanted
to be at home, but I knew, too, that Stella would see me
pass if I did not go in, and perhaps think I was afraid, and
that thought I could not endure.

"Good morning, Mary Katherine," Stella always said,
reaching over to wipe the counter with a damp rag, "how
are you today?"

"Very well, thank you."

"And Constance Blackwood, is she well?"

"Very well, thank you."

"And how is *he?*"

"As well as can be expected. Black coffee, please."

If anyone else came in and sat down at the counter I
would leave my coffee without seeming hurried, and
leave, nodding goodbye to Stella. "Keep well," she always said automatically as I went out.

I chose the library books with care. There were books
in our house, of course; our father's study had books covering two walls, but I liked fairy tales and books of history, and Constance liked books about food. Although
Uncle Julian never took up a book, he liked to see Constance reading in the evenings while he worked at his papers, and sometimes he turned his head to look at her and
nod.

"What are you reading, my dear? A pretty sight, a
lady with a book."

"I'm reading something called *The Art of Cooking,*
Uncle Julian."

"Admirable."

We never sat quietly for long, of course, with Uncle

Julian in the room, but I do not recall that Constance and I have ever opened the library books which are still on our kitchen shelf. It was a fine April morning when I came out of the library; the sun was shining and the false glorious promises of spring were everywhere, showing oddly through the village grime. I remember that I stood on the library steps holding my books and looking for a minute at the soft hinted green in the branches against the sky and wishing, as I always did, that I could walk home across the sky instead of through the village. From the library steps I could cross the street directly and walk on the other side along to the grocery, but that meant that I must pass the general store and the men sitting in front. In this village the men stayed young and did the gossiping and the women aged with grey evil weariness and stood silently waiting for the men to get up and come home. I could leave the library and walk up the street on this side until I was opposite the grocery and then cross; that was preferable, although it took me past the post office and the Rochester house with the piles of rusted tin and the broken automobiles and the empty gas tins and the old mattresses and plumbing fixtures and wash tubs that the Harler family brought home and—I genuinely believe—loved.

The Rochester house was the loveliest in town and had once had a walnut-panelled library and a second-floor ballroom and a profusion of roses along the veranda; our mother had been born there and by rights it should have belonged to Constance. I decided as I always did that it would be safer to go past the post office and the

Rochester house, although I disliked seeing the house where our mother was born. This side of the street was generally deserted in the morning, since it was shady, and after I went into the grocery I would in any case have to pass the general store to get home, and passing it going and coming was more than I could bear.

Outside the village, on Hill Road and River Road and Old Mountain, people like the Clarkes and the Carringtons had built new lovely homes. They had to come through the village to get to Hill Road and River Road because the main street of the village was also the main highway across the state, but the Clarke children and the Carrington boys went to private schools and the food in the Hill Road kitchens came from the towns and the city; mail was taken from the village post office by car along the River Road and up to Old Mountain, but the Mountain people mailed their letters in the towns and the River Road people had their hair cut in the city.

I was always puzzled that the people of the village, living in their dirty little houses on the main highway or out on Creek Road, smiled and nodded and waved when the Clarkes and the Carringtons drove by; if Helen Clarke came into Elbert's Grocery to pick up a can of tomato sauce or a pound of coffee her cook had forgotten everyone told her "Good morning," and said the weather was better today. The Clarkes' house is newer but no finer than the Blackwood house. Our father brought home the first piano ever seen in the village. The Carringtons own the paper mill but the Blackwoods own all the land between the highway and the river. The

Shepherds of Old Mountain gave the village its town hall, which is white and peaked and set in a green lawn with a cannon in front. There was some talk once of putting in zoning laws in the village and tearing down the shacks on Creek Road and building up the whole village to match the town hall, but no one ever lifted a finger; maybe they thought the Blackwoods might take to attending town meetings if they did. The villagers get their hunting and fishing licenses in the town hall, and once a year the Clarkes and the Carringtons and the Shepherds attend town meeting and solemnly vote to get the Harler junk yard off Main Street and take away the benches in front of the general store, and each year the villagers gleefully outvote them. Past the town hall, bearing to the left, is Blackwood Road, which is the way home. Blackwood Road goes in a great circle around the Blackwood land and along every inch of Blackwood Road is a wire fence built by our father. Not far past the town hall is the big black rock which marks the entrance to the path where I unlock the gate and lock it behind me and go through the woods and am home.

The people of the village have always hated us.

I played a game when I did the shopping. I thought about the children's games where the board is marked into little spaces and each player moves according to a throw of the dice; there were always dangers, like "lose one turn" and "go back four spaces" and "return to start," and little helps, like "advance three spaces" and "take an extra turn." The library was my start and the

black rock was my goal. I had to move down one side of
Main Street, cross, and then move up the other side until
I reached the black rock, when I would win. I began
well, with a good safe turn along the empty side of Main
Street, and perhaps this would turn out to be one of the
very good days; it was like that sometimes, but not often
on spring mornings. If it was a very good day I would
later make an offering of jewelry out of gratitude.

I walked quickly when I started, taking a deep breath
to go on with and not looking around; I had the library
books and my shopping bag to carry and I watched my
feet moving one after the other; two feet in our mother's
old brown shoes. I felt someone watching me from inside the post office—we did not accept mail, and we did
not have a telephone; both had become unbearable six
years before—but I could bear a quick stare from the
office; that was old Miss Dutton, who never did her staring out in the open like other folks, but only looked out
between blinds or from behind curtains. I never looked at
the Rochester house. I could not bear to think of our
mother being born there. I wondered sometimes if the
Harler people knew that they lived in a house which
should have belonged to Constance; there was always so
much noise of crashing tinware in their yard that they
could not hear me walking. Perhaps the Harlers thought
that the unending noise drove away demons, or perhaps
they were musical and found it agreeable; perhaps the
Harlers lived inside the way they did outside, sitting in
old bathtubs and eating their dinner off broken plates set
on the skeleton of an old Ford car, rattling cans as they

ate, and talking in bellows. A spray of dirt always lay across the sidewalk where the Harlers lived.

Crossing the street (lose one turn) came next, to get to the grocery directly opposite. I always hesitated, vulnerable and exposed, on the side of the road while the traffic went by. Most Main Street traffic was going through, cars and trucks passing through the village because the highway did, so the drivers hardly glanced at me; I could tell a local car by the quick ugly glance from the driver and I wondered, always, what would happen if I stepped down from the curb onto the road; would there be a quick, almost unintended swerve toward me? Just to scare me, perhaps, just to see me jump? And then the laughter, coming from all sides, from behind the blinds in the post office, from the men in front of the general store, from the women peering out of the grocery doorway, all of them watching and gloating, to see Mary Katherine Blackwood scurrying out of the way of a car. I sometimes lost two or even three turns because I waited so carefully for the road to clear in both directions before I crossed.

In the middle of the street I came out of the shade and into the bright, misleading sunshine of April; by July the surface of the road would be soft in the heat and my feet would stick, making the crossing more perilous (Mary Katherine Blackwood, her foot caught in the tar, cringing as a car bore down on her; go back, all the way, and start over), and the buildings would be uglier. All of the village was of a piece, a time, and a style; it was as though the people needed the ugliness of the village, and fed on it. The houses and the stores seemed to have been set up in contemptuous haste to provide shelter for the drab and the unpleasant, and the Rochester house and the Blackwood house and even the town hall had been brought here perhaps accidentally from some far lovely country where people lived with grace. Perhaps the fine houses had been captured—perhaps as punishment for the Rochesters and the Blackwoods and their secret bad hearts?—and were held prisoner in the village; perhaps their slow rot was a sign of the ugliness of the villagers. The row of stores along Main Street was unchangingly grey. The people who owned the stores lived above them, in a row of second-story apartments, and the curtains in the regular line of second-story windows were pale and without life; whatever planned to be colorful lost its heart quickly in the village. The blight on the village never came from the Blackwoods; the villagers belonged here and the village was the only proper place for them.

I always thought about rot when I came toward the row of stores; I thought about burning black painful rot that ate away from inside, hurting dreadfully. I wished it on the village.

I had a shopping list for the grocery; Constance made it out for me every Tuesday and Friday before I left home. The people of the village disliked the fact that we always had plenty of money to pay for whatever we wanted; we had taken our money out of the bank, of course, and I knew they talked about the money hidden in our house, as though it were great heaps of golden coins and Constance and Uncle Julian and I sat in the evenings, our library books forgotten, and played with it, running our hands through it and counting and stacking and tumbling it, jeering and mocking behind locked doors. I imagine that there were plenty of rotting hearts in the village coveting our heaps of golden coins but they were cowards and they were afraid of Blackwoods. When I took my grocery list out of my shopping bag I took out the purse too so that Elbert in the grocery would know that I had brought money and he could not refuse to sell to me.

It never mattered who was in the grocery. I was always served at once; Mr. Elbert or his pale greedy wife always came right away from wherever they were in the store to get me what I wanted. Sometimes, if their older boy was helping out in school vacation, they hurried to make sure that he was not the one who waited on me and once when a little girl—a child strange to the village, of course—came close to me in the grocery Mrs. Elbert pulled her back so roughly that she screamed and then there was a long still minute while everyone waited before Mrs. Elbert took a breath and said, "Anything else?" I always stood perfectly straight and stiff when the children came close, because I was afraid of them. I was afraid that they might touch me and the mothers would come at me like a flock of taloned hawks; that was always the picture I had in my mind—birds descending, striking, gashing with razor claws. Today I had a great many things to buy for Constance, and it was a relief to see that there were no children in the store and not many

women; take an extra turn, I thought, and said to Mr.
Elbert, "Good morning."

He nodded to me; he could not go entirely without
greeting me and yet the women in the store were watching. I turned my back to them, but I could feel them
standing behind me, holding a can or a half-filled bag of
cookies or a head of lettuce, not willing to move until I
had gone out through the door again and the wave of
talk began and they were swept back into their own lives.
Mrs. Donell was back there somewhere; I had seen her as
I came in, and I wondered as I had before if she came on
purpose when she knew I was coming, because she always
tried to say something; she was one of the few who spoke.

"A roasting chicken," I said to Mr. Elbert, and across
the store his greedy wife opened the refrigerated case
and took out a chicken and began to wrap it. "A small
leg of lamb," I said, "my Uncle Julian always fancies a
roasted lamb in the first spring days." I should not have
said it, I knew, and a little gasp went around the store
like a scream. I could make them run like rabbits, I
thought, if I said to them what I really wanted to, but
they would only gather again outside and watch for me
there. "Onions," I said politely to Mr. Elbert, "coffee,
bread, flour. Walnuts," I said, "and sugar; we are very
low on sugar." Somewhere behind me there was a little
horrified laugh, and Mr. Elbert glanced past me, briefly,
and then to the items he was arranging on the counter.
In a minute Mrs. Elbert would bring my chicken and
my meat, wrapped, and set them down by the other

things; I need not turn around until I was ready to go. "Two quarts of milk," I said. "A half pint of cream, a pound of butter." The Harrises had stopped delivering dairy goods to us six years ago and I brought milk and butter home from the grocery now. "And a dozen eggs." Constance had forgotten to put eggs on the list, but there had been only two at home. "A box of peanut brittle," I said; Uncle Julian would clatter and crunch over his papers tonight, and go to bed sticky.

"The Blackwoods always did set a fine table." That was Mrs. Donell, speaking clearly from somewhere behind me, and someone giggled and someone else said "Shh." I never turned; it was enough to feel them all there in back of me without looking into their flat grey faces with the hating eyes. I wish you were all dead, I thought, and longed to say it out loud. Constance said, "Never let them see that you care," and "If you pay any attention they'll only get worse," and probably it was true, but I wished they were dead. I would have liked to come into the grocery some morning and see them all, even the Elberts and the children, lying there crying with the pain and dying. I would then help myself to groceries, I thought, stepping over their bodies, taking whatever I fancied from the shelves, and go home, with perhaps a kick for Mrs. Donell while she lay there. I was never sorry when I had thoughts like this; I only wished they would come true. "It's wrong to hate them," Constance said, "it only weakens *you*," but I hated them anyway, and wondered why it had been worth while creating them in the first place.

Mr. Elbert put all my groceries together on the counter and waited, looking past me into the distance. "That's all I want today," I told him, and without looking at me he wrote the prices on a slip and added, then passed the slip to me so I could make sure he had not cheated me. I always made a point of checking his figures carefully, although he never made a mistake; there were not many things I could do to get back at them, but I did what I could. The groceries filled my shopping bag and another bag besides, but there was no way of getting them home except by carrying them. No one would ever offer to help me, of course, even if I would let them.

Lose two turns. With my library books and my groceries, going slowly, I had to walk down the sidewalk past the general store and into Stella's. I stopped in the doorway of the grocery, feeling around inside myself for some thought to make me safe. Behind me the little stirrings and coughings began. They were getting ready to talk again, and across the width of the store the Elberts were probably rolling their eyes at each other in relief. I froze my face hard. Today I was going to think about taking our lunch out into the garden, and while I kept my eyes open just enough to see where I was walking—our mother's brown shoes going up and down—in my mind I was setting the table with a green cloth and bringing out yellow dishes and strawberries in a white bowl. Yellow dishes, I thought, feeling the eyes of the men looking at me as I went by, and Uncle Julian shall have a nice soft egg with toast broken into it, and I will remember to ask Constance to put a shawl across his shoulders because it is still very early spring. Without looking I could see the grinning and the gesturing; I wished they were all dead and I was walking on their bodies. They rarely spoke directly to me, but only to each other. "That's one of the Blackwood girls," I heard one of them say in a high mocking voice, "one of the Blackwood girls from Blackwood Farm." "Too bad about the Blackwoods," someone else said, just loud enough, "too bad about those poor girls." "Nice farm out there," they said, "nice land to farm. Man could get rich, farming the Blackwood land. If he had a million years and three heads, and didn't care what grew, a man could get rich. Keep their land pretty well locked up, the Blackwoods do." "Man could get rich." "Too bad about the Blackwood girls." "Never can tell what'll grow on Blackwood land."

I am walking on their bodies, I thought, we are having lunch in the garden and Uncle Julian is wearing his shawl. I always held my groceries carefully along here, because one terrible morning I had dropped the shopping bag and the eggs broke and the milk spilled and I gathered up what I could while they shouted, telling myself that whatever I did I would not run away, shovelling cans and boxes and spilled sugar wildly back into the shopping bag, telling myself not to run away.

In front of Stella's there was a crack in the sidewalk that looked like a finger pointing; the crack had always been there. Other landmarks, like the handprint Johnny Harris made in the concrete foundation of the town hall and the Mueller boy's initials on the library porch, had been put in in times that I remembered; I was in the third grade at the school when the town hall was built. But the crack in the sidewalk in front of Stella's had always been there, just as Stella's had always been there. I remember roller-skating across the crack, and being careful not to step on it or it would break our mother's back, and riding a bicycle past here with my hair flying behind; the villagers had not openly disliked us then although our father said they were trash. Our mother told me once that the crack was here when she was a girl in the Rochester house, so it must have been here when she married our father and went to live on Blackwood Farm, and I suppose the crack was there, like a finger pointing, from the time when the village was first put together out of old grey wood and the ugly people with their evil faces were brought from some impossible place and set down in the houses to live.

Stella bought the coffee urn and put in the marble counter with the insurance money when her husband died, but otherwise there had been no change in Stella's since I could remember; Constance and I had come in here to spend pennies after school and every afternoon we picked up the newspaper to take home for our father to read in the evening; we no longer bought newspapers, but Stella still sold them, along with magazines and penny candy and grey postcards of the town hall.

"Good morning, Mary Katherine," Stella said when I sat down at the counter and put my groceries on the floor; I sometimes thought when I wished all the village people dead that I might spare Stella because she was the closest to kind that any of them could be, and the only one who managed to keep hold of any color at all. She was round and pink and when she put on a bright print dress it stayed looking bright for a little while before it merged into the dirty grey of the rest. "How are you today?" she asked.

"Very well, thank you."

"And Constance Blackwood, is she well?"

"Very well, thank you."

"And how is *he?*"

"As well as can be expected. Black coffee, please." I really preferred sugar and cream in my coffee, because it is such bitter stuff, but since I only came here out of pride I needed to accept only the barest minimum for token.

If anyone came into Stella's while I was there I got up and left quietly, but some days I had bad luck. This morning she had only set my coffee down on the counter when there was a shadow against the doorway, and Stella looked up, and said, "Good morning, Jim." She went down to the other end of the counter and waited, expecting him to sit down there so I could leave without being noticed, but it was Jim Donell and I knew at once that today I had bad luck. Some of the people in the village had real faces that I knew and could hate individually; Jim Donell and his wife were among these, because they were deliberate instead of just hating dully and from habit like the others. Most people would have stayed down at the end of the counter where Stella waited, but Jim Donell came right to the end where I was sitting and took the stool next to me, as close to me as he could come because, I knew, he wanted this morning to be bad luck for me.

"They tell me," he said, swinging to sit sideways on his stool and look at me directly, "they tell me you're moving away."

I wished he would not sit so close to me; Stella came toward us on the inside of the counter and I wished she would ask him to move so I could get up and leave without having to struggle around him. "They tell me you're moving away," he said solemnly.

"No," I said, because he was waiting.

"Funny," he said, looking from me to Stella and then back. "I could have swore someone told me you'd be going soon."

"No," I said.

"Coffee, Jim?" Stella asked.

"Who do you think would of started a story like that, Stella? Who do you think would want to tell me they're moving away when they're not doing any such thing?" Stella shook her head at him, but she was trying not to smile. I saw that my hands were tearing at the paper napkin in my lap, ripping off a little corner, and I forced my hands to be still and made a rule for myself: Whenever I saw a tiny scrap of paper I was to remember to be kinder to Uncle Julian.

"Can't ever tell how gossip gets around," Jim Donnell said. Perhaps someday soon Jim Donnell would die; perhaps there was already a rot growing inside him that was going to kill him. "Did you ever hear anything like the gossip in this town?" he asked Stella.

"Leave her alone, Jim," Stella said.

Uncle Julian was an old man and he was dying, dying regrettably, more surely than Jim Donell and Stella and anyone else. The poor old Uncle Julian was dying and I made a firm rule to be kinder to him. We would have a picnic lunch on the lawn. Constance would bring his shawl and put it over his shoulders, and I would lie on the grass.

"I'm not bothering anybody, Stell. Am I bothering anybody? I'm just asking Miss Mary Katherine Blackwood here how it happens everyone in town is saying she and her big sister are going to be leaving us soon. Moving away. Going somewheres else to live." He stirred his coffee; from the corner of my eye I could see the spoon going around and around and around, and I wanted to laugh. There was something so simple and silly about the spoon going around while Jim Donell talked; I wondered if he would stop talking if I reached out and took hold of the spoon. Very likely he would, I told myself wisely, very likely he would throw the coffee in my face.

"Going somewheres else," he said sadly.

"Cut it out," Stella said.

I would listen more carefully when Uncle Julian told his story. I was already bringing peanut brittle; that was good.

"Here I was all upset," Jim Donell said, "thinking the town would be losing one of its fine old families. That would be really too bad." He swung the other way around on the stool because someone else was coming through the doorway; I was looking at my hands in my lap and of course would not turn around to see who was coming, but then Jim Donell said "Joe," and I knew it was Dunham, the carpenter; "Joe, you ever hear anything like this? Here all over town they're saying that the Blackwoods are moving away, and now Miss Mary Katherine Blackwood sits right here and speaks up and tells me they're not."

There was a little silence. I knew that Dunham was scowling, looking at Jim Donell and at Stella and at me, thinking over what he had heard, sorting out the words and deciding what each one meant. "That so?" he said at last.

"Listen, you two," Stella said, but Jim Donell went right on, talking with his back to me, and his legs stretched out so I could not get past him and outside. "I was saying to people only this morning it's too bad when the old families go. Although you could rightly say a good number of the Blackwoods are gone already." He laughed, and slapped the counter with his hand. "Gone already," he said again. The spoon in his cup was still, but he was talking on. "A village loses a lot of style when the fine old people go. Anyone would think," he said slowly, "that they wasn't wanted."

"That's right," Dunham said, and he laughed.

"The way they live up in their fine old private estate, with their fences and their private path and their stylish way of living." He always went on until he was tired. When Jim Donell thought of something to say he said it as often and in as many ways as possible, perhaps because he had very few ideas and had to wring each one dry. Besides, each time he repeated himself he thought it was funnier; I knew he might go on like this until he was really sure that no one was listening any more, and I made a rule for myself: Never think anything more than once, and I put my hands quietly in my lap. I am living on the moon, I told myself, I have a little house all by myself on the moon.

"Well," Jim Donell said; he smelled, too. "I can always tell people I used to know the Blackwoods. They never did anything to *me* that I can remember, always perfectly polite to *me*. Not," he said, and laughed, "that I ever got invited to take my dinner with them, nothing like that."

"That's enough right there," Stella said, and her voice was sharp. "You go pick on someone else, Jim Donell."

"Was I picking on anyone? You think I *wanted* to be asked to dinner? You think I'm *crazy?*"

"Me," Dunham said, "I can always tell people I fixed their broken step once and never got paid for it." That was true. Constance had sent me out to tell him that we wouldn't pay carpenter's prices for a raw board nailed crookedly across the step when what he was supposed to do was build it trim and new. When I went out and told him we wouldn't pay he grinned at me and spat, and picked up his hammer and pried the board loose and threw it on the ground. "Do it yourself," he said to me, and got into his truck and drove away. "Never did get paid for it," he said now.

"That must of been an oversight, Joe. You just go

right up and speak to Miss Constance Blackwood and she'll see you get what's coming to you. Just if you get invited to dinner, Joe, you just be sure and say no thank you to Miss Blackwood."

Dunham laughed. "Not me," he said. "I fixed their step for them and never did get paid for it."

"Funny," Jim Donell said, "them getting the house fixed up and all, and planning to move away all the time."

"Mary Katherine," Stella said, coming down inside the counter to where I was sitting, "you go along home. Just get up off that stool and go along home. There won't be any peace around here until you go."

"Now, *that's* the truth," Jim Donell said. Stella looked at him, and he moved his legs and let me pass. "You just say the word, Miss Mary Katherine, and we'll all come out and help you pack. Just you say the word, Merricat."

"And you can tell your sister from me—" Dunham started to say, but I hurried, and by the time I got outside all I could hear was the laughter, the two of them and Stella.

I liked my house on the moon, and I put a fireplace in it and a garden outside (what would flourish, growing on the moon? I must ask Constance) and I was going to have lunch outside in my garden on the moon. Things on the moon were very bright, and odd colors; my little house would be blue. I watched my small brown feet go in and out, and let the shopping bag swing a little by my side; I had been to Stella's and now I needed only to pass the town hall, which would be empty except for the people who made out dog licenses and the people who

counted traffic fines from the drivers who followed the
highway into the village and on through, and the people
who sent out notices about water and sewage and gar-
bage and forbade other people to burn leaves or to fish;
these would all be buried somewhere deep inside the
town hall, working busily together; I had nothing to
fear from them unless I fished out of season. I thought of
catching scarlet fish in the rivers on the moon and saw
that the Harris boys were in their front yard, clamoring
and quarrelling with half a dozen other boys. I had not
been able to see them until I came past the corner by the
town hall, and I could still have turned back and gone
the other way, up the main highway to the creek, and
then across the creek and home along the other half of
the path to our house, but it was late, and I had the groceries, and the creek was nasty to wade in our mother's
brown shoes, and I thought, I am living on the moon, and
I walked quickly. They saw me at once, and I thought
of them rotting away and curling in pain and crying out
loud; I wanted them doubled up and crying on the
ground in front of me.

"Merricat," they called, "Merricat, Merricat," and
moved all together to stand in a line by the fence.

I wondered if their parents taught them, Jim Donell
and Dunham and dirty Harris leading regular drills of
their children, teaching them with loving care, making
sure they pitched their voices right; how else could so
many children learn so thoroughly?

Merricat, said Connie, would you like a cup of tea?
Oh no, said Merricat, you'll poison me.

Merricat, said Connie, would you like to go to sleep?
Down in the boneyard ten feet deep!

I was pretending that I did not speak their language; on the moon we spoke a soft, liquid tongue, and sang in the starlight, looking down on the dead dried world; I was almost halfway past the fence.

"Merricat, Merricat!"

"Where's old Connie—home cooking dinner?"

"Would you like a cup of tea?"

It was strange to be inside myself, walking steadily and rigidly past the fence, putting my feet down strongly but without haste that they might have noticed, to be inside and know that they were looking at me; I was hiding very far inside but I could hear them and see them still from one corner of my eye. I wished they were all lying there dead on the ground.

"Down in the boneyard ten feet deep."

"Merricat!"

Once when I was going past, the Harris boys' mother came out onto the porch, perhaps to see what they were all yelling so about. She stood there for a minute watching and listening and I stopped and looked at her, looking into her flat dull eyes and knowing I must not speak to her and knowing I would. "Can't you make them stop?" I asked her that day, wondering if there was anything in this woman I could speak to, if she had ever run joyfully over grass, or had watched flowers, or known delight or love. "Can't you make them stop?"

"Kids," she said, not changing her voice or her look or her air of dull enjoyment, "don't call the lady names."

"Yes, ma," one of the boys said soberly.

"Don't go near no fence. Don't call no lady names."

And I walked on, while they shrieked and shouted and the woman stood on the porch and laughed.

Merricat, said Connie, would you like a cup of tea?
Oh, no, said Merricat, you'll poison me.

Their tongues will burn, I thought, as though they had eaten fire. Their throats will burn when the words come out, and in their bellies they will feel a torment hotter than a thousand fires.

"Goodbye, Merricat," they called as I went by the end of the fence, "don't hurry back."

"Goodbye, Merricat, give our love to Connie."

"Goodbye, Merricat," but I was at the black rock and there was the gate to our path.

~~~~~~~~~~~~~~~~~~~~~~~~~~~~~~~~~~~~~~~~~~~~~~~~~~~~~~~~~~~~

## 2

I HAD TO PUT DOWN THE SHOPPING BAG TO OPEN THE LOCK
on the gate; it was a simple padlock and any child could
have broken it, but on the gate was a sign saying PRIVATE
NO TRESPASSING and no one could go past that. Our
father had put up the signs and the gates and the locks
when he closed off the path; before, everyone used
the path as a short-cut from the village to the highway four-corners where the bus stopped; it saved them
perhaps a quarter of a mile to use our path and walk past

25

62414

our front door. Our mother disliked the sight of anyone
who wanted to walk past our front door, and when
our father brought her to live in the Blackwood house,
one of the first things he had to do was close off the path
and fence in the entire Blackwood property, from the
highway to the creek. There was another gate at the
other end of the path, although I rarely went that way,
and that gate too had a padlock and a sign saying PRIVATE
NO TRESPASSING. "The highway's built for common people," our mother said, "and my front door is private."

Anyone who came to see us, properly invited, came
up the main drive which led straight from the gateposts
on the highway up to our front door. When I was small
I used to lie in my bedroom at the back of the house and
imagine the driveway and the path as a crossroad meeting before our front door, and up and down the driveway went the good people, the clean and rich ones
dressed in satin and lace, who came rightfully to visit,
and back and forth along the path, sneaking and weaving and sidestepping servilely, went the people from the
village. They can't get in, I used to tell myself over and
over, lying in my dark room with the trees patterned
in shadow on the ceiling, they can't ever get in any more;
the path is closed forever. Sometimes I stood inside the
fence, hidden by the bushes, and watched people walking on the highway to get from the village to the four
corners. As far as I knew, no one from the village had
ever tried to use the path since our father locked the
gates.

When I had moved the shopping bag inside, I carefully locked the gate again, and tested the padlock to make sure it held. Once the padlock was securely fastened behind me I was safe. The path was dark, because once our father had given up any idea of putting his land to profitable use he had let the trees and bushes and small flowers grow as they chose, and except for one great meadow and the gardens our land was heavily wooded, and no one knew its secret ways but me. When I went along the path, going easily now because I was home, I knew each step and every turn. Constance could put names to all the growing things, but I was content to know them by their way and place of growing, and their unfailing offers of refuge. The only prints on the path were my own, going in and out to the village. Past the turn I might find a mark of Constance's foot, because she sometimes came that far to wait for me, but most of Constance's prints were in the garden and in the house. Today she had come to the end of the garden, and I saw her as soon as I came around the turn; she was standing with the house behind her, in the sunlight, and I ran to meet her.

"Merricat," she said, smiling at me, "look how far I came today."

"It's too far," I said. "First thing I know you'll be following me into the village."

"I might, at that," she said.

Even though I knew she was teasing me I was chilled, but I laughed. "You wouldn't like it much," I told her. "Here, lazy, take some of these packages. Where's my cat?"

"He went off chasing butterflies because you were late. Did you remember eggs? I forgot to tell you."

"Of course. Let's have lunch on the lawn."

When I was small I thought Constance was a fairy princess. I used to try to draw her picture, with long golden hair and eyes as blue as the crayon could make them, and a bright pink spot on either cheek; the pictures always surprised me, because she *did* look like that; even at the worst time she was pink and white and golden, and nothing had ever seemed to dim the brightness of her. She was the most precious person in my world, always. I followed her across the soft grass, past the flowers she tended, into our house, and Jonas, my cat, came out of the flowers and followed me.

Constance waited inside the tall front door while I came up the steps behind her, and then I put my packages down on the table in the hall and locked the door. We would not use it again until afternoon, because almost all of our life was lived toward the back of the house, on the lawn and the garden where no one else ever came. We left the front of the house turned toward the highway and the village, and went our own ways behind its stern, unwelcoming face. Although we kept the house well, the rooms we used together were the back ones, the kitchen and the back bedrooms and the little warm room off the kitchen where Uncle Julian lived; outside was Constance's chestnut tree and the wide, lovely reach of lawn and Constance's flowers and then, beyond, the vegetable garden Constance tended and, past that, the trees which shaded the creek. When we sat on the back lawn no one could see us from anywhere.

I remembered that I was to be kinder to Uncle Julian when I saw him sitting at his great old desk in the kitchen corner playing with his papers. "Will you let Uncle Julian have peanut brittle?" I asked Constance.

"After his lunch," Constance said. She took the groceries carefully from the bags; food of any kind was precious to Constance, and she always touched foodstuffs with quiet respect. I was not allowed to help; I was not allowed to prepare food, nor was I allowed to gather mushrooms, although I sometimes carried vegetables in from the garden, or apples from the old trees. "We'll have muffins," Constance said, almost singing because she was sorting and putting away the food. "Uncle Julian will have an egg, done soft and buttery, and a muffin and a little pudding."

"Pap," said Uncle Julian.

"Merricat will have something lean and rich and salty."

"Jonas will catch me a mouse," I said to my cat on my knee.

"I'm always so happy when you come home from the village," Constance said; she stopped to look and smile at me. "Partly because you bring home food, of course. But partly because I miss you."

"I'm always happy to get home from the village," I told her.

"Was it very bad?" She touched my cheek quickly with one finger.

"You don't want to know about it."

"Someday I'll go." It was the second time she had spoken of going outside, and I was chilled.

"Constance," Uncle Julian said. He lifted a small scrap of paper from his desk and studied it, frowning. "I do not seem to have any information on whether your father took his cigar in the garden as usual that morning."

"I'm sure he did," Constance said. "That cat's been fishing in the creek," she told me. "He came in all mud." She folded the grocery bag and put it with the others in the drawer, and set the library books on the shelf where they were going to stay forever. Jonas and I were expected to stay in our corner, out of the way, while Constance worked in the kitchen, and it was a joy to watch her, moving beautifully in the sunlight, touching foods so softly. "It's Helen Clarke's day," I said. "Are you frightened?"

She turned to smile at me. "Not a bit," she said. "I'm getting better all the time, I think. And today I'm going to make little rum cakes."

"And Helen Clarke will scream and gobble them."

Even now, Constance and I still saw some small society, visiting acquaintances who drove up the driveway to call. Helen Clarke took her tea with us on Fridays, and Mrs. Shepherd or Mrs. Rice or old Mrs. Crowley stopped by occasionally on a Sunday after church to tell us we would have enjoyed the sermon. They came dutifully, although we never returned their calls, and stayed a proper few minutes and sometimes brought flowers from their gardens, or books, or a song that Constance

might care to try over on her harp; they spoke politely
and with little runs of laughter, and never failed to invite
us to their houses although they knew we would never
come. They were civil to Uncle Julian, and patient with
his talk, they offered to take us for drives in their cars,
they referred to themselves as our friends. Constance
and I always spoke well of them to each other, because
they believed that their visits brought us pleasure. They
never walked on the path. If Constance offered them a
cutting from a rosebush, or invited them to see a happy
new arrangement of colors, they went into the garden,
but they never offered to step beyond their defined
areas; they walked along the garden and got into their
cars by the front door and drove away down the driveway and out through the big gates. Several times Mr.
and Mrs. Carrington had come to see how we were getting along, because Mr. Carrington had been a very good
friend of our father's. They never came inside or took
any refreshment, but they drove to the front steps and
sat in their car and talked for a few minutes. "How are
you getting along?" they always asked, looking from
Constance to me and back; "how are you managing all
by yourselves? Is there anything you need, anything we
can do? How are you getting along?" Constance always
invited them in, because we had been brought up to believe that it was discourteous to keep guests talking outside, but the Carringtons never came into the house. "I
wonder," I said, thinking about them, "whether the
Carringtons would bring me a horse if I asked them. I
could ride it in the long meadow."

Constance turned and looked at me for a minute, frowning a little. "You will not ask them," she said at last. "We do not ask from anyone. Remember that."

"I was teasing," I said, and she smiled again. "I really only want a winged horse, anyway. We could fly you to the moon and back, my horse and I."

"I remember when you used to want a griffin," she said. "Now, Miss Idleness, run out and set the table."

"They quarrelled hatefully that last night," Uncle Julian said. " 'I won't have it,' she said, 'I won't stand for it, John Blackwood,' and 'We have no choice,' he said. I listened at the door, of course, but I came too late to hear what they quarrelled about; I suppose it was money."

"They didn't often quarrel," Constance said.

"They were almost invariably civil to one another, Niece, if that is what you mean by not quarrelling; a most unsatisfactory example for the rest of us. My wife and I preferred to shout."

"It hardly seems like six years, sometimes," Constance said. I took the yellow tablecloth and went outside to the lawn to start the table; behind me I heard her saying to Uncle Julian, "Sometimes I feel I would give anything to have them all back again."

When I was a child I used to believe that someday I would grow up and be tall enough to touch the tops of the windows in our mother's drawing room. They were summer windows, because the house was really intended to be only a summer house and our father had only put in a heating system because there was no other house for our family to move to in the winters; by rights we should have had the Rochester house in the village, but that was long lost to us. The windows in the drawing room of our house reached from the floor to the ceiling, and I could never touch the top; our mother used to tell visitors that the light blue silk drapes on the windows had been made up fourteen feet long. There were two tall windows in the drawing room and two tall windows in the dining room across the hall, and from the outside they looked narrow and thin and gave the house a gaunt high look. Inside, however, the drawing room was lovely. Our mother had brought golden-legged chairs from the Rochester house, and her harp was here, and the room shone in reflections from mirrors and sparkling glass. Constance and I only used the room when Helen Clarke came for tea, but we kept it perfectly. Constance stood on a stepladder to wash the tops of the windows, and we dusted the Dresden figurines on the mantel, and with a cloth on the end of a broom I went around the wedding-cake trim at the tops of the walls, staring up into the white fruit and leaves, brushing away at cupids and ribbon knots, dizzy always from looking up and walking backward, and laughing at Constance when she caught me. We polished the floors and mended tiny tears in the rose brocade on the sofas and chairs. There was a golden valance over each high window, and golden scrollwork around the fireplace, and our mother's portrait hung in the drawing room; "I cannot bear to see my lovely room untidy," our mother used to say, and so

Constance and I had never been allowed in here, but now
we kept it shining and silky.

Our mother had always served tea to her friends from
a low table at one side of the fireplace, so that was where
Constance always set her table. She sat on the rose sofa
with our mother's portrait looking down on her, and I
sat in my small chair in the corner and watched. I was
allowed to carry cups and saucers and pass sandwiches
and cakes, but not to pour tea. I disliked eating anything
while people were looking at me, so I had my tea afterwards, in the kitchen. That day, which was the last time
Helen Clarke ever came for tea, Constance had set the
table as usual, with the lovely thin rose-colored cups our
mother had always used, and two silver dishes, one with
small sandwiches and one with the very special rum
cakes; two rum cakes were waiting for me in the kitchen,
in case Helen Clarke ate all of these. Constance sat quietly on the sofa; she never fidgeted, and her hands were
neatly in her lap. I waited by the window, watching for
Helen Clarke, who was always precisely on time. "Are
you frightened?" I asked Constance once, and she said,
"No, not at all." Without turning I could hear from her
voice that she was quiet.

I saw the car turn into the driveway and then saw that
there were two people in it instead of one; "Constance,"
I said, "she's brought someone else."

Constance was still for a minute, and then she said
quite firmly, "I think it will be all right."

I turned to look at her, and she was quiet. "I'll send
them away," I said. "She knows better than this."

"No," Constance said. "I really think it will be all right. You watch me."

"But I won't *have* you frightened."

"Sooner or later," she said, "sooner or later I will have to take a first step."

I was chilled. "I want to send them away."

"No," Constance said. "Absolutely not."

The car stopped in front of the house, and I went into the hall to open the front door, which I had unlocked earlier because it was not courteous to unlock the door in a guest's face. When I came onto the porch I saw that it was not quite as bad as I had expected; it was not a stranger Helen Clarke had with her, but little Mrs. Wright, who had come once before and been more frightened than anyone else. She would not be too much for Constance, but Helen Clarke ought not to have brought her without telling me.

"Good afternoon, Mary Katherine," Helen Clarke said, coming around the car and to the steps, "isn't this a lovely spring day? How is dear Constance? I brought Lucille." She was going to handle it brazenly, as though people brought almost-strangers every day to see Constance, and I disliked having to smile at her. "You remember Lucille Wright?" she asked me, and poor little Mrs. Wright said in a small voice that she had so wanted to come again. I held the front door open and they came into the hall. They had not worn coats because it was such a fine day, but Helen Clarke had the common sense to delay a minute anyway; "Tell dear Constance we've come," she said to me, and I knew she was giving me

time to tell Constance who was here, so I slipped into
the drawing room, where Constance sat quietly, and
said, "It's Mrs. Wright, the frightened one."

Constance smiled. "Kind of a weak first step," she
said. "It's going to be fine, Merricat."

In the hall Helen Clarke was showing off the staircase to Mrs. Wright, telling the familiar story about the
carving and the wood brought from Italy; when I came
out of the drawing room she glanced at me and then
said, "This staircase is one of the wonders of the county,
Mary Katherine. Shame to keep it hidden from the
world. Lucille?" They moved into the drawing room.

Constance was perfectly composed. She rose and
smiled and said she was glad to see them. Because Helen
Clarke was ungraceful by nature, she managed to make
the simple act of moving into a room and sitting down a
complex ballet for three people; before Constance had
quite finished speaking Helen Clarke jostled Mrs. Wright
and sent Mrs. Wright sideways like a careening croquet
ball off into the far corner of the room where she sat
abruptly and clearly without intention upon a small and
uncomfortable chair. Helen Clarke made for the sofa
where Constance sat, nearly upsetting the tea table,
and although there were enough chairs in the room and
another sofa, she sat finally uncomfortably close to Constance, who detested having anyone near her but me.
"Now," Helen Clarke said, spreading, "it's good to see
you again."

"So kind of you to have us," Mrs. Wright said, leaning forward. "Such a lovely staircase."

"You look well, Constance. Have you been working in the garden?"

"I couldn't help it, on a day like this." Constance laughed; she was doing very well. "It's so exciting," she said across to Mrs. Wright. "Perhaps you're a gardener, too? These first bright days are so exciting for a gardener."

She was talking a little too much and a little too fast, but no one noticed it except me.

"I do love a garden," Mrs. Wright said in a little burst. "I do so love a garden."

"How is Julian?" Helen Clarke asked before Mrs. Wright had quite finished speaking. "How is old Julian?"

"Very well, thank you. He is expecting to join us for a cup of tea this afternoon."

"Have you met Julian Blackwood?" Helen Clarke asked Mrs. Wright, and Mrs. Wright, shaking her head, began, "I would love to meet him, of course; I have heard so much—" and stopped.

"He's a touch . . . eccentric," Helen Clarke said, smiling at Constance as though it had been a secret until now. I was thinking that if eccentric meant, as the dictionary said it did, *deviating from regularity*, it was Helen Clarke who was far more eccentric than Uncle Julian, with her awkward movements and her unexpected questions, and her bringing strangers here to tea; Uncle Julian lived smoothly, in a perfectly planned pattern, rounded and sleek. She ought not to call people things they're not, I thought, remembering that I was to be kinder to Uncle Julian.

"Constance, you've always been one of my closest friends," she was saying now, and I wondered at her; she really could not see how Constance withdrew from such words. "I'm going to give you just a word of advice, and remember, it comes from a friend."

I must have known what she was going to say, because I was chilled; all this day had been building up to what Helen Clarke was going to say right now. I sat low in my chair and looked hard at Constance, wanting her to get up and run away, wanting her not to hear what was just about to be said, but Helen Clarke went on, "It's spring, you're young, you're lovely, you have a right to be happy. Come back into the world."

Once, even a month ago when it was still winter, words like that would have made Constance draw back and run away; now, I saw that she was listening and smiling, although she shook her head.

"You've done penance long enough," Helen Clarke said.

"I would so like to give a little luncheon—" Mrs. Wright began.

"You've forgotten the milk; I'll get it." I stood up and spoke directly to Constance and she looked around at me, almost surprised.

"Thank you, dear," she said.

I went out of the drawing room and into the hall and started toward the kitchen; this morning the kitchen had been bright and happy and now, chilled, I saw that it was dreary. Constance had looked as though suddenly, after all this time of refusing and denying, she had come to see that it might be possible, after all, to go outside. I realized now that this was the third time in one day that the subject had been touched, and three times makes it real. I could not breathe; I was tied with wire, and my head was huge and going to explode; I ran to the back door and opened it to breathe. I wanted to run; if I could have run to the end of our land and back I would have been all right, but Constance was alone with them in the drawing room and I had to hurry back. I had to content myself with smashing the milk pitcher which waited on the table; it had been our mother's and I left the pieces on the floor so Constance would see them. I took down the second-best milk pitcher, which did not match the cups; I was allowed to pour milk, so I filled it and took it to the drawing room.

"—do with Mary Katherine?" Constance was saying, and then she turned and smiled at me in the doorway. "Thank you, dear," she said, and glanced at the milk pitcher and at me. "Thank you," she said again, and I put the pitcher down on the tray.

"Not too much at first," Helen Clarke said. "That *would* look odd, I grant you. But a call or two on old friends, perhaps a day in the city shopping—no one would recognize you in the city, you know."

"A little luncheon?" Mrs. Wright said hopefully.

"I'll have to think." Constance made a little, laughing, bewildered gesture, and Helen Clarke nodded.

"You'll need some clothes," she said.

I came from my place in the corner to take a cup of tea from Constance and carry it over to Mrs. Wright, whose hand trembled when she took it. "Thank you, my dear," she said. I could see the tea trembling in the cup; it was only her second visit here, after all.

"Sugar?" I asked her; I couldn't help it, and besides, it was polite.

"Oh, no," she said. "No, thank you. No sugar."

I thought, looking at her, that she had dressed to come here today; Constance and I never wore black but Mrs. Wright had perhaps thought it was appropriate, and today she wore a plain black dress with a necklace of pearls. She had worn black the other time, too, I re-called; always in good taste, I thought, except in our mother's drawing room. I went back to Constance and took up the plate of rum cakes and brought them to Mrs. Wright; that was not kind either, and she should have had the sandwiches first, but I wanted her to be unhappy, dressed in black in our mother's drawing room. "My sis-ter made these this morning," I said.

"Thank you," she said. Her hand hesitated over the plate and then she took a rum cake and set it carefully on the edge of her saucer. I thought that Mrs. Wright was being almost hysterically polite, and I said, "Do take two. Everything my sister cooks is delicious."

"No," she said. "Oh, no. Thank you."

Helen Clarke was eating sandwiches, reaching down past Constance to take one after another. She wouldn't behave like this anywhere else, I thought, only here. She never cares what Constance thinks or I think of her man-ners; she only supposes we are so very glad to see her. Go away, I told her in my mind. Go away, go away. I wondered if Helen Clarke saved particular costumes for her visits to our house. "This," I could imagine her saying, turning out her closet, "no sense in throwing *this* away, I can keep it for visiting dear Constance." I began dressing Helen Clarke in my mind, putting her in a bathing suit on a snow bank, setting her high in the hard branches of a tree in a dress of flimsy pink ruffles that caught and pulled and tore; she was tangled in the tree and screaming and I almost laughed.

"Why not ask some people here?" Helen Clarke was saying to Constance. "A few old friends—there are many people who have wanted to keep in touch with you, Constance dear—a few old friends some evening. For dinner? No," she said, "perhaps not for dinner. Perhaps not, not at first."

"I myself—" Mrs. Wright began again; she had set her cup of tea and the little rum cake carefully on the table next to her.

"Although why not for dinner?" Helen Clarke said. "After all, you have to take the plunge sometime."

I was going to have to say something. Constance was not looking at me, but only at Helen Clarke. "Why not invite some good people from the village?" I asked loudly.

"Good heavens, Mary Katherine," Helen Clarke said. "You really startled me." She laughed. "I don't recall that the Blackwoods ever mingled socially with the villagers," she said.

"They hate us," I said.

"*I* don't listen to their gossip, and I hope you don't.

And, Mary Katherine, you know as well as I do that nine-tenths of that feeling is nothing but your imagination, and if you'd go halfway to be friendly there'd never be a word said against you. Good heavens. I grant you there might have been a little feeling once, but on your side it's just been exaggerated out of all proportion."

"People *will* gossip," Mrs. Wright said reassuringly.

"I've been saying right along that I was a close friend of the Blackwoods and not the least bit ashamed of it, either. You want to come to people of your *own* kind, Constance. They don't talk about *us*."

I wished they would be more amusing; I thought that now Constance was looking a little tired. If they would leave soon I would brush Constance's hair until she fell asleep.

"Uncle Julian is coming," I said to Constance. I could hear the soft sound of the wheel chair in the hall and I got up to open the door.

Helen Clarke said, "Do you suppose that people would really be afraid to visit here?" and Uncle Julian stopped in the doorway. He had put on his dandyish tie for company at tea, and washed his face until it was pink. "Afraid?" he said. "To visit here?" He bowed to Mrs. Wright from his chair and then to Helen Clarke. "Madam," he said, and "Madam." I knew that he could not remember either of their names, or whether he had ever seen them before.

"You look well, Julian," Helen Clarke said.

"Afraid to visit here? I apologize for repeating your

words, madam, but I am astonished. My niece, after all, was acquitted of murder. There could be no possible danger in visiting here *now*."

Mrs. Wright made a little convulsive gesture toward her cup of tea and then set her hands firmly in her lap.

"It could be said that there is danger everywhere," Uncle Julian said. "Danger of poison, certainly. My niece can tell you of the most unlikely perils—garden plants more deadly than snakes and simple herbs that slash like knives through the lining of your belly, madam. My niece—"

"Such a lovely garden," Mrs. Wright said earnestly to Constance. "I'm sure I don't know how you do it."

Helen Clarke said firmly, "Now, that's all been forgotten long ago, Julian. No one ever thinks about it any more."

"Regrettable," Uncle Julian said. "A most fascinating case, one of the few genuine mysteries of our time. Of my time, particularly. My life work," he told Mrs. Wright.

"Julian," Helen Clarke said quickly; Mrs. Wright seemed mesmerized. "There is such a thing as good taste, Julian."

"Taste, madam? Have you ever tasted arsenic? I assure you that there is one moment of utter incredulity before the mind can accept—"

A moment ago poor little Mrs. Wright would probably have bitten her tongue out before she mentioned the subject, but now she said, hardly breathing, "You mean you remember?"

"Remember." Uncle Julian sighed, shaking his head happily. "Perhaps," he said with eagerness, "perhaps you are not familiar with the story? Perhaps I might—"

"Julian," Helen Clarke said, "Lucille does not want to hear it. You should be ashamed to ask her."

I thought that Mrs. Wright very much did want to hear it, and I looked at Constance just as she glanced at me; we were both very sober, to suit the subject, but I knew she was as full of merriment as I; it was good to hear Uncle Julian, who was so lonely most of the time.

And poor, poor Mrs. Wright, tempted at last beyond endurance, was not able to hold it back any longer. She blushed deeply, and faltered, but Uncle Julian was a tempter and Mrs. Wright's human discipline could not resist forever. "It happened right in this house," she said like a prayer.

We were all silent, regarding her courteously, and she whispered, "I *do* beg your pardon."

"Naturally, in this house," Constance said. "In the dining room. We were having dinner."

"A family gathering for the evening meal," Uncle Julian said, caressing his words. "Never supposing it was to be our last."

"Arsenic in the sugar," Mrs. Wright said, carried away, hopelessly lost to all decorum.

"I used that sugar." Uncle Julian shook his finger at her. "I used that sugar myself, on my blackberries. Luckily," and he smiled blandly, "fate intervened. Some of us, that day, she led inexorably through the gates of death. Some of us, innocent and unsuspecting, took, unwillingly, that one last step to oblivion. Some of us took very little sugar."

"I never touch berries," Constance said; she looked directly at Mrs. Wright and said soberly, "I rarely take sugar on anything. Even now."

"It counted strongly against her at the trial," Uncle Julian said. "That she used no sugar, I mean. But my niece has never cared for berries. Even as a child it was her custom to refuse berries."

"Please," Helen Clarke said loudly, "it's *outrageous*, it really is; I can't bear to hear it talked about. Constance—Julian—what will Lucille think of you?"

"No, really," Mrs. Wright said, lifting her hands.

"I won't sit here and listen to another word," Helen Clarke said. "Constance must start thinking about the future; this dwelling on the past is not wholesome; the poor darling has suffered enough "

"Well, I miss them all, of course," Constance said. "Things have been much different with all of them gone, but I'm sure I don't think of myself as suffering."

"In some ways," Uncle Julian sailed on, "a piece of extraordinarily good fortune for me. I am a survivor of the most sensational poisoning case of the century. I have all the newspaper clippings. I knew the victims, the accused, intimately, as only a relative living in the very house *could* know them. I have exhaustive notes on all that happened. I have never been well since."

"I said I didn't want to talk about it," Helen Clarke said.

Uncle Julian stopped. He looked at Helen Clarke, and

then at Constance. "Didn't it really happen?" he asked after a minute, fingers at his mouth.

"Of course it really happened." Constance smiled at him.

"I have the newspaper clippings," Uncle Julian said uncertainly. "I have my notes," he told Helen Clarke, "I have written down everything."

"It was a terrible thing." Mrs. Wright was leaning forward earnestly and Uncle Julian turned to her.

"Dreadful," he agreed. "Frightful, madam." He maneuvered his wheel chair so his back was to Helen Clarke. "Would you like to view the dining room?" he asked. "The fatal board? I did not give evidence at the trial, you understand; my health was not equal, then or now, to the rude questions of strangers." He gave a little flick of his head in Helen Clarke's direction. "I wanted badly to take the witness stand. I flatter myself that I would not have appeared to disadvantage. But of course she was acquitted after all."

"Certainly she was acquitted," Helen Clarke said vehemently. She reached for her huge pocketbook and took it up onto her lap and felt in it for her gloves. "No one ever thinks about it any more." She caught Mrs. Wright's eye and prepared to rise.

"The dining room . . . ?" Mrs. Wright said timidly. "Just a glance?"

"Madam." Uncle Julian contrived a bow from his wheel chair, and Mrs. Wright hurried to reach the door and open it for him. "Directly across the hall," Uncle Julian said, and she followed. "I admire a decently curious woman, madam; I could see at once that you were devoured with a passion to view the scene of the tragedy; it happened in this very room, and we still have our dinner in here every night."

We could hear him clearly; he was apparently moving around our dining-room table while Mrs. Wright watched him from the doorway. "You will perceive that our table is round. It is overlarge now for the pitiful remnant of our family, but we have been reluctant to disturb what is, after all, a monument of sorts; at one time, a picture of this room would have commanded a large price from any of the newspapers. We were a large family once, you recall, a large and happy family. We had small disagreements, of course, we were not all of us overblessed with patience; I might almost say that there were quarrels. Nothing serious; husband and wife, brother and sister, did not always see eye to eye."

"Then why did she—"

"Yes," Uncle Julian said, "that *is* perplexing, is it not? My brother, as head of the family, sat naturally at the head of the table, there, with the windows at his back and the decanter before him. John Blackwood took pride in his table, his family, his position in the world."

"She never even met him," Helen Clarke said. She looked angrily at Constance. "I remember your father well."

Faces fade away out of memory, I thought. I wondered if I would recognize Mrs. Wright if I saw her in the village. I wondered if Mrs. Wright in the village would walk past me, not seeing; perhaps Mrs. Wright was so timid that she never looked up at faces at all. Her cup of tea and her little rum cake still sat on the table, untouched.

"*And* I was a good friend of your mother's, Constance. That's why I fccl able to speak to you openly, for your own good. Your mother would have wanted—"

"—my sister-in-law, who was, madam, a delicate woman. You will have noticed her portrait in the drawing room, and the exquisite line of the jawbone under the skin. A woman born for tragedy, perhaps, although inclined to be a little silly. On her right at this table, myself, younger then, and not an invalid; I have only been helpless since that night. Across from me, the boy Thomas—did you know I once had a nephew, that my brother had a son? Certainly, you would have read about him. He was ten years old and possessed many of his father's more forceful traits of character."

"He used the most sugar," Mrs. Wright said.

"Alas," Uncle Julian said. "Then, on either side of my brother, his daughter Constance and my wife Dorothy, who had done me the honor of casting in her lot with mine, although I do not think that she anticipated anything so severe as arsenic on her blackberries. Another child, my niece Mary Katherine, was not at table."

"She was in her room," Mrs. Wright said.

"A great child of twelve, sent to bed without her supper. But she need not concern us."

I laughed, and Constance said to Helen Clarke, "Merricat was always in disgrace. I used to go up the back stairs with a tray of dinner for her after my father had left the dining room. She was a wicked, disobedient child," and she smiled at me.

"An unhealthy environment," Helen Clarke said. "A child should be punished for wrongdoing, but she should be made to feel that she is still loved. *I* would never have tolerated the child's wildness. And now we really *must* . . ." She began to put on her gloves again.

"—spring lamb roasted, with a mint jelly made from Constance's garden mint. Spring potatoes, new peas, a salad, again from Constance's garden. I remember it perfectly, madam. It is still one of my favorite meals. I have also, of course, made very thorough notes of everything about that meal and, in fact, that entire day. You will see at once how the dinner revolves around my niece. It was early summer, her garden was doing well—the weather was lovely that year, I recall; we have not seen such another summer since, or perhaps I am only getting older. We relied upon Constance for various small delicacies which only she could provide; I am of course not referring to arsenic."

"Well, the blackberries were the important part." Mrs. Wright sounded a little hoarse.

"What a mind you have, madam! So precise, so unerring. I can see that you are going to ask me why she should conceivably have used arsenic. My niece is not capable of such subtlety, and her lawyer luckily said so at the trial. Constance can put her hand upon a bewildering array of deadly substances without ever leaving home; she could feed you a sauce of poison hemlock, a member of the parsley family which produccs immediate

paralysis and death when eaten. She might have made a
marmalade of the lovely thornapple or the baneberry,
she might have tossed the salad with *Holcus lanatus*,
called velvet grass, and rich in hydrocyanic acid. I have
notes on all these, madam. Deadly nightshade is a relative
of the tomato; would we, any of us, have had the pre-
science to decline if Constance served it to us, spiced and
made into pickle? Or consider just the mushroom family,
rich as that is in tradition and deception. We were all
fond of mushrooms—my niece makes a mushroom omelette you must taste to believe, madam—and the common death cup—"

"She should not have been doing the cooking," said
Mrs. Wright strongly.

"Well, of course, there is the root of our trouble. Certainly she should not have been doing the cooking if her
intention was to destroy all of us with poison; we would
have been blindly unselfish to encourage her to cook under such circumstances. But she was acquitted. Not only
of the deed, but of the intention."

"What was wrong with Mrs. Blackwood doing her
own cooking?"

"Please." Uncle Julian's voice had a little shudder in it,
and I knew the gesture he was using with it even though
he was out of my sight. He would have raised one hand,
fingers spread, and he would be smiling at her over his
fingers; it was a gallant, Uncle Julian, gesture; I had seen
him use it with Constance. "I personally preferred to
chance the arsenic," Uncle Julian said.

"We must go home," Helen Clarke said. "I don't know

what's come over Lucille. I *told* her before we came not
to mention this subject."

"I am going to put up wild strawberries this year,"
Constance said to me. "I noticed a considerable patch of
them near the end of the garden."

"It's terribly tactless of her, and she's keeping *me* waiting."

"—the sugar bowl on the sideboard, the heavy silver
sugar bowl. It is a family heirloom; my brother prized it
highly. You will be wondering about that sugar bowl, I
imagine. Is it still in use? you are wondering; has it been
cleaned? you may very well ask; was it thoroughly
washed? I can reassure you at once. My niece Constance
washed it before the doctor or the police had come, and
you will allow that it was not a felicitous moment to wash
a sugar bowl. The other dishes used at dinner were still
on the table, but my niece took the sugar bowl to the
kitchen, emptied it, and scrubbed it thoroughly with
boiling water. It was a curious act."

"There was a spider in it," Constance said to the teapot.
We used a little rose-covered sugar bowl for the lump
sugar for tea.

"—there was a spider in it, she said. That was what
she told the police. That was why she washed it."

"Well," Mrs. Wright said, "it does seem as though she
might have thought of a better reason. Even if it *was* a
real spider—I mean, you don't wash—I mean, you just
take the spider *out*."

"What reason would *you* have given, madam?"

"Well, I've never killed anybody, so I don't know—I

mean, I don't know what I'd say. The first thing that came into my head, I suppose. I mean, she must have been upset."

"I assure you the pangs were fearful; you say you have never tasted arsenic? It is not agreeable. I am extremely sorry for all of them. I myself lingered on in great pain for several days; Constance would, I am sure, have demonstrated only the deepest sympathy for me, but by then, of course, she was largely unavailable. They arrested her at once."

Mrs. Wright sounded more forceful, almost unwillingly eager. "I've always thought, ever since we moved up here, that it would be a wonderful chance to meet you people and *really* find out what happened, because of course there's always that one question, the one nobody has ever been able to answer; of course I hardly expected to *talk* to you about it, but look." There was the sound of a dining-room chair being moved; Mrs. Wright had clearly decided to settle down. "First," she said, "she bought the arsenic."

"To kill rats," Constance said to the teapot, and then turned and smiled at me.

"To kill rats," Uncle Julian said. "The only other popular use for arsenic is in taxidermy, and my niece could hardly pretend a working knowledge of that subject."

"She cooked the dinner, she set the table."

"I confess I am surprised at that woman," Helen Clarke said. "She seems such a quiet little body."

"It was Constance who saw them dying around her

like flies—I do beg your pardon—and never called a doctor until it was too late. She washed the sugar bowl."

"There was a spider in it," Constance said.

"She told the police those people deserved to die."

"She was excited, madam. Perhaps the remark was misconstrued. My niece is not hard-hearted; besides, she thought at the time that I was among them and although I deserve to die—we all do, do we not?—I hardly think that my niece is the one to point it out."

"She told the police that it was all her fault."

"Now there," Uncle Julian said, "I think she made a mistake. It was certainly true that she thought at first that her cooking had caused all this, but in taking full blame I think that she was over-eager. I would have advised her against any such attitude had I been consulted; it smacks of self-pity."

"But the great, the unanswered question, is *why*? Why did she do it? I mean, unless we agree that Constance was a homicidal maniac—"

"You have met her, madam."

"I have what? Oh, my goodness yes. I completely forgot. I cannot seem to remember that that pretty young girl is actually—well. Your mass murderer must have a reason, Mr. Blackwood, even if it is only some perverted, twisted—oh, dear. She is such a charming girl, your niece; I cannot remember when I have taken to anyone as I have to her. But if she *is* a homicidal maniac—"

"I'm leaving." Helen Clarke stood up and slammed her pocketbook emphatically under her arm. "Lucille," she said, "I am leaving. We have overstayed all limits of decency; it's after five o'clock."

Mrs. Wright scurried out of the dining room, distraught. "I'm so sorry," she said. "We were chatting and I lost track of time. Oh, dear." She ran to her chair to gather up her pocketbook.

"You haven't even touched your tea," I said, wanting to see her blush.

"Thank you," she said; she looked down at her teacup and blushed. "It was delicious."

Uncle Julian stopped his wheel chair in the center of the room and folded his hands happily before him. He looked at Constance and then raised his eyes to gaze on a corner of the ceiling, sober and demure.

"Julian, goodbye," Helen Clark said shortly. "Constance, I'm sorry we stayed so long; it was inexcusable. Lucille?"

Mrs. Wright looked like a child who knows it is going to be punished, but she had not forgotten her manners. "Thank you," she said to Constance, putting her hand out and then taking it back again quickly. "I had a very nice time. Goodbye," she said to Uncle Julian. They went into the hall and I followed, to lock the door after they had gone. Helen Clarke started the car before poor Mrs. Wright had quite finished getting herself inside, and the last I heard of Mrs. Wright was a little shriek as the car started down the driveway. I was laughing when I came back into the drawing room, and I went over and kissed Constance. "A very nice tea party," I said.

"That *impossible* woman." Constance put her head

back against the couch and laughed. "Ill bred, pretentious, stupid. Why she keeps coming I'll never know."

"She wants to reform you." I took up Mrs. Wright's
teacup and her rum cake and brought them over to
the tea tray. "Poor little Mrs. Wright," I said.

"You were teasing her, Merricat."

"A little bit, maybe. I can't help it when people are
frightened; I always want to frighten them more."

"Constance?" Uncle Julian turned his wheel chair to
face her. "How was I?"

"Superb, Uncle Julian." Constance stood up and went
over to him and touched his old head lightly. "You didn't
need your notes at all."

"It really happened?" he asked her.

"It certainly did. I'll take you in to your room and you
can look at your newspaper clippings."

"I think not right now. It has been a superlative afternoon, but I think I am a little tired. I will rest till dinner."

Constance pushed the wheel chair down the hall and I
followed with the tea tray. I was allowed to carry dirty
dishes but not to wash them, so I set the tray on the
kitchen table and watched while Constance stacked the
dishes by the sink to wash later, swept up the broken
milk pitcher on the floor, and took out the potatoes to
start for dinner. Finally I had to ask her; the thought had
been chilling me all afternoon. "Are you going to do
what she said?" I asked her. "What Helen Clarke said?"

She did not pretend not to understand. She stood there
looking down at her hands working, and smiled a little.
"I don't know," she said.

~~~~~~~~~~~~~~~~~~~~~~~~~~~~~~~~~~~~~~~~~~~~~~~~~~~~~~~~~

## 3

A CHANGE WAS COMING, AND NOBODY KNEW IT BUT ME. Constance suspected, perhaps; I noticed that she stood occasionally in her garden and looked not down at the plants she was tending, and not back at our house, but outward, toward the trees which hid the fence, and sometimes she looked long and curiously down the length of the driveway, as though wondering how it would feel to walk along it to the gates. I watched her. On Saturday morning, after Helen Clarke had come to tea, Constance looked at the driveway three times. Uncle Julian was not well on Saturday morning, after tiring himself at tea, and stayed in his bed in his warm room next to the kitchen, looking out of the window beside his pillow, calling now and then to make Constance notice him. Even Jonas was fretful—he was running up a storm, our mother used to say—and could not sleep quietly; all during those days when the change was coming Jonas stayed restless. From a deep sleep he would start suddenly, lifting his head as though listening, and then, on his feet and moving in one quick ripple, he ran up the stairs and across the beds and around through the doors in and out and then down the stairs and across the hall and over the chair in the dining room and around the table and through the kitchen and out into the garden where he would slow, sauntering, and then pause to lick a paw and flick an ear and take a look at the day. At night we could hear him running, feel him cross our feet as we lay in bed, running up a storm.

All the omens spoke of change. I woke up on Saturday morning and thought I heard them calling me; they want me to get up, I thought before I came fully awake and remembered that they were dead; Constance never called me to wake up. When I dressed and came downstairs that morning she was waiting to make my breakfast, and I told her, "I thought I heard them calling me this morning."

"Hurry with your breakfast," she said. "It's another lovely day."

After breakfast on the good mornings when I did not have to go into the village I had my work to do. Always on Wednesday mornings I went around the fence. It was necessary for me to check constantly to be sure that the wires were not broken and the gates were securely locked. I could make the repairs myself, winding the wire back together where it had torn, tightening loose strands, and it was a pleasure to know, every Wednesday morning, that we were safe for another week.

On Sunday mornings I examined my safeguards, the box of silver dollars I had buried by the creek, and the doll buried in the long field, and the book nailed to the tree in the pine woods; so long as they were where I had put them nothing could get in to harm us. I had always buried things, even when I was small; I remember that once I quartered the long field and buried something in each quarter to make the grass grow higher as I grew taller, so I would always be able to hide there. I once buried six blue marbles in the creek bed to make the river beyond run dry. "Here is treasure for you to bury," Constance used to say to me when I was small, giving me a penny, or a bright ribbon; I had buried all my baby teeth as they came out one by one and perhaps someday they would grow as dragons. All our land was enriched with my treasures buried in it, thickly inhabited just below the surface with my marbles and my teeth and my colored stones, all perhaps turned to jewels by now, held together under the ground in a powerful taut web which never loosened, but held fast to guard us.

On Tuesdays and Fridays I went into the village, and on Thursday, which was my most powerful day, I went into the big attic and dressed in their clothes.

Mondays we neatened the house, Constance and I, going into every room with mops and dustcloths, carefully setting the little things back after we had dusted, never altering the perfect line of our mother's tortoise-shell comb. Every spring we washed and polished the house for another year, but on Mondays we neatened; very little dust fell in their rooms, but even that little could not be permitted to stay. Sometimes Constance tried to neaten Uncle Julian's room, but Uncle Julian disliked being disturbed and kept his things in their own places, and Constance had to be content with washing his medicine glasses and changing his bed. I was not allowed in Uncle Julian's room.

On Saturday mornings I helped Constance. I was not allowed to handle knives, but when she worked in the garden I cared for her tools, keeping them bright and clean, and I carried great baskets of flowers, sometimes, or vegetables which Constance picked to make into food. The entire cellar of our house was filled with food. All the Blackwood women had made food and had taken pride in adding to the great supply of food in our cellar. There were jars of jam made by great-grandmothers, with labels in thin pale writing, almost unreadable by now, and pickles made by great-aunts and vegetables put up by our grandmother, and even our mother had left behind her six jars of apple jelly. Constance had worked all her life at adding to the food in the cellar, and her rows and rows of jars were easily the handsomest, and shone among the others. "You bury food the way I bury treasure," I told her sometimes, and she answered me once: "The food comes from the ground and can't be permitted to stay there and rot; *some*thing has to be done with it." All the Blackwood women had taken the food that came from the ground and preserved it, and the deeply colored rows of jellies and pickles and bottled vegetables and fruit, maroon and amber and dark rich green stood side by side in our cellar and would stand there forever, a poem by the Blackwood women. Each year Constance and Uncle Julian and I had jam or preserve or pickle that Constance had made, but we never touched what belonged to the others; Constance said it would kill us if we ate it.

This Saturday morning I had apricot jam on my toast, and I thought of Constance making it and putting it away carefully for me to eat on some bright morning, never dreaming that a change would be coming before the jar was finished.

"Lazy Merricat," Constance said to me, "stop dreaming over your toast; I want you in the garden on this lovely day."

She was arranging Uncle Julian's tray, putting his hot milk into a jug painted with yellow daisies, and trimming his toast so it would be tiny and hot and square; if anything looked large, or difficult to eat, Uncle Julian would leave it on the plate. Constance always took Uncle Julian's tray in to him in the morning because he slept painfully and sometimes lay awake in the darkness waiting for the first light and the comfort of Constance with his tray. Some nights, when his heart hurt him badly, he might take one more pill than usual, and then lie all morning drowsy and dull, unwilling to sip from his hot milk, but wanting to know that Constance was busy in the kitchen next door to his bedroom, or in the garden where he could see her from his pillow. On his very good mornings she brought him into the kitchen for his breakfast, and he would sit at his old desk in the corner, spilling crumbs among his notes, studying his papers while he ate. "If I am spared," he always said to Constance, "I will write the book myself. If not, see that my notes are entrusted to some worthy cynic who will not be too concerned with the truth."

I wanted to be kinder to Uncle Julian, so this morning I hoped he would enjoy his breakfast and later come out into the garden in his wheel chair and sit in the sun. "Maybe there will be a tulip open today," I said, looking out through the open kitchen door into the bright sunlight.

"Not until tomorrow, I think," said Constance, who always knew. "Wear your boots if you wander today; it will still be quite wet in the woods."

"There's a change coming," I said.

"It's spring, silly," she said, and took up Uncle Julian's tray. "Don't run off while I'm gone; there's work to be done."

She opened Uncle Julian's door and I heard her say good morning to him. When he said good morning back his voice was old and I knew that he was not well. Constance would have to stay near him all day.

"Is your father home yet, child?" he asked her.

"No, not today," Constance said. "Let me get your other pillow. It's a lovely day."

"He's a busy man," Uncle Julian said. "Bring me a pencil, my dear; I want to make a note of that. He's a very busy man."

"Take some hot milk; it will make you warm."

"You're not Dorothy. You're my niece Constance."

"Drink."

"Good morning, Constance."

"Good morning, Uncle Julian."

I decided that I would choose three powerful words, words of strong protection, and so long as these great words were never spoken aloud no change would come. I wrote the first word—*melody*—in the apricot jam on my toast with the handle of a spoon and then put the toast in my mouth and ate it very quickly. I was one-third safe. Constance came out of Uncle Julian's room carrying the tray.

"He's not well this morning," she said. "He left most of his breakfast and he's very tired."

"If I had a winged horse I could fly him to the moon; he would be more comfortable there."

"Later I'll take him out into the sunshine, and perhaps make him a little eggnog."

"Everything's safe on the moon."

She looked at me distantly. "Dandelion greens," she

said. "And radishes. I thought of working in the vegetable garden this morning, but I don't want to leave Uncle Julian. I hope that the carrots . . ." She tapped her
fingers on the table, thinking. "Rhubarb," she said.

I carried my breakfast dishes over to the sink and set
them down; I was deciding on my second magic word,
which I thought might very well be *Gloucester*. It was
strong, and I thought it would do, although Uncle Julian
might take it into his head to say almost anything and no
word was truly safe when Uncle Julian was talking.

"Why not make a pie for Uncle Julian?"

Constance smiled. "You mean, why not make a pie
for Merricat? Shall I make a rhubarb pie?"

"Jonas and I dislike rhubarb."

"But it has the prettiest colors of all; nothing is so
pretty on the shelves as rhubarb jam."

"Make it for the shelves, then. Make me a dandelion
pie."

"Silly Merricat," Constance said. She was wearing her
blue dress, the sunlight was patterned on the kitchen
floor, and color was beginning to show in the garden outside. Jonas sat on the step, washing, and Constance began
to sing as she turned to wash the dishes. I was two-thirds
safe, with only one magic word to find.

Later Uncle Julian still slept and Constance thought
to take five minutes and run down to the vegetable garden to gather what she could; I sat at the kitchen table
listening for Uncle Julian so I could call Constance if he
awakened, but when she came back he was still quiet. I
ate tiny sweet raw carrots while Constance washed the

vegetables and put them away. "We will have a spring salad," she said.

"We eat the year away. We eat the spring and the summer and the fall. We wait for something to grow and then we eat it."

"Silly Merricat," Constance said.

At twenty minutes after eleven by the kitchen clock she took off her apron, glanced in at Uncle Julian, and went, as she always did, upstairs to her room to wait until I called her. I went to the front door and unlocked it and opened it just as the doctor's car turned into the drive. He was in a hurry, always, and he stopped his car quickly and ran up the steps; "Good morning, Miss Blackwood," he said, going past me and down the hall, and by the time he had reached the kitchen he had his coat off and was ready to put it over the back of one of the kitchen chairs. He went directly to Uncle Julian's room without a glance at me or at the kitchen, and then when he opened Uncle Julian's door he was suddenly still, and gentle. "Good morning, Mr. Blackwood," he said, his voice easy, "how are things today?"

"Where's the old fool?" Uncle Julian said, as he always did. "Why didn't Jack Mason come?"

Dr. Mason was the one Constance called the night they all died.

"Dr. Mason couldn't make it today," the doctor said, as he always did. "I'm Dr. Levy. I've come to see you instead."

"Rather have Jack Mason."

"I'll do the best I can."

"Always said I'd outlive the old fool." Uncle Julian laughed thinly. "Why are you pretending with me? Jack Mason died three years ago."

"Mr. Blackwood," the doctor said, "it is a pleasure to have you as a patient." He closed the door very quietly. I thought of using *digitalis* as my third magic word, but it was too easy for someone to say, and at last I decided on *Pegasus*. I took a glass from the cabinet, and said the word very distinctly into the glass, then filled it with water and drank. Uncle Julian's door opened, and the doctor stood in the doorway for a minute.

"Remember, now," he said. "And I'll see you next Saturday."

"Quack," Uncle Julian said.

The doctor turned, smiling, and then the smile disappeared and he began to hurry again. He took up his coat and went off down the hall. I followed him and by the time I came to the front door he was already going down the steps. "Goodbye, Miss Blackwood," he said, not looking around, and got into his car and started at once, going faster and faster until he reached the gates and turned onto the highway. I locked the front door and went to the foot of the stairs. "Constance?" I called.

"Coming," she said from upstairs. "Coming, Merricat."

Uncle Julian was better later in the day, and sat out in the warm afternoon sun, hands folded in his lap, half-dreaming. I lay near him on the marble bench our mother had liked to sit on, and Constance knelt in the dirt, both hands buried as though she were growing, kneading the dirt and turning it, touching the plants on their roots.

"It was a fine morning," Uncle Julian said, his voice going on and on, "a fine bright morning, and none of them knew it was their last. She was downstairs first, my niece Constance. I woke up and heard her moving in the kitchen—I slept upstairs then, I could still go upstairs, and I slept with my wife in our room—and I thought, this is a fine morning, never dreaming then that it was their last. Then I heard my nephew—no, it was my brother; my brother came downstairs first after Constance. I heard him whistling. Constance?"

"Yes?"

"What was the tune my brother used to whistle, and always off-key?"

Constance thought, her hands in the ground, and hummed softly, and I shivered.

"Of course. I never had a head for music; I could remember what people looked like and what they said and what they did but I could never remember what they sang. It was my brother who came downstairs after Constance, never caring of course if he woke people with his noise and his whistling, never thinking that perhaps I might still be asleep, although as it happened I was already awake." Uncle Julian sighed, and lifted his head to look curiously, once, around the garden. "He never knew it was his last morning on earth. He might have been quieter, I think, if he did know. I heard him in the kitchen with Constance and I said to my wife—she was awake, too; his noise had awakened her—I said to my wife, you had better get dressed; we live here with my brother and his wife, after all, and we must remember to show them that we are friendly and eager to help out wherever we can; dress and go down to Constance in the kitchen. She did as she was told; our wives always did as they were told, although my sister-in-law lay in bed late that morning; perhaps *she* had a premonition and wanted to take her earthly rest while she could. I heard them all. I heard the boy go downstairs. I thought of dressing; Constance?"

"Yes, Uncle Julian?"

"I could still dress myself in those days, you know, although that *was* the last day. I could still walk around by myself, and dress myself, and feed myself, and I had no pain. I slept well in those days as a strong man should. I was not young, but I was strong and I slept well and I could still dress myself."

"Would you like a rug over your knees?"

"No, my dear, I thank you. You have been a good niece to me, although there are some grounds for supposing you an undutiful daughter. My sister-in-law came downstairs before I did. We had pancakes for breakfast, tiny thin hot pancakes, and my brother had two fried eggs and my wife—although I did not encourage her to eat heavily, since we were living with my brother—took largely of sausage. Homemade sausage, made by Constance. Constance?"

"Yes, Uncle Julian?"

"I think if I had known it was her last breakfast I would have permitted her more sausage. I am surprised, now I think of it, that no one suspected it was their last morning; they might not have grudged my wife more sausage *then*. My brother sometimes remarked upon what we ate, my wife and I; he was a just man, and never stinted his food, so long as we did not take too much. He watched my wife take sausage that morning, Constance. I saw him watching her. We took little enough from him, Constance. He had pancakes and fried eggs and sausage but I felt that he was going to speak to my wife; the boy ate hugely. I am pleased that the breakfast was particularly good that day."

"I could make you sausage next week, Uncle Julian; I think homemade sausage would not disagree with you if you had very little."

"My brother never grudged our food if we did not take too much. My wife helped to wash the dishes."

"I was very grateful to her."

"She might have done more, I think now. She entertained my sister-in-law, and she saw to our clothes, and she helped with the dishes in the mornings, but I believe that my brother thought that she might have done more. He went off after breakfast to see a man on business."

"He wanted an arbor built; it was his plan to start a grape arbor."

"I am sorry about that; we might now be eating jam from our own grapes. I was always better able to chat after he was gone; I recall that I entertained the ladies that morning, and we sat here in the garden. We talked about music; my wife was quite musical although she had never learned to play. My sister-in-law had a delicate touch; it was always said of her that she had a delicate touch, and she played in the evenings usually. Not that evening, of course. She was not able to play that evening. In the morning we thought she would play in the evening as usual. Do you recall that I was very entertaining in the garden that morning, Constance?"

"I was weeding the vegetables," Constance said. "I could hear you all laughing."

"I was quite entertaining; I am happy for that now." He was quiet for a minute, folding and refolding his hands. I wanted to be kinder to him, but I could not fold his hands for him, and there was nothing I could bring him, so I lay still and listened to him talk. Constance frowned, staring at a leaf, and the shadows moved softly across the lawn.

"The boy was off somewhere," Uncle Julian said at last in his sad old voice. "The boy had gone off somewhere—was he fishing, Constance?"

"He was climbing the chestnut tree."

"I remember. Of course. I remember all of it very clearly, my dear, and I have it all down in my notes. It was the last morning of all and I would not like to forget. He was climbing the chestnut tree, shouting down to us from very high in the tree, and dropping twigs until my sister-in-law spoke sharply to him. She disliked the twigs falling into her hair, and my wife disliked it too, although she would never have been the first to speak. I think my wife was civil to your mother, Constance. I would hate to think not; we lived in my brother's house and ate his food. I know my brother was home for lunch."

"We had a rarebit," Constance said. "I had been working with the vegetables all morning and I had to make something quickly for lunch."

"It was a rarebit we had. I have often wondered why the arsenic was never put into the rarebit. It is an interesting point, and one I shall bring out forcefully in my book. Why was the arsenic not put into the rarebit? They would have lost some hours of life on that last day, but it would all have been over with that much sooner. Constance, if there is one dish you prepare which I strongly dislike, it is a rarebit. I have never cared for rarebit."

"I know, Uncle Julian. I never serve it to you."

"It would have been most suitable for the arsenic. I had a salad instead, I recall. There was an apple pudding for dessert, left over from the night before."

"The sun is going down." Constance rose and brushed the dirt from her hands. "You'll be chilly unless I take you indoors."

"It would have been far more suitable in the rarebit, Constance. Odd that the point was never brought out at the time. Arsenic is tasteless, you know, although I swear a rarebit is not. Where am I going?"

"You are going indoors. You will rest in your room for an hour until your dinner, and after dinner I will play for you, if you like."

"I cannot afford the time, my dear. I have a thousand details to remember and note down, and not a minute to waste. I would hate to lose any small thing from their last day; my book must be complete. I think, on the whole, it was a pleasant day for all of them, and of course it is much better that they never supposed it was to be their last. I think I am chilly, Constance."

"You will be tucked away in your room in a minute."

I came slowly behind them, unwilling to leave the darkening garden; Jonas came after me, moving toward the light in the house. When Jonas and I came inside Constance was just closing the door to Uncle Julian's room, and she smiled at me. "He's practically asleep already," she said softly.

"When I'm as old as Uncle Julian will you take care of me?" I asked her.

"If I'm still around," she said, and I was chilled. I sat in my corner holding Jonas and watched her move quickly and silently around our bright kitchen. In a few minutes she would ask me to set the table for the three of us in the dining room, and then after dinner it would be night and we would sit warmly together in the kitchen where we were guarded by the house and no one from outside could see so much as a light.

## 4

~~~~~~~~~~~~~~~~~~~~~~~~~~~~~~~~~~~~~~~~~~~~~~~~~~~~~~~~~~~~~

ON SUNDAY MORNING THE CHANGE WAS ONE DAY NEARER.
I was resolute about not thinking my three magic words
and would not let them into my mind, but the air of
change was so strong that there was no avoiding it;
change lay over the stairs and the kitchen and the
garden like fog. I would not forget my magic words;
they were MELODY GLOUCESTER PEGASUS, but I refused
to let them into my mind. The weather was uneasy on
Sunday morning and I thought that perhaps Jonas would

succeed after all in running up a storm; the sun shone into the kitchen but there were clouds moving quickly across the sky and a sharp little breeze that came in and out of the kitchen while I had my breakfast.

"Wear your boots if you wander today," Constance told me.

"I don't expect that Uncle Julian will sit outdoors today; it will be far too cool for him."

"Pure spring weather," Constance said, and smiled out at her garden.

"I love you, Constance," I said.

"I love you too, silly Merricat."

"Is Uncle Julian better?"

"I don't think so. He had his tray while you were still asleep, and I thought he seemed very tired. He said he had an extra pill during the night. I think perhaps he is getting worse."

"Are you worried about him?"

"Yes. Very."

"Will he die?"

"Do you know what he said to me this morning?" Constance turned, leaning against the sink, and looked at me with sadness. "He thought I was Aunt Dorothy, and he held my hand and said, 'It's terrible to be old, and just lie here wondering when it will happen.' He almost frightened me."

"You should have let me take him to the moon," I said.

"I gave him his hot milk and then he remembered who I was."

I thought that Uncle Julian was probably really very

happy, with both Constance and Aunt Dorothy to take
care of him, and I told myself that long thin things would
remind me to be kinder to Uncle Julian; this was to be a
day of long thin things, since there had already been a
hair in my toothbrush, and a fragment of a string was
caught on the side of my chair and I could see a splinter
broken off the back step. "Make him a little pudding," I
said.

"Perhaps I will." She took out the long thin slicing
knife and set it on the sink. "Or a cup of cocoa. And
dumplings with his chicken tonight."

"Do you need me?"

"No, my Merricat. Run along, and wear your boots."

The day outside was full of changing light, and Jonas
danced in and out of shadows as he followed me. When I
ran Jonas ran, and when I stopped and stood still he
stopped and glanced at me and then went briskly off in
another direction, as though we were not acquainted,
and then he sat down and waited for me to run again. We
were going to the long field which today looked like an
ocean, although I had never seen an ocean; the grass was
moving in the breeze and the cloud shadows passed back
and forth and the trees in the distance moved. Jonas disappeared into the grass, which was tall enough for me to
touch with my hands while I walked, and he made small
crooked movements of his own; for a minute the grass
would all bend together under the breeze and then there
would be a hurrying pattern across it where Jonas was
running. I started at one corner and walked diagonally
across the long field toward the opposite corner, and in

the middle I came directly to the rock covering the spot where the doll was buried; I could always find it although much of my buried treasure was forever lost. The rock was undisturbed and so the doll was safe. I am walking on buried treasure, I thought, with the grass brushing against my hands and nothing around me but the reach of the long field with the grass blowing and the pine woods at the end; behind me was the house, and far off to my left, hidden by trees and almost out of sight, was the wire fence our father had built to keep people out.

When I left the long field I went between the four apple trees we called our orchard, and along the path toward the creek. My box of silver dollars buried by the creek was safe. Near the creek, well hidden, was one of my hiding places, which I had made carefully and used often. I had torn away two or three low bushes and smoothed the ground; all around were more bushes and tree branches, and the entrance was covered by a branch which almost touched the ground. It was not really necessary to be so secret, since no one ever came looking for me here, but I liked to lie inside with Jonas and know that I could never be found. I used leaves and branches for a bed, and Constance had given me a blanket. The trees around and overhead were so thick that it was always dry inside and on Sunday morning I lay there with Jonas, listening to his stories. All cat stories start with the statement: "My mother, who was the first cat, told me this," and I lay with my head close to Jonas and listened. There was no change coming, I thought here, only spring; I was wrong to be so frightened. The days would get warmer, and Uncle Julian would sit in the sun, and Constance would laugh when she worked in the garden, and it would always be the same. Jonas went on and on ("And then we sang! And then we sang!") and the leaves moved overhead and it would always be the same.

1 found a nest of baby snakes near the creek and killed them all; I dislike snakes and Constance had never asked me not to. I was on my way back to the house when I found a very bad omen, one of the worst. My book nailed to a tree in the pine woods had fallen down. I decided that the nail had rusted away and the book—it was a little notebook of our father's, where he used to record the names of people who owed him money, and people who ought, he thought, to do favors for him—was useless now as protection. I had wrapped it very thoroughly in heavy paper before nailing it to the tree, but the nail had rusted and it had fallen. I thought I had better destroy it, in case it was now actively bad, and bring something else out to the tree, perhaps a scarf of our mother's, or a glove. It was really too late, although I did not know it then; he was already on his way to the house. By the time I found the book he had probably already left his suitcase in the post office and was asking directions. All Jonas and I knew then was that we were hungry, and we ran together back to the house, and came with the breeze into the kitchen.

"Did you really forget your boots?" Constance said. She tried to frown and then laughed. "Silly Merricat."

"Jonas had no boots. It's a wonderful day."

"Perhaps tomorrow we'll go to gather mushrooms."

"Jonas and I are hungry *today*."

By then he was already walking through the village toward the black rock, with all of them watching him and wondering and whispering as he passed.

It was the last of our slow lovely days, although, as Uncle Julian would have pointed out, we never suspected it then. Constance and I had lunch, giggling and never knowing that while we were happy he was trying the locked gate, and peering down the path, and wandering the woods, shut out for a time by our father's fence. The rain started while we sat in the kitchen, and we left the kitchen door open so we could watch the rain slanting past the doorway and washing the garden; Constance was pleased, the way any good gardener is pleased with rain. "We'll see color out there soon," she said.

"We'll always be here together, won't we, Constance?"

"Don't you ever want to leave here, Merricat?"

"Where could we go?" I asked her. "What place would be better for us than this? Who wants us, outside? The world is full of terrible people."

"I wonder sometimes." She was very serious for a minute, and then she turned and smiled at me. "Don't you worry, my Merricat. Nothing bad will happen."

That must have been just about the minute he found the entrance and started up the driveway, hurrying in the rain, because I had only a minute or two left before I saw him. I might have used that minute or two for so many things: I might have warned Constance, somehow, or I might have thought of a new, safer, magic word, or I might have pushed the table across the kitchen doorway; as it happened, I played with my spoon, and looked at Jonas, and when Constance shivered I said, "I'll get your sweater for you." That was what brought me into the hall as he was coming up the steps. I saw him through the dining-room window and for a minute, chilled, I could not breathe. I knew the front door was locked; I thought of that first. "Constance," I said softly, not moving, "there's one outside. The kitchen door, quickly." I thought she had heard me, because I heard her move in the kitchen, but Uncle Julian had called at that moment, and she went in to him, leaving the heart of our house unguarded. I ran to the front door and leaned against it and heard his steps outside. He knocked, quietly at first and then firmly, and I leaned against the door, feeling the knocks hit at me, knowing how close he was. I knew already that he was one of the bad ones; I had seen his face briefly and he was one of the bad ones, who go around and around the house, trying to get in, looking in the windows, pulling and poking and stealing souvenirs.

He knocked again, and then called out, "Constance? Constance?"

Well, they always knew her name. They knew her name and Uncle Julian's name and how she wore her hair and the color of the three dresses she had to wear in court and how old she was and how she talked and moved and when they could they looked close in her face to see if she was crying. "I want to talk to Constance," he said outside, the way they always did.

It had been a long time since any of them came, but I had not forgotten how they made me feel. At first, they were always there, waiting for Constance, just wanting to see her. "Look," they said, nudging each other and pointing, "there she is, that one, that's the one, Constance." "Doesn't *look* like a murderess, does she?" they told each other; "listen, see if you can get a picture of her when she shows again." "Let's just take some of these flowers," they said comfortably to each other; "get a rock or something out of the garden, we can take it home to show the kids."

"Constance?" he said outside. "Constance?" He knocked again. "I want to talk to Constance," he said, "I have something important to say to her."

They always had something important they wanted to tell Constance, whether they were pushing at the door or yelling outside or calling on the telephone or writing the terrible terrible letters. Sometimes they wanted Julian Blackwood, but they never asked for me. I had been sent to bed without my supper, I had not been allowed in the courtroom, no one had taken my picture. While they were looking at Constance in the courtroom I had been lying on the cot at the orphanage, staring at the ceiling, wishing they were all dead, waiting for Constance to come and take me home.

"Constance, *can* you hear me?" he called outside. "Please listen for just a minute."

I wondered if he could hear me breathing on the inside of the door; I knew what he would do next. First he would back away from the house, sheltering his eyes from the rain, and look up at the windows upstairs, hoping to see a face looking down. Then he would start toward the side of the house, following the walk which was only supposed to be used by Constance and me. When he found the side door, which we never opened, he would knock there, calling Constance. Sometimes they went away when no one answered at either the front door or the side; the ones who were faintly embarrassed at being here at all and wished they had not bothered to come in the first place because there was really nothing to see and they could have saved their time or gone somewhere else —they usually hurried off when they found they were not going to get in to see Constance, but the stubborn ones, the ones I wished would die and lie there dead on the driveway, went around and around the house, trying every door and tapping on the windows. "We got a *right* to see her," they used to shout, "she killed all those people, didn't she?" They drove cars up to the steps and parked there. Most of them locked their cars carefully, making sure all the windows were shut, before they came to pound at the house and call to Constance. They had picnics on the lawn and took pictures of each other standing in front of the house and let their dogs run in the garden. They wrote their names on the walls and on the front door.

"Look," he said outside, "you've *got* to let me in."

I heard him go down the steps and knew he was looking up. The windows were all locked. The side door was locked. I knew better than to try to look out through the narrow glass panels on either side of the door; they always noticed even the slightest movement, and if I had even barely touched the dining-room drapes he would have been running at the house, shouting, "There she is, there she is." I leaned against the front door and thought about opening it and finding him dead on the driveway.

He was looking up at a blank face of a house looking down because we always kept the shades drawn on the upstairs windows; he would get no answer there and I had to find Constance a sweater before she shivered any more. It was safe to go upstairs, but I wanted to be back with Constance while he was waiting outside, so I ran up the stairs and snatched a sweater from the chair in Constance's room and ran downstairs and down the hall into the kitchen and he was sitting at the table in my chair.

"I had three magic words," I said, holding the sweater. "Their names were MELODY GLOUCESTER PEGASUS, and we were safe until they were said out loud."

"Merricat," Constance said; she turned and looked at me, smiling. "It's our cousin, our cousin Charles Blackwood. I knew him at once; he looks like Father."

"Well, Mary," he said. He stood up; he was taller now that he was inside, bigger and bigger as he came closer to me. "Got a kiss for your cousin Charles?"

Behind him the kitchen door was open wide; he was the first one who had ever gotten inside and Constance had let him in. Constance stood up; she knew better than to touch me but she said "Merricat, Merricat" gently and held out her arms to me. I was held tight, wound round with wire, I couldn't breathe, and I had to run. I threw the sweater on the floor and went out the door and down

to the creek where I always went. Jonas found me after
a while and we lay there together, protected from the
rain by the trees crowding overhead, dim and rich in the
kind of knowing, possessive way trees have of pressing
closer. I looked back at the trees and listened to the soft
sound of the water. There was no cousin, no Charles
Blackwood, no intruder inside. It was because the book
had fallen from the tree; I had neglected to replace it at
once and our wall of safety had cracked. Tomorrow I
would find some powerful thing and nail it to the tree.
I fell asleep listening to Jonas, just as the shadows were
coming down. Sometime during the night Jonas left me
to go hunting, and I woke a little when he came back,
pressing against me to get warm. "Jonas," I said, and he
purred comfortably. When I woke up the early morning
mists were wandering lightly along the creek, curling
around my face and touching me. I lay there laughing,
feeling the almost imaginary brush of the mist across my
eyes, and looking up into the trees.

*5*

⁓⁓⁓⁓⁓⁓⁓⁓⁓⁓⁓⁓⁓⁓⁓⁓⁓⁓⁓⁓⁓⁓⁓⁓⁓

WHEN I CAME INTO THE KITCHEN, STILL TRAILING MIST
from the creek, Constance was arranging Uncle Julian's
breakfast tray. Uncle Julian was clearly feeling well this
morning, since Constance was giving him tea instead of
hot milk; he must have awakened early and asked for tea.
I went to her and put my arms around her and she turned
and hugged me.

"Good morning, my Merricat," she said.

"Good morning, my Constance. Is Uncle Julian better today?"

"Much, much better. And the sun is going to shine after yesterday's rain. And I am going to make a chocolate mousse for your dinner, my Merricat."

"I love you, Constance."

"And I love you. Now what will you have for breakfast?"

"Pancakes. Little tiny hot ones. And two fried eggs. Today my winged horse is coming and I am carrying you off to the moon and on the moon we will eat rose petals."

"Some rose petals are poisonous."

"Not on the moon. Is it true that you can plant a leaf?"

"Some leaves. Furred leaves. You can put them in water and they grow roots and then you plant them and they grow into a plant. The kind of a plant they were when they started, of course, not just any plant."

"I'm sorry about that. Good morning, Jonas. You are a furred leaf, I think."

"Silly Merricat."

"I like a leaf that grows into a different plant. All furry."

Constance was laughing. "Uncle Julian will never get his breakfast if I listen to you," she said. She took up the tray and went into Uncle Julian's room. "Hot tea coming," she said.

"Constance, my dear. A glorious morning, I think. A splendid day to work."

"And to sit in the sun."

Jonas sat in the sunlit doorway, washing his face. I

was hungry; perhaps it would be kind to Uncle Julian today if I put a feather on the lawn at the spot where Uncle Julian's chair would go; I was not allowed to bury things in the lawn. On the moon we wore feathers in our hair, and rubies on our hands. On the moon we had gold spoons.

"Perhaps today is a good day to begin a new chapter. Constance?"

"Yes, Uncle Julian?"

"Do you think I should begin chapter forty-four today?"

"Of course."

"Some of the early pages need a little brushing up. A work like this is never done."

"Shall I brush your hair?"

"I think I will brush it myself this morning, thank you. A man's head should be his own responsibility, after all. I have no jam."

"Shall I get you some?"

"No, because I see that I have somehow eaten all my toast. I fancy a broiled liver for my lunch, Constance."

"You shall have it. Shall I take your tray?"

"Yes, thank you. And I will brush my hair."

Constance came back into the kitchen and set down the tray. "And now for you, my Merricat," she said.

"And Jonas."

"Jonas had his breakfast long ago."

"Will you plant a leaf for me?"

"One of these days." She turned her head and listened. "He is still asleep," she said.

"Who is still asleep? Will I watch it grow?"

"Cousin Charles is still asleep," she said, and the day fell apart around me. I saw Jonas in the doorway and Constance by the stove but they had no color. I could not breathe, I was tied around tight, everything was cold.

"He was a ghost," I said.

Constance laughed, and it was a sound very far away. "Then a ghost is sleeping in Father's bed," she said. "And ate a very hearty dinner last night. While you were gone," she said.

"I dreamed that he came. I fell asleep on the ground and dreamed that he came, but then I dreamed him away." I was held tight; when Constance believed me I could breathe again.

"We talked for a long time last night."

"Go and look," I said, not breathing, "go and look; he isn't there."

"Silly Merricat," she said.

I could not run; I had to help Constance. I took my glass and smashed it on the floor. "Now he'll go away," I said.

Constance came to the table and sat down across from me, looking very serious. I wanted to go around the table and hug her, but she still had no color. "My Merricat," she said slowly, "Cousin Charles is here. He *is* our cousin. As long as his father was alive—that was Arthur Blackwood, Father's brother—Cousin Charles could not come to us, or try to help us, because his father would not allow him. His father," she said, and smiled a little, "thought very badly of us. He refused to take care of you during the trial, did you know that? And he never let our names be mentioned in his house."

"Then why do you mention his name in our house?"

"Because I am trying to explain. As soon as his father died Cousin Charles hurried here to help us."

"How can he help us? We're very happy, aren't we, Constance?"

"Very happy, Merricat. But please be pleasant to Cousin Charles."

I could breathe a little; it was going to be all right. Cousin Charles was a ghost, but a ghost that could be driven away. "He'll go away," I said.

"I don't suppose he plans to stay forever," Constance said. "He only came for a visit, after all."

I would have to find something, a device, to use against him. "Has Uncle Julian seen him?"

"Uncle Julian knows he is here, but Uncle Julian was too unwell last night to leave his room. He had his dinner on a tray, only a little soup. I was glad he asked for tea this morning."

"Today we neaten the house."

"Later, after Cousin Charles is awake. And I'd better sweep up that broken glass before he comes down."

I watched her while she swept up the glass; today would be a glittering day, full of tiny sparkling things. There was no point in hurrying with my breakfast, because today I could not go out until we had neatened the house, so I lingered, drinking milk slowly and watching Jonas. Before I was finished Uncle Julian called Constance to come and help him into his chair, and she brought him into the kitchen and put him by his table and his papers.

"I really think I shall commence chapter forty-four," he said, patting his hands together. "I shall commence, I think, with a slight exaggeration and go on from there into an outright lie. Constance, my dear?"

"Yes, Uncle Julian?"

"I am going to say that my wife was beautiful."

Then we were all silent for a minute, puzzled by the sound of a foot stepping upstairs where there had always been silence before. It was unpleasant, this walking overhead. Constance always stepped lightly, and Uncle Julian never walked; this footstep was heavy and even and bad.

"That is Cousin Charles," Constance said, looking up.

"Indeed," said Uncle Julian. He carefully arranged a paper before him and took up a pencil. "I am anticipating considerable pleasure from the society of my brother's son," he said. "Perhaps he can fill in some details on the behavior of his family during the trial. Although, I confess, I have somewhere set down notes on a possible conversation they might have had . . ." He turned to one of his notebooks. "This will delay chapter forty-four, I suspect."

I took Jonas and went to my corner, and Constance went into the hall to meet Charles when he came down the stairs. "Good morning, Cousin Charles," she said.

"Good morning, Connie." It was the same voice as he had used last night. I got further into my corner as she brought him into the kitchen, and Uncle Julian touched his papers and turned to face the doorway.

"Uncle Julian. I am pleased to meet you at last."

"Charles. You are Arthur's son, but you resemble my brother John, who is dead."

"Arthur's dead, too. That's why I'm here."

"He died wealthy, I trust? I was the only brother with no knack for money."

"As a matter of fact, Uncle Julian, my father left nothing."

"A pity. *His* father left a considerable sum. It came to a considerable sum, even divided among the three of us. I always knew my share would melt away, but I had not suspected it of my brother Arthur. Perhaps your mother was an extravagant woman? I do not remember her very clearly. I recall that when my niece Constance wrote to her uncle during the trial, it was his wife who answered, requesting that the family connection be severed."

"I wanted to come before, Uncle Julian."

"I daresay. Youth is always curious. And a woman of such notoriety as your cousin Constance would present a romantic figure to a young man. Constance?"

"Yes, Uncle Julian?"

"Have I had my breakfast?"

"Yes."

"I will have another cup of tea, then. This young man and I have a great deal to discuss."

I still could not see him clearly, perhaps because he was a ghost, perhaps because he was so very big. His great round face, looking so much like our father's, turned from Constance to Uncle Julian and back, smiling and opening its mouth to talk. I moved as far into my corner as I could, but finally the big face turned at me.

"Why, there's Mary," it said. "Good morning, Mary."

I put my face down to Jonas.

"Shy?" he asked Constance. "Never mind. Kids always take to me."

Constance laughed. "We don't see many strangers," she said. She was not at all awkward or uncomfortable; it was as though she had been expecting all her life that Cousin Charles would come, as though she had planned exactly what to do and say, almost as though in the house of her life there had always been a room kept for Cousin Charles.

He stood up and came closer to me. "That's a handsome cat," he said. "Does it have a name?"

Jonas and I looked at him and then I thought that Jonas's name might be the safest thing to speak to him first. "Jonas," I said.

"Jonas? Is he your special pet?"

"Yes," I said. We looked at him, Jonas and I, not daring to blink or turn away. The big white face was close, still looking like our father, and the big mouth was smiling.

"We're going to be good friends, you and Jonas and I," he said.

"What will you have for breakfast?" Constance asked him, and she smiled at me because I had told him Jonas's name.

"Whatever you're serving," he said, turning away from me at last.

"Merricat had pancakes."

"Pancakes would be great. A good breakfast in charming company on a beautiful day; what more could I ask?"

"Pancakes," observed Uncle Julian, "are an honored dish in this family, although I rarely take them myself; my health permits only the lightest and daintiest foods. Pancakes were served for breakfast on that last—"

"Uncle Julian," Constance said, "your papers are spilling on the floor."

"Let me get them, sir." Cousin Charles kneeled to gather the papers and Constance said, "After breakfast you'll see my garden."

"A chivalrous young man," Uncle Julian said, accepting his papers from Charles. "I thank you; I am not able myself to leap across a room and kneel on the floor and I am gratified to find someone who can. I believe that you are a year or so older than my niece?"

"I'm thirty-two," Charles said.

"And Constance is approximately twenty-eight. We long ago gave up the practice of birthdays, but twenty-eight should be about right. Constance, I should not be talking so on an empty stomach. Where is my breakfast?"

"You finished it an hour ago, Uncle Julian. I am making you a cup of tea, and pancakes for Cousin Charles."

"Charles is intrepid. Your cooking, although it is of a very high standard indeed, has certain disadvantages."

"I'm not afraid to eat anything Constance cooks," Charles said.

"Really?" said Uncle Julian. "I congratulate you. I was referring to the effect a weighty meal like pancakes is apt to have on a delicate stomach. I suppose *your* reference was to arsenic."

"Come and have your breakfast," Constance said.

I was laughing, although Jonas hid my face. It took Charles a good half-minute to pick up his fork, and he kept smiling at Constance. Finally, knowing that Constance and Uncle Julian and Jonas and I were watching him, he cut off a small piece of pancake and brought it to his mouth, but could not bring himself to put it inside. Finally he set the fork with the piece of pancake down on his plate and turned to Uncle Julian. "You know, I was thinking," he said. "Maybe while I'm here there are things I could do for you—dig in the garden, maybe, or run errands. I'm pretty good at hard work."

"You had dinner here last night and woke up alive this morning," Constance said; I was laughing but she suddenly looked almost cross.

"What?" Charles said. "Oh." He looked down at his fork as though he had forgotten it and at last he picked it up and put the piece of pancake into his mouth very quickly, and chewed it and swallowed it and looked up at Constance. "Delicious," he said, and Constance smiled.

"Constance?"

"Yes, Uncle Julian?"

"I think I shall not, after all, begin chapter forty-four this morning. I think I shall go back to chapter seventeen, where I recall that I made some slight mention of your cousin and his family, and their attitude during the trial. Charles, you are a clever young man. I am eager to hear your story."

"It was all so long ago," Charles said.

"You should have kept notes," Uncle Julian said.

"I mean," Charles said, "can't it all be forgotten? There's no point in keeping those memories alive."

"Forgotten?" Uncle Julian said. "Forgotten?"

"It was a sad and horrible time and it's not going to do Connie here any good at all to keep talking about it."

"Young man, you are speaking slightingly, I believe, of my work. A man does not take his work lightly. A man has his work to do, and he does it. Remember that, Charles."

"I'm just saying that I don't want to talk about Connie and that bad time."

"I shall be forced to invent, to fictionalize, to imagine."

"I refuse to discuss it any further."

"Constance?"

"Yes, Uncle Julian?" Constance looked very serious.

"It *did* happen? I remember that it happened," said Uncle Julian, fingers at his mouth.

Constance hesitated, and then she said, "Of course it did, Uncle Julian."

"My notes . . . " Uncle Julian's voice trailed off, and he gestured at his papers.

"Yes, Uncle Julian. It was real."

I was angry because Charles ought to be kind to Uncle Julian. I remembered that today was to be a day of sparkles and light, and I thought that I would find something bright and pretty to put near Uncle Julian's chair.

"Constance?"

"Yes?"

"May I go outside? Am I warm enough?"

"I think so, Uncle Julian." Constance was sorry, too. Uncle Julian was shaking his head back and forth sadly and he had put down his pencil. Constance went into Uncle Julian's room and brought out his shawl, which she put around his shoulders very gently. Charles was eating his pancakes bravely now, and did not look up; I wondered if he cared that he had not been kind to Uncle Julian.

"Now you will go outside," Constance said quietly to Uncle Julian, "and the sun will be warm and the garden will be bright and you will have broiled liver for your lunch."

"Perhaps not," Uncle Julian said. "Perhaps I had better have just an egg."

Constance wheeled him gently to the door and eased his chair carefully down the step. Charles looked up from his pancakes but when he started to rise to help her she shook her head. "I'll put you in your special corner," she said to Uncle Julian, "where I can see you every minute and five times an hour I'll wave hello to you."

We could hear her talking all the time she was wheeling Uncle Julian to his corner. Jonas left me and went to sit in the doorway and watch them. "Jonas?" Charles said, and Jonas turned toward him. "Cousin Mary doesn't like me," Charles said to Jonas. I disliked the way he was talking to Jonas and I disliked the way Jonas appeared to be listening to him. "How can I make Cousin Mary like me?" Charles said, and Jonas looked quickly at me and then back to Charles. "Here I've come to visit my two dear cousins," Charles said, "my two dear cousins and my old uncle whom I haven't seen for years, and my Cousin Mary won't even be polite to me. What do you think, Jonas?"

There were sparkles at the sink where a drop of water was swelling to fall. Perhaps if I held my breath until the drop fell Charles would go away, but I knew that was not true; holding my breath was too easy.

"Oh, well," Charles said to Jonas, "*Constance* likes me, and I guess that's all that matters."

Constance came to the doorway, waited for Jonas to move, and when he did not, stepped over him. "More pancakes?" she said to Charles.

"No, thanks. I'm trying to get acquainted with my little cousin."

"It won't be long before she's fond of you." Constance was looking at me. Jonas had fallen to washing himself, and I thought at last of what to say.

"Today we neaten the house," I said.

Uncle Julian slept all morning in the garden. Constance went often to the back bedroom windows to look down on him while we worked and stood sometimes, with the dustcloth in her hands, as though she were forgetting to come back and dust our mother's jewel box that held our mother's pearls, and her sapphire ring, and her brooch with diamonds. I looked out the window only once, to see Uncle Julian with his eyes closed and Charles standing nearby. It was ugly to think of Charles walking among the vegetables and under the apple trees and across the lawn where Uncle Julian slept.

"We'll let Father's room go this morning," Constance said, "because Charles is living there." Some time later she said, as though she had been thinking about it, "I wonder if it would be right for me to wear Mother's pearls. I have never worn pearls."

"They've always been in the box," I said. "You'd have to take them out."

"It's not likely that anyone would care," Constance said.

"*I* would care, if you looked more beautiful."

Constance laughed, and said, "I'm silly now. Why should I want to wear pearls?"

"They're better off in the box where they belong."

Charles had closed the door of our father's room so I could not look inside, but I wondered if he had moved our father's things, or put a hat or a handkerchief or a glove on the dresser beside our father's silver brushes. I wondered if he had looked into the closet or into the drawers. Our father's room was in the front of the house, and I wondered if Charles had looked down from the windows and out over the lawn and the long driveway to the road, and wanted to be on that road and away home.

"How long did it take Charles to get here?" I asked Constance.

"Four or five hours, I think," she said. "He came by bus to the village, and had to walk from there."

"Then it will take him four or five hours to get home again?"

"I suppose so. When he goes."

"But first he will have to walk back to the village?"

"Unless you take him on your winged horse."

"I don't have any winged horse," I said.

"Oh, Merricat," Constance said. "Charles is *not* a bad man."

There were sparkles in the mirrors and inside our mother's jewel box the diamonds and the pearls were shining in the darkness. Constance made shadows up and down the hall when she went to the window to look down on Uncle Julian and outside the new leaves moved quickly in the sunlight. Charles had only gotten in because the magic was broken; if I could re-seal the protection around Constance and shut Charles out he would have to leave the house. Every touch he made on the house must be erased.

"Charles is a ghost," I said, and Constance sighed.

I polished the doorknob to our father's room with my dustcloth, and at least one of Charles' touches was gone.

When we had neatened the upstairs rooms we came downstairs together, carrying our dustcloths and the broom and dustpan and mop like a pair of witches walking home. In the drawing room we dusted the golden-legged chairs and the harp, and everything sparkled at us, even the blue dress in the portrait of our mother. I dusted the wedding cake trim with a cloth on the end of a broom, staggering, and looking up and pretending that the ceiling was the floor and I was sweeping, hovering busily in space looking down at my broom, weightless and flying until the room swung dizzily and I was again on the floor looking up.

"Charles has not yet seen this room," Constance said. "Mother was so proud of it; I ought to have showed it to him right away."

"May I have sandwiches for my lunch? I want to go down to the creek."

"Sooner or later you're going to have to sit at the table with him, Merricat."

"Tonight at dinner. I promise."

We dusted the dining room and the silver tea service and the high wooden backs of the chairs. Constance went every few minutes into the kitchen to look out the back door and check on Uncle Julian, and once I heard her laugh and call, "Watch out for the mud down there," and I knew she was talking to Charles.

"Where did you let Charles sit last night at dinner?" I asked her once.

"In Father's chair," she said, and then, "He has a perfect right to sit there. He's a guest, and he even *looks* like Father."

"Will he sit there tonight?"

"Yes, Merricat."

I dusted our father's chair thoroughly, although it was small use if Charles was to sit there again tonight. I would have to clean all the silverware.

When we had finished neatening the house we came back to the kitchen. Charles was sitting at the kitchen table smoking his pipe and looking at Jonas, who was looking back at him. The pipe smoke was disagreeable in our kitchen, and I disliked having Jonas look at Charles. Constance went on out the back door to get Uncle Julian, and we could hear him say, "Dorothy? I was not asleep, Dorothy."

"Cousin Mary doesn't like me," Charles said again to Jonas. "I wonder if Cousin Mary knows how I get even with people who don't like me? Can I help you with that chair, Constance? Have a nice nap, Uncle?"

Constance made sandwiches for Jonas and me, and we ate them in a tree; I sat in a low fork and Jonas sat on a small branch near me, watching for birds.

"Jonas," I told him, "you are not to listen any more to Cousin Charles," and Jonas regarded me in wide-eyed astonishment, that I should attempt to make decisions for him. "Jonas," I said, "he is a ghost," and Jonas closed his eyes and turned away.

It was important to choose the exact device to drive Charles away. An imperfect magic, or one incorrectly used, might only bring more disaster upon our house. I thought of my mother's jewels, since this was a day of sparkling things, but they might not be strong on a dull day, and Constance would be angry if I took them out of the box where they belonged, when she herself had decided against it. I thought of books, which are always strongly protective, but my father's book had fallen from the tree and let Charles in; books, then, were perhaps powerless against Charles. I lay back against the tree trunk and thought of magic; if Charles had not gone away before three days I would smash the mirror in the hall.

He sat across from me at dinner, in our father's chair, with his big white face blotting out the silver on the sideboard behind him. He watched while Constance cut up Uncle Julian's chicken and put it correctly on the plate, and he watched when Uncle Julian took the first bite and turned it over and over in his mouth.

"Here is a biscuit, Uncle Julian," Constance said. "Eat the soft inside."

Constance had forgotten and put dressing on my salad, but I would not have eaten anyway with that big white face watching. Jonas, who was not allowed chicken, sat on the floor beside my chair.

"Does he always eat with you?" Charles asked once, nodding his head at Uncle Julian.

"When he's well enough," Constance said.

"I wonder how you stand it," Charles said.

"I tell you, John," Uncle Julian said suddenly to Charles, "investments are not what they were when Father made his money. He was a shrewd man, but he never understood that times change."

"Who's he talking to?" Charles asked Constance.

"He thinks you are his brother John."

Charles looked at Uncle Julian for a long minute, and then shook his head and returned to his chicken.

"That was my dead wife's chair on your left, young man," Uncle Julian said. "I well recall the last time she sat there; we—"

"None of that," Charles said, and shook his finger at Uncle Julian; he had been holding his chicken in his hands to eat it, and his finger sparkled with grease. "We're not going to talk about it any more, Uncle."

Constance was pleased with me because I had come to the table and when I looked at her she smiled at me. She knew that I disliked eating when anyone was watching me, and she would save my plate and bring it to me later in the kitchen; she did not remember, I saw, that she had put dressing on my salad.

"Noticed this morning," Charles said, taking up the platter of chicken and looking into it carefully, "that there was a broken step out back. How about I fix it for you one of these days? I might as well earn my keep."

"It would be very kind of you," Constance said. "That step has been a nuisance for a long time."

"And I want to run into the village to get some pipe tobacco, so I can pick up anything you need there."

"But I go to the village on Tuesday," I said, startled.

"You do?" He looked at me across the table, big white face turned directly at me. I was quiet; I remembered that walking to the village was the first step on Charles' way home.

"Merricat, dear, I think if Charles doesn't mind it might be a good idea. I never feel quite comfortable when you're away in the village." Constance laughed. "I'll give you a list, Charles, and the money, and you shall be the grocery boy."

"You keep the money in the house?"

"Of course."

"Doesn't sound very wise."

"It's in Father's safe."

"Even so."

"I assure you, sir," Uncle Julian said, "I made a point of examining the books thoroughly before committing myself. I cannot have been deceived."

"So I'm taking little Cousin Mary's job away from her," Charles said, looking at me again. "You'll have to find something else for her to do, Connie."

I had made sure of what to say to him before I came to the table. "The *Amanita phalloides*," I said to him, "holds three different poisons. There is amanitin, which works slowly and is most potent. There is phalloidin, which acts at once, and there is phallin, which dissolves red corpuscles, although it is the least potent. The first symptoms do not appear until seven to twelve hours after eating, in some cases not before twenty-four or even forty hours. The symptoms begin with violent stomach pains, cold sweat, vomiting—"

"Listen," Charles said. He put down his chicken. "You stop that," he said.

Constance was laughing. "Oh, Merricat," she said, laughing through the words, "you *are* silly. I taught her," she told Charles, "there are mushrooms by the creek and in the fields and I made her learn the deadly ones. Oh, Merricat."

"Death occurs between five and ten days after eating," I said.

"I don't think that's very funny," Charles said.

"Silly Merricat," Constance said.

*6*

~~~~~~~~~~~~~~~~~~~~~~~~~~~~~~~~~~~~~~~~~~~~~~~~~~~~~~~~~~~~~~

THE HOUSE WAS NOT SECURE JUST BECAUSE CHARLES HAD
gone out of it and into the village; for one thing, Constance had given him a key to the gates. There had originally been a key for each of us; our father had a key, and
our mother, and the keys were kept on a rack beside the
kitchen door. When Charles started out for the village
Constance gave him a key, perhaps our father's key, and
a shopping list, and the money to pay for what he bought.
   "You shouldn't keep money in the house like this," he

said, holding it tight in his hand for a minute before he reached into a back pocket and took out a wallet. "Women alone like you are, you shouldn't keep money in the house."

I was watching him from my corner of the kitchen but I would not let Jonas come to me while Charles was in the house. "Are you sure you put everything down?" he asked Constance. "Hate to make two trips."

I waited until Charles was well along, perhaps almost to the black rock, and then I said, "He forgot the library books."

Constance looked at me for a minute. "Miss Wickedness," she said. "You wanted him to forget."

"How could he know about the library books? He doesn't belong in this house; he has nothing to do with our books."

"Do you know," Constance said, looking into a pot on the stove, "I think that soon we will be picking lettuce; the weather has stayed so warm."

"On the moon," I said, and then stopped.

"On the moon," Constance said, turning to smile at me, "you have lettuce all year round, perhaps?"

"On the moon we have everything. Lettuce, and pumpkin pie and *Amanita phalloides*. We have cat-furred plants and horses dancing with their wings. All the locks are solid and tight, and there are no ghosts. On the moon Uncle Julian would be well and the sun would shine every day. You would wear our mother's pearls and sing, and the sun would shine all the time."

"I wish I could go to your moon. I wonder if I should

start the gingerbread now; it will be cold if Charles is late."

"I'll be here to eat it," I said.

"But Charles said he loved gingerbread."

I was making a little house at the table, out of the library books, standing one across two set on edge. "Old witch," I said, "you have a gingerbread house."

"I do not," Constance said. "I have a lovely house where I live with my sister Merricat."

I laughed at her; she was worrying at the pot on the stove and she had flour on her face. "Maybe he'll never come back," I said.

"He has to; I'm making gingerbread for him."

Since Charles had taken my occupation for Tuesday morning I had nothing to do. I wondered about going down to the creek, but I had no reason to suppose that the creek would even be there, since I never visited it on Tuesday mornings; would the people in the village be waiting for me, glancing from the corners of their eyes to see if I was coming, nudging one another, and then turn in astonishment when they saw Charles? Perhaps the whole village would falter and slow, bewildered at the lack of Miss Mary Katherine Blackwood? I giggled, thinking of Jim Donell and the Harris boys peering anxiously up the road to see if I was coming.

"What's funny?" Constance asked, turning to see.

"I was thinking that you might make a gingerbread man, and I could name him Charles and eat him."

"Oh, Merricat, *please*."

I could tell that Constance was going to be irritable,

partly because of me and partly because of the gingerbread, so I thought it wiser to run away. Since it was a
free morning, and I was uneasy at going out of doors, it
might be a good time to search out a device to use against
Charles, and I started upstairs; the smell of baking gingerbread followed me almost halfway to the top. Charles
had left his door open, not wide, but enough for me to
get a hand inside.

When I pushed a little the door opened wide and I
looked in at our father's room, which now belonged to
Charles. Charles had made his bed, I noticed; his mother
must have taught him. His suitcase was on a chair, but
it was closed; there were things belonging to Charles on
the dresser where our father's possessions had always
been kept; I saw Charles' pipe, and a handkerchief, things
that Charles had touched and used dirtying our father's
room. One drawer of the dresser was a little open, and
I thought again of Charles picking over our father's
clothes. I walked very softly across the room because I
did not want Constance to hear me from downstairs, and
looked into the open drawer. I thought that Charles
would not be pleased to know that I had caught him
looking at our father's things, and something from this
drawer might be extraordinarily powerful, since it would
carry a guilt of Charles. I was not surprised to find that
he had been looking at our father's jewelry; inside the
drawer was a leather box which held, I knew, a watch
and chain made of gold, and cuff links, and a signet ring.
I would not touch our mother's jewelry, but Constance

had not said anything about our father's jewelry, had not even come into this room to neaten, so I thought I could open the box and take something out. The watch was inside, in a small private box of its own, resting on a satin lining and not ticking, and the watch chain was curled beside it. I would not touch the ring; the thought of a ring around my finger always made me feel tied tight, because rings had no openings to get out of, but I liked the watch chain, which twisted and wound around my hand when I picked it up. I put the jewelry box carefully back inside the drawer and closed the drawer and went out of the room and closed the door after me, and took the watch chain into my room, where it curled again into a sleeping gold heap on the pillow.

I had intended to bury it, but I was sorry when I thought how long it had been there in the darkness in the box in our father's drawer, and I thought that it had earned a place up high, where it could sparkle in the sunlight, and I decided to nail it to the tree where the book had come down. While Constance made gingerbread in the kitchen, and Uncle Julian slept in his room, and Charles walked in and out of the village stores, I lay on my bed and played with my golden chain.

"That's my brother's gold watch chain," Uncle Julian said, leaning forward curiously. "I thought he was buried in it."

Charles' hand was shaking as he held it out; I could see it shaking against the yellow of the wall behind him. "In a tree," he said, and his voice was shaking too. "I found it nailed to a tree, for God's sake. What kind of a house *is* this?"

"It's not important," Constance said. "Really, Charles, it's not important."

"Not important? Connie, this thing's made of *gold*."

"But no one wants it."

"One of the links is smashed," Charles said, mourning over the chain. "I could have worn it; what a hell of a way to treat a valuable thing. We could have sold it," he said to Constance.

"But why?"

"I certainly did think he was buried in it," Uncle Julian said. "He was never a man to give things away easily. I suppose he never knew they kept it from him."

"It's worth money," Charles said, explaining carefully to Constance. "This is a gold watch chain, worth possibly a good deal of money. Sensible people don't go around nailing this kind of valuable thing to trees."

"Lunch will be cold if you stand there worrying."

"I'll take it up and put it back in the box where it belongs," Charles said. No one but me noticed that he knew where it had been kept. "Later," he said, looking at me, "we'll find out how it got on the tree."

"Merricat put it there," Constance said. "Please do come to lunch."

"How do you know? About Mary?"

"She always does." Constance smiled at me. "Silly Merricat."

"Does she indeed?" said Charles. He came slowly over to the table, looking at me.

"He was a man very fond of his person," Uncle Julian said. "Given to adorning himself, and not overly clean."

It was quiet in the kitchen; Constance was in Uncle Julian's room, putting him to bed for his afternoon nap. "Where would poor Cousin Mary go if her sister turned her out?" Charles asked Jonas, who listened quietly. "What would poor Cousin Mary do if Constance and Charles didn't love her?"

I cannot think why it seemed to me that I might simply ask Charles to go away. Perhaps I thought that he had to be asked politely just once; perhaps the idea of going away had just not come into his mind and it was necessary to put it there. I decided that asking Charles to go away was the next thing to do, before he was everywhere in the house and could never be eradicated. Already the house smelled of him, of his pipe and his shaving lotion, and the noise of him echoed in the rooms all day long; his pipe was sometimes on the kitchen table and his gloves or his tobacco pouch or his constant boxes of matches were scattered through our rooms. He walked into the village each afternoon and brought back newspapers which he left lying anywhere, even in the kitchen where Constance might see them. A spark from his pipe had left a tiny burn on the rose brocade of a chair in the drawing room; Constance had not yet noticed it and I thought not to tell her because I hoped that the house, injured, would reject him by itself.

"Constance," I asked her on a bright morning; Charles had been in our house for three days then, I thought; "Constance, has he said anything yet about leaving?"

She was increasingly cross with me when I wanted Charles to leave; always before Constance had listened and smiled and only been angry when Jonas and I had been wicked, but now she frowned at me often, as though I somehow looked different to her. "I've told you," she said to me, "I've told you and told you that I won't hear any more silliness about Charles. He is our cousin and he has been invited to visit us and he will probably go when he is ready."

"He makes Uncle Julian sicker."

"He's only trying to keep Uncle Julian from thinking about sad things all the time. And I agree with him. Uncle Julian should be cheerful."

"Why should he be cheerful if he's going to die?"

"I haven't been doing my duty," Constance said.

"I don't know what that means."

"I've been hiding here," Constance said slowly, as though she were not at all sure of the correct order of the words. She stood by the stove in the sunlight with color in her hair and eyes and not smiling, and she said slowly, "I have let Uncle Julian spend all his time living in the past and particularly re-living that one dreadful day. I have let you run wild; how long has it been since you combed your hair?"

I could not allow myself to be angry, and particularly

not angry with Constance, but I wished Charles dead. Constance needed guarding more than ever before and if I became angry and looked aside she might very well be lost. I said very cautiously, "On the moon . . ."

"On the moon," Constance said, and laughed unpleasantly. "It's all been my fault," she said. "I didn't realize how wrong I was, letting things go on and on because I wanted to hide. It wasn't fair to you or to Uncle Julian."

"And Charles is also mending the broken step?"

"Uncle Julian should be in a hospital, with nurses to take care of him. And you—" She opened her eyes wide suddenly, as though seeing her old Merricat again, and then she held out her arms to me. "Oh, Merricat," she said, and laughed a little. "Listen to me scolding you; how silly I am."

I went to her and put my arms around her. "I love you, Constance."

"You're a good child, Merricat," she said.

That was when I left her and went outside to talk to Charles. I knew I would dislike talking to Charles, but it was almost too late to ask him politely and I thought I should ask him once. Even the garden had become a strange landscape with Charles' figure in it; I could see him standing under the apple trees and the trees were crooked and shortened beside him. I came out the kitchen door and walked slowly toward him. I was trying to think charitably of him, since I would never be able to speak kindly until I did, but whenever I thought of his big white face grinning at me across the table or watching me whenever I moved I wanted to beat at him until he went away, I wanted to stamp on him after he was dead, and see him lying dead on the grass. So I made my mind charitable toward Charles and came up to him slowly.

"Cousin Charles?" I said, and he turned to look at me. I thought of seeing him dead. "Cousin Charles?"

"Well?"

"I have decided to ask you please to go away."

"All right," he said. "You asked me."

"Please will you go away?"

"No," he said.

I could not think of anything further to say. I saw that he was wearing our father's gold watch chain, even with the crooked link, and I knew without seeing that our father's watch was in his pocket. I thought that tomorrow he would be wearing our father's signet ring, and I wondered if he would make Constance put on our mother's pearls.

"You stay away from Jonas," I said.

"As a matter of fact," he said, "come about a month from now, I wonder who *will* still be here? You," he said, "or me?"

I ran back into the house and straight up to our father's room, where I hammered with a shoe at the mirror over the dresser until it cracked across. Then I went into my room and rested my head on the window sill and slept.

I was remembering these days to be kinder to Uncle Julian. I was sorry because he was spending more and more time in his room, taking both his breakfast and his lunch on a tray and only eating his dinners in the dining room under the despising eye of Charles.

"Can't you feed him or something?" Charles asked Constance. "He's got food all over himself."

"I didn't mean to," Uncle Julian said, looking at Constance.

"Ought to wear a baby bib," Charles said, laughing.

While Charles sat in the kitchen in the mornings eating hugely of ham and potatoes and fried eggs and hot biscuits and doughnuts and toast, Uncle Julian drowsed in his room over his hot milk and sometimes when he called to Constance, Charles said, "Tell him you're busy; you don't have to go running every time he wets his bed; he just likes being waited on."

I always had my breakfast earlier than Charles on those sunny mornings, and if he came down before I finished I would take my plate out and sit on the grass under the chestnut tree. Once I brought Uncle Julian a new leaf from the chestnut tree and put it on his window sill. I stood outside in the sunlight and looked in at him lying still in the dark room and tried to think of ways I might be kinder. I thought of him lying there alone dreaming old Uncle Julian dreams, and I went into the kitchen and said to Constance, "Will you make Uncle Julian a little soft cake for his lunch?"

"She's too busy now," Charles said with his mouth full. "Your sister works like a slave."

"Will you?" I asked Constance.

"I'm sorry," Constance said. "I have so much to do."

"But Uncle Julian is going to die."

"Constance is too busy," Charles said. "Run along and play."

I followed Charles one afternoon when he went to the village. I stopped by the black rock, because it was not one of my days for going into the village, and watched Charles go down the main street. He stopped and talked for a minute to Stella, who was standing in the sunlight outside her shop, and he bought a paper; when I saw him sit down on the benches with the other men I turned and went back to our house. If I went into the village shopping again Charles would be one of the men who watched me going past. Constance was working in her garden and Uncle Julian slept in his chair in the sun, and when I sat quietly on my bench Constance asked, not looking up at me, "Where have you been, Merricat?"

"Wandering. Where is my cat?"

"I think," Constance said, "that we are going to have to forbid your wandering. It's time you quieted down a little."

"Does 'we' mean you and Charles?"

"Merricat." Constance turned toward me, sitting back against her feet and folding her hands before her. "I never realized until lately how wrong I was to let you and Uncle Julian hide here with me. We should have faced the world and tried to live normal lives; Uncle Julian should have been in a hospital all these years, with good care and nurses to watch him. We should have been living like other people. You should . . ." She stopped, and waved her hands helplessly. "You should have boy friends," she said finally, and then began to laugh because she sounded funny even to herself.

"I have Jonas," I said, and we both laughed and Uncle Julian woke up suddenly and laughed a thin old cackle.

"You are the silliest person I ever saw," I told Constance, and went off to look for Jonas. While I was wandering Charles came back to our house; he brought a newspaper and a bottle of wine for his dinner and our father's scarf which I had used to tie shut the gate, because Charles had a key.

"I could have worn this scarf," he said irritably, and I heard him from the vegetable garden where I had found Jonas sleeping in a tangle of young lettuce plants. "It's an expensive thing, and I like the colors."

"It belonged to Father," Constance said.

"That reminds me," Charles said. "One of these days I'd like to look over the rest of his clothes." He was quiet for a minute; I thought he was probably sitting down on my bench. Then he went on, very lightly. "Also," he said, "while I'm here, I ought to go over your father's papers. There might be something important."

"Not *my* papers," Uncle Julian said. "That young man is not to put a finger on *my* papers."

"I haven't even seen your father's study," Charles said.

"We don't use it. Nothing in there is ever touched."

"Except the safe, of course," Charles said.

"Constance?"

"Yes, Uncle Julian?"

"I want you to have my papers afterwards. No one else is to touch my papers, do you hear me?"

"Yes, Uncle Julian."

I was not allowed to open the safe where Constance kept our father's money. I was allowed to go into the study, but I disliked it and never even touched the doorknob. I hoped Constance would not open the study for Charles; he already had our father's bedroom, after all, and our father's watch and his gold chain and his signet ring. I was thinking that being a demon and a ghost must be very difficult, even for Charles; if he ever forgot, or let his disguise drop for a minute, he would be recognized at once and driven away; he must be extremely careful to use the same voice every time, and present the same face and the same manner without a slip; he must be constantly on guard against betraying himself. I wondered if he would turn back to his true form when he was dead. When it grew cooler and I knew that Constance would be taking Uncle Julian indoors I left Jonas asleep on the lettuce plants and came back into the house. When I came into the kitchen Uncle Julian was poking furiously at the papers on his table, trying to get them into a small heap, and Constance was peeling potatoes. I could hear Charles moving around upstairs, and for a minute the kitchen was warm and glowing and bright.

"Jonas is asleep in the lettuce," I said.

"There is nothing I like more than cat fur in my salad," Constance said amiably.

"It is time that I had a box," Uncle Julian announced. He sat back and looked angrily at his papers. "They must all be put into a box, this very minute. Constance?"

"Yes, Uncle Julian; I can find you a box."

"If I put all my papers in a box and put the box in my room, then that dreadful young man cannot touch them. He *is* a dreadful young man, Constance."

"Really, Uncle Julian, Charles is very kind."

"He is dishonest. His father was dishonest. Both my brothers were dishonest. If he tries to take my papers you must stop him; I cannot permit tampering with my papers and I will not tolerate intrusion. You must tell him this, Constance. He is a bastard."

"Uncle Julian—"

"In a purely metaphorical sense, I assure you. Both my brothers married women of very strong will. That is merely a word used—among men, my dear; I apologize for submitting you to such a word—to categorize an undesirable fellow."

Constance turned without speaking and opened the door which led to the cellar stairs and to the rows and rows of food preserved at the very bottom of our house. She went quietly down the stairs, and we could hear Charles moving upstairs and Constance moving downstairs.

"William of Orange was a bastard," Uncle Julian said to himself; he took up a bit of paper and made a note. Constance came back up the cellar stairs with a box which she brought to Uncle Julian. "Here is a clean box," she said.

"What for?" Uncle Julian asked.

"To put your papers in."

"That young man is not to touch my papers, Constance. I will not have that young man going through my papers."

"This is all my fault," Constance said, turning to me. "He should be in a hospital."

"I will put my papers in that box, Constance, my dear, if you will be kind enough to hand it to me."

"He has a happy time," I said to Constance.

"I should have done everything differently."

"It would certainly not be kind to put Uncle Julian in a hospital."

"But I'll have to if I—" and Constance stopped suddenly, and turned back to the sink and the potatoes. "Shall I put walnuts in the applesauce?" she asked.

I sat very quietly, listening to what she had almost said. Time was running shorter, tightening around our house, crushing me. I thought it might be time to smash the big mirror in the hall, but then Charles' feet were coming heavily down the stairs and through the hall and into the kitchen.

"Well, well, everybody's here," he said. "What's for dinner?"

That evening Constance played for us in the drawing room, the tall curve of her harp making shadows against our mother's portrait and the soft notes falling into the air like petals. She played "Over the Sea to Skye" and "Flow Gently, Sweet Afton" and "I Saw a Lady," and other songs our mother used to play, but I never remember that our mother's fingers touched the strings so lightly with such a breath of melody. Uncle Julian kept himself awake, listening and dreaming, and even Charles did not quite dare to put his feet on the furniture in the drawing room, although the smoke from his pipe drifted against the wedding cake ceiling and he moved restlessly while Constance played.

"A delicate touch," Uncle Julian said once. "All the Blackwood women had a gifted touch."

Charles stopped by the fireplace to knock his pipe against the grate. "Pretty," he said, taking down one of the Dresden figurines. Constance stopped playing and he turned to look at her. "Valuable?"

"Not particularly," Constance said. "My mother liked them."

Uncle Julian said, "My particular favorite was always 'Bluebells of Scotland'; Constance, my dear, would you—"

"No more now," Charles said. "Now Constance and I want to talk, Uncle. We've got plans to make."

# 7

〰〰〰〰〰〰〰〰〰〰〰〰〰〰〰〰〰〰〰

THURSDAY WAS MY MOST POWERFUL DAY. IT WAS THE right day to settle with Charles. In the morning Constance decided to make spice cookies for dinner; that was too bad, because if any of us had known we could have told her not to bother, that Thursday was going to be the last day. Even Uncle Julian did not suspect, however; he felt a little stronger on Thursday morning and late in the morning Constance brought him into the kitchen which smelled richly of spice cookies and he continued putting his papers into the box. Charles had taken a hammer and found nails and a board and was pounding away mercilessly at the broken step; from the kitchen window I could see that he was doing it very badly and I was pleased; I wished the hammer to pound his thumb. I stayed in the kitchen until I was certain that they would all keep where they were for a while and then I went upstairs and into our father's room, walking softly so Constance would not know I was there. The first thing to do was stop our father's watch which Charles had started. I knew he was not wearing it to mend the broken step because he was not wearing the chain, and I found the watch and the chain and our father's signet ring on our father's dresser with Charles' tobacco pouch and four books of matches. I was not allowed to touch matches but in any case I would not have touched Charles' matches. I took up the watch and listened to it ticking because Charles had started it; I could not turn it all the way back to where it had formerly been because he had kept it going for two or three days, but I twisted the winding knob backward until there was a small complaining crack from the watch and the ticking stopped. When I was sure that he could never start it ticking again I put it back gently where I had found it; one thing, at least, had been released from Charles' spell and I thought that I had at last broken through his tight skin of invulnerability. I need not bother about the chain, which was broken, and I disliked the ring. Eliminating Charles from everything he had touched was almost impossible, but it seemed to me that if I altered our father's room, and perhaps later the kitchen and the drawing room and the study, and even finally the garden, Charles would be lost, shut off from what he recognized, and would have to concede that this was not the house he had come to visit and so would go away. I altered our father's room very quickly, and almost without noise.

During the night I had gone out in the darkness and brought in a large basket filled with pieces of wood and broken sticks and leaves and scraps of glass and metal from the field and the wood. Jonas came back and forth with me, amused at our walking silently while everyone slept. When I altered our father's room I took the books from the desk and blankets from the bed, and I put my glass and metal and wood and sticks and leaves into the empty places. I could not put the things which had been our father's into my own room, so I carried them softly up the stairs to the attic where everything else of theirs was kept. I poured a pitcher of water onto our father's bed; Charles could not sleep there again. The mirror over the dresser was already smashed; it would not reflect Charles. He would not be able to find books or clothes and would be lost in a room of leaves and broken sticks. I tore down the curtains and threw them on the floor; now Charles would have to look outside and see the driveway going away and the road beyond.

I looked at the room with pleasure. A demon-ghost would not easily find himself here. I was back in my own room, lying on the bed and playing with Jonas when

I heard Charles down below in the garden shouting to Constance. "This is too much," he was saying, "simply too much."

"What now?" Constance asked; she had come to the kitchen door and I could hear Uncle Julian somewhere below saying, "Tell that young fool to stop his bellowing."

I looked out quickly; the broken step had clearly been too much for Charles because the hammer and the board lay on the ground and the step was still broken; Charles was coming up the path from the creek and he was carrying something; I wondered what he had found now.

"Did you ever hear of anything like this?" he was saying; even though he was close now he was still shouting. "Look at this, Connie, just *look* at it."

"I suppose it belongs to Merricat," Constance said.

"It does *not* belong to Merricat, or anything like it. This is *money*."

"I remember," Constance said. "Silver dollars. I remember when she buried them."

"There must be twenty or thirty dollars here; this is outrageous."

"She likes to bury things."

Charles was still shouting, shaking my box of silver dollars back and forth violently. I wondered if he would drop it; I would like to have seen Charles on the ground, scrabbling after my silver dollars.

"It's not her money," he was shouting, "she has no right to hide it."

I wondered how he had happened to find the box where I had buried it; perhaps Charles and money found each other no matter how far apart they were, or perhaps Charles was engaged in systematically digging up every inch of our land. "This is terrible," he was shouting, "terrible; she has no right."

"No harm is done," Constance said. I could see that she was puzzled and somewhere inside the kitchen Uncle Julian was pounding and calling her.

"How do you know there isn't more?" Charles held the box out accusingly. "How do you know that crazy kid hasn't buried thousands of dollars all over, where we'll *never* find it?"

"She likes to bury things," Constance said. "Coming, Uncle Julian."

Charles followed her inside, still holding the box tenderly. I supposed I could bury the box again after he had gone, but I was not pleased. I came to the top of the stairs and watched Charles proceeding down the hall to the study; he was clearly going to put my silver dollars into our father's safe. I ran down the stairs quickly and quietly and out through the kitchen. "Silly Merricat," Constance said to me as I passed; she was putting spice cookies in long rows to cool.

I was thinking of Charles. I could turn him into a fly and drop him into a spider's web and watch him tangled and helpless and struggling, shut into the body of a dying buzzing fly; I could wish him dead until he died. I could fasten him to a tree and keep him there until he grew into the trunk and bark grew over his mouth. I could bury him in the hole where my box of silver dollars had been so safe until he came; if he was under the ground I could walk over him stamping my feet.

He had not even bothered to fill in the hole. I could imagine him walking here and noticing the spot where the ground was disturbed, stopping to poke in it and then digging wildly with both his hands, scowling and finally greedy and shocked and gasping when he found my box of silver dollars. "Don't blame *me*," I said to the hole; I would have to find something else to bury here and I wished it could be Charles.

The hole would hold his head nicely. I laughed when I found a round stone the right size, and scratched a face on it and buried it in the hole. "Goodbye, Charles," I said. "Next time don't go around taking other people's things."

I stayed by the creek for an hour or so; I was staying by the creek when Charles finally went upstairs and into the room which was no longer his and no longer our father's. I thought for one minute that Charles had been in my shelter, but nothing was disturbed, as it would have been if Charles had come scratching around. He had been near enough to bother me, however, so I cleared out the grass and leaves I usually slept on, and shook out my blanket, and put in everything fresh. I washed the flat rock where I sometimes ate my meals, and put a better branch across the entrance. I wondered if Charles would come back looking for more silver dollars and I wondered if he would like my six blue marbles. I was finally hungry and went back to our house, and there in the kitchen was Charles, still shouting.

"I can't *believe* it," he was saying, quite shrill by now, "I simply can't *believe* it."

I wondered how long Charles was going to go on shouting. He made a black noise in our house and his voice was getting thinner and higher; perhaps if he shouted long enough he would squeak. I sat on the kitchen step next to Jonas and thought that perhaps Constance might laugh out loud if Charles squeaked at her. It never happened, however, because as soon as he saw that I was sitting on the step he was quiet for a minute and then when he spoke he had brought his voice down and made it slow.

"So you're back," he said. He did not move toward me but I felt his voice as though he were coming closer. I did not look at him; I looked at Jonas, who was looking at him.

"I haven't quite decided what I'm going to do with you," he said. "But whatever I do, you'll remember it."

"Don't bully her, Charles," Constance said. I did not like her voice either because it was strange and I knew she was uncertain. "It's all my fault, anyway." That was her new way of thinking.

I thought I would help Constance, perhaps make her laugh. "*Amanita pantherina*," I said, "highly poisonous. *Amanita rubescens*, edible and good. The *Cicuta maculata* is the water hemlock, one of the most poisonous of wild plants if taken internally. The *Apocynum canna-*

*binum* is not a poisonous plant of the first importance, but the snakeberry—"

"Stop it," Charles said, still quiet.

"Constance," I said, "we came home for lunch, Jonas and I."

"First you will have to explain to Cousin Charles," Constance said, and I was chilled.

Charles was sitting at the kitchen table, with his chair pushed back and turned a little to face me in the doorway. Constance stood behind him, leaning against the sink. Uncle Julian sat at his table, stirring papers. There were rows and rows of spice cookies cooling and the kitchen still smelled of cinnamon and nutmeg. I wondered if Constance would give Jonas a spice cookie with his supper but of course she never did because that was the last day.

"Now listen," Charles said. He had brought down a handful of sticks and dirt, perhaps to prove to Constance that they had really been in his room, or perhaps because he was going to clean it away handful by handful; the sticks and dirt looked wrong on the kitchen table and I thought that perhaps one reason Constance looked so sad was the dirt on her clean table. "Now listen," Charles said.

"I cannot work in here if that young man is going to talk all the time," Uncle Julian said. "Constance, tell him he must be quiet for a little while."

"You, too," Charles said in that soft voice. "I have put up with enough from both of you. One of you fouls my room and goes around burying money and the other one can't even remember my name."

"Charles," I said to Jonas. I was the one who buried money, certainly, so I was not the one who could not remember his name; poor old Uncle Julian could not bury anything and could not remember Charles' name. I would remember to be kinder to Uncle Julian. "Will you give Uncle Julian a spice cookie for his dinner?" I asked Constance. "And Jonas one too?"

"Mary Katherine," Charles said, "I am going to give you one chance to explain. Why did you make that mess in my room?"

There was no reason to answer him. He was not Constance, and anything I said to him might perhaps help him to get back his thin grasp on our house. I sat on the door step and played with Jonas's ears, which flicked and snapped when I tickled them.

"Answer me," Charles said.

"How often must I tell you, John, that I know nothing whatsoever about it?" Uncle Julian slammed his hand down onto his papers and scattered them. "It is a quarrel between the women and none of my affair. I do not involve myself in my wife's petty squabbles and I strongly advise you to do the same. It is not fitting for men of dignity to threaten and reproach because women have had a falling out. You lose stature, John, you lose stature."

"Shut up," Charles said; he was shouting again and I was pleased. "Constance," he said, lowering his voice a

little, "this is terrible. The sooner you're out of it the
better."

"—will not be told to shut up by my own brother.
We will leave your house, John, if that is really your
desire. I ask you, however, to reflect. My wife and I—"

"It's my fault, all of it," Constance said. I thought she
was going to cry. It was unthinkable for Constance to
cry again after all these years, but I was held tight, I was
chilled, and I could not move to go over to her.

"You are evil," I said to Charles. "You are a ghost and
a demon."

"What the *hell?*" Charles said.

"Don't pay any attention," Constance told him.
"Don't listen to Merricat's nonsense."

"You are a very selfish man, John, perhaps even a
scoundrel, and overly fond of the world's goods; I
sometimes wonder, John, if you are every bit the gentleman."

"It's a crazy house," Charles said with conviction.
"Constance, this is a crazy house."

"I'll clean your room, right away. Charles, please
don't be angry." Constance looked at me wildly, but I
was held tight and could not see her.

"Uncle Julian." Charles got up and went over to
where Uncle Julian sat at his table.

"Don't you touch my papers," Uncle Julian said, trying to cover them with his hands. "You get away from
my papers, you bastard."

"What?" said Charles.

"I apologize," Uncle Julian said to Constance. "Not

language fitting for your ears, my dear. Just tell this young bastard to stay away from my papers."

"Look," Charles said to Uncle Julian, "I tell you I've had enough of this. I am not going to touch your silly papers and I am not your brother John."

"Of course you are not my brother John; you are not tall enough by half an inch. You are a young bastard and I desire that you return to your father, who, to my shame, is my brother Arthur, and tell him I said so. In the presence of your mother, if you choose; she is a strong-willed woman but lacks family feeling. She desired that the family connection be severed. I have consequently no objection to your repeating my high language in her presence."

"That has all been forgotten, Uncle Julian; Constance and I—"

"I think you have forgotten *yourself*, young man, to take such a tone to me. I am pleased that you are repentant, but you have taken far too much of my time. Please be extremely quiet now."

"Not until I have finished with your niece Mary Katherine."

"My niece Mary Katherine has been a long time dead, young man. She did not survive the loss of her family; I supposed you knew that."

"What?" Charles turned furiously to Constance.

"My niece Mary Katherine died in an orphanage, of neglect, during her sister's trial for murder. But she is of very little consequence to my book, and so we will have done with her."

"She is sitting right here." Charles waved his hands, and his face was red.

"Young man." Uncle Julian put down his pencil and half-turned to face Charles. "I have pointed out to you, I believe, the importance of my work. You choose constantly to interrupt me. I have had enough. You must either be quiet or you must leave this room."

I was laughing at Charles and even Constance was smiling. Charles stood staring at Uncle Julian, and Uncle Julian, going through his papers, said to himself, "Damned impertinent puppy," and then, "Constance?"

"Yes, Uncle Julian?"

"Why have my papers been put into this box? I shall have to take them all out again and rearrange them. Has that young man been near my papers? Has he?"

"No, Uncle Julian."

"He takes a great deal upon himself, I think. When is he going away?"

"I'm not going away," Charles said. "I am going to stay."

"Impossible," Uncle Julian said. "We have not the room. Constance?"

"Yes, Uncle Julian?"

"I would like a chop for my lunch. A nice little chop, neatly broiled. Perhaps a mushroom."

"Yes," Constance said with relief, "I should start lunch." As though she were happy to be doing it at last she came to the table to brush away the dirt and leaves that Charles had left there. She brushed them into a paper bag and threw the bag into the wastebasket, and then

she came back with a cloth and scrubbed the table.
Charles looked at her and at me and at Uncle Julian. He
was clearly baffled, unable to grasp his fingers tightly
around anything he saw or heard; it was a joyful sight,
to see the first twistings and turnings of the demon
caught, and I was very proud of Uncle Julian. Constance
smiled down at Charles, happy that no one was shouting
any more; she was not going to cry now and perhaps she
too was getting a quick glimpse of a straining demon because she said, "You look tired, Charles. Go and rest till
lunch."

"Go and rest where?" he said and he was still angry.
"I am not going to stir out of here until something is
done about that girl."

"Merricat? Why should anything be done? I said I
would clean your room."

"Aren't you even going to punish her?"

"Punish me?" I was standing then, shivering against
the door frame. "Punish me? You mean send me to bed
without my dinner?"

And I ran. I ran until I was in the field of grass, in the
very center where it was safe, and I sat there, the grass
taller than my head and hiding me. Jonas found me, and
we sat there together where no one could ever see us.

After a very long time I stood up again because I knew
where I was going. I was going to the summerhouse. I
had not been near the summerhouse for six years, but
Charles had blackened the world and only the summerhouse would do. Jonas would not follow me; he disliked

the summerhouse and when he saw me turning onto the overgrown path which led there he went another way as though he had something important to do and would meet me somewhere later. No one had ever liked the summerhouse very much, I remembered. Our father had planned it and had intended to lead the creek near it and build a tiny waterfall, but something had gotten into the wood and stone and paint when the summerhouse was built and made it bad. Our mother had once seen a rat in the doorway looking in and nothing after that could persuade her there again, and where our mother did not go, no one else went.

I had never buried anything around here. The ground was black and wet and nothing buried would have been quite comfortable. The trees pressed too closely against the sides of the summerhouse, and breathed heavily on its roof, and the poor flowers planted here once had either died or grown into huge tasteless wild things. When I stood near the summerhouse and looked at it I thought it the ugliest place I had ever seen; I remembered that our mother had quite seriously asked to have it burned down.

Inside was all wet and dark. I disliked sitting on the stone floor but there was no other place; once, I recalled, there had been chairs here and perhaps even a low table but these were gone now, carried off or rotted away. I sat on the floor and placed all of them correctly in my mind, in the circle around the dining-room table. Our father sat at the head. Our mother sat at the foot. Uncle Julian sat on one hand of our mother, and our brother

Thomas on the other; beside my father sat our Aunt Dorothy and Constance. I sat between Constance and Uncle Julian, in my rightful, my own and proper, place at the table. Slowly I began to listen to them talking.

"—to buy a book for Mary Katherine. Lucy, should not Mary Katherine have a new book?"

"Mary Katherine should have anything she wants, my dear. Our most loved daughter must have anything she likes."

"Constance, your sister lacks butter. Pass it to her at once, please."

"Mary Katherine, we love you."

"You must never be punished. Lucy, you are to see to it that our most loved daughter Mary Katherine is never punished."

"Mary Katherine would never allow herself to do anything wrong; there is never any need to punish her."

"I have heard, Lucy, of disobedient children being sent to their beds without dinner as a punishment. That must not be permitted with our Mary Katherine."

"I quite agree, my dear. Mary Katherine must never be punished. Must never be sent to bed without her dinner. Mary Katherine will never allow herself to do anything inviting punishment."

"Our beloved, our dearest Mary Katherine must be guarded and cherished. Thomas, give your sister your dinner; she would like more to eat."

"Dorothy—Julian. Rise when our beloved daughter rises."

"Bow all your heads to our adored Mary Katherine."

~~~~~~~~~~~~~~~~~~~~~~~~~~~~~~~~~~~~~~~~~~~~~~~~~~~~~

I HAD TO GO BACK FOR DINNER; IT WAS VITAL THAT I SIT at the dinner table with Constance and Uncle Julian and Charles. It was unthinkable that they should sit there, eating their dinner and talking and passing food to one another, and see my place empty. As Jonas and I came along the path and through the garden in the gathering darkness I looked at the house with all the richness of love I contained; it was a good house, and soon it would be cleaned and fair again. I stopped for a minute, look-

141

ing, and Jonas brushed my leg and spoke softly, in curiosity.

"I'm looking at our house," I told him and he stood quietly beside me, looking up with me. The roof pointed firmly against the sky, and the walls met one another compactly, and the windows shone darkly; it was a good house, and nearly clean. There was light from the kitchen window and from the windows of the dining room; it was time for their dinner and I must be there. I wanted to be inside the house, with the door shut behind me.

When I opened the kitchen door to go inside I could feel at once that the house still held anger, and I wondered that anyone could keep one emotion so long; I could hear his voice clearly from the kitchen, going on and on.

"—*must* be done about her," he was saying, "things simply can*not* continue like this."

Poor Constance, I thought, having to listen and listen and watch the food getting cold. Jonas ran ahead of me into the dining room, and Constance said, "Here she is."

I stood in the dining-room doorway and looked carefully for a minute. Constance was wearing pink, and her hair was combed back nicely; she smiled at me when I looked at her, and I knew she was tired of listening. Uncle Julian's wheel chair was pushed up tight against the table and I was sorry to see that Constance had tucked his napkin under his chin; it was too bad that Uncle Julian should not be allowed to eat freely. He was eating meat loaf, and peas which Constance had preserved one fragrant summer day; Constance had cut the meat loaf into small pieces and Uncle Julian mashed meat loaf and peas with the back of his spoon and stirred them before trying to get them into his mouth. He was not listening, but the voice went on and on.

"So you decided to come back again, did you? And high time, too, young lady; your sister and I have been trying to decide how to teach you a lesson."

"Wash your face, Merricat," Constance said gently. "And comb your hair; we do not want you untidy at table, and your Cousin Charles is already angry with you."

Charles pointed his fork at me. "I may as well tell you, Mary, that your tricks are over for good. Your sister and I have decided that we have had just exactly enough of hiding and destroying and temper."

I disliked having a fork pointed at me and I disliked the sound of the voice never stopping; I wished he would put food on the fork and put it into his mouth and strangle himself.

"Run along, Merricat," Constance said, "your dinner will be cold." She knew I would not eat dinner sitting at that table and she would bring me my dinner in the kitchen afterward, but I thought that she did not want to remind Charles of that and so give him one more thing to talk about. I smiled at her and went into the hall, with the voice still talking behind me. There had not been this many words sounded in our house for a long time, and it was going to take a while to clean them out. I walked heavily going up the stairs so they could hear that I was surely going up, but when I reached the top I went as softly as Jonas behind me.

Constance had cleaned the room where he was living. It looked very empty, because all she had done was take things out; she had nothing to put back because I had carried all of it to the attic. I knew the dresser drawers were empty, and the closet, and the bookshelves. There was no mirror, and a broken watch and a smashed chain lay alone on the dresser top. Constance had taken away the wet bedding, and I supposed she had dried and turned the mattress, because the bed was made up again. The long curtains were gone, perhaps to be washed. He had been lying on the bed, because it was disarranged, and his pipe, still burning, lay on the table beside the bed; I supposed that he had been lying here when Constance called him to dinner, and I wondered if he had looked around and around the altered room, trying to find something familiar, hoping that perhaps the angle of the closet door or the light on the ceiling would bring everything back to him again. I was sorry that Constance had to turn the mattress alone; usually I helped her but perhaps he had come and offered to do it for her. She had even brought him a clean saucer for his pipe; our house did not have ashtrays and when he kept trying to find places to put down his pipe Constance had brought a set of chipped saucers from the pantry shelf and given them to him to hold his pipe. The saucers were pink, with gold leaves around the rim; they were from a set older than any I remembered.

"Who used them?" I asked Constance, when she

brought them into the kitchen. "Where are their cups?"

"I've never seen them used; they come from a time before I was in the kitchen. Some great-grandmother brought them with her dowry and they were used and broken and replaced and finally put away on the top shelf of the pantry; there are only these saucers and three dinner plates."

"They belong in the pantry," I said. "Not put around the house."

Constance had given them to Charles and now they were scattered, instead of spending their little time decently put away on a shelf. There was one in the drawing room and one in the dining room and one, I supposed, in the study. They were not fragile, because the one now in the bedroom had not cracked although the pipe on it was burning. I had known all day that I would find something here; I brushed the saucer and the pipe off the table into the wastebasket and they fell softly onto the newspapers he had brought into the house.

I was wondering about my eyes; one of my eyes—the left—saw everything golden and yellow and orange, and the other eye saw shades of blue and grey and green; perhaps one eye was for daylight and the other was for night. If everyone in the world saw different colors from different eyes there might be a great many new colors still to be invented. I had reached the staircase to go downstairs before I remembered and had to go back to wash, and comb my hair. "What took you so long?" he asked when I sat down at the table. "What have you been doing up there?"

"Will you make me a cake with pink frosting?" I asked Constance. "With little gold leaves around the edge? Jonas and I are going to have a party."

"Perhaps tomorrow," Constance said.

"We are going to have a long talk after dinner," Charles said.

"*Solanum dulcamara*," I told him.

"What?" he said.

"Deadly nightshade," Constance said. "Charles, please let it wait."

"I've had enough," he said.

"Constance?"

"Yes, Uncle Julian?"

"I have cleaned my plate." Uncle Julian found a morsel of meat loaf on his napkin and put it into his mouth. "What do I have now?"

"Perhaps a little more, Uncle Julian? It is a pleasure to see you so hungry."

"I feel considerably better tonight. I have not felt so hearty for days."

I was pleased that Uncle Julian was well and I knew he was happy because he had been so discourteous to Charles. While Constance was cutting up another small piece of meat loaf Uncle Julian looked at Charles with an evil shine in his old eyes, and I knew he was going to say something wicked. "Young man," he began at last, but Charles turned his head suddenly to look into the hall.

"I smell smoke," Charles said.

Constance paused and lifted her head and turned to

the kitchen door. "The stove?" she said and got up quickly to go into the kitchen.

"Young man—"

"There is certainly smoke." Charles went to look into the hall. "I smell it out here," he said. I wondered whom he thought he was talking to; Constance was in the kitchen and Uncle Julian was thinking about what he was going to say, and I had stopped listening. "There *is* smoke," Charles said.

"It's not the stove." Constance stood in the kitchen doorway and looked at Charles.

Charles turned and came closer to me. "If this is anything you've done . . ." he said.

I laughed because it was clear that Charles was afraid to go upstairs and follow the smoke; then Constance said, "Charles—your pipe—" and he turned and ran up the stairs. "I've asked him and asked him," Constance said.

"Would it start a fire?" I asked her, and then Charles screamed from upstairs, screamed, I thought, with the exact sound of a bluejay in the woods. "That's Charles," I said politely to Constance, and she hurried to go into the hall and look up. "What *is* it?" she asked, "Charles, what *is* it?"

"Fire," Charles said, crashing down the stairs, "Run, run; the whole damn house is on fire," he screamed into Constance's face, "and you haven't got a *phone*."

"My papers," Uncle Julian said. "I shall collect my papers and remove them to a place of safety." He pushed against the edge of the table to move his chair away. "Constance?"

"Run," Charles said, at the front door now, wrenching at the lock, "*run*, you fool."

"I have not done much running in the past few years, young man. I see no cause for this hysteria; there is time to gather my papers."

Charles had the front door open now, and turned on the doorsill to call to Constance. "Don't try to carry the safe," he said, "put the money in a bag. I'll be back as fast as I can get help. Don't panic." He ran, and we could hear him screaming "Fire! Fire! Fire!" as he ran toward the village.

"Good heavens," Constance said, almost amused. Then she took Uncle Julian's chair to help him into his room and I went into the hall and looked upstairs. Charles had left the door to our father's room standing open and I could see the movement of fire inside. Fire burns upward, I thought; it will burn their things in the attic. Charles had left the front door open too, and a line of smoke reached down the stairs and drifted outside. I did not see any need to move quickly or to run shrieking around the house because the fire did not seem to be hurrying itself. I wondered if I could go up the stairs and shut the door to our father's room and keep the fire inside, belonging entirely to Charles, but when I started up the stairs I saw a finger of flame reach out to touch the hall carpet and some heavy object fell crashing in our father's room. There would be nothing of

Charles in there now; even his pipe must have been consumed.

"Uncle Julian is gathering his papers," Constance said, coming into the hall to stand beside me. She had Uncle Julian's shawl over her arm.

"We will have to go outside," I said. I knew that she was frightened, so I said, "We can stay on the porch, behind the vines, in the darkness."

"We neatened it just the other day," she said. "It has no *right* to burn." She began to shiver as though she were angry, and I took her by the hand and brought her through the open front door and just as we turned back for another look the lights came into the driveway with the disgusting noise of sirens and we were held in the doorway in the light. Constance put her face against me to hide, and then there was Jim Donell, the first one to leap from the fire engine and run up the steps. "Out of the way," he said, and pushed past us and into our house. I took Constance along the porch to the corner where the vines grew thick, and she moved into the corner and pressed against the vines. I held her hand tight, and together we watched the great feet of the men stepping across our doorsill, dragging their hoses, bringing filth and confusion and danger into our house. More lights moved into the driveway and up to the steps, and the front of the house was white and pale and uncomfortable at being so clearly visible; it had never been lighted before. The noise was too much for me to hear all together, but somewhere in the noise was Charles' voice,

still going on and on. "Get the safe in the study," he said
a thousand times.

Smoke squeezed out the front door, coming between
the big men pushing in. "Constance," I whispered, "Constance, don't watch them."

"Can they see me?" she whispered back. "Is anyone
looking?"

"They're all watching the fire. Be very quiet."

I looked carefully out between the vines. There was a
long row of cars, and the village fire engine, all parked
as close to the house as they could get, and everyone in
the village was there, looking up and watching. I saw
faces laughing, and faces that looked frightened, and
then someone called out, very near to us, "What about
the women, and the old man? Anyone see them?"

"They had plenty of warning," Charles shouted from
somewhere, "they're all right."

Uncle Julian could manage his chair well enough to
get out the back door, I thought, but it did not seem that
the fire was going near the kitchen or Uncle Julian's
room; I could see the hoses and hear the men shouting,
and they were all on the stairs and in the front bedrooms
upstairs. I could not get through the front door, and
even if I could leave Constance there was no way to go
around to the back door without going down the steps
in the light with all of them watching. "Was Uncle
Julian frightened?" I whispered to Constance.

"I think he was annoyed," she said. A few minutes
later she said, "It will take a great deal of scrubbing to
get that hall clean again," and sighed. I was pleased that

she thought of the house and forgot the people outside.
"Jonas?" I said to her; "where is he?"

I could see her smile a little in the darkness of the vines.
"He was annoyed, too," she said. "He went out the back
door when I took Uncle Julian in to get his papers."

We were all right. Uncle Julian might very well forget that there was a fire at all if he became interested in
his papers, and Jonas was almost certainly watching
from the shadow of the trees. When they had finished
putting out Charles' fire I would take Constance back
inside and we could start to clean our house again. Constance was quieter, although more and more cars came
down the driveway and the unending pattern of feet
went back and forth across our doorsill. Except for Jim
Donell, who wore a hat proclaiming him "Chief," it was
impossible to identify any one person, any more than it
was possible to put a name to any of the faces out in
front of our house, looking up and laughing at the fire.

I tried to think clearly. The house was burning; there
was fire inside our house, but Jim Donell and the other,
anonymous, men in hats and raincoats were curiously
able to destroy the fire which was running through the
bones of our house. It was Charles' fire. When I listened
particularly for the fire I could hear it, a singing hot
noise upstairs, but over and around it, smothering it, were
the voices of the men inside and the voices of the people
watching outside and the distant sound of cars on the
driveway. Next to me Constance was standing quietly,
sometimes looking at the men going into the house, but
more often covering her eyes with her hands; she was

excited, I thought, but not in any danger. Every now
and then it was possible to hear one voice raised above
the others; Jim Donell shouted some word of instruc-
tion, or someone in the crowd called out. "Why not let
it burn?" a woman's voice came loudly, laughing, and
"Get the safe out of the study downstairs"; that was
Charles, safely in the crowd out front.

"Why not let it burn?" the woman called insistently,
and one of the dark men going in and out of our front
door turned and waved and grinned. "We're the firemen," he called back, "we *got* to put it out."

"Let it burn," the woman called.

Smoke was everywhere, thick and ugly. Sometimes
when I looked out the faces of the people were clouded
with smoke, and it came out the front door in frightening waves. Once there was a crash from inside the house
and voices speaking quickly and urgently, and the faces
outside turned up happily in the smoke, mouths open.
"Get the safe," Charles called out wildly, "two or three
of you men get the safe out of the study; the whole
house is going."

"Let it burn," the woman called.

I was hungry and I wanted my dinner, and I wondered
how long they could make the fire last before they put
it out and went away and Constance and I could go back
inside. One or two of the village boys had edged onto
the porch dangerously close to where we stood, but
they only looked inside, not at the porch, and tried to
stand on their toes and see past the fireman and the hoses.
I was tired and I wished it would all be over. I realized

then that the light was lessening, the faces on the lawn less distinct, and a new tone came into the noise; the voices inside were surer, less sharp, almost pleased, and the voices outside were lower, and disappointed.

"It's going out," someone said.

"Under control," another voice added.

"Did a lot of damage, though." There was laughter. "Sure made a mess of the old place."

"Should of burned it down years ago."

"And them in it."

They mean us, I thought, Constance and me.

"Say—anybody *seen* them?"

"No such luck. Firemen threw them out."

"Too bad."

The light was almost gone. The people outside stood now in shadows, their faces narrowed and dark, with only the headlights of the cars to light them; I saw the flash of a smile, and somewhere else a hand raised to wave, and the voices went on regretfully.

"Just about over."

"Pretty good fire."

Jim Donell came through the front door. Everyone knew him because of his size and his hat saying CHIEF. "Say, Jim," someone called, "why don't you let it burn?"

He lifted both his hands to make everyone be quiet. "Fire's all out, folks," he said.

Very carefully he put up his hands and took off his hat saying CHIEF and while everyone watched he walked slowly down the steps and over to the fire engine and set his hat down on the front seat. Then he bent down, searching thoughtfully, and finally, while everyone watched, he took up a rock. In complete silence he turned slowly and then raised his arm and smashed the rock through one of the great tall windows of our mother's drawing room. A wall of laughter rose and grew behind him and then, first the boys on the steps and then the other men and at last the women and the smaller children, they moved like a wave at our house.

"Constance," I said, "Constance," but she had her hands over her eyes.

The other of the drawing-room windows crashed, this time from inside, and I saw that it had been shattered by the lamp which always stood by Constance's chair in the drawing room.

Above it all, most horrible, was the laughter. I saw one of the Dresden figurines thrown and break against the porch rail, and the other fell unbroken and rolled along the grass. I heard Constance's harp go over with a musical cry, and a sound which I knew was a chair being smashed against the wall.

"Listen," said Charles from somewhere, "will a couple of you guys help me with this safe?"

Then, through the laughter, someone began, "Merricat, said Constance, would you like a cup of tea?" It was rhythmic and insistent. I am on the moon, I thought, please let me be on the moon. Then I heard the sound of dishes smashing and at that minute realized that we stood outside the tall windows of the dining room and they were coming very close.

"Constance," I said, "we have to run."

She shook her head, her hands over her face.

"They'll find us in a minute. Please, Constance dearest; run with me."

"I can't," she said, and from just inside the dining-room window a shout went up: "Merricat, said Constance, would you like to go to sleep?" and I pulled Constance away a second before the window went; I thought a chair had been thrown through it, perhaps the dining-room chair where our father used to sit and Charles used to sit. "Hurry," I said, no longer able to be quiet in all that noise, and pulling Constance by the hand I ran toward the steps. As we came into the light she threw Uncle Julian's shawl across her face to hide it.

A little girl ran out of the front door carrying something, and her mother, behind her, caught her by the back of the dress and slapped her hands. "Don't you put that stuff in your mouth," the mother screamed, and the little girl dropped a handful of Constance's spice cookies.

"Merricat, said Constance, would you like a cup of tea?"

"Merricat, said Constance, would you like to go to sleep?"

"Oh, no, said Merricat, you'll poison me."

We had to get down the steps and into the woods to be safe; it was not far but the headlights of the cars shone across the lawn. I wondered if Constance would slip and fall, running through the light, but we had to get to the woods and there was no other way. We hesitated near the steps, neither one of us quite daring to go farther, but the windows were broken and inside they were throwing our dishes and our glasses and our silverware and even the pots Constance used in cooking; I wondered if my stool in the corner of the kitchen had been smashed yet. While we stood still for a last minute, a car came up the driveway, and another behind it; they swung to a stop in front of the house, sending more light onto the lawn. "What the holy devil is going *on* here?" Jim Clarke said, rolling out of the first car, and Helen Clarke, on the other side, opened her mouth and stared. Shouting and pushing, and not seeing us at all, Jim Clarke made his way through our door and into our house, "What the holy goddam devil is going *on* here?" he kept saying and outside Helen Clarke never saw us, but only stared at our house. "Crazy fools," Jim Clarke yelled inside, "crazy drunken fools." Dr. Levy came out of the second car and hurried toward the house. "Has everyone gone crazy in here?" Jim Clarke was saying from inside, and there was a shout of laughter. "Would you like a cup of tea?" someone inside screamed, and they laughed. "Ought to bring it down brick by brick," someone said inside.

The doctor came up the steps running, and pushed us aside without looking. "Where is Julian Blackwood?" he asked a woman in the doorway, and the woman said, "Down in the boneyard ten feet deep."

It was time; I took Constance tightly by the hand, and we started carefully down the steps. I would not run yet because I was afraid that Constance might fall, so I brought her slowly down the steps; no one could see us yet except Helen Clarke and she stared at the house. Behind us I heard Jim Clarke shouting; he was trying to make the people leave our house, and before we reached the bottom step there were voices behind us.

"There they are," someone shouted and I think it was Stella. "There they are, there they are, there they are," and I started to run but Constance stumbled and then they were all around us, pushing and laughing and trying to get close to see. Constance held Uncle Julian's shawl across her face so they could not look at her, and for a minute we stood very still, pressed together by the feeling of people all around us.

"Put them back in the house and start the fire all over again."

"We fixed things up nice for you girls, just like you always wanted it."

"Merricat, said Constance, would you like a cup of tea?"

For one terrible minute I thought that they were going to join hands and dance around us, singing. I saw Helen Clarke far away, pressed hard against the side of her car; she was crying and saying something and even though I could not hear her through the noise I knew she was saying "I want to go home, please, I want to go home."

"Merricat, said Constance, would you like to go to sleep?"

They were trying not to touch us; whenever I turned they fell back a little; once, between two shoulders I saw Harler of the junk yard wandering across the porch

of our house, picking up things and setting them to one
side in a pile. I moved a little, holding Constance's hand
tight, and as they fell back we ran suddenly, going toward the trees, but Jim Donell's wife and Mrs. Mueller came in front of us, laughing and holding out their
arms, and we stopped. I turned, and gave Constance a
little pull, and we ran, but Stella and the Harris boys
crossed in front of us, laughing, and the Harris boys
shouting "Down in the boneyard ten feet deep," and we
stopped. Then I turned toward the house, running again
with Constance pulled behind me, and Elbert the grocer
and his greedy wife were there, holding their hands to
halt us, almost dancing together, and we stopped. I went
then to the side, and Jim Donell stepped in front of us,
and we stopped.

"Oh, no, said Merricat, you'll poison me," Jim Donell
said politely, and they came around us again, circling
and keeping carefully out of reach. "Merricat, said Constance, would you like to go to sleep?" Over it all was
the laughter, almost drowning the singing and the shouting and the howling of the Harris boys.

"Merricat, said Constance, would you like a cup of
tea?"

Constance held to me with one hand and with the
other hand she kept Uncle Julian's shawl across her face.
I saw an opening in the circle around us, and ran again
for the trees, but all the Harris boys were there, one
on the ground with laughter, and we stopped. I turned
again and ran for the house but Stella came forward and
we stopped. Constance was stumbling, and I wondered

if we were going to fall onto the ground in front of them, lying there where they might step on us in their dancing, and I stood still; I could not possibly let Constance fall in front of them.

"That's all now," Jim Clarke said from the porch. His voice was not loud, but they all heard. "That's enough," he said. There was a small polite silence, and then someone said, "Down in the boneyard ten feet deep," and the laughter rose.

"Listen to me," Jim Clarke said, raising his voice, "listen to me. Julian Blackwood is dead."

Then they were quiet at last. After a minute Charles Blackwood said from the crowd around us, "Did she kill him?" They went back from us, moving slowly in small steps, withdrawing, until there was a wide clear space around us and Constance standing clearly with Uncle Julian's shawl across her face. "Did she kill him?" Charles Blackwood asked again.

"She did not," said the doctor, standing in the doorway of our house. "Julian died as I have always known he would; he has been waiting a long time."

"Now go quietly," Jim Clarke said. He began to take people by the shoulders, pushing a little at their backs, turning them toward their cars and the driveway. "Go quickly," he said, "There has been a death in this house."

It was so quiet, in spite of many people moving across the grass and going away, that I heard Helen Clarke say, "Poor Julian."

I took a cautious step toward the darkness, pulling Constance a little so that she followed me. "Heart," the doctor said on the porch, and I went another step. No one turned to look at us. Car doors slammed softly and motors started. I looked back once. A little group was standing around the doctor on the steps. Most of the lights were turned away, heading down the driveway. When I felt the shadows of the trees fall on us, I moved quickly; one last step and we were inside. Pulling Constance, I hurried under the trees, in the darkness; when I felt my feet leave the grass of the lawn and touch the soft mossy ground of the path through the woods and knew that the trees had closed in around us I stopped and put my arms around Constance. "It's all over," I told her, and held her tight. "It's all right," I said, "all right now."

I knew my way in the darkness or in the light. I thought once how good it was that I had straightened my hiding place and freshened it, so it would now be pleasant for Constance. I would cover her with leaves, like children in a story, and keep her safe and warm. Perhaps I would sing to her or tell her stories; I would bring her bright fruits and berries and water in a leaf cup. Someday we would go to the moon. I found the entrance to my hiding place and led Constance in and took her to the corner where there was a fresh pile of leaves and a blanket. I pushed her gently until she sat down and I took Uncle Julian's shawl away from her and covered her with it. A little purr came from the corner and I knew that Jonas had been waiting here for me.

I put branches across the entrance; even if they came

with lights they would not see us. It was not entirely dark; I could see the shadow that was Constance and when I put my head back I saw two or three stars, shining from far away between the leaves and the branches and down onto my head.

One of our mother's Dresden figurines is broken, I thought, and I said aloud to Constance, "I am going to put death in all their food and watch them die."

Constance stirred, and the leaves rustled. "The way you did before?" she asked.

It had never been spoken of between us, not once in six years.

"Yes," I said after a minute, "the way I did before."

with lights they would not see us. It was not entirely dark; I could see the shadow that was Constance, and when I put my head back I saw face or three stars, also far away between the leaves and the branches and down onto my head.

One of our mother's Dresden figurines is missing, I thought; and I said aloud to Constance, "I am going to put death in all their food and watch them die."

Constance stirred, and the leaves rustled. "The way you did before," she asked.

It had never been spoken of between us, not once in six years.

"Yes," I said after a minute, "the way I did before."

# 9

~~~~~~~~~~~~~~~~~~~~~~~~~~~~~~~~~~~~~~~~~~~~~~~~~~~~

SOMETIME DURING THE NIGHT AN AMBULANCE CAME
and took Uncle Julian away, and I wondered if they
missed his shawl, which was wound around Constance
as she slept. I saw the ambulance lights turning into the
driveway, with the small red light on top, and I heard
the distant sounds of Uncle Julian's leaving, the voices
speaking gently because they were in the presence of
the dead, and the doors opening and closing. They called
to us two or three times, perhaps to ask if they might

have Uncle Julian, but their voices were subdued and no one came into the woods. I sat by the creek, wishing that I had been kinder to Uncle Julian. Uncle Julian had believed that I was dead, and now he was dead himself; bow your heads to our beloved Mary Katherine, I thought, or you will be dead.

The water moved sleepily in the darkness and I wondered what kind of a house we would have now. Perhaps the fire had destroyed everything and we would go back tomorrow and find that the past six years had been burned and they were waiting for us, sitting around the dining-room table waiting for Constance to bring them their dinner. Perhaps we would find ourselves in the Rochester house, or living in the village or on a houseboat on the river or in a tower on top of a hill; perhaps the fire might be persuaded to reverse itself and abandon our house and destroy the village instead; perhaps the villagers were all dead now. Perhaps the village was really a great game board, with the squares neatly marked out, and I had been moved past the square which read "Fire; return to Start," and was now on the last few squares, with only one move to go to reach home.

Jonas's fur smelled of smoke. Today was Helen Clarke's day to come to tea, but there would be no tea today, because we would have to neaten the house, although it was not the usual day for neatening the house. I wished that Constance had made sandwiches for us to bring down to the creek, and I wondered if Helen Clarke would try to come to tea even though the house

was not ready. I decided that from now on I would not
be allowed to hand tea cups.

When it first began to get light I heard Constance
stirring on the leaves and I went into my hiding place to
be near her when she awakened. When she opened her
eyes she looked first at the trees above her, and then at
me and smiled.

"We are on the moon at last," I told her, and she
smiled.

"I thought I dreamed it all," she said.

"It really happened," I said.

"Poor Uncle Julian."

"They came in the night and took him away, and we
stayed here on the moon."

"I'm glad to be here," she said. "Thank you for bringing me."

There were leaves in her hair and dirt on her face and
Jonas, who had followed me into my hiding place, stared
at her in surprise; he had never seen Constance with a
dirty face before. For a minute she was quiet, no longer
smiling, looking back at Jonas, realizing that she was
dirty, and then she said, "Merricat, what are we going
to do?"

"First we must neaten the house, even though it is not
the usual day."

"The house," she said. "Oh, Merricat."

"I had no dinner last night," I told her.

"Oh, *Merricat.*" She sat up and untangled herself
quickly from Uncle Julian's shawl and the leaves; "Oh,

Merricat, poor baby," she said. "We'll hurry," and she scrambled to her feet.

"First you had better wash your face."

She went to the creek and wet her handkerchief and scrubbed at her face while I shook out Uncle Julian's shawl and folded it, thinking how strange and backward everything was this morning; I had never touched Uncle Julian's shawl before. I already saw that the rules were going to be different, but it was odd to be folding Uncle Julian's shawl. Later, I thought, I would come back here to my hiding place and clean it, and put in fresh leaves.

"Merricat, you'll starve."

"We have to watch," I said, taking her hand to slow her. "We have to go very quietly and carefully; some of them may still be around waiting."

I went first down the path, walking silently, with Constance and Jonas behind me. Constance could not step as silently as I could, but she made very little sound and of course Jonas made no sound at all. I took the path that would bring us out of the woods at the back of the house, near the vegetable garden, and when I came to the edge of the woods I stopped and held Constance back while we looked carefully to see if there were any of them left. For one first minute we saw only the garden and the kitchen door, looking just as always, and then Constance gasped and said, "Oh, *Merricat*," with a little moan, and I held myself very still, because the top of our house was gone.

I remembered that I had stood looking at our house with love yesterday, and I thought how it had always been so tall, reaching up into the trees. Today the house ended above the kitchen doorway in a nightmare of black and twisted wood; I saw part of a window frame still holding broken glass and I thought: that was my window; I looked out that window from my room.

There was no one there, and no sound. We moved together very slowly toward the house, trying to understand its ugliness and ruin and shame. I saw that ash had drifted among the vegetable plants; the lettuce would have to be washed before I could eat it, and the tomatoes. No fire had come this way, but everything, the grass and the apple trees and the marble bench in Constance's garden, had an air of smokiness and everything was dirty. As we came closer to the house we saw more clearly that the fire had not reached the ground floor, but had had to be content with the bedrooms and the attic. Constance hesitated at the kitchen door, but she had opened it a thousand times before and it ought surely to recognize the touch of her hand, so she took the latch and lifted it. The house seemed to shiver when she opened the door, although one more draft could hardly chill it now. Constance had to push at the door to make it open, but no burned timber crashed down, and there was not, as I half thought there might be, a sudden rushing falling together, as a house, seemingly solid but really made only of ash, might dissolve at a touch.

"My kitchen," Constance said. "My kitchen."

She stood in the doorway, looking. I thought that we had somehow not found our way back correctly through the night, that we had somehow lost ourselves and come back through the wrong gap in time, or the wrong door, or the wrong fairy tale. Constance put her hand against the door frame to steady herself, and said again, "My kitchen, Merricat."

"My stool is still there," I said.

The obstacle which made the door hard to open was the kitchen table, turned on its side. I set it upright, and we went inside. Two of the chairs had been smashed, and the floor was horrible with broken dishes and glasses and broken boxes of food and paper torn from the shelves. Jars of jam and syrup and catsup had been shattered against the walls. The sink where Constance washed her dishes was filled with broken glass, as though glass after glass had been broken there methodically, one after another. Drawers of silverware and cooking ware had been pulled out and broken against the table and the walls, and silverware that had been in the house for generations of Blackwood wives was lying bent and scattered on the floor. Tablecloths and napkins hemmed by Blackwood women, and washed and ironed again and again, mended and cherished, had been ripped from the dining-room sideboard and dragged across the kitchen. It seemed that all the wealth and hidden treasure of our house had been found out and torn and soiled; I saw broken plates which had come from the top shelves in the cupboard, and our little sugar bowl with roses lay almost at my feet, handles gone. Constance bent down and picked up a silver spoon. "This was our grandmother's wedding pattern," she said, and set the spoon on the table. Then she said, "The preserves," and turned to the cellar door; it was closed and I hoped that perhaps they had not seen it, or had perhaps not had time to go down the stairs. Constance picked her way carefully across the floor and opened the cellar door and looked down. I thought of the jars and jars so beautifully preserved lying in broken sticky heaps in the cellar, but Constance went down a step or two and said, "No, it's all right; nothing here's been touched." She closed the cellar door again and made her way across to the sink to wash her hands and dry them on a dishtowel from the floor. "First, your breakfast," she said.

Jonas sat on the doorstep in the growing sunlight looking at the kitchen with astonishment; once he raised his eyes to me and I wondered if he thought that Constance and I had made this mess. I saw a cup not broken, and picked it up and set it on the table, and then thought to look for more things which might have escaped. I remembered that one of our mother's Dresden figurines had rolled safely onto the grass and I wondered if it had hidden successfully and preserved itself; I would look for it later.

Nothing was orderly, nothing was planned; it was not like any other day. Once Constance went into the cellar and came back with her arms full. "Vegetable soup," she said, almost singing, "and strawberry jam, and chicken soup, and pickled beef." She set the jars on the kitchen table and turned slowly, looking down at the floor. "There," she said at last, and went to a corner to pick up a small saucepan. Then on a sudden thought she set down the saucepan and made her way into the pantry. "Merricat," she called with laughter, "they didn't find the flour in the barrel. Or the salt. Or the potatoes."

They found the sugar, I thought. The floor was gritty, and almost alive under my feet, and I thought of course; of course they would go looking for the sugar and have a lovely time; perhaps they had thrown handfuls of sugar at one another, screaming, "Blackwood sugar, Blackwood sugar, want a taste?"

"They got to the pantry shelves," Constance went on, "the cereals and the spices and the canned food."

I walked slowly around the kitchen, looking at the floor. I thought that they had probably tumbled things by the armload, because cans of food were scattered and bent as though they had been tossed into the air, and the boxes of cereal and tea and crackers had been trampled under foot and broken open. The tins of spices were all together, thrown into a corner unopened; I thought I could still smell the faint spicy scent of Constance's cookies and then saw some of them, crushed on the floor.

Constance came out of the pantry carrying a loaf of bread. "Look what they didn't find," she said, "and there are eggs and milk and butter in the cooler." Since they had not found the cellar door they had not found the cooler just inside, and I was pleased that they had not discovered eggs to mix into the mess on the floor.

At one time I found three unbroken chairs and set them where they belonged around the table. Jonas sat in my corner, on my stool, watching us. I drank chicken soup from a cup without a handle, and Constance washed a knife to spread butter on the bread. Although I did not perceive it then, time and the orderly pattern of our old days had ended; I do not know when I found the three chairs and when I ate buttered bread, whether I had found the chairs and then eaten bread, or whether I had eaten first, or even done both at once. Once Constance turned suddenly and put down her knife; she started for the closed door to Uncle Julian's room and then turned back, smiling a little. "I thought I heard him waking," she said, and sat down again.

We had not yet been out of the kitchen. We still did not know how much house was left to us, or what we might find waiting beyond the closed doors into the dining room and the hall. We sat quietly in the kitchen, grateful for the chairs and the chicken soup and the sunlight coming through the doorway, not yet ready to go further.

"What will they do with Uncle Julian?" I asked.

"They will have a funeral," Constance said with sadness. "Do you remember the others?"

"I was in the orphanage."

"They let me go to the funerals of the others. I can remember. They will have a funeral for Uncle Julian, and the Clarkes will go, and the Carringtons, and certainly little Mrs. Wright. They will tell each other how sorry they are. They will look to see if we are there."

I felt them looking to see if we were there, and I shivered.

"They will bury him with the others."

"I would like to bury something for Uncle Julian," I said.

Constance was quiet, looking at her fingers which lay still and long on the table. "Uncle Julian is gone, and the others," she said. "Most of our house is gone, Merricat; we are all that is left."

"Jonas."

"Jonas. We are going to lock ourselves in more securely than ever."

"But today is the day Helen Clarke comes to tea."

"No," she said. "Not again. Not here."

As long as we sat quietly together in the kitchen it was possible to postpone seeing the rest of the house. The library books were still on their shelf, untouched, and I supposed that no one had wanted to touch books belonging to the library; there was a fine, after all, for destroying library property.

Constance, who was always dancing, seemed now unwilling to move; she sat on at the kitchen table with her hands spread before her, not looking around at the destruction, and almost dreaming, as though she never believed that she had wakened this morning at all. "We must neaten the house," I said to her uneasily, and she smiled across at me.

When I felt that I could not wait for her any longer I said, "I'm going to look," and got up and went to the dining-room door. She watched me, not moving. When I opened the door to the dining room there was a shocking smell of wetness and burned wood and destruction, and glass from the tall windows lay across the floor and the silver tea service had been swept off the sideboard and stamped into grotesque, unrecognizable shapes. Chairs were broken here, too; I remembered that they had taken up chairs and hurled them at windows and walls. I went through the dining room and into the front hall. The front door stood wide open and early sunlight lay in patterns along the floor of the hall, touching broken glass and torn cloth; after a minute I recognized the cloth as the drawing-room draperies which our mother had once had made up fourteen feet long. No one was outside; I stood in the open doorway and saw that the lawn was marked with the tires of cars and the feet which had danced, and where the hoses had gone there were puddles and mud. The front porch was littered, and I remembered the neat pile of partly broken furniture which Harler the junk dealer had set together last night. I wondered if he planned to come today with a truck and gather up everything he could, or if he had only put the pile together because he loved great piles of broken things and could not resist stacking junk wherever he found it. I waited in the doorway to be sure that no one was watching, and then I ran down the steps across the grass and found our mother's Dresden figurine unbroken where it had hidden against the roots of a bush; I thought to take it to Constance.

She was still sitting quietly at the kitchen table, and when I put the Dresden figurine down before her she looked for a minute and then took it in her hands and held it against her cheek. "It was all my fault," she said. "Somehow it was all my fault."

"I love you, Constance," I said.

"And I love you, Merricat."

"And will you make that little cake for Jonas and me? Pink frosting, with gold leaves around the edge?"

She shook her head, and for a minute I thought she was not going to answer me, and then she took a deep breath, and stood up. "First," she said, "I'm going to clean this kitchen."

"What are you going to do with that?" I asked her, touching the Dresden figurine with the very tip of my finger.

"Put it back where it belongs," she said, and I followed her as she opened the door to the hall and made her way down the hall to the drawing-room doorway. The hall was less littered than the rooms, because there had been less in it to smash, but there were fragments carried from the kitchen, and we stepped on spoons and dishes which had been thrown here. I was shocked when we came into the drawing room to see our mother's portrait looking down on us graciously while her drawing room lay destroyed around her. The white wedding cake trim was blackened with smoke and soot and would never be clean again; I disliked seeing the drawing room even more than the kitchen or the dining room, because we had always kept it so tidy, and our mother had loved this room. I wondered which of them had pushed over Constance's harp and I remembered that I had heard it cry out as it fell. The rose brocade on the chairs was torn and dirty, smudged with the marks of wet feet that had kicked at the chairs and stamped on the sofa. The windows were broken here too, and with the drapes torn down we were clearly visible from outside.

"I think I can close the shutters," I said, as Constance hesitated in the doorway, unwilling to come further into the room. I stepped out onto the porch through the broken window, thinking that no one had ever come this way before, and found that I could unhook the shutters easily. The shutters were as tall as the windows; originally it was intended that a man with a ladder would close the shutters when the summers were ended and the family went away to a city house, but so many years had passed since the shutters were closed that the hooks had rusted and I needed only to shake the heavy shutters to pull the hooks away from the house. I swung the shutters closed, but I could only reach the lower bolt to hold them; there were two more bolts high above my head; perhaps some night I might come out here with a ladder, but the lower bolt would have to hold them now. After I had closed the shutters on both tall drawing-room windows I went along the porch and in, formally, through the front door and into the drawing room where Constance stood in dimness now, without the sunlight. Constance went to the mantel and set the Dresden figurine in its place below the portrait of our mother and for one quick minute the great shadowy room came back together again, as it should be, and then fell apart forever.

We had to walk carefully because of the broken things

on the floor. Our father's safe lay just inside the drawing-room door, and I laughed and even Constance smiled, because it had not been opened and it had clearly not been possible to carry it any farther than this. "Foolishness," Constance said, and touched the safe with her toe.

Our mother had always been pleased when people admired her drawing room, but now no one could come to the windows and look in, and no one would ever see it again. Constance and I closed the drawing-room door behind us and never opened it afterwards. Constance waited just inside the front door while I went onto the porch again and closed the shutters over the tall dining-room windows, and then I came inside and we shut and locked the front door and we were safe. The hall was dark, with two narrow lines of sunlight coming through the two narrow glass panels set on either side of the door; we could look outside through the glass, but no one could see in, even by putting their eyes up close, because the hall inside was dark. Above us the stairs were black and led into blackness or burned rooms with, incredibly, tiny spots of sky showing through. Until now, the roof had always hidden us from the sky, but I did not think that there was any way we could be vulnerable from above, and closed my mind against the thought of silent winged creatures coming out of the trees above to perch on the broken burnt rafters of our house, peering down. I thought it might be wise to barricade the stairs by putting something—a broken chair, perhaps—across. A mattress, soaked and dirty, lay halfway down the stairs;

this was where they had stood with the hoses and fought the fire back and out. I stood at the foot of the stairs, looking up, wondering where our house had gone, the walls and the floors and the beds and the boxes of things in the attic; our father's watch was burned away, and our mother's tortoise-shell dressing set. I could feel a breath of air on my cheek; it came from the sky I could see, but it smelled of smoke and ruin. Our house was a castle, turreted and open to the sky.

"Come back to the kitchen," Constance said. "I can't stay out here."

Like children hunting for shells, or two old ladies going through dead leaves looking for pennies, we shuffled along the kitchen floor with our feet, turning over broken trash to find things which were still whole, and useful. When we had been along and across and diagonally through the kitchen we had gathered together a little pile of practical things on the kitchen table, and there was quite enough for the two of us. There were two cups with handles, and several without, and half a dozen plates, and three bowls. We had been able to rescue all the cans of food undamaged, and the cans of spice went neatly back onto their shelf. We found most of the silverware and straightened most of it as well as we could and put it back into its proper drawers. Since every Blackwood bride had brought her own silverware and china and linen into the house we had always had dozens of butter knives and soup ladles and cake servers; our mother's best silverware had been in a tarnish-proof box in the dining-room sideboard, but they had found it and scattered it on the floor.

One of our whole cups was green with a pale yellow inside, and Constance said that one could be mine. "I never saw anyone use it before," she said. "I suppose a grandmother or a great-great-aunt brought that set to the house as her wedding china. There once were plates to match." The cup which Constance chose was white with orange flowers, and one of the plates matched that. "I remember when we used those dishes," Constance said; "they were the everyday china when I was very small. The china we used for best then was white, with gold edges. Then Mother bought new best china and the white and gold china was used for everyday and these flowered dishes went onto the pantry shelf with the other half-broken sets. These last few years I have always used Mother's everyday china, except when Helen Clarke came to tea. We will take our meals like ladies," she said, "using cups with handles."

When we had taken out everything we wanted and could use, Constance got the heavy broom and swept all the rubble into the dining room. "Now we won't have to look at it," she said. She swept the hall clear so we could go from the kitchen to the front door without passing through the dining room, and then we closed all the doors to the dining room and never opened them again. I thought of the Dresden figurine standing small and courageous under our mother's portrait in the dark drawing room and I remembered that we would never dust it again. Before Constance swept away the torn cloth that had been the drawing-room drapes I asked her to cut me off a piece of the cord which had once drawn them open and shut, and she cut me a piece with a gold tassel on the end; I wondered if it might be the right thing to bury for Uncle Julian.

When we had finished and Constance had scrubbed the kitchen floor our house looked clean and new; from the front door to the kitchen door everything was clear and swept. So many things were gone from the kitchen that it looked bare, but Constance put our cups and plates and bowls on a shelf, and found a pan to give Jonas milk, and we were quite safe. The front door was locked, and the kitchen door was locked and bolted, and we were sitting at the kitchen table drinking milk from our two cups and Jonas was drinking from his pan when a knocking started on the front door. Constance ran to the cellar, and I stopped just long enough to be sure that the kitchen door was bolted, and then followed her. We sat on the cellar stairs in the darkness, and listened. Far away, at the front door, the knocking went on and on, and then a voice called, "Constance? Mary Katherine?"

"It's Helen Clarke," Constance said in a whisper.

"Do you think she has come for her tea?"

"No. Never again."

As we had both known she would, she came around the house, calling us. When she knocked on the kitchen door we held our breath, neither of us moving, because the top half of the kitchen door was glass, and we knew she could see in, but we were safely on the cellar stairs and she could not open the door.

"Constance? Mary Katherine? Are you *in* there?" She shook the door handle as people do when they want a door to open and think to catch it unaware and slip in before the lock can hold. "Jim," she said, "I *know* they're in there. I can see something cooking on the stove. You've got to open the door," she said, raising her voice. "Constance, come and talk to me; I want to see you. Jim," she said, "they're in there and they can hear me, I know it."

"I'm sure they can hear you," Jim Clarke said. "They can probably hear you in the village."

"But I'm sure they misunderstood the people last night; I'm sure Constance was upset, and I *must* tell them that nobody meant any harm. Constance, listen to me, please. We want you and Mary Katherine to come to our house until we can decide what to do with you. Everything's all right, really it is; we're going to forget all about it."

"Do you think she will push over the house?" I whispered to Constance, and Constance shook her head wordlessly.

"Jim, do you think you could break down the door?"

"Certainly not. Leave them alone, Helen, they'll come out when they're ready."

"But Constance takes these things so *seriously*. I'm sure she's frightened now."

"Leave them alone."

"They cannot be left alone, that is absolutely the worst

possible thing for them. I want them out of there and home with me where I can take care of them."

"They don't seem to want to come," Jim Clarke said.

"Constance? Constance? I know you're in there; come and open the door."

I was thinking that we might very well put a cloth or a piece of cardboard over the window in the kitchen door; it simply would not do to have Helen Clarke constantly peering in to watch pots cooking on the stove. We could pin the curtains together across the kitchen windows, and perhaps if the windows were all covered we could sit quietly at the table when Helen Clarke came pounding outside and not have to hide on the cellar stairs.

"Let's leave," Jim Clarke said. "They're not going to answer you."

"But I want to take them home with me."

"We did what we could. We'll come back another time, when they'll feel more like seeing you."

"Constance? Constance, *please* answer me."

Constance sighed, and tapped her fingers irritably and almost noiselessly on the stair rail. "I wish she'd hurry," she said into my ear, "my soup is going to boil over."

Helen Clarke called again and again, going back around the house to their car, calling "Constance? Constance?" as though we might be somewhere in the woods, up a tree perhaps, or under the lettuce leaves, or waiting to spring out at her from behind a bush. When we heard their car start, distantly, we came up out of the cellar and Constance turned off her soup and I went along the hall to the front door to be sure they had gone and that the door was safely locked. I saw their car turn out of the driveway and thought I could still hear Helen Clarke calling "Constance? Constance?"

"She certainly wanted her tea," I said to Constance when I came back to the kitchen.

"We have only two cups with handles," Constance said. "She will never take tea here again."

"It's a good thing Uncle Julian's gone, or one of us would have to use a broken cup. Are you going to neaten Uncle Julian's room?"

"Merricat." Constance turned from the stove to look at me. "What are we going to do?"

"We've neatened the house. We've had food. We've hidden from Helen Clarke. What *are* we going to do?"

"Where are we going to sleep? How are we going to know what time it is? What will we wear for clothes?"

"Why do we need to know what time it is?"

"Our food won't last forever, even the preserves."

"We can sleep in my hiding place by the creek."

"No. That's all right for hiding, but you must have a real bed."

"I saw a mattress on the stairs. From my own old bed, perhaps. We can pull it down and clean it and dry it in the sun. One corner is burned."

"Good," said Constance. We went together to the stairs and took hold of the mattress awkwardly; it was unpleasantly wet and dirty. We dragged it, pulling together, along the hall, with little scraps of wood and glass coming with it, and got it across Constance's clean kitchen floor to the kitchen door. Before unlocking the door I looked out carefully, and even when the door was opened I went out first to look around in every direction, but it was safe. We dragged the mattress out onto the lawn, and put it in the sun near our mother's marble bench.

"Uncle Julian used to sit right here," I said.

"It would be a good day, today, for Uncle Julian to sit in the sun."

"I hope he was warm when he died. Perhaps he remembered the sun for a minute."

"I had his shawl; I hope he didn't wish for it. Merricat, I am going to plant something here, where he used to sit."

"I am going to bury something for him. What will you plant?"

"A flower." Constance leaned, and touched the grass softly. "Some kind of a yellow flower."

"It's going to look funny, right in the middle of the lawn."

"We'll know why it's there, and no one else will ever see it."

"And I will bury something yellow, to keep Uncle Julian warm."

"First, however, my lazy Merricat, you will get a pot of water and scrub that mattress clean. And I will wash the kitchen floor again."

We were going to be very happy, I thought. There were a great many things to do, and a whole new pattern of days to arrange, but I thought we were going to be very happy. Constance was pale, and still saddened by what they had done to her kitchen, but she had scrubbed every shelf, and washed the table again and again, and washed the windows and the floor. Our dishes were bravely on their shelf, and the cans and unbroken boxes of food we had rescued made a substantial row in the pantry.

"I could train Jonas to bring back rabbits for stew," I told her, and she laughed, and Jonas looked back at her blandly.

"That cat is so used to living on cream and rum cakes and buttered eggs that I doubt if he could catch a grasshopper," she said.

"I don't think I could care for a grasshopper stew."

"At any rate, right *now* I am making an onion pie."

While Constance washed the kitchen I found a heavy cardboard carton which I took apart carefully, and so had several large pieces of cardboard to cover the glass window in the kitchen door. The hammer and the nails were in the tool shed where Charles Blackwood had put them after trying to mend the broken step, and I nailed cardboard across the kitchen door until the glass was completely covered and no one could see in. I nailed more cardboard across the two kitchen windows, and the kitchen was dark, but safe. "It would be safer to let the kitchen windows get dirty," I told Constance, but she was shocked, and said, "I wouldn't live in a house with dirty windows."

When we had finished the kitchen was very clean but could not sparkle because there was so little light, and I knew that Constance was not pleased. She loved sunshine and brightness and cooking in a light lovely kitchen.

"We can keep the door open," I said, "if we watch carefully all the time. We'll hear if any cars stop in front of the house. When I can," I said, "I will try to think of a way to build barricades along the sides of the house so no one will be able to come around here to the back."

"I am sure Helen Clarke will try again."

"At any rate she cannot look in now."

The afternoon was drawing in; even with the door open the sunlight came only a short way across the floor, and Jonas came to Constance at the stove, asking for his supper. The kitchen was warm and comfortable and familiar and clean. It would be nice to have a fireplace in here, I thought; we could sit beside a fire, and then I thought no, we have already had a fire.

"I will go and make sure that the front door is locked," I said.

The front door was locked and no one was outside. When I came back into the kitchen Constance said, "Tomorrow I will clean Uncle Julian's room. We have so little house left that it should all be very clean."

"Will you sleep in there? In Uncle Julian's bed?"

"No, Merricat. I want you to sleep in there. It's the only bed we have."

"I am not allowed in Uncle Julian's room."

She was quiet for a minute, looking at me curiously, and then asked, "Even though Uncle Julian's gone, Merricat?"

"Besides, I found the mattress, and cleaned it, and it came from my bed. I want it on the floor in my corner."

"Silly Merricat. Anyway, I'm afraid we'll both have

the floor tonight. The mattress will not dry before to-morrow, and Uncle Julian's bed is not clean."

"I can bring branches from my hiding place, and leaves."

"On my clean kitchen floor?"

"I'll get the blanket, though, and Uncle Julian's shawl."

"You're going out? Now? All that way?"

"No one's outside," I said. "It's almost dark and I can go very safely. If anyone comes, close the door and lock it; if I see that the door is closed I will wait by the creek until I can come safely home. And I will take Jonas for protection."

I ran all the way to the creek, but Jonas was faster, and was waiting for me when I got to my hiding place. It was good to run, and good to come back again to our house and see the kitchen door standing open and the warm light inside. When Jonas and I came in I shut the door and bolted it and we were ready for the night.

"It's a good dinner," Constance said, warm and happy from cooking. "Come and sit down, Merricat." With the door shut she had had to turn on the ceiling light, and our dishes on the table were neatly set. "Tomorrow I will try to polish the silverware," she said, "and we must bring in things from the garden."

"The lettuce is full of ashes."

"Tomorrow, too," Constance said, looking at the black squares of cardboard which covered the windows, "I am going to try to think of some kind of curtains to hide your cardboard."

"Tomorrow I will barricade the sides of the house.

Tomorrow Jonas will catch us a rabbit. Tomorrow I will guess for you what time it is."

Far away, in the front of the house, a car stopped, and we were silent, looking at one another; now, I thought, now we will know how safe we are, and I got up and made sure that the kitchen door was bolted; I could not see out through the cardboard and I was sure that they could not see in. The knocking started at the front door, but there was no time to make sure that the front door was locked. They knocked only for a moment, as though certain that we would not be in the front of the house, and then we heard them stumbling in the darkness as they tried to find their way around the side of the house to the back. I heard Jim Clarke's voice, and another which I remembered was the voice of Dr. Levy.

"Can't see a thing," Jim Clarke said. "Black as sin out here."

"There's a crack of light at one of the windows."

Which one, I wondered; which window still showed a crack?

"They're in there, all right," Jim Clarke said. "No place else they could be."

"I just want to know if they're hurt, or sick; don't like to think of them shut up in there needing help."

"I'm supposed to bring them home with me," Jim Clarke said.

They came to the back door; their voices were directly outside, and Constance reached out her hand across the table to me; if it seemed that they might be able to look in we could run together for the cellar. "Damn place is all boarded up," Jim Clarke said, and I thought, good, oh, that's good. I had forgotten that there would be real boards in the tool shed; I never thought of anything but cardboard which is much too weak.

"Miss Blackwood?" the doctor called, and one of them knocked on the door. "Miss Blackwood? It's Dr. Levy."

"And Jim Clarke. Helen's husband. Helen's very worried about you."

"Are you hurt? Sick? Do you need help?"

"Helen wants you to come to our house; she's waiting there for you."

"Listen," the doctor said, and I thought he had his face up very close to the glass, almost touching it. He talked in a very friendly voice, and quietly. "Listen, no one's going to hurt you. We're your friends. We came all the way over here to help you and make sure you were all right and we don't want to bother you. As a matter of fact, we promise not to bother you at all, ever again, if you'll just once say that you're well and safe. Just one word."

"You can't just let people go on worrying and worrying about you," Jim Clarke said.

"Just one word," the doctor said. "All you have to do is say you're all right."

They waited; I could feel them pressing their faces close to the glass, longing to see inside. Constance looked at me across the table and smiled a little, and I smiled back; our safeguards were good and they could not see in.

"Listen," the doctor said, and he raised his voice a little; "listen, Julian's funeral is tomorrow. We thought you'd want to know."

"There are a lot of flowers already," Jim Clarke said. "You'd be really pleased to see all the flowers. We sent flowers, and the Wrights, and the Carringtons. I think you'd feel a little different about your friends if you could see the flowers we all sent Julian."

I wondered why we would feel different if we saw who sent Uncle Julian flowers. Certainly Uncle Julian buried in flowers, swarmed over by flowers, would not resemble the Uncle Julian we had seen every day. Perhaps masses of flowers would warm Uncle Julian dead; I tried to think of Uncle Julian dead and could only remember him asleep. I thought of the Clarkes and the Carringtons and the Wrights pouring armfuls of flowers down onto poor old Uncle Julian, helplessly dead.

"You're not gaining anything by driving away your friends, you know. Helen said to tell you—"

"Listen." I could feel them pushing against the door. "No one's going to bother you. Just tell us, are you all right?"

"We're not going to keep coming, you know. There's a limit to how much friends can take."

Jonas yawned. In silence Constance turned, slowly and carefully, back to face her place at the table, and took up a buttered biscuit and took a tiny silent bite. I wanted to laugh, and put my hands over my mouth; Constance eating a biscuit silently was funny, like a doll pretending to eat.

"*Damn* it," Jim Clarke said. He knocked on the door. "*Damn* it," he said.

"For the last time," the doctor said, "we know you're in there; for the last time will you just—"

"Oh, come away," Jim Clarke said. "It's not worth all the yelling."

"Listen," the doctor said, and I thought he had his mouth against the door, "one of these days you're going to *need* help. You'll be sick, or hurt. You'll *need* help. *Then* you'll be quick enough to—"

"Leave them be," Jim Clarke said. "Come on."

I heard their footsteps going around the side of the house and wondered if they were tricking us, pretending to walk away and then coming silently back to stand without sound outside the door, waiting. I thought of Constance silently eating a biscuit inside and Jim Clarke silently listening outside and a little cold chill went up my back; perhaps there would never be noise in the world again. Then the car started at the front of the house and we heard it drive away and Constance put her fork down on her plate with a little crash and I breathed again and said, "Where have they got Uncle Julian, do you suppose?"

"At that same place," Constance said absently, "in the city. Merricat," she said, looking up suddenly.

"Yes, Constance?"

"I want to say I'm sorry. I was wicked last night."

I was still and cold, looking at her and remembering.

"I was very wicked," she said. "I never should have reminded you of why they all died."

"Then don't remind me now." I could not move my hand to reach over and take hers.

"I wanted you to forget about it. I never wanted to speak about it, ever, and I'm sorry I did."

"I put it in the sugar."

"I know. I knew then."

"You never used sugar."

"No."

"So I put it in the sugar."

Constance sighed. "Merricat," she said, "we'll never talk about it again. Never."

I was chilled, but she smiled at me kindly and it was all right.

"I love you, Constance," I said.

"And I love you, my Merricat."

Jonas sat on the floor and slept on the floor and I thought it ought not to be so difficult for me. Constance should have had leaves and soft moss under her blanket but we could not dirty the kitchen floor again. I put my blanket in the corner near my stool because it was the place I knew best, and Jonas got up onto the stool and sat there, looking down on me. Constance lay on the floor near the stove; it was dark, but I could see the paleness of her face across the kitchen. "Are you comfortable?" I asked her, and she laughed.

"I've spent a lot of time in this kitchen," she said, "but I never before tried lying on its floor. I've taken such good care of it that it has to make me welcome, I think."

"Tomorrow we bring in lettuce."

*10*

~~~~~~~~~~~~~~~~~~~~~~~~~~~~~~~~~~~~~

SLOWLY THE PATTERN OF OUR DAYS GREW, AND SHAPED itself into a happy life. In the mornings when I awakened I would go at once down the hall to make sure the front door was locked. We were most active in the very early morning because no one was ever around. We had not realized that, with the gates opened and the path exposed to public use, the children would come; one morning I stood beside the front door, looking out through the narrow pane of glass, and saw children playing on our

front lawn. Perhaps the parents had sent them to explore
the way and make sure it was navigable, or perhaps
children can never resist playing anywhere; they seemed
a little uneasy playing in front of our house, and their
voices were subdued. I thought that perhaps they were
only pretending to play, because they were children and
were supposed to play, but perhaps they were actually
sent here to look for us, thinly disguised as children.
They were not really convincing, I decided as I watched
them; they moved gracelessly, and never once glanced,
that I could see, at our house. I wondered how soon they
would creep onto the porch, and press their small faces
against the shutters, trying to see through cracks. Constance came up behind me and looked out over my shoulder. "They are the children of the strangers," I told her.
"They have no faces."

"They have eyes."

"Pretend they are birds. They can't see us. They don't
know it yet, they don't want to believe it, but they won't
ever see us again."

"I suppose that now they've come once, they'll come
again."

"All the strangers will come, but they can't see inside.
And now may I please have my breakfast?"

The kitchen was always dark in the mornings until I
unbolted the kitchen door and opened it to let the sunlight in. Then Jonas went to sit on the step and bathe and
Constance sang while she made our breakfast. After
breakfast I sat on the step with Jonas while Constance
washed the kitchen.

Barricading the sides of the house had been easier than I expected; I managed it in one night with Constance holding a flashlight for me. At either side of our house there was a spot where the trees and bushes grew close to the house, sheltering the back and narrowing the path which was the only way around. I brought piece after piece from the pile of junk Mr. Harler had made on our front porch, and heaped the broken boards and furniture across the narrowest spot. It would not really keep anyone out, of course; the children could climb over it easily, but if anyone did try to get past there would be enough noise and falling of broken boards to give us plenty of time to close and bolt the kitchen door. I had found some boards around the tool shed, and nailed them rudely across the glass of the kitchen door, but I disliked putting them across the sides of the house as a barricade, where anyone might see them and know how clumsily I built. Perhaps, I told myself, I might try my hand at mending the broken step.

"What are you laughing about now?" Constance asked me.

"I am thinking that we are on the moon, but it is not quite as I supposed it would be."

"It is a very happy place, though." Constance was bringing breakfast to the table: scrambled eggs and toasted biscuits and blackberry jam she had made some golden summer. "We ought to bring in as much food as we can," she said. "I don't like to think of the garden waiting there for us to come and gather growing things.

And I'd feel much better if we had more food put securely away in the house."

"I will go on my winged horse and bring you cinnamon and thyme, emeralds and clove, cloth of gold and cabbages."

"And rhubarb."

We were able to leave the kitchen door open when we went down to the vegetable garden, because we could see clearly whether anyone was approaching my barricades and run back to the house if we needed to. I carried the basket and we brought back lettuce, still grey with ash, and radishes, and tomatoes and cucumbers and, later, berries, and melons. Usually I ate fruit and vegetables still moist from the ground and the air, but I disliked eating anything while it was still dirty with the ash from our burned house. Most of the dirt and the soot had blown away and the air around the garden was fresh and clean, but the smoke was in the ground and I thought it would always be there.

As soon as we were safely settled Constance had opened Uncle Julian's room and cleaned it. She brought out the sheets from Uncle Julian's bed, and the blankets, and washed them in the kitchen sink and set them outside to dry in the sunlight. "What are you going to do with Uncle Julian's papers?" I asked her, and she rested her hands against the edge of the sink, hesitating.

"I suppose I'll keep them all in the box," she said at last. "I suppose I'll put the box down in the cellar."

"And preserve it?"

"And preserve it. He would like to think that his pa-

pers were treated respectfully. And I would not want
Uncle Julian to suspect that his papers were not preserved."

"I had better go and see that the front door is locked."
The children were often outside on our front lawn,
playing their still games and not looking at our house,
moving awkwardly in little dashing runs, and slapping
one another without cause. Whenever I checked to make
sure that the front door was locked I looked out to see
if the children were there. Very often I saw people walking on our path now, using it to go from one place to another, and putting their feet down where once only my
feet had gone; I thought they used the path without
wanting to, as though each of them had to travel it once
to show that it could be done, but I thought that only a
few, the defiant hating ones, came by more than once.

I dreamed away the long afternoon while Constance
cleaned Uncle Julian's room; I sat on the doorsill with
Jonas asleep beside me, and looked out on the quiet safe
garden.

"Look, Merricat," Constance said, coming to me with
an armful of clothes, "look, Uncle Julian had two suits,
and a topcoat and a hat."

"He walked upright once; he told us so himself."

"I can just barely remember him, years ago, going off
one day to buy a suit, and I suppose it was one of these
suits he bought; they are neither of them much worn."

"What would he have been wearing on the last day
with them? What tie did he have on at dinner? He would
surely like to have it remembered."

She looked at me for a minute, not smiling. "It would hardly have been one of these; when I came to get him afterwards, at the hospital, he was wearing pajamas and a robe."

"Perhaps he should have one of these suits now."

"He was probably buried in an old suit of Jim Clarke's." Constance started for the cellar, and then stopped. "Merricat?"

"Yes, Constance?"

"Do you realize that these things of Uncle Julian's are the only clothes left in our house? All of mine burned, and all of yours."

"And everything of theirs in the attic."

"I have only this pink dress I have on."

I looked down. "And I am wearing brown."

"And yours needs washing, and mending; how *can* you tear your clothes so, my Merricat?"

"I shall weave a suit of leaves. At once. With acorns for buttons."

"Merricat, be serious. We will have to wear Uncle Julian's clothes."

"I am not allowed to touch Uncle Julian's things. I shall have a lining of moss, for cold winter days, and a hat made of bird feathers."

"That may be all very well for the moon, Miss Foolishness. On the moon you may wear a suit of fur like Jonas, for all of me. But right here in our house you are going to be clothed in one of your Uncle Julian's old shirts, and perhaps his trousers too."

"Or Uncle Julian's bathrobe and pajamas, I suppose.

No; I am not allowed to touch Uncle Julian's things; I will wear leaves."

"But you are allowed. I tell you that you are allowed."

"No."

She sighed. "Well," she said, "you'll probably see me wearing them." Then she stopped, and laughed, and looked at me, and laughed again.

"Constance?" I said.

She put Uncle Julian's clothes over the back of a chair, and, still laughing, went into the pantry and opened one of the drawers. I remembered what she was after and I laughed too. Then she came back and put an armload of tablecloths down beside me.

"These will do you very nicely, elegant Merricat. Look; how will you feel in this, with a border of yellow flowers? Or this handsome red and white check? The damask, I am afraid, is too stiff for comfort, and besides it has been darned."

I stood up and held the red and white checked table-cloth against me. "You can cut a hole for my head," I said; I was pleased.

"I have no sewing things. You will simply have to tie it around your waist with a cord or let it hang like a toga."

"I will use the damask for a cloak; who else wears a damask cloak?"

"Merricat, oh, Merricat." Constance dropped the tablecloth she was holding and put her arms around me. "What have I done to my baby Merricat?" she said. "No

house. No food. And dressed in a tablecloth; what have
I *done?*"

"Constance," I said, "I love you, Constance."

"Dressed in a tablecloth like a rag doll."

"Constance. We are going to be very happy, Constance."

"Oh, Merricat," she said, holding me.

"Listen to me, Constance. We are going to be very
happy."

I dressed at once, not wanting to give Constance more
time to think. I chose the red and white check, and when
Constance had cut a hole for my head I took my gold
cord with the tassel that Constance had cut from the
drawing-room drapes and tied it around me for a belt
and looked, I thought, very fine. Constance was sad at
first, and turned away sadly when she saw me, and
scrubbed furiously at the sink to get my brown dress
clean, but I liked my robe, and danced in it, and before
long she smiled again and then laughed at me.

"Robinson Crusoe dressed in the skins of animals," I
told her. "He had no gay cloths with a gold belt."

"I must say you never looked so bright before."

"You will be wearing the skins of Uncle Julian; I prefer my tablecloth."

"I believe the one you are wearing now was used for
summer breakfasts on the lawn many years ago. Red and
white check would never be used in the dining room, of
course."

"Some days I shall be a summer breakfast on the lawn,

and some days I shall be a formal dinner by candlelight, and some days I shall be—"

"A very dirty Merricat. You have a fine gown, but your face is dirty. We have lost almost everything, young lady, but at least we still have clean water and a comb."

One thing was most lucky about Uncle Julian's room: I persuaded Constance to bring out his chair and wheel it through the garden to reinforce my barricade. It looked strange to see Constance wheeling the empty chair, and for a minute I tried to see Uncle Julian again, riding with his hands in his lap, but all that remained of Uncle Julian's presence were the worn spots on the chair, and a handkerchief tucked under the cushion. The chair would be powerful in my barricade, however, staring out always at intruders with a blank menace of dead Uncle Julian. I was troubled to think that Uncle Julian might vanish altogether, with his papers in a box and his chair on the barricade and his toothbrush thrown away and even the smell of Uncle Julian gone from his room, but when the ground was soft Constance planted a yellow rosebush at Uncle Julian's spot on the lawn, and one night I went down to the creek and buried Uncle Julian's initialled gold pencil by the water, so the creek would always speak his name. Jonas took to going into Uncle Julian's room, where he had never gone before, but I did not go inside.

Helen Clarke came to our door twice more, knocking and calling and begging us to answer, but we sat quietly, and when she found that she could not come around the house because of my barricade she told us from the front door that she would not come back, and she did not. One evening, perhaps the evening of the day Constance planted Uncle Julian's rosebush, we heard a very soft knock at our front door while we sat at the table eating dinner. It was far too soft a knock for Helen Clarke, and I left the table and hurried silently down the hall to be sure that the front door was locked, and Constance followed me, curious. We pressed silently against the door and listened.

"Miss Blackwood?" someone said outside, in a low voice; I wondered if he suspected we were so close to him. "Miss Constance? Miss Mary Katherine?"

It was not quite dark outside, but inside where we stood we could only see one another dimly, two white faces against the door. "Miss Constance?" he said again. "Listen."

I thought that he was moving his head from side to side to make sure that he was not seen. "Listen," he said, "I got a chicken here."

He tapped softly on the door. "I hope you can hear me," he said. "I got a chicken here. My wife fixed it, roasted it nice, and there's some cookies and a pie. I hope you can hear me."

I could see that Constance's eyes were wide with wonder. I stared at her and she stared at me.

"I sure hope you can hear me, Miss Blackwood. I broke one of your chairs and I'm sorry." He tapped against the door again, very softly. "Well," he said. "I'll just set this basket down on your step here. I hope you heard me. Goodbye."

We listened to quiet footsteps going away, and after a minute Constance said, "What shall we do? Shall we open the door?"

"Later," I said. "I'll come when it's really dark."

"I wonder what kind of pie it is. Do you think it's as good as my pies?"

We finished our dinner and waited until I was sure that no one could possibly see the front door opening, and then we went down the hall and I unlocked the door and looked outside. The basket sat on the doorstep, covered with a napkin. I brought it inside and locked the door while Constance took the basket from me and carried it to the kitchen. "Blueberry," she said when I came. "Quite good, too; it's still warm."

She took out the chicken, wrapped in a napkin, and the little package of cookies, touching each lovingly and with gentleness. "Everything's still warm," she said. "She must have baked them right after dinner, so he could bring them right over. I wonder if she made two pies, one for the house. She wrapped everything while it was still warm and told him to bring them over. These cookies are not crisp enough."

"I'll take the basket back and leave it on the porch, so he'll know we found it."

"No, no." Constance caught me by the arm. "Not until I've washed the napkins; what would she think of me?"

Sometimes they brought bacon, home-cured, or fruit,

or their own preserves, which were never as good as the preserves Constance made. Mostly they brought roasted chicken; sometimes a cake or a pie, frequently cookies, sometimes a potato salad or coleslaw. Once they brought a pot of beef stew, which Constance took apart and put back together again according to her own rules for beef stew, and sometimes there were pots of baked beans or macaroni. "We are the biggest church supper they ever had," Constance said once, looking at a loaf of home-made bread I had just brought inside.

These things were always left on the front doorstep, always silently and in the evenings. We thought that the men came home from work and the women had the baskets ready for them to carry over; perhaps they came in darkness not to be recognized, as though each of them wanted to hide from the others, and bringing us food was somehow a shameful thing to do in public. There were many women cooking, Constance said. "Here is one," she explained to me once, tasting a bean, "who uses ketchup, and too much of it; and the last one used more molasses." Once or twice there was a note in the basket: "This is for the dishes," or "We apologize about the cur-tains," or "Sorry for your harp." We always set the bas-kets back where we had found them, and never opened the front door until it was completely dark and we were sure that no one was near. I always checked carefully afterwards to make certain that the front door was locked.

I discovered that I was no longer allowed to go to the creek; Uncle Julian was there, and it was much too far

from Constance. I never went farther away than the edge
of the woods, and Constance went only as far as the vegetable garden. I was not allowed to bury anything more,
nor was I allowed to touch stone. Every day I looked
over the boards across the kitchen windows and when I
found small cracks I nailed on more boards. Every morning I checked at once to make sure the front door
was locked, and every morning Constance washed the
kitchen. We spent a good deal of time at the front door,
particularly during the afternoons, when most people
came by; we sat, one on either side of the front door,
looking out through the narrow glass panels which I had
covered almost entirely with cardboard so that we had
each only a small peephole and no one could possibly see
inside. We watched the children playing, and the people
walking past, and we heard their voices and they were all
strangers, with their wide staring eyes and their evil open
mouths. One day a group came by bicycle; there were
two women and a man, and two children. They parked
their bicycles in our driveway and lay down on our front
lawn, pulling at the grass and talking while they rested.
The children ran up and down our driveway and over
and around the trees and bushes. This was the day that
we learned that the vines were growing over the burned
roof of our house, because one of the women glanced
sideways at the house and said that the vines almost hid
the marks of burning. They rarely turned squarely to
look at our house face to face, but looked from the corners of their eyes or from over a shoulder or through
their fingers. "It used to be a lovely old house, I hear,"

said the woman sitting on our grass. "I've heard that it was quite a local landmark at one time."

"Now it looks like a tomb," the other woman said.

"Shh," the first woman said, and gestured toward the house with her head. "I heard," she said loudly, "that they had a staircase which was very fine. Carved in Italy, I heard."

"They can't hear you," the other woman said, amused. "And who cares if they do, anyway?"

"Shhh."

"No one knows for sure if there's anyone inside or not. The local people tell some tall tales."

"Shh. Tommy," she called to one of the children, "don't you go near those steps."

"Why?" said the child, backing away.

"Because the ladies live in there, and they don't like it."

"Why?" said the child, pausing at the foot of the steps and giving a quick look backward at our front door.

"The ladies don't like little boys," the second woman said; she was one of the bad ones; I could see her mouth from the side and it was the mouth of a snake.

"What would they do to me?"

"They'd hold you down and make you eat candy full of poison; I heard that dozens of bad little boys have gone too near that house and never been seen again. They catch little boys and they—"

"Shh. *Honestly*, Ethel."

"Do they like little girls?" The other child drew near.

"They hate little boys *and* little girls. The difference is, they *eat* the little girls."

"Ethel, stop. You're terrifying the children. It isn't true, darlings; she's only teasing you."

"They never come out except at night," the bad woman said, looking evilly at the children, "and then when it's dark they go hunting little children."

"Just the same," the man said suddenly, "I don't want to see the kids going too near that house."

Charles Blackwood came back only once. He came in a car with another man late one afternoon when we had been watching for a long time. All the strangers had gone, and Constance had just stirred and said, "Time to put on the potatoes," when the car turned into the driveway and she settled back to watch again. Charles and the other man got out of the car in front of the house and walked directly to the foot of the steps, looking up, although they could not see us inside. I remembered the first time Charles had come and stood looking up at our house in just the same manner, but this time he would never get in. I reached up and touched the lock on the front door to make sure it was fastened, and on the other side of the doorway Constance turned and nodded to me; she knew, too, that Charles would never get in again.

"See?" Charles said, outside, at the foot of our steps. "There's the house, just like I said. It doesn't look as bad as it did, now the vines have grown so. But the roof's been burned away, and the place was gutted inside."

"Are the ladies in there?"

"Sure." Charles laughed, and I remembered his laughter and his big staring white face and from inside the door I wished him dead. "They're in there all right," he said. "And so is a whole damn fortune."

"You *know* that?"

"They've got money in there's never even been counted. They've got it buried all over, and a safe full, and God knows where else they've hidden it. They never come out, just hide away inside with all that money."

"Look," the other man said, "they know you, don't they?"

"Sure. I'm their cousin. I came here on a visit once."

"You think there's any chance you might get one of them to talk to you? Maybe come to the window or something, so I could get a picture?"

Charles thought. He looked at the house and at the other man, and thought. "If you sell this, to the magazine or somewhere, do I get half?"

"Sure, it's a promise."

"I'll try it," Charles said. "You get back behind the car, out of sight. They certainly won't come out if they see a stranger." The other man went back to the car and took out a camera and settled himself on the other side of the car where we could not see him. "Okay," he called, and Charles started up the steps to our front door.

"Connie?" he called. "Hey, Connie? It's Charles; I'm back."

I looked at Constance and thought she had never seen Charles so truly before.

"Connie?"

She knew now that Charles was a ghost and a demon, one of the strangers.

"Let's forget all that happened," Charles said. He came close to the door and spoke pleasantly, with a little pleading tone. "Let's be friends again."

I could see his feet. One of them was tapping and tapping on the floor of our porch. "I don't know what you've got against me," he said, "and I've been waiting and waiting for you to let me know I could come back again. If I did anything to offend you, I'm really sorry."

I wished Charles could see inside, could see us sitting on the floor on either side of the front door, listening to him and looking at his feet, while he talked beggingly to the door three feet above our heads.

"Open the door," he said very softly. "Connie, will you open the door for me, for Cousin Charles?"

Constance looked up to where his face must be and smiled unpleasantly. I thought it must be a smile she had been saving for Charles if he ever came back again.

"I went to see old Julian's grave this morning," Charles said. "I came back to visit old Julian's grave and to see you once more." He waited a minute and then said with a little break in his voice, "I put a couple of flowers— *you* know—on the old fellow's grave; he was a fine old guy, and he was always pretty good to me."

Beyond Charles' feet I saw the other man coming out from behind the car with his camera. "Look," he called, "you're wasting your breath. And I haven't got all day."

"Don't you understand?" Charles had turned away

from the door, but his voice still had the little break in it. "I've *got* to see her once more. I was the cause of it all."

"What?"

"Why do you suppose two old maids shut themselves up in a house like this? God knows," Charles said, "I didn't mean it to turn out this way."

I thought Constance was going to speak then, or at least laugh out loud, and I reached across and touched her arm, warning her to be quiet, but she did not turn her head to me.

"If I could just *talk* to her," Charles said. "You can get some pictures of the house, anyway, with me standing here. Or knocking at the door; I could be knocking frantically at the door."

"You could be stretched across the doorsill dying of a broken heart, for all of me," the other man said. He went to the car and put his camera inside. "Waste of time."

"And all that money. Connie," Charles called loudly, "will you for heaven's sake open that door?"

"You know," the other man said from the car, "I'll just bet you're never going to see those silver dollars again."

"Connie," Charles said, "you don't know what you're doing to me; I never deserved to be treated like this. *Please*, Connie."

"You want to walk back to town?" the other man said. He closed the car door.

Charles turned away from the door and then turned back. "All right, Connie," he said, "this is it. If you let me go this time, you'll never see me again. I mean it, Connie."

"I'm leaving," the other man said from the car.

"I mean it, Connie, I really do." Charles started down the steps, talking over his shoulder. "Take a last look," he said. "I'm going. One word could make me stay."

I did not think he was going to go in time. I honestly did not know whether Constance was going to be able to contain herself until he got down the steps and safely into the car. "Goodbye, Connie," he said from the foot of the steps and then turned away and went slowly toward the car. He looked for a minute as though he might wipe his eyes or blow his nose, but the other man said, "Hurry *up*," and Charles looked back once more, raised his hand sadly, and got into the car. Then Constance laughed, and I laughed, and for a minute I saw Charles in the car turn his head quickly, as though he had heard us laughing, but the car started, and drove off down the driveway, and we held each other in the dark hall and laughed, with the tears running down our cheeks and echoes of our laughter going up the ruined stairway to the sky.

"I am so happy," Constance said at last, gasping. "Merricat, I am so happy."

"I told you that you would like it on the moon."

The Carringtons stopped their car in front of our house one Sunday after church and sat quietly in the car looking at our house, as though supposing that we would come out if there was anything the Carringtons could do for us. Sometimes I thought of the drawing room and the dining room, forever closed away, with our mother's lovely broken things lying scattered, and the dust sifting gently down to cover them; we had new landmarks in the house, just as we had a new pattern for our days. The crooked, broken-off fragment which was all that was left of our lovely stairway was something we passed every day and came to know as intimately as we had once known the stairs themselves. The boards across the kitchen windows were ours, and part of our house, and we loved them. We were very happy, although Constance was always in terror lest one of our two cups should break, and one of us have to use a cup without a handle. We had our well-known and familiar places: our chairs at the table, and our beds, and our places beside the front door. Constance washed the red and white tablecloth and the shirts of Uncle Julian's which she wore, and while they were hanging in the garden to dry I wore a tablecloth with a yellow border, which looked very handsome with my gold belt. Our mother's old brown shoes were safely put away in my corner of the kitchen, since in the warm summer days I went barefoot like Jonas. Constance disliked picking many flowers, but there was always a bowl on the kitchen table with roses or daisies, although of course she never picked a rose from Uncle Julian's rosebush.

I sometimes thought of my six blue marbles, but I was not allowed to go to the long field now, and I thought that perhaps my six blue marbles had been buried to protect a house which no longer existed and had no connection with the house where we lived now, and where we were very happy. My new magical safeguards were the lock on the front door, and the boards over the windows, and the barricades along the sides of the house. In the evenings sometimes we saw movement in the darkness on the lawn, and heard whispers.

"Don't; the ladies might be watching."

"You think they can see in the dark?"

"I heard they see everything that goes on."

Then there might be laughter, drifting away into the warm darkness.

"They will soon be calling this Lover's Lane," Constance said.

"After Charles, no doubt."

"The least Charles could have done," Constance said, considering seriously, "was shoot himself through the head in the driveway."

We learned, from listening, that all the strangers could see from outside, when they looked at all, was a great ruined structure overgrown with vines, barely recognizable as a house. It was the point halfway between the village and the highway, the middle spot on the path, and no one ever saw our eyes looking out through the vines.

"You can't go on those steps," the children warned each other; "if you do, the ladies will get you."

Once a boy, dared by the others, stood at the foot of the steps facing the house, and shivered and almost cried and almost ran away, and then called out shakily, "Merricat, said Constance, would you like a cup of tea?" and then fled, followed by all the others. That night we found on the doorsill a basket of fresh eggs and a note reading, "He didn't mean it, please."

"Poor child," Constance said, putting the eggs into a bowl to go into the cooler. "He's probably hiding under the bed right now."

"Perhaps he had a good whipping to teach him manners."

"We will have an omelette for breakfast."

"I wonder if I *could* eat a child if I had the chance."

"I doubt if I could cook one," said Constance.

"Poor strangers," I said. "They have so much to be afraid of."

"Well," Constance said, "I am afraid of spiders."

"Jonas and I will see to it that no spider ever comes near you. Oh, Constance," I said, "we are so happy."